Programming ar Automating Cisc Networks

Ryan Tischer, CCIE No. 11459

Jason Gooley, CCIE No. 38759 (R&S & SP)

Cisco Press

800 East 96th Street

Indianapolis, Indiana 46240 USA

Programming and Automating Cisco Networks

Ryan Tischer
Jason Gooley

Published by:
Cisco Press
800 East 96th Street
Indianapolis, IN 46240 USA

Printed in the United States of America

1 16

Library of Congress Control Number: 2016942372

ISBN-13: 978-1-58714-465-3

ISBN-10: 1-58714-465-4

Warning and Disclaimer

This book is designed to provide information about network programmability and automation of Cisco Data Center, Campus, and WAN networks. Every effort has been made to make this book as complete and as accurate as possible, but no warranty or fitness is implied.

The information is provided on an "as is" basis. The authors, Cisco Press, and Cisco Systems, Inc. shall have neither liability nor responsibility to any person or entity with respect to any loss or damages arising from the information contained in this book or from the use of the discs or programs that may accompany it.

The opinions expressed in this book belong to the author and are not necessarily those of Cisco Systems, Inc.

Trademark Acknowledgments

All terms mentioned in this book that are known to be trademarks or service marks have been appropriately capitalized. Cisco Press or Cisco Systems, Inc., cannot attest to the accuracy of this information. Use of a term in this book should not be regarded as affecting the validity of any trademark or service mark.

Special Sales

For information about buying this title in bulk quantities, or for special sales opportunities (which may include electronic versions; custom cover designs; and content particular to your business, training goals, marketing focus, or branding interests), please contact our corporate sales department at corpsales@pearsoned.com or (800) 382-3419.

For government sales inquiries, please contact governmentsales@pearsoned.com.

For questions about sales outside the U.S., please contact intlcs@pearson.com.

Feedback Information

At Cisco Press, our goal is to create in-depth technical books of the highest quality and value. Each book is crafted with care and precision, undergoing rigorous development that involves the unique expertise of members from the professional technical community.

Readers' feedback is a natural continuation of this process. If you have any comments regarding how we could improve the quality of this book, or otherwise alter it to better suit your needs, you can contact us through email at feedback@ciscopress.com. Please make sure to include the book title and ISBN in your message.

We greatly appreciate your assistance.

Editor-in-Chief: Mark Taub

Product Line Manager: Brett Bartow

Alliances Manager, Cisco Press: Ronald Fligge

Managing Editor: Sandra Schroeder

Development Editor: Ellie C. Bru

Project Editor: Mandie Frank

Copy Editor: Lori Martinsek

Technical Editor(s): Joe Clarke, Omar Sultan

Editorial Assistant: Vanessa Evans

Cover Designer: Chuti Prasertsith

Composition: codeMantra

Indexer: Erika Millen

Proofreader: Kamalakannan

cisco

Americas Headquarters
Cisco Systems, Inc.
San Jose, CA

Asia Pacific Headquarters
Cisco Systems (USA) Pte. Ltd.
Singapore

Europe Headquarters
Cisco Systems International BV
Amsterdam, The Netherlands

Cisco has more than 200 offices worldwide. Addresses, phone numbers, and fax numbers are listed on the Cisco Website at **www.cisco.com/go/offices.**

About the Authors

Ryan Tischer, CCIE No. 11459 is a Technical Solution Architect at Cisco where he focuses on SDN, Cloud, and network programmability. He has worked in IT for 20 years, specifically focused on design, deployment, and operations of networking technologies. Ryan holds a BA in Information Technology from the University of Massachusetts, Lowell and a MS in Network Engineering from Depaul University. Ryan lives with his wife and children in the Milwaukee, WI area. Ryan blogs at http://Policyetc.com.

Jason Gooley, CCIE No. 38759 (R&S & SP), is a very enthusiastic engineer that is passionate about helping others in the industry succeed. Jason has more than 20 years of experience in the Information Technology and Telecommunications industry. Jason currently works at Cisco as a Strategic Systems Engineer where he specializes in SD-WAN, campus, and data center network design. In addition, Jason works with Learning@Cisco on certification development, mentoring, and training. Jason is also a Program Committee member and organizer for the Chicago Network Operators Group (CHINOG). Jason lives in Illinois with his wife Jamie and their daughter Kaleigh.

About the Technical Reviewers

Joe Clarke, CCIE No. 5384 is a Global TAC engineer. He has contributed to network management products and technologies by finding and fixing bugs, as well as implementing maintenance and troubleshooting components in Cisco Prime.

Joe helps to support and enhance the embedded automation and programmability technologies, such as the Embedded Event Manager, Tcl, NETCONF/RESTCONF, and ONE Platform Kit (onePK). Joe is a top-rated speaker at Cisco's annual user conference, CiscoLive!, as well as certified as a Cisco Certified Internetworking Expert, Certified Java Programmer, and VMware Certified Professional. Joe provides network consulting and design support for the Internet Engineering Task Force (IETF) conference network infrastructure deployments. He has authored numerous technical documents on Cisco network management, automation, and programmability products and technologies. Joe is co-author of more than 20 Cisco patents. He is an alumnus of the University of Miami and holds a Bachelor of Science degree in computer science. Outside of Cisco, Joe is a member of the FreeBSD project. He is a committer in the project focusing mainly on the GNOME Desktop. He also maintains the FreeBSD ports Tinderbox application, which facilitates the automated packaging and testing of FreeBSD third-party ports.

Omar Sultan currently leads a team of sales managers and product managers focused on Cisco's web and cloud customers. At Cisco since 1999, Omar has focused on helping the company successfully enter new markets and is currently focused on the software and hardware technologies that underpin web-scale infrastructure. A geek at heart, Omar has been involved with IT since VAXes roamed the earth. Omar has been involved in every aspect of IT from cabling to coding to systems and networking, which has left him the perspective that data centers should really be viewed as their own class of quirky complex life forms.

Dedications

Ryan Tischer:

This book is dedicated to my wife Jennifer and my children Madeline, Alexander, and Elaina. When the road gets rough, you are the reason I do not give up. When scary arrives, you are the source for my courage. When good enough is reached, you make me push for better. When things don't go my way, you make me substitute my cuss words.

ILMF4EVER

Special thank you to my parents—Stop saying I turned out all right; there's still time.

To my friends—I know the best place for chili.

A message to my children—

Whatever your life has in store for you, be ...

curious

passionate

thoughtful

Break ground and glass

Be anything but boring.

—Ryan

Jason Gooley:

I would like to dedicate this book to my family. To my wife Jamie for being so endlessly supportive of me with my various "projects." Without you, I would not have been able to make it this far. To my daughter Kaleigh, who at the time of this writing is just 15 months old: It is extremely difficult to leave your side when all I want to do is spend time with you. I feel like I have already missed so much just writing this paragraph! To my father and brother for always having my back and believing in me. To my late mother, you have been the guiding light that has kept me on the right path.

Acknowledgments

Ryan Tischer:

I'd like to give special recognition to the amazing engineers, managers, sales teams, and customers I have the privilege of working with. I am humbled to be a part of this community, and I fully recognize that without your inspiration, encouragement, and knowledge, this book would not be possible. I have been truly blessed to have managers and co-workers who believe in me, told me when I screwed up, and gave me the opportunity of a lifetime. Special thank you to INSBU for building wickedly-cool products and letting me play.

A big thank you to Joe Clark, Omar Sultan, Brett Bartow, and Eleanor Bru for their amazing work on this book.

Finally, I'd like to thank my co-author Jason Gooley. I approached him with this project at the very last minute, and he's worked very hard to keep the book on time, while not sacrificing technical depth or content.

Jason Gooley:

First, thank you to Brett Bartow, Eleanor Bru, and the rest of the Cisco Press team for all of the support during creation of this book. It was a pleasure to work with such an amazing group of professionals.

I would like to thank the entire Cisco Commercial Midwest Select Operation for supporting me during this process. Thank you to my manager and all of my teammates on the Illinois Select team for the continued reinforcement of this project.

A special thanks to Anthony Sequeira, Keith Barker, Andre Laurent, and Luke Kaelin for all the mentoring and words of encouragement. I can't thank you enough for all of your support over the years.

Thank you, Ryan, for giving me the opportunity to write this book with you. It has been an absolute blast, and I am honored to be a part of it.

Finally, I would like to thank all my friends and family who have patiently waited for me to finish this project, so I would be able to go outside and play. You know who you are!

Contents at a Glance

Contents

Reader Services

Register your copy at www.ciscopress.com/title/ISBN for convenient access to downloads, updates, and corrections as they become available. To start the registration process, go to www.ciscopress.com/register and log in or create an account.* Enter the product ISBN 9781587144653 and click Submit. Once the process is complete, you will find any available bonus content under Registered Products.

*Be sure to check the box that you would like to hear from us to receive exclusive discounts on future editions of this product.

Icons Used in This Book

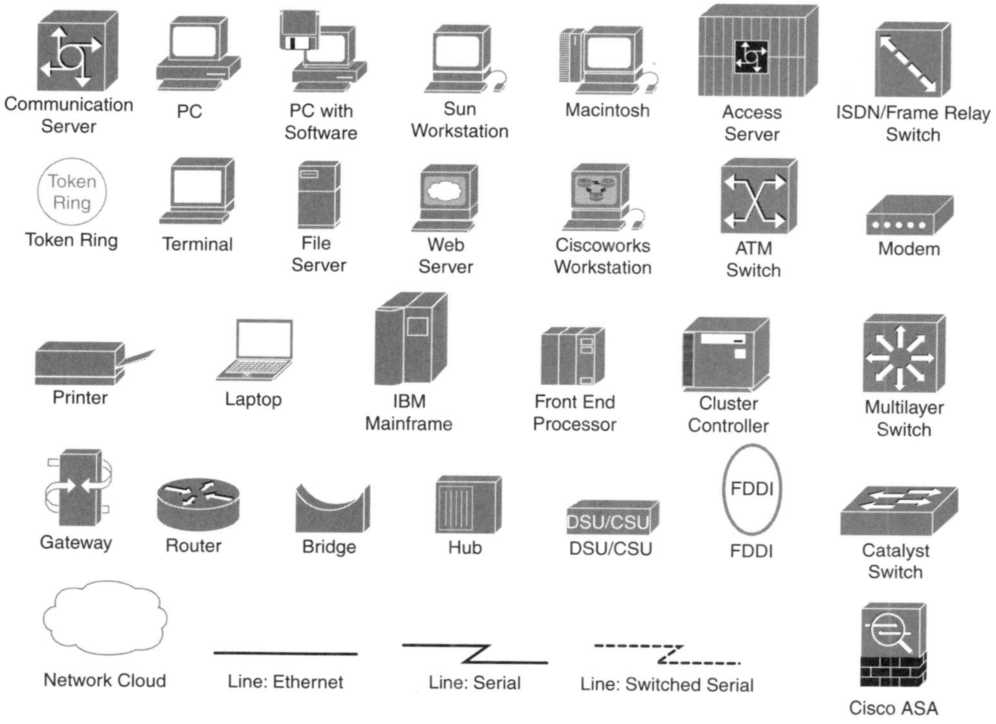

Command Syntax Conventions

The conventions used to present command syntax in this book are the same conventions used in the IOS Command Reference. The Command Reference describes these conventions as follows:

- **Boldface** indicates commands and keywords that are entered literally as shown. In actual configuration examples and output (not general command syntax), boldface indicates commands that are manually input by the user (such as a show command).
- *Italic* indicates arguments for which you supply actual values.
- Vertical bars (|) separate alternative, mutually exclusive elements.
- Square brackets ([ ]) indicate an optional element.
- Braces ({ }) indicate a required choice.
- Braces within brackets ([{ }]) indicate a required choice within an optional element.

Introduction

This book was designed with the focus on utilizing Cisco ACI Cisco Nexus 9000, Cisco UCS Director, Cisco (JSON), Python, Linux, Cisco APIC-EM, ConfD, and Data Models in a production environment as effectively as possible. Industry leaders were consulted for technical accuracy throughout this book.

Who Should Read This Book?

This book is designed for those network engineers and operators who want to implement, manage, and maintain Cisco networking solutions in modern environments. This book discusses automation and programming tools and techniques across the Cisco data center, campus, and LAN and WAN technologies.

How This Book Is Organized

Chapter 1, "Introduction: Why Network Programmability:" Network programmability can solve business problems, reduce operating expenses and increase business agility. Current network management is slow and prone to errors because it's a closed, box-by-box, CLI-driven system that requires constant and expensive attention. Network programmability serves as a tool kit to automate network configurations and troubleshooting, significantly reducing nonoperational states. Additionally network programmability allows the network to participate or add value to dynamic application environments, that is, DevOps, web, security, by facilitating a tight bond between applications and infrastructure.

Chapter 2, "Foundational Skills:" A basic introduction into software engineering and DEVOPS.

Chapter 3, "Next-Generation Cisco Data Center Networking:" This chapter discusses Cisco portfolio and where the reader could possibly implement network programmability and automation.

Chapter 4, "On-Box Programmability and Automation with Cisco Nexus NX-OS:" This chapter discusses writing software designed to run on the Nexus switch.

Chapter 5, "Off-Box Programmability and Automation with Cisco Nexus NX-OS:" This chapter discusses writing software to run on other systems and access Nexus switches remotely.

Chapter 6, "Network Programmability with Cisco ACI:" Chapter 6 discusses writing software to interact and enhance Cisco ACI.

Chapter 7, "On-Box Automation and Operations Tools:" This chapter discusses some of the automation and operations tools that are available on many Cisco platforms.

Chapter 8, "Network Automation Tools for Campus Environments:" Automation tools can be off-box as well as on-box. This chapter covers some of the tools available for Cisco campus networks including SDN, controllers, and more.

Chapter 9, "Piecing It All Together:" This chapter summarizes the contents of this book by giving our perspective on the many tools that are available to interact with Cisco networks.

Chapter 1

Introduction: Why Network Programmability

It's 8 p.m. when the phone rings. Web traffic is up over 1000% after your company's mobile application is casually mentioned during the Superbowl. The web team just added twenty-five more servers to the cluster. However, none of the VMs can communicate. As the lead network engineer, you instantly understand the issues:

1. Switch ports are configured for different VLANS.
2. Access control lists are misconfigured.
3. QoS is wrong.
4. Firewall ports need to be opened.
5. Load balancer needs the pool updated.

You report back to the president of the company that you're confident you can make all these changes in about a week, but only if he extends your outage window.

You never get a chance to make those changes. What could have been new customers and millions in revenue was lost because of a bad application experience. Revenue was lost due to the network impeding application delivery. Also you lost your job.

This example represents the issue with the network today in that how we manage it has not changed in thirty years. It's still box-by-box, CLI driven, and all too often, so complex that simple changes have undesired results. In contrast, modern applications, which often are key to the success of the business, are incredibly dynamic and a static network infrastructure deteriorates the application experience. Network programmability enables the network to not only participate in this new environment but to enhance the application experience. Network programmability allows for consistent and dynamic infrastructure configurations by automating deployments and simplifying the network.

The network, like all infrastructure, exists solely to support applications, and how applications are developed has recently gone through a significant change. Information technology departments used to be a necessary evil largely focused on cost reduction.

However, modern enterprises use technology, specifically software, to differentiate from their competitors. This shift set new expectations for software development and thus forced slow, uptime-focused IT processes to respond faster, be more flexible, and reduce operational costs associated with provisioning and managing infrastructure.

Traditionally, software development focuses on "close-to-perfect-as-possible" releases that greatly increase time to delivery and leave consumers waiting for new features and bug fixes. New software development methodologies, such as continuous integration/continuous deployment (CI/CD), or DevOps in general, focus on small and frequent software rollouts that quickly bring new products and features to market to meet customer demands. A key component of CI/CD is automated testing procedures that quickly detect issues with code and help prevent major software bugs. If or when software bugs make their way into production, the small size of the rollouts allows developers to rollback and fix issues with minimal impact to the users.

There is an old saying in information technology that applies to modern software development, "Good, fast, or cheap—pick two," as shown in Figure 1-1.

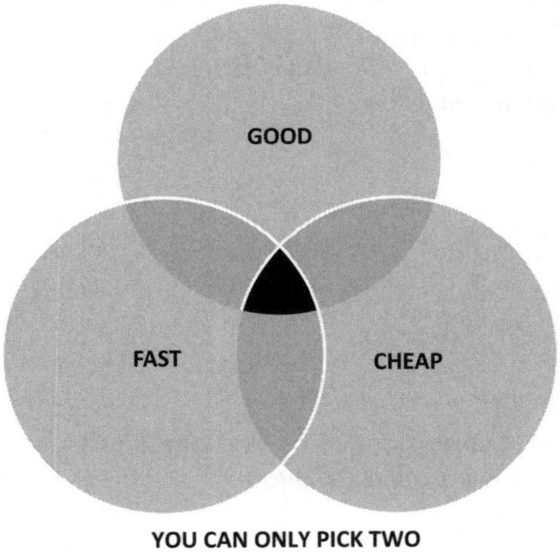

Figure 1-1 *Good, fast, or cheap—pick two*

The shift in both importance and delivery of software puts new demands on infrastructure. Server teams responded by virtualizing the server and automating deployments. The result was most IT teams could spin up a new virtual machine in minutes. However, the network takes much longer. Network services, for example firewall and load balancers, take even more time. In response, many networks do not use network hardware to full potential and are dumbed down to minimal configurations: no ACL's, no QoS, and trunking every VLAN to every host. Commercial overlay tools, such as VMware NSX, attempt agile networking by bypassing network hardware. However, they lack features and have scale/performance issues. Because software overlays do not have an interface to hardware, they cannot use it to enhance application delivery. Network programmability and automation utilizes both hardware and software to and enables agile network infrastructure. Agile network infrastructure can respond to and add value to dynamic business software.

What Is Network Programmability

Network programmability is a set of tools to deploy, manage, and troubleshoot a network device. A programmability-enabled network is driven by intelligent software that can deal with a single node or a group of nodes or even or address the network a single unified element. The tool chain uses application programming interfaces or APIs, which serve as the interface to the device or controller. The tool chain also utilizes software that uses the API to gather data or intelligently build configurations. The term network programmability can have different meanings, depending on perspective. To a network engineer, programmability means interacting with a device or group of devices (driving configurations, troubleshooting, etc.) with a software that sits (logically) above the device. To a developer, network programmability means abstracting the network such that it appears as a single device that can be manipulated with specialized software or within existing software. Both perspectives are correct and drive toward the same goals of using the network to enhance and secure application delivery.

The software component of network programmability can encompass different purposes and either run on the device (on-box) or remotely (off-box). Software built to interact with the network and can address how and/or why the interaction is required. In the case of driving configurations, "How" software addresses the specific device changes when a human determines that configuration is required. "Why" software adds intelligence to automatically react to network or external events, for example, a WAN outage or sudden influx of traffic. In some cases, the software will be purposely built to interact with the network—for example, day zero deployments or a component of a larger applications, such as Microsoft SharePoint. Figure 1-2 describes the relationship between software, the API, and the network.

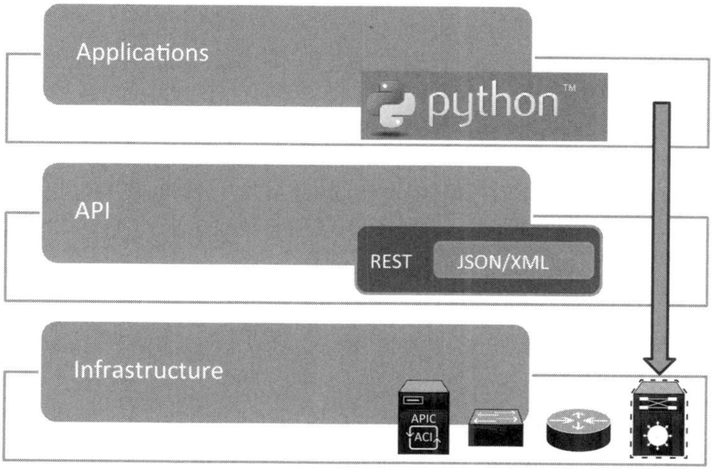

Figure 1-2 *What is network programmability?*

Network Programmability Benefits

Some of the benefits of network programmability include:

1. Time and money cost savings
2. Customization
3. Reduction of human error
4. Innovation

Simplified Networking

The network is a distributed system, and every new feature required adds configuration complexity and more operational risk. Complexity can lead to increased cost and increased outages. Today a high percentage of the "network down" events are due to misconfiguration (human error). Managing the network programmatically simplifies network management by reducing system variance with automated configurations and streamlined troubleshooting.

For example, Quality of Service (QoS) is a critical business feature that, due to complexity, is not commonly configured and is frequently configured incorrectly. A simple change, such as adding a new application, requires a human to access every network device and make a configuration change. Network programmability can simplify QoS deployment and configuration by using a simple application to quickly deliver consistent and accurate configuration changes. Simplified networking reduces man-hours spent operating the network to time spent innovating with the network.

Network Innovation with Programmability

Network programmability can transition the network from simple transport to a source of innovation. Today the network is a distributed system of single-purpose appliances that, in most cases, has excess resources. Network programmability unlocks these resources to solve business problems and enhance the application experience. The network is the most logical place for innovation because it has holistic application visibility with distributed policy enforcement. This allows the network to consistently check and adjust the user's application experience. Examples of network innovation include abnormal traffic detection, for example, a deep packet inspection (DPI) tool driving QoS policy, custom integrations to critical mission applications, and automated response to link failure.

Many organizations use redundant WAN links; however, due to cost considerations, the redundant link may only provide enough bandwidth for critical application traffic. Distributed network protocols, for example, OSPF or BGP, are excellent at re-routing traffic in the event of failure, but they generally cannot differentiate between high-priority and low-priority traffic. Network programmability enables automatic and intelligent configuration changes to be also based on business priority. During a failure, a reactive script could change ACLs to block nonpriority traffic from the backup link and even configure policy-based routing to send low-priority traffic over an Internet link, as shown in Figure 1-3.

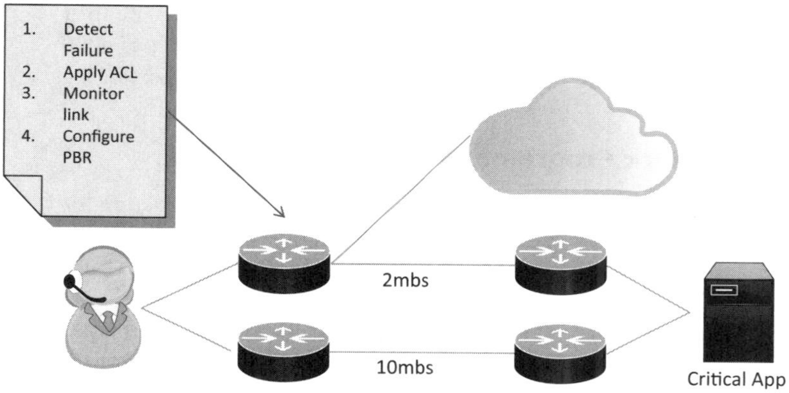

Figure 1-3 *Network innovation during WAN failure*

Network hardware provides a wealth of statistical information that can aid in detecting abnormal traffic or security issues. Data analytic tools can analyze n telemetry from network hardware detect patterns like abnormal flows, for example increased data rate or connections from new countries. If an issue is detected, network programmability can issue an updated QoS configuration to limit data flows or route traffic to a honey pot, as shown in Figure 1-4.

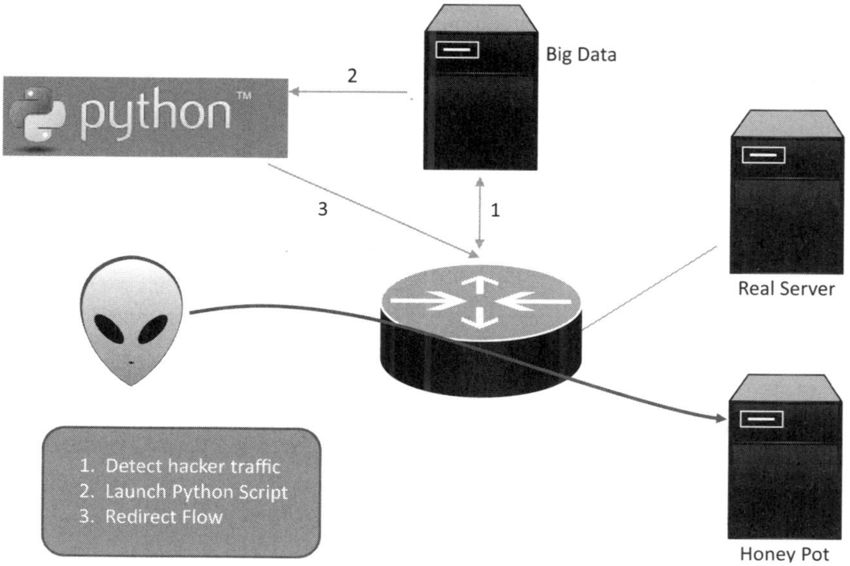

Figure 1-4 *Combined analytics and network programmability*

Traditionally, Cisco and other network vendors are the innovators in network software and network protocols. If a network administrator needs new features, they are faced with a long process of selling an idea and hoping the vendor will fund its development. Network programmability enables anyone to innovate by creating or extending software without his or her vendor. Network innovation helps organizations differentiate their products and solve problems using the network. Open NX-OS on Cisco Nexus 9000 enables use of the switch as a platform to run user-provided software/applications.

Cloud, SDN, and Network Programmability

The cloud is an operational model that automates and orchestrates infrastructure for application delivery. The cloud reduces information technology (IT) operational costs and/or increasing IT agility. It can be deployed on premises (private cloud), in a public provider, for example, Amazon AWS (public cloud), or a combination of public and private clouds (hybrid cloud). A hybrid cloud is very popular because it allows organizations to buy infrastructure for average volume and uses public resources (someone else's computer) for unexpected bursts.

Note The difference between automation and orchestration is that automation deals with a single element or single device, and orchestration assembles multiple elements or multiple devices to accomplish a task.

Cloud operational models are driven from a self-service catalog that provides an online shopping experience to consume IT resources and deliver applications. Self-service catalogs can be user facing or built for IT professionals, depending on business requirements. In either case, once the resources are approved for use, a tool chain allocates network, server, and storage resources to deliver a service to the user. The delivered service can consist of any IT resources; however, common models are software as a service (SaaS) or infrastructure as a service (IaaS). Organizations with software development teams also offer platform as a service (PaaS). Table 1-1 lists the common cloud services with example use cases.

Table 1-1 *Common Cloud Services and Use Cases*

Cloud Service	Example Use Case
Infrastructure as a service (IaaS)	Bare metal, Windows 2012, or Linux server
Platform as a service (PaaS)	Java, .Net or Python environment
Software as a service (SaaS)	Salesforce.com, SAP

Between the automation layer and the physical equipment are domain controllers. Domain controllers provide holistic management of the network by building a layer of abstraction between the physical infrastructure and its configuration. This allows the distributed network to be represented as a single device and provides simple integrations for cloud automation and orchestration tools, for example USC-Director or Cliqr. Automation and orchestration tools integrate to the controller through an API. Programmability of the network is written in a language proprietary to the tool or, in some cases, standard tools.

Controllers allow consumption of network resources without really understanding the network or even the language of network. Without a controller, the automation tool would have to understand the complexity of the network (protocols, hardware status, etc.) requiring significantly more integration work. Figure 1-5 demonstrates the relationship between infrastructure, controllers, and higher-level software tools.

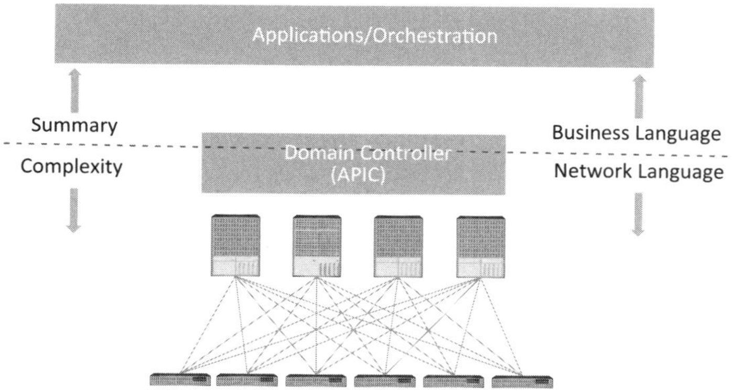

Figure 1-5 *Domain controllers*

Note Cisco Unified Computing System's (UCS) UCS Manager is a domain controller for compute resources.

The hybrid cloud operational model consists of automation, orchestration, and self-service tools. Clouds are built with multiple stacked tools, each providing an abstraction or summary of the infrastructure below it. For example, the Cisco Cloud stack leverages UCS-Director as an infrastructure automation engine which Cliqr, an orchestration tool, leverages to move toward deploying an application. Integration between the layers (or tools) is an open API that allows any tool (from any vendor) to be integrated and provide additional value. The Cisco hybrid cloud stack is represented in Figure 1-6.

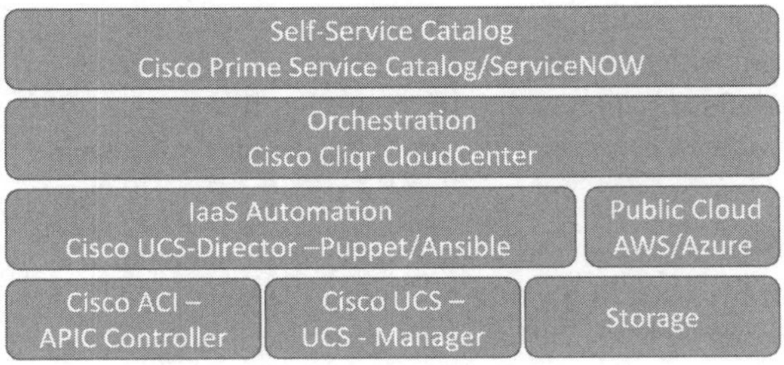

Figure 1-6 *Cisco Cloud Private Stack?*

SDN

Software-defined networking (SDN) sprang up in 2008 and is defined as a separation of the control and data plane of a network device. A separated and centralized, software-based control plane allows network operators to administrate the network as a single unit, which lowers operational costs, and through open interfaces, makes integration to applications much easier. The SDN controller serves as the network control plane and the single management interface for the network.

Cisco, with the release of Application Centric Infrastructure (ACI), entered into the SDN market, fulfilling the promises of SDN with considerable less complexity than existing solutions. ACI represents an SDN "easy button," which enables the network to be application-aware without changing the application. The controller in ACI, called the APIC (application policy infrastructure controller), allows the network to participate in cloud operational models. APIC differs from competitive SDN controllers in that it is not part of the control or data plane but instead relies on application centric policy to be instantiated to the hardware. The Cisco APIC features a robust API to interface and manage an ACI fabric programmatically.

Network programmability and SDN are similar in that they both can drive network element configurations. However, network programmability adds a software layer that can intelligently automate deployments or integrate with other systems. This software layer integrates with the API on the SDN controller. In this case, network controllers build an abstraction layer for the network by dealing with the details of the network physical infrastructure (link status, topology, etc.) while providing a simplified, single interface for programmability. A controller eliminates the requirement to understand and work with discrete network devices. Example use cases include driving automated configurations (rolling out a new service) or an analytics engine dynamically changing a path. The software layer can add intelligence to the network by integrating with business applications or other outside software. Figure 1-7 details the relationship between programmability, a SDN controller, and the physical infrastructure.

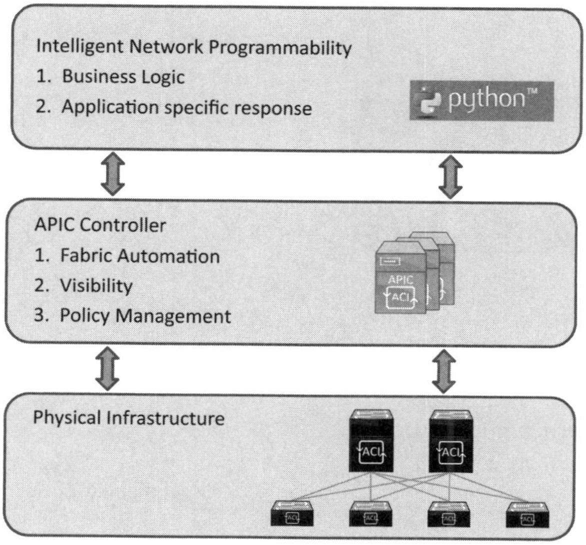

Figure 1-7 *SDN and network programmability*

Is Programmability a New Idea?

Network programmability is not a new idea. Legacy tools such as Expect or heavyweight vendor tools have been used to help manage networks for some time. In most cases, these tools provide limited business value because they are focused on interaction with CLI. CLI is built for humans to interact with a machine and is difficult to work with programmatically. Network programmability augments human-to-machine interaction with machine-to-machine interactions (M2M). M2M interaction is a two-way street where devices share information and state, enabling an application to effectively manage a business outcome, based on business-relevant events. M2M interactions are more direct because they do not require a translation and, therefore, can bypass slow and complex CLI parsers. Additionally, network programmability applications are agnostic about where they run, which language they are written in, and some cases care very little about mundane device details, such as version numbers. For example, a route could be expressed as an object. Then the object would be expressed across a variety of device types. Figure 1-8 demonstrates CLI versus a machine-friendly representation of a device state.

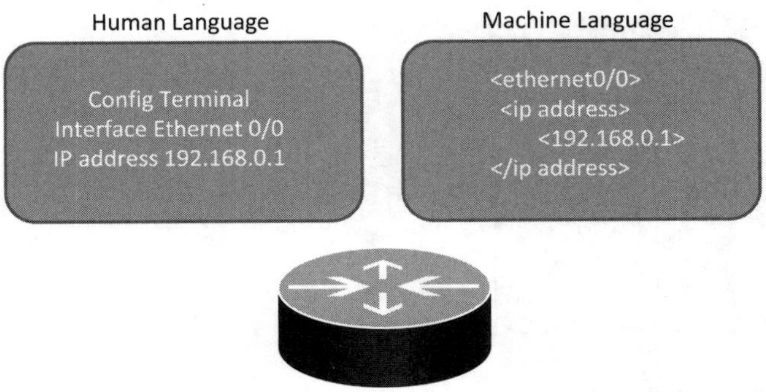

Figure 1-8 *Human language versus machine language*

Network Automation

The network programmability toolset is the foundation for advanced next-generation network automation. Network automation adds prebuilt intelligence that can assist with network deployments, operations, or troubleshooting. Like programmability, automation reduces cost and complexity, but it does so with an *if* statement to automatically invoke actions or changes, based on events. Network automation toolsets have been available for some time;, however, due to the complexity or cost, very few networks are automated. Network programmability, specifically open APIs and makes automation simpler and more accessible through standard tools. Examples are Python or common infrastructure automation tools like Puppet or Ansible. Network automation applications can be initiated by infrastructure events, such as a link failure or external events such as extreme weather or poorly performing applications. A common question for new automaton engineers is "When is a task worth automating?"

Questions to ask before automating a network task:

- Will automating this task save time?
- Will automating this task save money?
- Is the task prone to errors?

If the answer to one or more of these questions is yes, then the task is worth automating.

Automation Example

Handling link failure in WAN environments is a common use case for network automation. In the event of link failure, an automated response can either quickly resolve the issue or initiate a repair process, including opening a help desk ticket. Network automation can feed into IT automation by detecting whether the failure impacts any critical applications and moving the application to a different location, as shown in Figure 1-9.

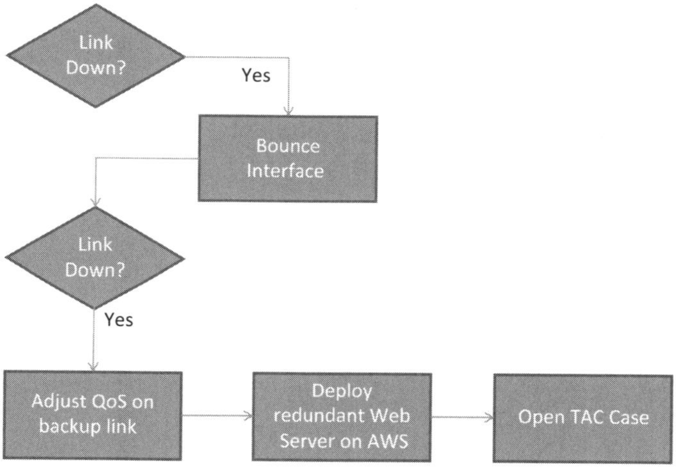

Figure 1-9 *Network automation workflow*

Summary

Network programmability changes the role of network administrators from operationally focused to innovation focused. Today's administrator is consumed by work orders and change requests, each of which require complex box-by-box CLI-based configuration across a tangled and distributed system. Network programmability frees a network administrator of operational burdens and allows them to focus on utilizing the network as a source of innovation.

Consider this book an argument for a change toward simplifying, automating, and adding (connected) intelligence to the network. Programmability is the future of network management because it saves time, saves money, and enables the next-generation network, which, however, requires a next-generation network engineer. The next-generation network engineer will require strong network skills in addition to programming skills. This book discusses foundational programming skills, Cisco APIs, and examples to enhance existing network engineers in campus WAN and data center networks. It paves the way to the next generation of network deployment and operations.

Chapter 2

Foundational Skills

This chapter is an introduction to the mind set and tools to build software. The topics discussed are designed to give the reader enough information for network programmability projects. However, the topics here are not comprehensive. The foundation skills covered are universal and apply to everything from complex web applications to simple network scripts.

Introduction to Software Development

Writing quality computer software, from simple scripts to multitier applications, requires an iterative process that begins with planning. Proper planning will save time, produce reusable code, and end with a better solution.

The first step in writing software is determining if software is the best solution to the problem. Software is awesome at solving countless problems, such as communications or organizing data; however, this adds components and complexity to a process. The software must produce a quicker, less expensive and/or better overall solution. For example, a sales organization may use customer relationship management software (CRM) to organize a sales process. In this case, is CRM software better than spreadsheets or even paper and pen? Most users would agree that CRM makes sale management easier, which produces more sales and happier customers. In this case, software used for sales management is justified. Factors, such as new revenue or increased productivity should be balanced against costs (time and resources to develop and maintain code) to evaluate a return on investment (ROI). In some cases, and especially with network programming and automation, ROI calculations can be simple. For example, if a task is required more than twice, it probably makes sense to automate with software. Due to unknown factors, It can be difficult to determine an ROI and is often imprecise. ROI calculation should be checked and rechecked during the software development process and adjustments made as needed.

> **Note** New programmers should not let ROI calculations impede experiences—in other words, just write code!

After a positive ROI is found (and the boss is convinced the project is a good use of time), the next step is the creation of pseudocode. Pseudocode is a framework of what the software hopes to accomplish without actually writing code. The good news about building pseudocode is that it can be used to document the final program and the architect does not have to know anything about programming. Building pseudocode is fairly easy and can help eliminate logic errors. A logic error occurs when the programmer writes functional code with nondesirable or inaccurate results.

Pseudocode for changing an NTP server in a data center network:

1. Identify every data center switch
2. Login to every data center switch
3. Delete previous NTP server
4. Configure NTP Server 192.168.0.55
5. Save Configuration

Once the basic steps are in place, it's easy to move them around. If you don't know every data center switch and want to use CDP to crawl the network, the pseudocode would be:

1. Login to a data center switch
2. Delete previous NTP server
3. Configure NTP Server 192.168.0.55
4. Save Configuration
5. Identify connected data center switches with CDP
6. Go to step 1

The basics are the same, with the additional step 6. The Go-to (repeat) is obvious because we built pseudocode. Once the pseudocode is done, we can move on to actually writing code.

At the most fundamental level, writing software is programming a computer to accomplish a task. The role of a programmer is to enumerate instructions for the computer to follow; however, this must be done from the context of the computer.

The computer is a blank slate and does not understand what, where, or why it is. Often programmers will fail to recognize the difference in human and computer thought and experience issues in creating software. For example, consider the human instructions to build a peanut butter and jelly sandwich:

1. Spread peanut butter over one slice of bread
2. Spread jelly over another slice of bread
3. Combine pieces of bread and enjoy.

Any seven-year-old English-speaking human could follow these instructions. However, if we gave this to a computer it would error on step one, word one.

```
"Error in 'Spread' (function not defined)"
```

A computer needs exact and detailed instructions to accomplish a task, and it is the mission of the programmer to translate those instructions into code.

```
Step 1. Locate self
Step 2. Locate peanut butter jar
Step 3. Open cupboard
Step 4. Move self to peanut butter jar
Step 5. Move hand to peanut butter jar
Step 6. Open hand ~10% larger than peanut butter jar
Step 7. Close hand around peanut butter jar
Step 101. Pick up knife
Step 102. Put knife into peanut butter jar
Step 103. Capture manageable amount of peanut butter on knife
Step 104. Move knife to bread
Step 105. Move knife from top of bread to bottom
Step 106. Move knife from bottom to top of bread
...
Step 1242. Enjoy
```

Common Constructs—Variables, Flow Control, Functions, and Objects

Today there are many quality-programming languages such as Ruby, Python, or Perl. However, they share common constructs. Learning common constructs is universal to using any language and is a fundamental skill for a programmer.

Variables

A variable is something unknown or dynamic. Variables could be usernames, number of switches, or types of jelly. The programmer will define variables in a program and define what *type* of data they will hold. Some languages require variables to be defined at the beginning of the code while some, notably Python, allow definition anywhere.

A best practice is to define variables in the beginning of your code unless the variable is temporary, for example, counters. In many languages, a variable is declared with its type (string, number, hash), and it must remain in that type. In some languages, declaration of a variable is done explicitly. For example in pseudo code, a variable to hold a number or assign data:

```
int NumUsers = 70
```

A variable is used to hold a string.

```
String greekGod = "Zeus"
```

Others, such as Python, are typed by the data. For example:

```
greekGod = "Zeus"
```

Quotes define a string or text in the variable.

The programmer can use any unique word to define a variable; however, it is best practice to use meaningful names and use consistent formatting. Variable name formatting varies from person to person; however, common formats include the "hump" where every other word is capitalized or using an underscore to define the type or scope, followed by the name.

Modern languages have many different types of variables, where strings, numbers, lists, and hashes are commonly used. The variable type (number, string, etc.) defines what can happen to the variable.

Variables that hold a number can be sorted or used in math functions. For example:

```
numZeuschildren = 70
num_zeusgrandchildren = 250
zeusOffspring = numZeuschildren + numZeusGrandChildren
print zeusOffspring
330
```

Strings can be searched, split, or concatenated.

```
zeusFirstname = "Zeus"
zeusLastname = "Horkios"
zeusFullname = zeusFirstname + zeusLastname
print zeusFullname
Zeus Horkios
```

Line 3 uses the "+" sign to concatenate or combine two strings.

A list is a variable that holds multiple items that can be of different type. For example, a list of letters in "Cisco" would be

networkCompany = ['C', 'i', 's', 'c', 'o']

Values in a list are separated by a comma and can be referenced by position. For example, to get the value of the third letter in in the list, use the following:

```
print networkCompany[3]
```

returns the single character "s."

A list can hold multiple data types and even other lists. For example the following list holds the word Cisco, the current year, and a list of Nexus 9000 switches.

networkCompany = ['C', 'i', 's', 'c', 'o' , 2016, ['9732', '9504', '9516']]

Hashes are another type of variable and are a list of key | value pairs. They help organize data with relationships. In the following example that shows data center switches, TOR1 is the key and the IP address is the value.

```
TOR1:192.168.50.50
TOR2:192.168.50.51
TOR3:192.168.50.52
```

Flow Control—Conditions

Conditions add logic and choice to a program. Back to the PB&J example, say there are two types of jelly in the fridge: grape (Zeus's favorite) and raspberry (Hera's favorite). Conditions are defined with an "if" and are followed by an action unique to that choice. The result of a condition is either true or false. For example:

```
if "Hera"
 jelly = "raspberry"
```

We can also use so-called else statements if the if statement is false:

```
if "Hera"
 jelly = "raspberry"
else
 jelly = "grape"
```

In some cases, we want to test an additional condition with else-if:

```
if "Hera"
 jelly = "raspberry"
else-if "Zeus"
 jelly = "grape"
else
 jelly = "none"
```

Flow Control—Loops

A loop is a tool to repeat something for a number of times. In general, two types of loops, **for** and **while**, exist. A **for** loop executes once for each item in a list or string, where a **while** loop evaluates before every iteration.

For example, the following shows a comparison between a **for** loop through a list and a **for** loop through a string:

```
list = [1, 2, 3]
for x in list:
 print x
Returns
1
2
3
```

```
for a in "cisco":
print a
Returns
c
i
s
c
o
```

The **while** loop executes the code block while the condition is true. If the condition starts false, the code will not execute.

```
x = 0
while x < 5:
 print "The variable is less than 5"
 x = x + 1
```

The line x = x +1 adds one to the value every iteration through the loop and returns

```
"The variable is less than 5"
"The variable is less than 5"
"The variable is less than 5"
"The variable is less than 5"
"The variable is less than 5"
```

Functions

Functions are defined by name, and have multiple uses:

- Modularize code to be smaller and reusable.
- Can repeat a task a number of times.
- Can be used to make a task more readable.
- Can optionally can take input or produce output.

The following example is a simple function to multiple an input by ten.

```
Function multipleBYten(inputNum)
 inputNum = inputNum * 10
 return inputNum
Function multipleBYhundo(inputNum)
 inputNum = inputNum * 10
 return inputNum
#Main code - Create variables byTen and ByHundred and use the above functions to
get the values
byTen = multipleBYten(10)
byHundred = multipleBYhundo(10)
#print the values
print "The value of 10*10 is " + byTen
print "The value of 100 * 10 is " + byHundred
output
print "The value of 10*10 is 100
print "The value of 100 * 10 is 1000
```

The function byTen inputs a number, multiplies the input by 10, and returns a value to the main.

We can also pass in variables to functions:

```
#Main code
paycheck = 10
byTen = multipleBYten(paycheck)
byHundred = multipleBYhundo(paycheck)
print byTen
print byHundred
```

Objects

Objects are a collection of data and procedures pertaining to a specific thing, for example a person, car, or router. Objects are built or instantiated from a template, called a class, which defines common properties about the object. If we were working with lots of routers in a WAN, we could build a class with the following:

```
Class Router
 IP address:
 SNMP community:
 Management protocol:
 Routing protocol:
 DNS:
```

> **Notice!** There is no data in the class; it is just the template.

To instantiate an object provide a unique name and the details for the object.

```
myRouter = Router("172.30.1.2", "admin", ssh, OSPF, "192.168.0.55")
```

Once the object is created, we can then work with the object with methods. Methods are actions for the object created within the object.

```
Class Router
 IPaddress:
 SNMP community:
 Management protocol:
 Routing protocol:
 DNS:
Method showIP
 print IPaddress
```

To use the method, reference the object name and the method

```
myRouter.showIP
```

Objects and object-oriented programming (OOP) are very advanced and take years to master but are useful when dealing with elements of Cisco ACI.

A Basic Introduction to Python

Python is a powerful, easy-to-use, and hard-to-mess-up interactive programming language that offers the next-generation network engineer a toolkit to interact with network devices. Python programs can be simple top-down scripts or drive robust object-oriented applications, for example, Open Stack. Python can be an interpreted or a byte-code compiled language, where most Python is interpreted. Text in interpreted languages is immediately executable and can feed line by line into the interpreter. For this reason interpreted languages are easier to use and debug, but interpreted languages have a performance penalty. Python syntax is intuitive, includes built-in help, and is designed for enhanced readability. Finally, Python can be extended with thousands of free importable libraries.

The Python interpreter is included by default on Cisco NX-OS, Mac OS X, and Linux systems. Microsoft users have to install Python via a free download (https://www.python.org/downloads/). The interpreter features an interactive shell that is often used to quickly build or test code. To invoke the Python interpreter shell, type **python** from the operating system command prompt or NX-OS CLI, as shown in the following example.

```
bash-3.2$ python
Python 2.7.10 (v2.7.10:15c95b7d81dc, May 23 2015, 09:33:12)
[GCC 4.2.1 (Apple Inc. build 5666) (dot 3)] on darwin
Type "help", "copyright", "credits" or "license" for more information.
>>>
```

When the interpreter is invoked, it displays the version of Python, in this case Python 2.7. The **>>>** indicates the user is in the interpreter and it is ready for Python commands.

Note—Python versions At the time of this publication, the current version of Python is 3.4; however, most users leverage 2.7.X. This book will focus on 2.7.10, but most examples will work in 3.3.

To print "Hello World" in Python, use the built-in **print** command to pass "Hello World" to standard output.

```
>>> print "Hello World"
Hello World
>>>
```

Variables in Python can be declared at any point in the program and are automatically typed, based on the data. The following example defines a variable "a" and assigns the string of "Hello World." The variable "a" is now typed as a string.

```
>>> a = "Hello World"
>>> print a
Hello World
>>>
```

Variables can also hold numbers. The following example creates a variable named "A" and assigns the value of 10

```
>>> A = 10
>>> print a
Hello World
>>> print A
10
>>>
```

Notice! Python is case sensitive; a and A are different.

More on Strings

Building and manipulating strings is a key skill to working with Cisco network devices. A string in Python is an array of characters, each in a unique (indexed) position. The following example shows an array in which the data stored in "a" is "Hello World" where a[0] is the letter "H." Python and most languages are 0 based, which is to say the data always starts in the zero position.

```
>>> print a
Hello World
>>> print a[0]
H
>>> print a[1]
e
>>> print a[2]
l
>>> print a[3]
l
>>> print a[4]
o
>>>
```

The variable type dictates what types of operations or methods can be performed on the data. Python methods are built in tools to manipulate a variable. As an example, a string can be searched, split, or concatenated. The following is a string split.

```
>>> print a
Hello World
>>> a.split(" ")
['Hello', 'World']
>>> a.split(" ")[0]
'Hello'
>>>
```

This example uses the built-in Python method **split**. To use **split** (or any other Python method) connect the variable name to method with a period (**a.split**) followed by the input parameter for the method, in this case a blank space.

The **find** method can be used to search a string:

```
>>> print a
Hello World
>>> a.find("Hello")
0
>>> a.find("World")
6
>>>
```

a.find returns the position of the beginning of the searched word. In this case the word "Hello" starts at position 0 and "World" starts at 6.

The **+** sign will concatenate two strings:

```
>>> a = "Hello"
>>> b = "World"
>>> print a+b
HelloWorld
>>>
```

a+b returns "HelloWorld", which is missing a space and is not correct. A space can be added using concatenation three times:

```
>>> print a + " " + b
Hello World
>>>
```

Other variables such as numbers can be converted into strings with the **str** command.

```
>>> a = 5
>>> str(a)
'5'
>>>
```

Help!

One of the very nice features of Python is the built-in help. To list all of the built in methods for variable use dir(variable name)

The following example demonstrates available methods for the string stored in variable "a."

```
>>> a = "Hello World"
>>> dir(a)
… '_formatter_field_name_split', '_formatter_parser', 'capitalize', 'center',
'count', 'decode', 'encode', 'endswith', 'expandtabs', 'find', 'format', 'index',
'isalnum', 'isalpha', 'isdigit', 'islower', 'isspace', 'istitle', 'isupper',
'join', 'ljust', 'lower', 'lstrip', 'partition', 'replace', 'rfind', 'rindex',
'rjust', 'rpartition', 'rsplit', 'rstrip', 'split', 'splitlines', 'startswith',
'strip', 'swapcase', 'title', 'translate', 'upper', 'zfill']
>>>
```

Python help has built-in documentation accessed by help (**a.split**) as shown in the following example.

```
>>>help(a.split)
split(…)
 S.split([sep [,maxsplit]]) -> list of strings
 Return a list of the words in the string S, using sep as the
```

```
 delimiter string. If maxsplit is given, at most maxsplit
 splits are done. If sep is not specified or is None, any
 whitespace string is a separator and empty strings are removed
 from the result.
(END)
```

In addition to the built-in Python documentation, online documentation and examples can be found at https://docs.python.org.

Flow Control

Flow control enables a coder to direct code, based on variables or other input. Flow control introduces logic into an application with conditions, iteration, and loops.

Python Conditions

Conditions in Python use **if**, **else**, and **elif** (**else-if**) statements. **If** statements compare two or more values and follow a specific path, based on the truth of the expression. If the expression is true, the code under the **if** statement is executed; if not, the code block is skipped. Python **if** statements require indentation.

```
>>> if 1 < 2:
... print "True"
 File "<stdin>", line 2
 print "True"
 ^
IndentationError: expected an indented block
>>>
```

The above code failed due to an indentation error. Python requires indentation. The following shows the correct code.

```
>>> if 1 < 2:
... print "True"
...
True
>>> if 1 > 2:
... print "This will not Print"
...
>>>
```

Many times data must be evaluated against many options. While it is possible to have multiple **if** statements, **else** and **elif** are used to clean up code and make it more readable. The following example evaluates the value of “a” to determine if it is less than, greater than, or equal to 5.

```
>>> a = 5
>>> if a < 5:
... print "a is less then 5"
... elif a > 5:
... print "a is greater then 5"
... elif a == 5:
... print "a is equal to 5"
... else:
... print "a is not normal"
...
a is equal to 5
>>>
```

Python compares two values, using operators. Table 2-1 lists the operator symbol and its purpose.

Table 2-1 *Python Operators*

Purpose	Symbol
Less than	<
Greater than	>
Less than or equal	<=
Greater than or equal	>=
Equals	==
Not equal	!=

Python Loops

The **for** loop in Python will execute code a certain number of times for every element in a sequence.

```
>>> for x in range(0,5):
... print "Hello World"
...
Hello World
Hello World
Hello World
Hello World
Hello World
>>>
```

The **for** loop defines the variable x and executes the code block for each number in the range of 0–5. The following is the same code, however the code prints the value of x.

```
>>> for x in range(0,5):
... print x
...
0
1
2
3
4
>>>
```

A **for** loop can iterate through any data including a string.

```
>>> a = "cisco"
>>> for x in a:
... print x
...
c
i
s
c
o
>>>
```

While Loop

A **while** loop will repeat a code block while the initial condition is true, as shown in the following example.

```
>>> a = 0
>>> while a != 100:
... a = a + 20
... print a
...
20
40
60
80
100
>>>
```

The previous example sets the value of a to 0. The while loop adds the value of a to itself and adds 20. This loop runs while the value of a does not equal 100.

Other data types in Python are:

- lists
- tuples
- hashes

Lists, tuples, and hashes are variable data structures that create a sequence of data but have different properties.

A list is created with comma-separated values within square brackets:

```
>>> ciscoNexus = ["9273", "9396", "93128"]
>>> print ciscoNexus
['9273', '9396', '93128']
```

Data within a list can be accessed by position:

```
>>> print ciscoNexus[0]
9273
```

Data within a list is mutable (can be changed):

```
>>> ciscoNexus[0] = "9372"
>>> print ciscoNexus[0]
9372
>>>
```

A tuple is created with comma-separated values within parentheses:

```
>>> ciscoNexus = ("9273", "9396", "93128")
>>> print ciscoNexus[0]
9273
>>>
```

Data within a tuple is immutable (can NOT be changed):

```
>>> ciscoNexus[0] = "something, anything"
Traceback (most recent call last):
 File "<stdin>", line 1, in <module>
TypeError: 'tuple' object does not support item assignment
>>>
```

Note "Traceback" is Python's way of saying something is wrong.

Hashes in Python are called dictionaries and are useful when working with associative data. Dictionaries are a map of unordered key/value pairs of where the key must be unique sting and the value can be any type of data. The values in a dictionary are mutable, however the keys are not. Dictionaries are useful in network programmability because device configuration is structured in a similar fashion.

For example, NTP server (key) = 172.32.1.1 (value).

Dictionaries are built, using curly brackets followed by the key|value separated by a colon.

```
>>> ntpServers = {"server1" : "172.32.1.1", "server2" : "172.32.1.2","server3" :
"172.32.1.3"}
>>> print ntpServers
{'server1': '172.32.1.1', 'server2': '172.32.1.2', 'server3': '172.32.1.3'}
>>>
```

Data within a dictionary can be accessed via the key:

```
>>> print ntpServers["server1"]
172.32.1.1
>>>
```

Data within a dictionary can be changed via the key:

```
>>> ntpServers["server3"] = "172.32.1.4"
>>> print ntpServers["server3"]
172.32.1.4
>>>
```

Data within a dictionary can be looped (iterate through):

```
>>> for key in ntpServers:
... print key + " = " + ntpServers[key]
...
server1 = 172.32.1.1
server2 = 172.32.1.2
server3 = 172.32.1.3
```

The line "print key + " = " + ntpServers[key] references every key in ntpServers and prints the value. Notice that the line requires indentation.

Python Functions

A function is separate block of code that is called within a program. Functions are useful when the code needs to used or run many times. Functions also clean up code and makes it more readable.

The Python key word **def** followed by a name defines a function. Optionally, functions have input defined by a variable.

```
>>> def someMath(x):
... a = x * x
... return a
```

The function someMath expects input and stores the input in the variable "x" The variable "x" only holds data for the life of the function. The second line of the function multiples "x" times "x" and store the value in "a". The final line of the function and returns the data in the variable "a"

To call the function, type the function name followed by the input in ():

```
>>>
>>> b = someMath(5)
>>> print b
25
>>>
```

In this case, the data returned is store in the global variable "b."

Python Files

The interactive Python interpreter is a great tool to test or debug code; however, in most cases Python code is executed from a file. The unenforced standard extension for Python files is **.py** and the file must have "execute" permissions. The first line in a Python file is referred to as a "shebang" and should point to the location of the Python interpreter, usually located at **/usr/bin/python**. The shebang starts with #! and tells the script to first run the interpreter and pass the location of the file as a parameter.

Python files can be run directly from the operating system; however, they must have operating system execute permissions. The **chmod** command sets the execute bit of SimpleMath.py.

```
Mac and Linux systems - chmod +x SimpleMath.py
```

The Python interpreter can also execute or run Python files.

```
python somecode.py
```

In-file documentation, commonly referred to as "code comments" is a coding best practice that helps you and other programmers understand the purpose of the code. Single line documentation starts with a **#** and is ignored by the interpreter. Multiline documentation opens and closes with three single quotes in a row. The following example demonstrates in-file documentation.

```
# single line documentation
'''
multiline documentation
in a python file
'''
```

Importing Libraries

Python is extremely extensible through built-in and third-party libraries. Libraries allow Python developers to import enhanced functionality into their programs. Python's standard library is included with the base installation and provides tools for common tasks such as operating system manipulation and using regular expressions. Third-party libraries further extend Python's capabilities but must be installed into Python. Most third-party libraries are licensed under an open-source model and can be used without charge. Python libraries must be imported into the Python session, either in interactive mode or in a file. When the file is complete or the session is ended, the library is removed from memory. Libraries are imported, using the Python statement "**import**" to import the entire library. Alternately, to load specific attributes from a library, use the command "**from *library_name* import *attribute name***". The following Python code imports the entire sys library.

```
"import sys"
```

or to import a specific attribute of sys use

```
"from sys import executable"
```

Some common Python libraries are listed in Table 2-2.

Table 2-2 *Common Python Libraries*

Library	Capability
re	Works with regular expressions.
sys	Works with user input
datetime	Gets data and time information
os	Works with Operating System (OS), writes and opens files
requests	Working with web requests*
scrapy	Screen Scraping*
json	Working with JSON formatted data.*

*Not included in the standard Python distribution.

Installing Python Libraries

Python version 2.7.9 and greater includes package management tool (PIP) to manage and install third-party libraries. PIP will download the latest stable library and any package dependences. PIP requires an Internet connection.

> **Note** Python versions before 2.7.9 and Mac OS users will have to install PIP. OS X users use "sudo easy_install pip"

PIP downloads libraries from Python Package Index or PyPI. Libraries located by PyPI are user submitted and is maintained by the Python Software Foundation. The PyPI website is located at https://pypi.python.org and offers a package index, documentation, and community support.

Using PIP

The PyPi repository is searched via the **PIP** command line using:

```
pip search "Package Name"
```

For Example,

```
pip search requests
```

PIP search returns every package with the term **requests** in either the name or the description of the package. Use standard output modifiers to read the results.

```
pip search requests | more
```

Once the desired package is located use **PIP install** to install the package.

```
pip install requests
```

> **Note** Mac and Linux users—you have to be root to install or modify packages. Use the **sudo** command to escalate privileges.
>
> sudo pip install requests

pip show "package name" will display detailed information about an installed package. **pip list** displays all installed packages.

Using Common Python Libraries

Most Python programs will utilize an imported library. **re** (regular expressions), **sys** (Python system, including user input), and **datetime** (use date and time) are often utilized in network programmability scripts. Libraries must be imported for use **import re** imports the regular expression library.

Regular expressions, or regex, are a powerful tool to search and manipulate strings. The standard Python library "re" enables regular expressions. Regular expressions are built with a string of text with or without special characters. Special characters match characters are similar to wildcard and match specific pattern or occurrences.

Table 2-3 shows some of the common special characters.

Table 2-3 *Regular Expression Special Characters*

Character	Purposes
.	Matches any character, except a new line
^	Matches the start of a line
$	Matches the end of a line
*	Matches 0 or more of the preceding character
+	Matches 1 or more or the preceding character
{x} or {x,y}	Matches x or x and y copies or repetitions
[]	Matches a set

Python's re library has several methods to work with regular expressions, as listed in Table 2-4.

Table 2-4 *Regular Expression Common Methods*

Method	Description
re.findall	Searches entire string and store in a list
re.search	Searches the entire string
re.sub	Finds and replace
re.match	Searches the beginning of the string

Given a string (and an excellent Einstein quote):

```
>>> someText = "We cannot solve our problems with the same thinking we used when
we created them"
```

The method **re.findall** will output a list of occurrences from the search string:

```
>>> o = re.findall ("we", someText) #find all occurrences of "we" in the string
>>> print o
['we', 'we']
>>>
```

re.findall located both occurrences of "we," however ignored the "We." Regular expressions are case sensitive.

Adding the special character [] enables finding both the lower- and uppercase text.

```
>>> o = re.findall ("[Ww]e", someText)
>>> print o
['We', 'we', 'we']
```

Note The special character [ ], known as a character set, is very useful when looking for a set of options. In the above example [Ww], search for either a "W" or a "w". Character sets can be expanded to search for a range of characters for example, [0–9] will match any single digit or 3[5–9] will match any number between 35 and 39. Finally, character sets be negated with [^] to say anything but this set. For example, given the string of "123456," [^123] matches "456."

The method **re.match** is used to search starting from the beginning of the string.

print re.match ("we", someText) returns "None". Which says it did not find the string of "we" in the beginning of the variable someText.

print re.match ("We", someText) returns "<_sre.SRE_Match object at 0x1004b7f38>" which is the location of "We". It is rare that the location of the match is important; most of the time we are looking for what matched. The output text from **re.match** is stored in a group and is accessible by the group number. In the following code **group 0** returns **We.**

```
>>> o = re.match (".e", someText) # The . matches on any character
>>> print o.group(0)
We
```

Note The above example uses the regex special character "." that means "match any character." In this ca, capital and lowercase "w." The Dot is very powerful and in many cases, too powerful. For example, the expression ".e" matches "be," "de," "e," and so on. Use the Dot with caution.

Best practice is to use **re.match** followed immediately by an **if**, which ensures a match was found. The following code only prints "We" if the match was found.

```
o = re.match ("We", someText)
>>> if o:
… print o.group(0)
We
```

re.search will search through an entire string, however will stop in the first instance. The following example leverages re.search to find the first "we" in someText

```
>>> o = re.search("we", someText)
>>> print o.group(0)
```

This example returns "we" , which is the first "we" in someText. This can be verified with **o.span** which stores the start and end locations of the indexed string someText:

```
>>> print o.span()
(52, 54)
```

The location of the word can be verified by sting position, in this case position 52 and 53

>>> print someText[52]

w

>>> print someText[53]

e

re.sub will substitute a search string for inputted text:

```
>>> re.sub ("we", "WEEEE", someText)
'We cannot solve our problems with the same thinking WEEEE used when WEEEE created
them'
```

Regex quantifiers, "*", "+" and "{}" search for occurrences for characters. From someText, say we wanted to break the word *cannot* into two words.

```
>>> re.sub ("n{2}", "n n", someText)
'We can not solve our problems with the same thinking we used when we created
them'
```

The above expression says only find "nn" and replace it with "n n".

Regular expressions are an incredibility powerful tool when working with text. They can also be extremely complex. The following resources are recommended to learn more about regular expressions.

https://github.com/npaa/NPaA/blob/master/learn_regex.txt

http://regexr.com/

http://www.regular-expressions.info/

http://regexone.com/

Sys, short for system, enables Python programs to interact with the interpreter. **Sys** is most often used to interact with the command line and specifically to input arguments into a Python programs. The following example utilizes **sys** to check for user input, and echoes the input to standard output.

```
#!/usr/bin/python
#import sys from standard library
import sys
#echoes input
#Calculate number of arguments. sys.argv considers the script name an arg, so
# we subtract 1
numArg = len(sys.argv) - 1
#print the number of arguments
print " "
```

```
print "There are " + str(numArg) + " arguments"
print " "
#if the user enter "–help" display the help message"
if str(sys.argv[1]) == "-help":
 print "This is the help message"
 print "Enter a string, any string"
 print " "
#if input does not equal "–help" echo the input
else:
 print "The input was " + str(sys.argv[1])
```

Output

```
bash-3.2$ python sys_example.py -help
There are 1 arguments
This is the help message
Enter a string, any string
bash-3.2$ python sys_example.py Cisco
There are 1 arguments
The input was Cisco
bash-3.2$
```

Datetime allows the Python interpreter to access the system clock. **Datetime** is useful to complete tasks at a certain time or for logging output, as shown in the following example.

```
#!/usr/bin/python
#import system and date from datetime
import sys
from datetime import date
#assigns the current data to the var
todaysDate = str(date.today())
#Gets user input
myBirthday = str(sys.argv[1])
print " "
print " "
#checks if todays data is equal to users input
if todaysDate == myBirthday:
 print "Whoa - Happy Birthday!"
 print "Check under the chair for a prize"
else:
 print "it is not your birthday…Get back to work"
 print "Todays Date is " + todaysDate
print " "
print " "
```

Output

```
bash-3.2$ ./datatime_example.py 2016-04-11
Whoa - Happy Birthday!
Check under the chair for a prize
bash-3.2$ ./datatime_example.py 2016-05-02
it is not your birthday…Get back to work
Todays Date is 2016-04-11
bash-3.2$
```

The following is another example of a simple Python program.

```
SimpleMath.py
#!/usr/bin/python
#Single Line Documentation
#This program multiples a number
#File name SimpleMath.py
'''
Multiline documentation
Spawned by Ryan Tischer
use at your own risk!
'''
def someMath(x): #Function inputs a number, multiples it by its self and returns
the answer
 a = x * x # do the math
 return a #return the result
a = "Tricky question… let me think…"
#send the value of 5 to someMath
b = someMath(5)
#print results
print a
print "I found the answer… 5 multiplied by 5 is " +str(b) + " . That was easy!"
Results
Tricky question… let me think…
I found the answer… 5 multiplied by 5 is 25. That was easy!
```

Python is a powerful yet easy-to-use programming language. It supports a wide range of applications from simple configurations scripts to large open source projects and can be extended, using thousands of free libraries. Python has built-in documentation that helps new and experienced coders navigate and utilize features. Required formatting ensures code readability and reuse. Python's features and ease of use makes it the preferred language for building network programmability code. See the following resources to learn more about Python.

https://github.com/npaa/NPaA/blob/master/learn_python.txt

http://www.learnpython.org

https://www.codecademy.com/learn/python

https://www.python.org/about/gettingstarted/

APIs and SDKs

The software development kit or SDK is a tool kit to aid in software development for a specific platform. SDKs are downloaded and installed onto your development system. In most cases the use of the SDK is optional; however, they make software development much easier. Many Cisco products including, Cisco ACI, NX-OS, and UCS Director have a SDK. An SDK communicates over an API.

Application programming interfaces (APIs) are an interface for software to communicate with other software. The API allows software to interact or modify a device. APIs have been vendor specific, but there is a move to create vendor agnostic APIs, so a piece of code will work across hardware for different vendors. APIs will evolve over time with new capabilities, but a well-designed API will maintain backward compatibility. In most cases, the API will have to be enabled and require authentication. Most modern TCP/IP connected operating systems have an API, including Cisco NX-OS, Cisco ACI, and Cisco IOS-XE. APIs used by Cisco products are not language specific (Ruby, Python, etc.) however expect specific formatting. Modern APIs leverage the HTTP (REST) for secure data transport and XML or JSON for data encoding.

Web Technologies

Modern APIs communicate and exchange data via web-based technologies. Web-based technologies are well understood, can be encrypted, and use common formatting. REST is the most common web technology for connecting and exchanging to network devices.

Representational State Transfer or REST is a structure for communicating to a remote system with HTTP. REST works in a client-to-server manner, in which the client initiates a connection to a server (Figure 2-1). A system that is accessible via REST is said to be RESTful. The REST connection uses HTTP or, for secure connections, HTTPS and utilizes common HTTP verbs. Some common HTTP verb examples are found in Table 2-5.

REST is considered stateless (thus the word *state*) in that the RESTful server does not maintain any memory of a client connection. A RESTful server sees every client connection as new and the client's request as the current configuration state. In the event the client sends a state that already exists on the RESTful server, the server accepts the request but does not make any changes. Transacting with a RESTful server requires some type of data formatting.

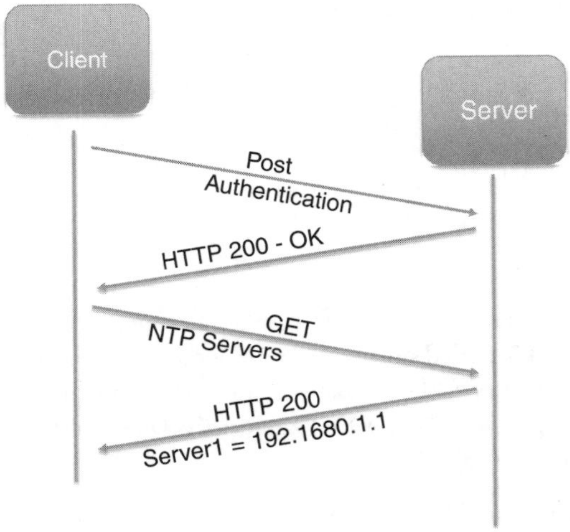

Figure 2-1 *REST Communication*

Table 2-5 *HTTP Verbs*

Verb Name	Action	Example
GET	Retrieves Data	Regular Web Surfing
POST	Creates Data	Web forms
PUT	Creates or updates data	Message boards
DELETE	Removes data	Remove configuration

Web Technologies—Data Formatting

A RESTful server will send and expect to receive formatted data. Formatted data ensures proper type and structure is when working with a remote system. XML and JSON are common data-encoding formats.

XML

XML is a markup language similar to HTML and designed to describe data in a human readable format. XML can be used to share data between machines. Data in XML is marked up with user-defined tags that describe the data within the tag. The following is a simple example of XML marked up data.

```
<favoriteBook> Hitchhikers Guide to the Galaxy</favoriteBook>
```

Table 2-6 dissects the XML tagging in the previous example.

Table 2-6 *XML Breakdown*

<favoriteBook>	Opening tag
Hitchhikers Guide to the Galaxy	The data
</favoriteBook>	End of the expression. Notice the </

XML is often structured hierarchically to better organize data.

```
<books>
 <book>Hitchhikers Guide to the Galaxy</book>
 <book>IT</book>
</books>
```

XML is very flexible and can be used to represent complex data, however using XML can be very complex. JSON is a lightweight alternative to XML.

JSON

Javascript Object Notation or JSON is a lightweight data-formatting tool. JSON was designed to describe data in plain text and be human readable. JSON is structured with user-defined KEY VALUE pairs. In the following example, favoriteBook is the KEY and "Hitchhikers guide to the Galaxy" is the value. JSON uses curly brackets to delineate data structure.

```
{
"favoriteBook" : "Hitchhikers Guide to the Galaxy"
}
```

Similar to XML, JSON is hierarchical. In the following, data books is the key with a value of key:value pairs.

```
{
 "books": {
 "book1": "Hitchhikers Guide to the Galaxy",
 "book2": "Monster Hunter International",
 "book3": "IT"
 }
}
```

JSON values may contain any data types, including lists. The following is a better way to represent the above data using a list of books:

```
{
 "books": {
 "book": [
 "Hitchhikers Guide to the Galaxy",
 "IT",
 "Monster Hunter International"
 ]
 }
}
```

REST, JSON, and XML make it very easy to send and receive data between systems. However, each requires a REST client. Google Postman is a freely available REST client that supports both JSON and XML.

Google Postman

Google Postman is a REST client accessed as an extension to Google's Chrome web browser and supports Windows, Mac, and Linux systems. Google's Postman is installed via the Google Chrome Web Store. Using Postman is similar to a web browser but supports sending and receiving formatted data.

Using Postman

This example will leverage Google Postman to retrieve weather data from OpenWeatherMap.org. The key shown in Figure 2-2 has been changed. Unique authentication keys can be created at http://www.openweathermap.com.

Note Open Weather Map is a free resource but requires a KEY to authenticate.

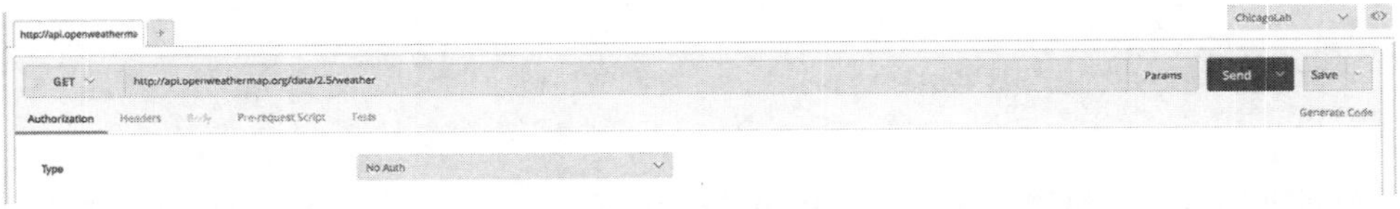

Figure 2-2 *Base Google Postman*

1. Similar to a normal web browser, enter the URL of the service. In this case the HTTP verb "GET" is used to get data from OpenWeatherMap.
2. Click **Send** (Figure 2-3).

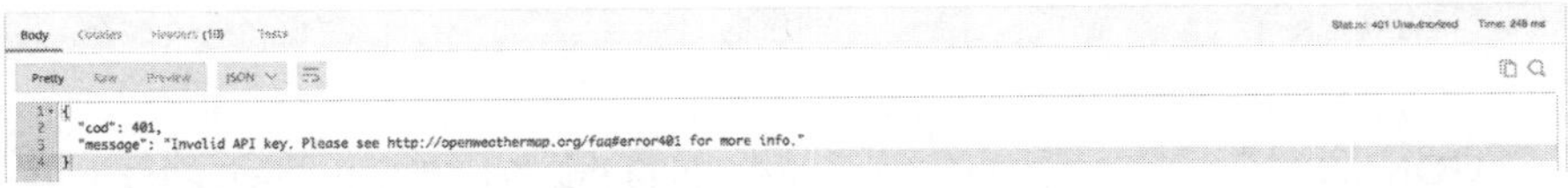

Figure 2-3 *Postman URL with no key*

The send key will send the URL to the server and display the response. The response in this case returns the HTTP error "401 – unauthorized". Additionally OpenWeatherMap.org was nice enough to include the message "Invalid API Key" with instructions on how to remedy the issue.

The authorization key is sent via a URL parameter. OpenWeatherMap.org expects the key of "APPID" and the value of a unique user key. The URL parameter is specified with the standard http '?" followed by the data.

Add URL parameter for authentication. Click **Send** (Figure 2-4).

Figure 2-4 *Postman URL with key and no parameters*

This response returns the HTTP code "200 OK" which signifies the request was good, however the OpenWeatherMap application returns the error message "404 - Error: Not found city" In other words the request authenticated fine, however the request failed to ask what city we want weather information for. To add a city add an additional key | value pair.

Note To find OpenWeatherMap city ids go,to http://openweathermap.org/find search by zip code using "?zip=94040,us"

Add URL Parameter for City and Imperial units

Figure 2-5 demonstrates a successful request to OpenWeatherMap, including the URL and parameters.

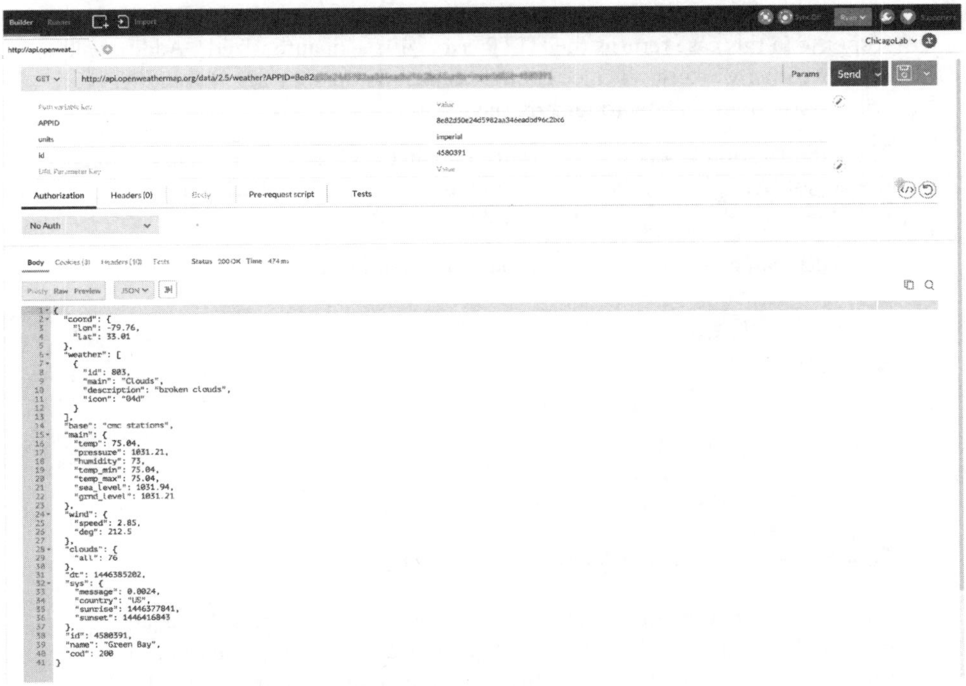

Figure 2-5 *Successful Open WeatherMap with Postman*

The final URL sent from Postman is:

http://api.openweathermap.org/data/2.5/weather?APPID=8e82&units=imperial&id=4580391

Open Weather Map's API is specific to their service and version number. The API is documented on their website, including city codes and unit conversion. Details about Open Weather Map's API can be found at http://openweathermap.org/api. Table 2-7 details the URL and parameters used to get weather information for Green Bay, Wisconsin.

Table 2-7 *URL Decode*

BASE URL	**http://api.openweathermap.org/data/2.5/weather**	**2.5 is a version number**
Parameter 1	weather?id=4580391	Green Bay, WI
Separator	&	
Parameter 2	units=imperial	Get results in Fahrenheit
Separator	&	
Parameter 3	APPID=8e82	Auth Key

Google Postman makes working with RESTful services easy. It supports variables, multiple URL parameters, and sharing of information through Postman collections. Collections can be downloaded and imported into Postman for many systems, including Nexus and ACI. The GitHub site for this publication includes Postman collections specific to network programmability. Finally, Postman includes a feature that automatically generates code for Python or other languages. Look for the "Generate Code" button in the upper right corner, and for the example in this book, use "Python/requests."

Using JSON in Python

Python has libraries to support HTTP/HTTPS communication and working with JSON-formatted data. The Python library "requests" supports sending and receiving data to RESTful services and is accessed via an import command. Requests is a third-party library and must be installed (use PIP).

```
>>> import requests
```

Requests supports HTTP verbs (as methods) and require a URL as input (as parameters). For example, some common methods supported by **requests** are shown in Table 2-8.

Table 2-8 *Common Requests Methods*

Example	Python Example
requests.get (URL)	requests.get ('http://www.yahoo.com')
requests.put (URL, Data)	requests.put ('http://192.168.0.5/post', data = {'NTP':'192.168.5.5'})
requests.delete (URL, Data)	requests.delete('https://192.168.0.5/delete', data = {'NTP':'192.168.5.5'})

Typically the results of the "requests" call are stored in a variable. Parameters in requests can either be in the URL or passed as parameters with no functional difference. In either case, it is best practice to store the data in a variable and pass the variable to requests, as shown in the following example.

```
myURL="http://api.openweathermap.org/data/2.5/weather?id=4580391&units=imperial&
APPID=8e82"

output = requests.get(myURL)

or

myURL="http://api.openweathermap.org/data/2.5/weather

myURLparms = {'id': '4580391', 'units': 'imperial', 'APPID':8e82 }

output = requests.get(myURL, myURLparms)
```

The data is returned as text, formatted in JSON. Requests has a built-in method to use the json response as a Python dictionary, for example:

```
jsonOutput = output.json()
```

Now the data in jsonOutput can be referenced by the keys, as shown in the following example.

```
print jsonOutput['name']
print jsonOutput['main']['temp']
Output
Green Bay
77.86
```

The standard Python library **json** is an additional library to work with **json. json** is accessed via an import.

```
>>> import json
```

The **json** library supports loading and unloading structured data into or out of JSON. Given the JSON data of:

```
{
 "books": {
 "book": [
 "Hitchhikers Guide to the Galaxy",
 "IT",
 "Monster Hunter International"
 ]
 }
}
```

The data is stored in a Python dictionary named obj.

>>> obj = {'books': {'book': ['Hitchhikers Guide to the Galaxy', 'IT', 'Monster Hunter International']}}

json.dumps loads the Python dictionary into a JSON-formatted string:

```
>>> json.dumps(obj)
'{"books": {"book": ["Hitchhikers Guide to the Galaxy", "IT", "Monster Hunter
International"]}}'
```

json.loads formats json data into a Python dictionary.

```
>>> object2 = json.dumps(obj)
>>> json.loads(object2)
{u'books': {u'book': [u'Hitchhikers Guide to the Galaxy', u'IT', u'Monster Hunter
International']}}
```

Note What is the "u"? The "u" prefix signal that the following sting is encoded, or better said in this example, decoded in Unicode. Unicode is a widely accepted representation of text in a computer or protocol.

Cisco networking devices input and export configurations and other data in JSON or XML. **json.dumps** and **json.loads** makes parsing and manipulating JSON formatted data fast and easy.

Basic Introduction to Version Control, Git, and GitHub

Version control enables a programmer to maintain a list of changes to a file or an entire project. Version control systems maintain a repository of all the files in a project and all changes to the files. In the event the software has an issue, changes can be compared or rolled back to a working state. Version control also enables multiple developers to simultaneously work on the same project. Git is a distributed version control system in that the repository is simultaneously maintained across multiple systems.

Git requires both a client and a server. Git software is open source and available for free download at https://git-scm.com. Git servers are deployed by IT or development teams to maintain and secure source code for a project. The Git client is available as command line or via a GUI. Private Git servers are not conducive to sharing code with the public.

GitHub is a public Git server. GitHub offers a place for the developer to share and distribute code for open-source projects. GitHub offers free accounts for public repositories and, for a reasonable fee, offers private repositories.

Note Git version control can be used with any files, for example, Cisco configurations.

To create a GitHub repository log in and click the Green Box labeled **Create repository**, as shown in Figure 2-6.

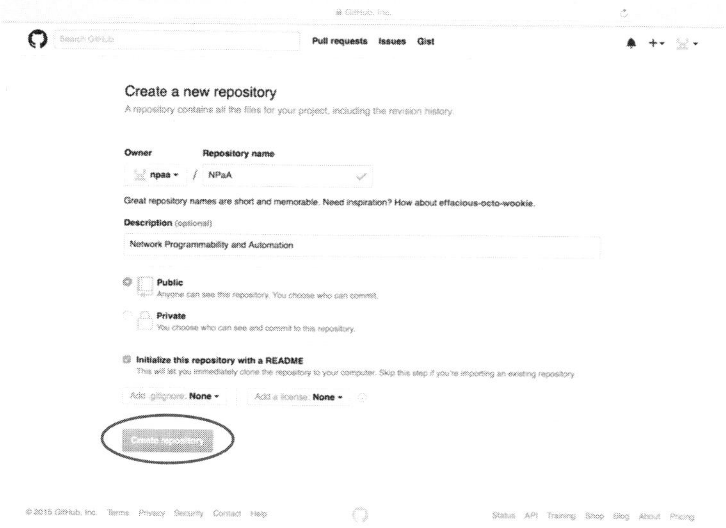

Figure 2-6 *Create GitHub Repository*

This example creates a repository under my username called "NPaA" and is initialized with a single README.md file (Figure 2-7). The README.md is displayed on GitHub similar to a home page and is designed to give basic information about the project.

To work with the repository, it must be cloned to a local system. A clone of a is a copy of the repository that is tracked for changes. In the event the clone is changed, it can be integrated and pushed back to the repository. Other developers working on the repository can use a Git command to re-sync their local clone.

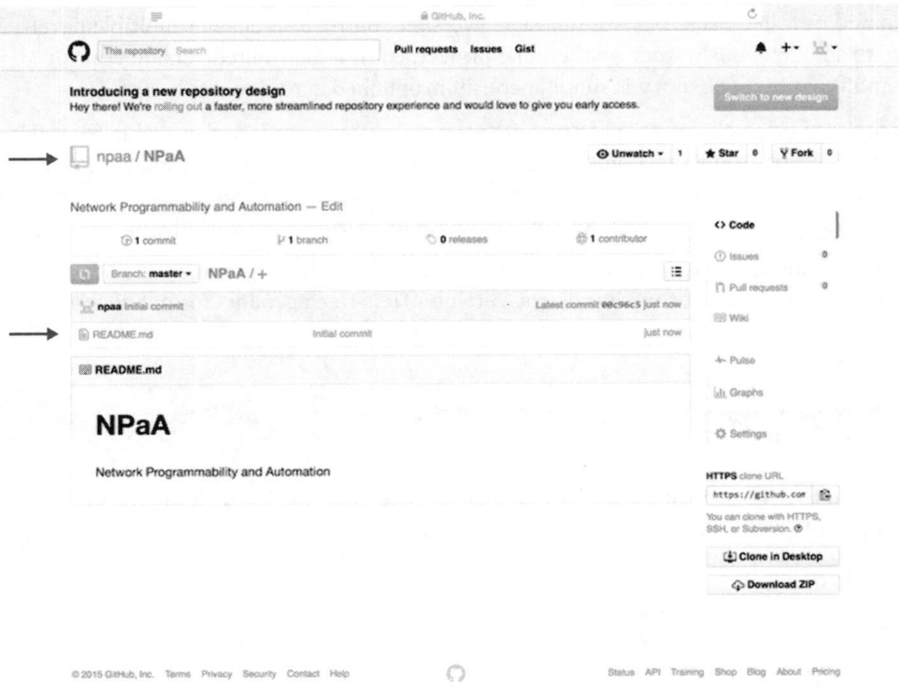

Figure 2-7 *GitHub Repository*

Git offers both command-line and GUI client tools for Mac, Windows, and Linux systems. The client should be downloaded from the aforementioned Git website and installed on the local system. The Git command line is similar on all systems, is much faster than GUIs and is recommended by developers. To clone a repository, copy the HTTPS link from the GitHub site and clone on the local system:

```
bash-3.2$ git clone https://github.com/npaa/NPaA.git
Cloning into 'NPaA'…
remote: Counting objects: 6, done.
remote: Compressing objects: 100% (3/3), done.
remote: Total 6 (delta 0), reused 3 (delta 0), pack-reused 0
```

```
Unpacking objects: 100% (6/6), done.
Checking connectivity…done.
bash-3.2$
```

The previous example clones the repository to the local system. The Git process creates a directory named for the repository name, in this case "NPaA" and copies any files from the repository. The clone process also creates a hidden .git directory which stores the versioning information.

```
bash-3.2$ cd NPaA/
bash-3.2$ ls -la
total 8
drwxr-xr-x 4 ryantischer staff 136 Nov 29 11:00 .
drwxr-xr-x+ 87 ryantischer staff 2958 Nov 29 11:00 ..
drwxr-xr-x 13 ryantischer staff 442 Nov 29 11:00 .git
-rw-r—r— 1 ryantischer staff 46 Nov 29 11:00 README.md
Bash-3.2$
```

Git—Add a File

Once the repository is cloned, files or directories can be added or changed.

```
bash-3.2$ touch testfile.txt
bash-3.2$
```

The following output creates an empty file called testfile.txt. The file is simply in the directory and has not yet been committed to the repository. The command "git status" is used to determine any changes between the local files and the GitHub repository.

```
bash-3.2$ git status
On branch master
Your branch is up-to-date with 'origin/master'.
Untracked files:
  (use "git add <file>…" to include in what will be committed)
  testfile.txt
nothing added to commit but untracked files present (use "git add" to track)
bash-3.2$
```

The output of "git status" highlights that the file testfile.txt is untracked. The command "git add ." will track all changes in the directory, however does not upload it to GitHub. Use the command "git add filename" to add a specific file.

```
bash-3.2$ git add.
bash-3.2$ git status
On branch master
Your branch is up-to-date with 'origin/master'.
Changes to be committed:
```

```
  (use "git reset HEAD <file>..." to unstage)
  new file: testfile.txt
bash-3.2$
```

Now Git tracks the file **testfile.txt**. The next step is to commit the change to the local repository.

```
bash-3.2$ git commit -m "Added testfile.txt"
[master af539af] Added testfile.txt
 1 file changed, 0 insertions(+), 0 deletions(-)
 create mode 100644 testfile.txt
bash-3.2$
```

git commit –m "message" commits the file to GitHub. Git requires a message with every commit and best practices dictate meaningful messages so you or other developers can understand what was done.

The final step is to push the commit to GitHub.

```
bash-3.2$ git push
Counting objects: 3, done.
Delta compression using up to 8 threads.
Compressing objects: 100% (2/2), done.
Writing objects: 100% (3/3), 279 bytes | 0 bytes/s, done.
Total 3 (delta 0), reused 0 (delta 0)
To https://github.com/npaa/NPaA.git
 00c96c5..3386665 master -> master
bash-3.2$
```

To review the change, refresh the repository page on GitHub; the result will be like that of Figure 2-8.

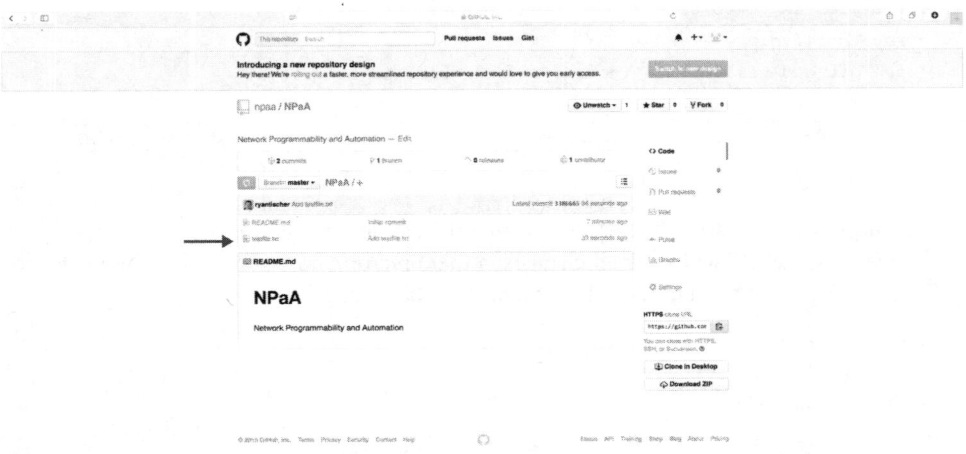

Figure 2-8 *Updated Git repository*

Table 2-9 summarizes the **Git** commands.

Table 2-9 *Summary of Git Commands*

git clone	Copies a repository to the local system
git add	Adds or update a file or files
git commit	Adds changes to local repository
git push	Syncs files to GitHub
git pull	Updates local repository with changes from the remote repository

Please consider placing any of your network programmability code in your personal GitHub account. Submitting code on GitHub allows other users to use, add, or improve your applications and enhances the networking community. Many employers use GitHub as a recruitment tool to better understand a candidate's skills and past experiences.

See the following resources to learn more about Git, including practice exercises.

https://github.com/npaa/NPaA/blob/master/learn_git.txt

https://try.github.io/levels/1/challenges/1

https://www.codecademy.com/learn/learn-git

Creating and Editing Source Code

A developer has many tools to create source code. Source code is plain text and can be written in plain-text editors. When using a plain-text editor, the developer is responsible for every component and formatting for the code. Any errors will be found during the compile process or in the case of Python at run time. Source code editors and integrated development environments (IDE) make software development easier with intelligent tools.

A source code editor can assist a developer with intelligent tools for example code autocomplete, automated formatting, and syntax highlighting. A source code editor will have a specific language library configured, such as Python or Java. Code autocomplete will recognize the user's input and offer suggestions for the remainder of the input. Additionally, autocomplete will recognize user-defined variables and functions. Autocomplete significantly reduces coding errors due to misspelling or typos. Automatic formatting will ensure indentation is correct (which, as you know, is critical with Python). Intelligent syntax highlighting will highlight keywords within a program and alert the developer if something is wrong.

IDEs contain enhanced tools in addition to a source code editor. IDEs provide a graphical user interface to design, develop, and debug a program. IDEs will also help when multiple users are working on a single program with version control and code checkout. The disadvantage to IDEs is they require time and training to use the IDE.

PyCharm is a free, open-source and easy to use Python IDE from Jetbrains. PyCharm makes building software very easy and is available on Mac, Windows, and Linux systems. PyCharm has built-in features including, autocomplete, code completion, syntax highlighting, and autoformatting that allow the developer to focus on writing quality code.

Note—PyCharm offers a competitively priced professional version that includes additional tools for example built in web and database development tools.

Getting Started with PyCharm

The latest version of PyCharm (4.5 at the time of this writing) is best downloaded with installation instructions from http://www.jetbrains.com/pycharm/. PyCharm requires a Python interpreter installed on the system.

PyCharm starts with a dialog box to Create or Open a project (Figure 2-9). A project is a collection of files, Python code, and libraries to support an application.

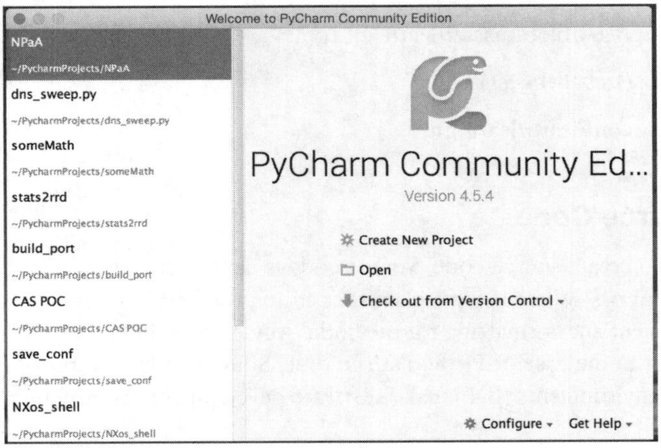

Figure 2-9 *Creating a Project and Setting up The Editor*

1. Select Create a New Project

   The next dialog box asks for a location for the project and the location of the Python interpreter (Figure 2-10). Choose the default 2.7 interpreter located at /usr/bin/python, and press **Create**.

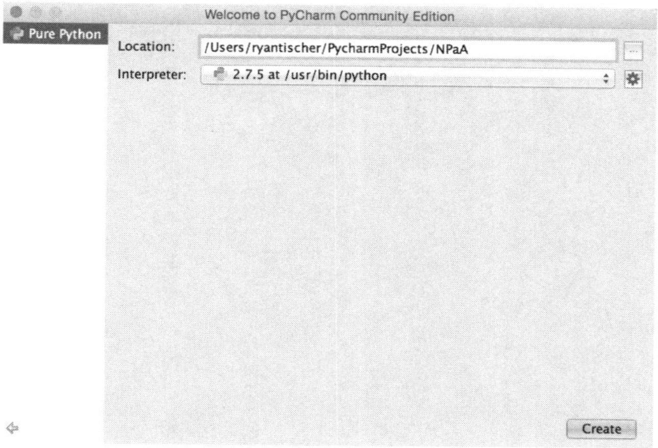

Figure 2-10 *Specifying the Project Location and Interpreter*

2. By default a project does not create any files. To create a file, right-click on project name and select **New > Python File** (Figure 2-11).

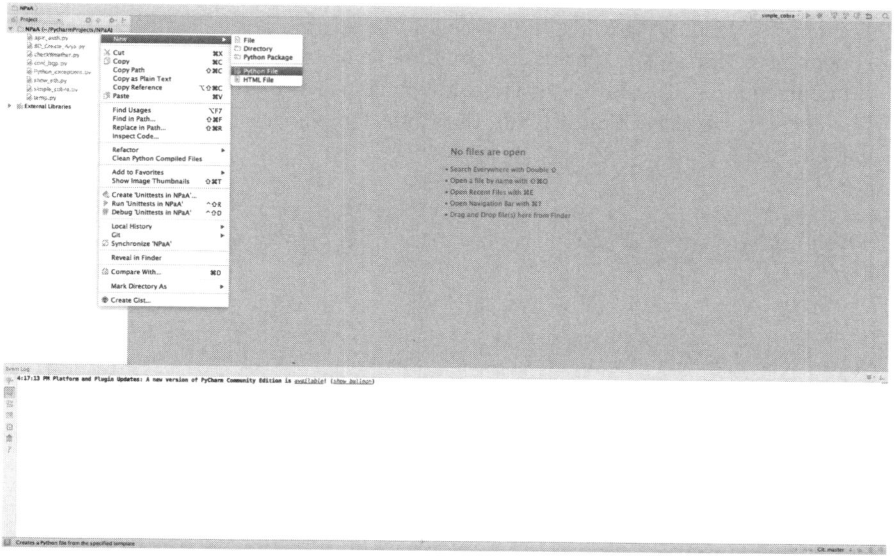

Figure 2-11 *Create a PyCharm Python file*

Once the Python file is named, PyCharm presents the main developer interface, as shown in Figure 2-12.

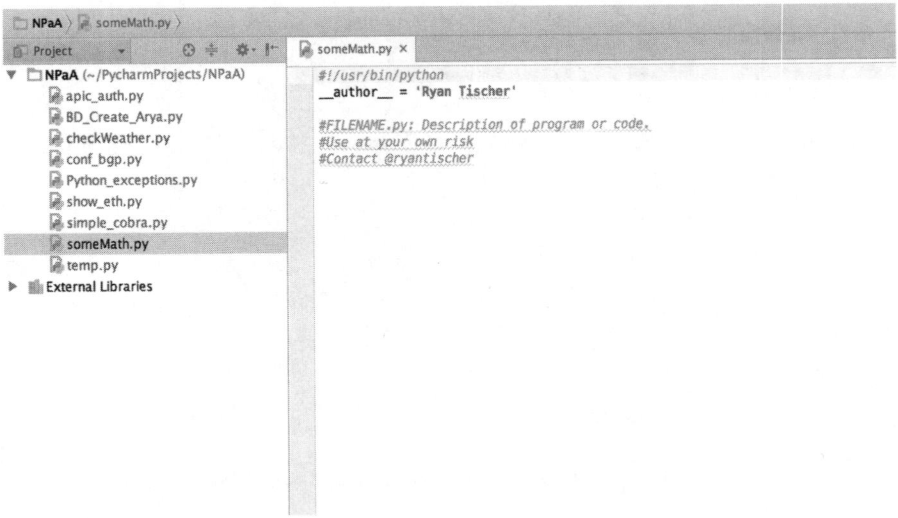

Figure 2-12 *PyCharm Python interface*

PyCharm initializes new files using the default file template. By default the template assigns the author tag to the username. Modifying the default template with additional documentation and comments serves as a reminder to build quality and consistent documentation. To modify the Default template navigate to File > Default Settings. In the window select **Editor > File and Code Templates > Python Script**, as shown in Figure 2-13.

Note VI/VIM fans rejoice! PyCharm supports VI commands Goto Tools | VIM Emulator.

Note Line numbers make things easier. Go to View | Active Editor > Show line numbers

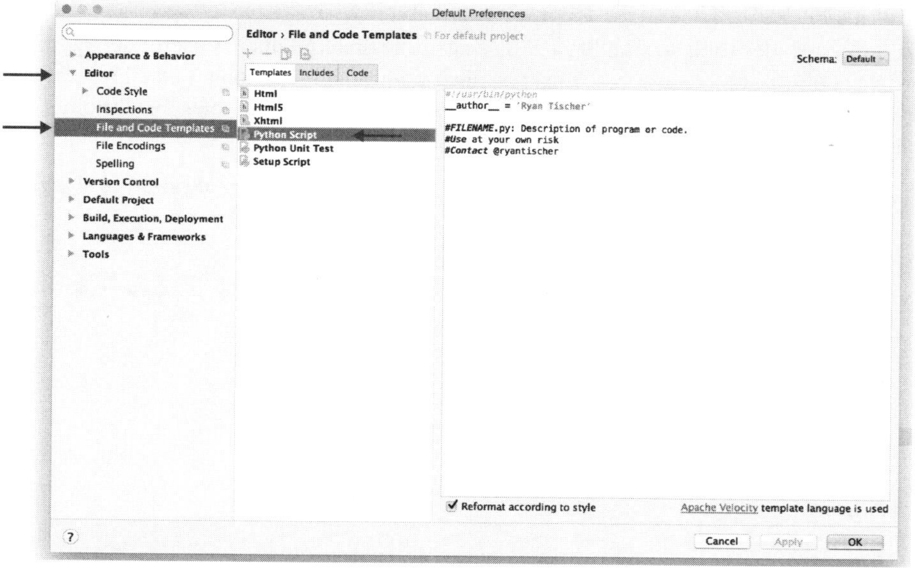

Figure 2-13 *PyCharm—Create Default Template*

PyCharm views support a bottom window for runtime output, debugging, and a terminal. The terminal can be used for OS-level tasks or instantiate an interactive Python interpreter. Quick access to the interpreter is useful for quickly troubleshooting code.

Writing Code in PyCharm—Get the Weather

This program will use requests and JSON to check the weather from Open Weather API.

To run the program go to **RUN > Run 'checkWeather'** or select ▶, in the upper left corner. The program output is shown in Figure 2-14.

```
#!/usr/bin/python
__author__ = 'Ryan Tischer'   __author__: 'Ryan Tischer'

# checkWeather.py: Gets weather data from .
# Use at your own risk
# Contact @ryantischer

#import
import requests


openWeatherAPI="http://api.openweathermap.org/data/2.5/weather?id=4580391&units=imperial&APPID=8e82d50e

output = requests.get(openWeatherAPI)

jsonOutput = output.json()
print jsonOutput['name']
print jsonOutput['main']['temp']
```

Figure 2-14 *checkWeather.py PyCharm output*

Debugging in PyCharm

PyCharm includes tools to simplify debugging code. Breakpoints is a useful debugging tool that stops code execution at a user-defined point, the breakpoint, and allows the developer to examine individual code segments or the value of variables. Breakpoints can help solve both program errors and logic issues.

1. To insert a breakpoint, go to **Run > Toggle Temporary Line Breakpoint**, as shown in Figure 2-15.

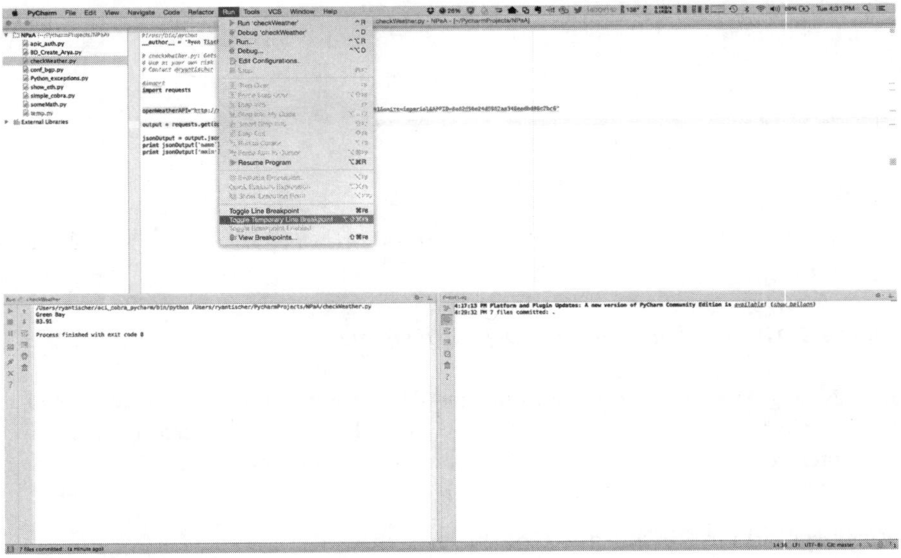

Figure 2-15 *PyCharm breakpoint1*

2. To debug the program use the Bug Icon (Figure 2-16) in the upper right corner.

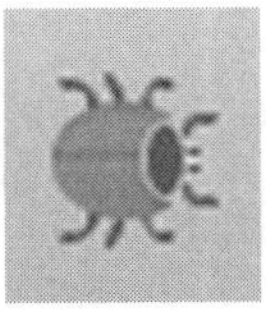

Figure 2-16 *PyCharm bug*

The output of the debugger details additional information about line 11 and the requests call, as shown in Figure 2-17.

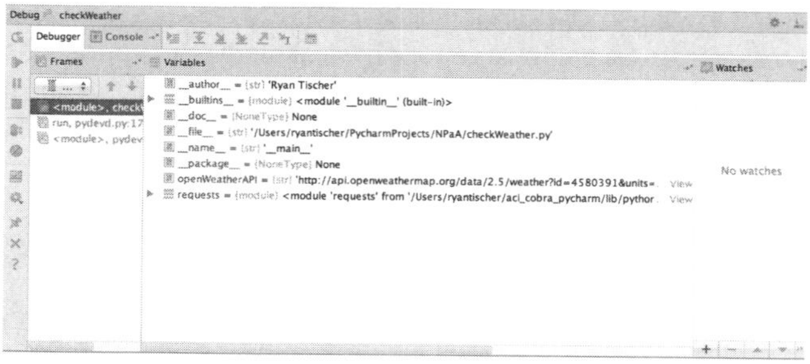

Figure 2-17 *Debugger output*

PyCharm is one of many quality IDEs that make building, debugging, and sharing source code easy. To learn more about using PyCharm, see the following resources.

https://github.com/npaa/NPaA/blob/master/learn_pycharm.txt

https://blog.jetbrains.com/pycharm/2016/01/introducing-getting-started-with-pycharm-video-tutorials/

https://www.jetbrains.com/help/pycharm/5.0/quick-start-guide.html

Introduction to Linux

Linux is a robust, scalable, and flexible operating system that powers everything from web servers to IoT sensors to network devices. Linux is the base operating system for many Cisco devices including Cisco NX-OS and Cisco IOS-XE. Next-generation network engineers will require Linux skills to administer and troubleshoot Cisco network equipment. Additionally, Linux offers an additional vector for network programmability.

Traditionally, Cisco devices hid the base operating system and only exposed the top-level CLI interface. Modern Linux-based network devices expose the OS and allow operations teams to administrate servers and network with the same tools. Cisco software for example (NX-OS) runs as an application and exposes additional compute resources for other applications. Disaggregation of the OS and network software allow for better software management.

Linux is packaged and most often used in distributions. A distribution is the Linux kernel packaged with other software often supported by a company or organization. Hundreds of distributions are available that focus on enterprise deployments, gaming, or security tool sets. Most Linux distributions are licensed under the GPL licenses and are free to use; however, organizations will charge for physical media or support contracts. Redhat, Ubuntu, and Suse are common Linux distributions for server, desktop, and cloud environments.

Note What is a GPL License? General Public License is a free software license that dictates software under it. GPL is free to use, change, or copy. More details about GPL can be found at http://www.gnu.org/licenses/gpl-3.0.en.html

Working in Linux

Linux offers both command line and GUI user interfaces. The GUI is appropriate for desktop environments; however, network devices, servers, and IoT devices are managed via the command line. The Linux command line is provided by the Bash application.

Bash is one of many shells available for Linux but is included in most Linux distributions. Bash serves two purposes: first, as the interface to the Linux system and second, as a powerful scripting tool. Bash scripting is covered in chapter three.

By default, Bash displays username@hostname followed by a character to signify it is ready for input:

```
admin@apic1:~>
```

Bash will take keyboard input and run any command located in the path. The path is a Bash environment variable stored under the name $PATH. The "$" signifies a variable. To view any Bash variable, use the command "echo."

```
admin@apic1:~> echo $PATH
/usr/bin/:/bin/:/usr/bin:/bin:/usr/sbin:/sbin:/usr/local/bin:/usr/local/sbin
```

Bash has several tools to make working in Bash easier. The history function records input and similar to Cisco network software command history is accessed via up and down arrows. Also similar to Cisco, Bash supports keyboard shortcuts for moving around the command line. Most common are CTL-A that moves the cursor to the front of the line and CTL-E that moves to the end. Finally and again similar to Cisco, Bash supports autocomplete via the TAB key.

The commands shown in Table 2-10 are very useful when working with Linux; most are located in /bin.

Table 2-10 *Summary of Linux Commands*

Command	Description
cat	Displays contents of a file.
cd	Changes directory
chmod	Changes the permissions of a file or directory
chown	Changes the owner of the file or directory
clear	Clears the screen
cp	Copies a file
df	Displays disk space utilization
grep	Performs pattern search
kill	Kills a process
less	Displays output one page at a time
ls	Lists a directory
man	Displays help for a command
mkdir	Makes a directory
mv	Moves a file
pwd	Displays current directory
rm	Removes a file or directory
su	Changes user
tail	Shows text from the end of a file
tar	Bundles or unbundles files
touch	Creates a file or updates file timestamps

Commands with output can be piped to other commands to parse the output.

For example the /etc/passwd file stores authentication information for users and can get very large. The tool "cat" can open and display the file, however by default it will scroll all the information very fast. The "cat" tool is used in combination or "piped" with "less" to display information one page at a time.

```
cat /etc/passwd | less
```

The **grep** tool searches for a text and displays the lines that match.

```
admin@apic1:etc> cat /etc/passwd | grep root
root:x:0:0:root:/root:/bin/bash
operator:x:11:0:operator:/root:/sbin/nologin
```

The **tail** command displays the last ten lines of a file but optionally accepts input to display any number of lines.

```
admin@apic1:etc> cat /etc/passwd | tail -5
quagga:x:92:92:Quagga routing suite:/var/run/quagga:/sbin/nologin
tss:x:59:59:Account by trousers:/dev/null:/sbin/nologin
shellinabox:x:494:485:Shellinabox:/var/lib/shellinabox:/sbin/nologin
rescue-user:x:10998:0:ishell:/var/run:/mgmt/usr/bin/loginshell
ishell:x:10999:0:ishell:/var/run:/mgmt/usr/bin/loginshell
```

Linux Architecture

The kernel in Linux is responsible for managing the underlying hardware. The Linux kernel is monolithic and thus contains software to manage all hardware (CPU, memory, network cards), virtual memory, and processes. Changes to the kernel, for example adding a new device driver, require loading the modules directly into the kernel. The kernel runs in a special ring of the CPU, labeled ring 0, and is the only software allowed in the space. Other processes run in userspace, which is assigned to the lower-privileged ring and interactions with the hardware go through the kernel, as shown in Figure 2-18.

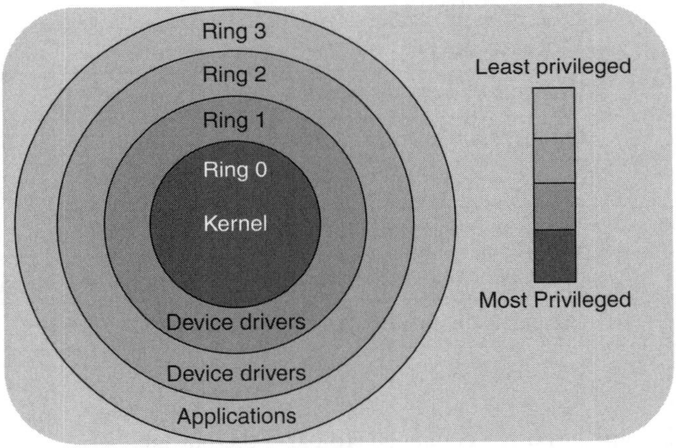

Figure 2-18 *Linux protection ring*

Source: http://en.wikipedia.org/wiki/Protection_ring#mediaviewer/File:Priv_rings.svg

In Linux, a process is a running instance of an application. Each process had an ID, called a PID, and an owner. By default, Linux includes many tools for displaying and managing process.

Display Linux Process

The **ps** tool is used to display running processes on a Linux machine. Without any parameters **ps** displays the process running for the current user:

```
admin@apic1:~> ps
 PID TTY TIME CMD
20349 pts/0 00:00:00 scriptcontainer
20350 pts/0 00:00:00 bash
20391 pts/0 00:00:00 ps
admin@apic1:~>
```

The common options for **ps**, **aux**, display all running processes: who owns the process and the resources consumed by the process. The command **ps aux** usually outputs multiple pages and is best used when piping the output to less:

```
admin@apic1:~> ps aux | less
USER PID %CPU %MEM VSZ RSS TTY STAT START TIME COMMAND
root 1 0.0 0.0 35764 2288 ? Ss Oct12 0:15 /sbin/init
root 2 0.0 0.0 0 0 ? S Oct12 0:00 [kthreadd]
root 3 0.0 0.0 0 0 ? S Oct12 4:19 [ksoftirqd/0]
root 6 0.0 0.0 0 0 ? S Oct12 0:00 [migration/0]
root 7 0.0 0.0 0 0 ? S Oct12 0:21 [watchdog/0]
root 8 0.0 0.0 0 0 ? S Oct12 0:00 [migration/1]
root 10 0.0 0.0 0 0 ? S Oct12 3:24 [ksoftirqd/1]
```

The command **top** is an interactive display of running process. **top** is similar to Windows task manager and is useful to understand what processes are consuming the most resources. To launch top type **top** in the shell. The output is shown in Figure 2-19.

```
top - 09:56:23 up 47 days, 22:23,  1 user,  load average: 1.66, 1.06, 0.77
Tasks: 339 total,   1 running, 338 sleeping,   0 stopped,   0 zombie
Cpu(s):  0.6%us,  0.7%sy,  0.0%ni, 98.6%id,  0.0%wa,  0.0%hi,  0.0%si,  0.0%st
Mem:  65704536k total, 12834208k used, 52870328k free,   700804k buffers
Swap:        0k total,        0k used,        0k free,  3946588k cached

  PID USER      PR  NI  VIRT  RES  SHR S %CPU %MEM    TIME+  COMMAND
32723 root      20   0  572m 219m  88m S  4.6  0.3   3308:58 svc_ifc_applian
32740 ifc       20   0  705m 348m  89m S  4.0  0.5   1923:07 svc_ifc_dbgr.bi
 5387 root      20   0  838m 428m  98m S  3.0  0.7   1725:42 nginx.bin
32725 root      20   0  705m 328m  88m S  2.7  0.5   1670:03 svc_ifc_bootmgr
32745 ifc       20   0  840m 423m  80m S  2.7  0.7   1769:51 svc_ifc_eventmg
32748 ifc       20   0  798m 460m  73m S  2.7  0.7   1604:51 svc_ifc_reader.
32734 ifc       20   0 1228m 859m  74m S  2.3  1.3   1788:29 svc_ifc_observe
32741 ifc       20   0  655m 311m  88m S  2.3  0.5   1663:19 svc_ifc_topomgr
32746 ifc       20   0 1046m 620m 105m S  2.3  1.0   1700:47 svc_ifc_policym
32749 ifc       20   0  509m 179m  69m S  2.3  0.3   1615:25 svc_ifc_vtap.bi
32751 ifc       20   0  635m 283m  70m S  2.3  0.4   1659:39 svc_ifc_idmgr.b
  449 root      20   0  520m 205m  86m S  2.0  0.3   1616:47 dhcpd.bin
32739 ifc       20   0  796m 342m 100m S  2.0  0.5   1700:33 svc_ifc_vmmmgr.
32752 ifc       20   0  726m 289m  76m S  2.0  0.5   1678:54 svc_ifc_scripth
32753 root      20   0  589m 222m  76m S  2.0  0.3   1934:14 svc_ifc_ae.bin
32733 root      20   0 63340 9576 2408 S  0.3  0.0  29:01.29 watcher.py
    1 root      20   0 35764 2288 1508 S  0.0  0.0   0:15.14 init
    2 root      20   0     0    0    0 S  0.0  0.0   0:00.69 kthreadd
    3 root      20   0     0    0    0 S  0.0  0.0   4:19.45 ksoftirqd/0
    6 root      RT   0     0    0    0 S  0.0  0.0   0:00.06 migration/0
    7 root      RT   0     0    0    0 S  0.0  0.0   0:21.20 watchdog/0
    8 root      RT   0     0    0    0 S  0.0  0.0   0:00.09 migration/1
   10 root      20   0     0    0    0 S  0.0  0.0   3:24.14 ksoftirqd/1
   12 root      RT   0     0    0    0 S  0.0  0.0   0:15.99 watchdog/1
   13 root      RT   0     0    0    0 S  0.0  0.0   0:00.10 migration/2
   15 root      20   0     0    0    0 S  0.0  0.0   3:55.04 ksoftirqd/2
   16 root      RT   0     0    0    0 S  0.0  0.0   0:16.06 watchdog/2
   17 root      RT   0     0    0    0 S  0.0  0.0   0:00.15 migration/3
   19 root      20   0     0    0    0 S  0.0  0.0   6:10.84 ksoftirqd/3
   20 root      RT   0     0    0    0 S  0.0  0.0   0:15.12 watchdog/3
   21 root      RT   0     0    0    0 S  0.0  0.0   0:00.11 migration/4
   23 root      20   0     0    0    0 S  0.0  0.0   7:06.77 ksoftirqd/4
   24 root      RT   0     0    0    0 S  0.0  0.0   0:14.93 watchdog/4
   25 root      RT   0     0    0    0 S  0.0  0.0   0:00.10 migration/5
   27 root      20   0     0    0    0 S  0.0  0.0   4:49.67 ksoftirqd/5
   28 root      RT   0     0    0    0 S  0.0  0.0   0:15.29 watchdog/5
   29 root      RT   0     0    0    0 S  0.0  0.0   0:00.10 migration/6
   31 root      20   0     0    0    0 S  0.0  0.0   4:04.16 ksoftirqd/6
   32 root      RT   0     0    0    0 S  0.0  0.0   0:20.25 watchdog/6
   33 root      RT   0     0    0    0 S  0.0  0.0   0:00.10 migration/7
   35 root      20   0     0    0    0 S  0.0  0.0   3:40.30 ksoftirqd/7
   36 root      RT   0     0    0    0 S  0.0  0.0   0:17.88 watchdog/7
   37 root      RT   0     0    0    0 S  0.0  0.0   0:00.09 migration/8
   39 root      20   0     0    0    0 S  0.0  0.0   4:39.79 ksoftirqd/8
   40 root      RT   0     0    0    0 S  0.0  0.0   0:17.94 watchdog/8
```

Figure 2-19 *Top Output*

The default display in top is to display processes sorted by CPU usage. Top supports changing sort order, filtering by owner and stopping (kill) a process. Some common **top** commands are listed in Table 2-11.

Table 2-11 *Common top Commands*

Command	Description
h	Displays Help screen
Shift-f	Changees sort order—"s" to sort
1	Displays data from all CPUs
z	Adds color
u	Filters by process owner
k	Kills a process by PID

Processes are spawned directly by the user, in the boot-up process or as part of a larger application. Systemd is a tool to manage Linux boot and processes within an application.

Systemd is a Linux boot (well known as initialization) tool. It is the default on some distributions, including Redhat and Ubuntu. Systemd boots the system in addition to managing Linux processes, for example Apache or MySQL. Systemd manages process as units. A unit contains the main process and any spawned process. In the event a process is stopped or restarted, systemd will stop everything in the unit. Systemd is the default is many modern Linux distributions.

Using Systemd

Administrators manage systemd, and through the command line tool, systemctl.

To start, stop, or restart a process, use the following command.

```
systemctl {start,stop,restart,reload} service.name
```

For example, to start apache2, you would type:

```
systemctl start apache2
```

The following example utilizes systemctl to list process running on the system.

```
UNIT LOAD ACTIVE SUB DESCRIPTION
accounts-daemon.service loaded active running Accounts Service
apache2.service loaded active running LSB: Apache2 web server
apparmor.service loaded active exited LSB: AppArmor initialization
apport.service loaded active exited LSB: automatic crash report generation
atd.service loaded active running Deferred execution scheduler
cron.service loaded active running Regular background program processing dae
dbus.service loaded active running D-Bus System Message Bus
getty@tty1.service loaded active running Getty on tty1
```

The following example utilizes systemctl to get status and the last ten log entries of a process.

```
tischer@NPaA:~$ systemctl status apache2
 apache2.service - LSB: Apache2 web server
 Loaded: loaded (/etc/init.d/apache2)
 Active: active (running) since Sun 2015-11-29 12:03:51 CST; 3min 50s ago
 Docs: man:systemd-sysv-generator(8)
 Process: 1059 ExecStop=/etc/init.d/apache2 stop (code=exited, status=0/SUCCESS)
 Process: 1092 ExecStart=/etc/init.d/apache2 start (code=exited, status=0/SUCCESS)
 CGroup: /system.slice/apache2.service
 ├─1106 /usr/sbin/apache2 -k start
 ├─1109 /usr/sbin/apache2 -k start
 └─1110 /usr/sbin/apache2 -k start
Nov 29 12:03:49 NPaA systemd[1]: Starting LSB: Apache2 web server…
Nov 29 12:03:49 NPaA apache2[1092]: * Starting web server apache2
Nov 29 12:03:50 NPaA apache2[1092]: AH00558: apache2: Could not reliably determine
the server's fu…sage
Nov 29 12:03:51 NPaA apache2[1092]: *
Nov 29 12:03:51 NPaA systemd[1]: Started LSB: Apache2 web server.
Hint: Some lines were ellipsized, use -l to show in full.
tischer@NPaA:~$
```

Systemd groups process in Linux control groups, commonly known as cgroups. Cgroups are a uniquely identified logical partition of processes. Cgroups limit resources, for example memory, CPU, or Disk I/O to a group. Additionally, cgroups support prioritization such that one group can have a larger share of resources, based on system or business priorities. Cgroups work closely with another Linux technology called namespaces.

Linux namespaces provide segmentation from other processes or cgroups on a system. Namespace segmentation enables a specific resource, for example a network interface or disk mount, to be assigned to a process. As of this text, there are six different namespaces that include network, process (PID), and mount (disk, filesystem). Together, cgroups and namespaces form an abstraction from the base OS and thus are the building blocks to Linux virtualization with containers.

Linux can be virtualized into containers, called LinuX Containers (LXC). LXC is an operating system-level virtualization that has better efficiency than traditional whole system virtualization, for example, Vmware ESXi. Containers share the kernel and common libraries across virtualized user spaces and thus have less duplication of process. LXC utilizes cgroups and namespaces to provide resource limitations (CPU, memory, etc.) and unique physical or virtual resources (NIC, process, etc.) respectively. LXC is available on Nexus 9000 series hardware and is useful to run third-party applications directly on the switch. LXC on the 9K is covered in the following chapter.

Linux File System and Permissions

The Linux file system is responsible for storing files and directories. File systems have a specific format that dictates how files and directories are stored on the disk. Modern Linux distributions use the ext4 format, which supports large partitions, encryption, and journaling. File system journaling keep track of disk writes for logging and disaster recovery.

In Linux configurations, applications, and so on are files, and those files are either text or binary. Text files can be opened and edited; binary files cannot. Every file in Linux has permissions that define who can read, write, or execute a file. Linux permissions are specified by owner and a group each with unique permissions. **Ls** with the **-l** flag displays a directory listing with permission information:

```
tischer@NPaA:~$ ls -l
total 2
-rw-rw-r— 1 tischer tischer 0 Nov 3 13:16 testfile1.txt
-rw-r—r— 1 root root 0 Nov 3 13:16 testfile2.txt
tischer@NPaA:~$
```

The first line of the output (starting with -rw-rw-r—) displays if the file is a directory and what permissions the file has. Permissions in Linux define which owners, groups, and all users can read, write, or execute a file. The owner of the file is listed, followed by the group. Linux permissions are displayed as:

	Owner			Group			All Users		
_	R	W	X	R	W	X	R	W	X
Type	Read	Write	Execute	Read	Write	Execute	Read	Write	Execute

Note The execute bit has a different meaning for directories. It means the contents can be searched.

Testfile2.txt in the previous output has the permissions -*rw*- r- _-r- -, which explains the user root, has read and write permissions, the group "root" only has read permissions, and all other users only have read permissions.

Linux permissions can be modified for access and security. Permissions are defined in octal with each permission (rwx) is represented by a number.

Read = 4

Write = 2

Execute = 1

	Owner			Group			All Users		
–	R	W	X	R	W	X	R	W	X
Type	Read	Write	Execute	Read	Write	Execute	Read	Write	Execute
Binary	4	2	1	4	2	1	4	2	1
Textfile.txt	6			4			4		

Adding the numbers together define the access. For example, the binary permissions for is testfile2.txt = 644. The command **chmod** modifies the permissions. For example:

```
chmod 777 testfile2.txt - assigns all permissions to all users.
chmod 700 testfile2.txt - assigns read, write and execute permission for the owner
chmod 755 testfile2.txt - assigns all permissions to the owner and execute permissions to all other users
```

Linux Directories

By default, Linux distributions install common tools in well-known directories.

- **/boot**—holds kernel
- **/etc**—holds config files
- **/bin**—holds systems commands
- **/sbin**—holds admin commands
- **/home**—holds user home directories
- **/usr**—holds applications
- **/var/log**—holds logs

Installing Applications on Linux

Linux supports tens of thousands of different commercial and open-source applications. Open-source applications can be installed from source, which requires a compile process or to make applications easier to install and they come packaged. Linux packages contain the necessary pre-compiled components for an application to install on the local system. RPM is a popular Linux packaging format.

Redhat Package manger or RPM is a popular packaging format. RPM allows system administrators to consistently install, upgrade, and maintain software on compatible systems. RPMs are manually moved to the system and installed with the RPM tool.

```
rpm -ivh packagename.rpm
```

Before the rpm tool installs a package, it will check for applications dependencies.

Most applications will have some dependencies, and if the dependencies are not on the local system, rpm will stop the install. The administrator is required to install any dependencies and retry the installation. The Yum tool further simplifies Linux application installation.

Yum is a RPM package management tool. It automates dependency issues and supports automated updates. Yum packages are located on open Internet-based repositories and thus require Internet access. Yum is used by some commercial distributions, notably Redhat and Redhat variants. Table 2-12 lists some of the common Yum commands.

Table 2-12 *Common Yum commands*

yum search *keyword*	Searches yum repository
yum info *package-name*	Retrieves information about a package
yum install *package-name*	Installs package from repository
yum remove *package-name*	Removes package from local system

Cisco Nexus 9000 supports Yum and installing RPMs on the system. Examples of installing and using packages on a Nexus 9K will be in Chapter 3.

> **Note** Apt is another popular package management tool used in Ubuntu and other Debian-based distributions. Apt is similar to Yum; it will automaticity resolve dependences and leverages repositories.

The next-generation network engineer will require a deep level of Linux skills to install, manage, and deploy network devices. Some Cisco devices have recently exposed the Linux OS and allow users to interact with the device at a much deeper level. To learn more about Linux and related tools see the following resources.

https://github.com/npaa/NPaA/blob/master/learn_linux.txt

https://training.linuxfoundation.org/free-linux-training/linux-training-videos

https://www.edx.org/course/introduction-linux-linuxfoundationx-lfs101x-0

http://www.ibm.com/developerworks/library/l-lpic1–102–5/

Where to Go for Help

Learning the foundational skills associated with network programmability and automation will take time and practice to master. Online resources, for example, blogs, videos, and tutorials, can supplement the foundational skills discussed in this chapter. As highlighted throughout this chapter the GitHub site for this book contains a technology-specific file that lists a number of online tools for additional study.

The GitHub site is located at https://github.com/npaa/NPaA. Cisco DevNet is another excellent resource for building Cisco-enabled applications.

DevNet is a developer program from Cisco, providing tools, training, and other resources that enable developers to produce Cisco-enabled applications. DevNet features a fully integrated developer program, comprising a website, an interactive community, coordinated developer tools, and sandboxes. DevNet provides a number of example applications and a lab environment, named Sandbox, to run and test development projects.

DevNet Sandbox is an online lab resource to build and test code in production-ready environments. Sandbox labs are available for data center, campus, and WAN environments and allows testing code and configuration on real Cisco hardware. DevNet sandbox features step-by-step labs and supports running all example applications discussed in this book.

Network Programmability user group (NPUG) is a free community to collaborate with other network coders. NPUG has chapters in many cities and offers both physical and virtual meetings. NPUG members are encouraged to share network programmability projects, ask questions, and discuss network generation network technology.

Note If no NPUG group is near you, start one!

NPUG can be found at https://netprog.atlassian.net/wiki/display/NPUG/NPUG

Summary

The skills discussed in this chapter cover the necessary fundamentals to begin working with next-generation network hardware and enhancing it with simple applications. Building software starts with planning and building pseudo code that highlights the applications goals. Python provides an easy-to-use language to build everything from simple scripts to complex applications that extend the network to directly solve business. Finally, many modern network devices run Linux, which changes how network engineers manage and troubleshoot network device in addition to providing enhanced network programmability options.

The next chapters discuss network programmability and automation with Cisco products. Use cases and examples are provided, using Python, Linux, and other tools to demonstrate how the network can be leveraged to solve business problems.

Chapter 3

Next-Generation Cisco Data Center Networking

Cisco's Nexus data center networking portfolio features best of breed products to build traditional data center solutions or next-generation spine/leaf architecture. The Nexus product line originally debuted with the Nexus 7000, 5000, and 3000 series and was significantly enhanced with the subsequent launch of the Nexus 9000.

At the heart of the first-generation Nexus 9000 is the popular Trident 2 network forwarding engine (NFE) from Broadcom. Known as the "T2," Broadcom's Trident 2 offers high speed, low latency, and low-cost data center switching; in addition, it supports next generation VXLAN bridging. Some Nexus 9000 models also utilize an additional switching ASIC, named the application leaf engine (ALE) for critical data center switching features. The ALE adds VXLAN routing, additional buffer memory, and increased telemetry with atomic counters. If the 9K switch has an ALE or not, the physical ports are connected to the T2 ASIC. The ALE ASIC is connected to the T2 as depicted in Figure 3-1.

Please note that VXLAN details are covered later in this chapter.

The combination of T2 and ALE form Cisco's Merchant + strategy, which combines the low cost, high performance of the T2 with Cisco hardware-driven features in the ALE. ALE features are available in both NX-OS and ACI mode and require no additional configuration or operational complexity. In order to provide line rate and deterministic performance, ACI policy is instantiated in the ALE. The Cisco Application Spine Engine (ASE) ASIC is purposely built for ACI spine switches and does not support NX-OS. Figure 3-2 provides additional details for Cisco's Merchant + ASIC strategy.

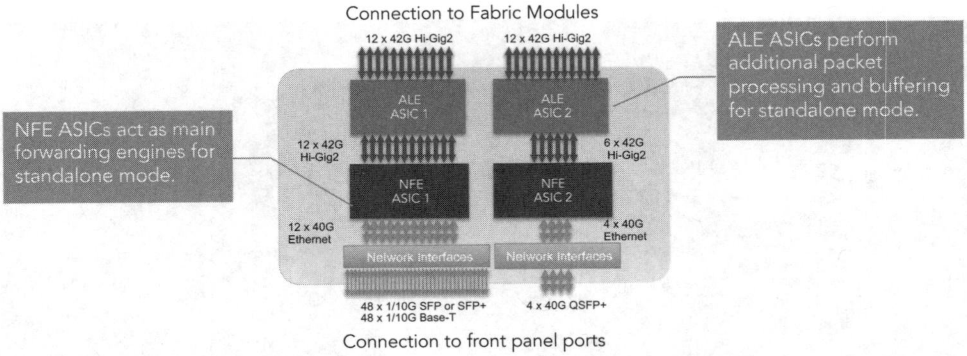

Figure 3-1 *Block Diagram for ALE-enabled Line Cards and 9300 Series Switches*

- Merchant +

Merchant ASIC - - - NFE (Broadcom T2) BROADCOM + CISCO

Custom ASIC - - - Cisco ALE (ACL Leaf Engine), ASE (ACI Spine Engine)

- Best Performance and Functionalities
- Optimal Pricing

	NFE	ALE	ASE
ASIC Technology	40 nm	28 nm	28 nm
40Gbps Ports	32 (24)	24 (24)	42 (42)
Buffer (MB)	12 MB	40 MB	23 MB
L2/ L3	L2/ L3	L2/ L3	L3

Figure 3-2 *Cisco Merchant +*

The recently released Nexus 9K devices (Nexus 9200K and 9300EX) depart from the Merchant + strategy with 100 percent Cisco-spun ASICs. The latest devices in the Nexus switching portfolio are built on 16 Nanometer Cloud Scale technology ASICs. Cloud Scale ASICs support high density 10-, 25-, 40-, 50- and 100-Gbps connectivity in addition to VXLAN routing and bridging and advanced Netflow and analytics.

> **Note** What is 16 Nanometer ASIC? Today's processors, either from Cisco, Intel, or any other chip manufacture, use silicon transistors. A transistor is a semiconductor (sometimes it conducts; sometimes it does not) used to build processors. An individual transistor is either on or off (1 or 0 in binary). 16 Nanometer talks to the size of the transistors in which small is better. Smaller transistors have better performance, use less power, and more can be fit on a chip. Today 16 Nanometers is the smallest available in a switching platform.

Note Cisco will continue to sell merchant silicon switches. However, Cisco offers price and feature completive alternatives.

The Cisco Nexus 9000 Series delivers proven high performance and density, low latency, and exceptional power efficiency in both modular and fixed broad-form factors. The Nexus 9000 is the market's most programmable data center switch operating in Cisco NX-OS software mode or in application centric infrastructure (ACI) mode, making it ideal in traditional or fully automated data center deployments. The Nexus 9000, powered by Cisco NX-OS, enables next-generation data center architecture.

Cisco NX-OS software is a data center-class operating system that was built with modularity, resiliency, and serviceability at its foundation. The self-healing and highly modular design of Cisco NX-OS makes zero-impact operations a reality and enables exceptional operational flexibility. Focused on modern requirements of the data center, Cisco NX-OS provides a robust and comprehensive feature set that fulfills the switching needs of present and future data centers.

NX-OS is an extensible network operating system that enables programmability and integration with other third-party software. NX-OS features a RESTful interface, delivered through the open source NGINX web server, to meet the needs of modern programmability. NX-API exposes the complete configuration and management capabilities of the CLI through web-based APIs. NX-API can be used for a multitude of applications, including automating network configurations, streamline troubleshooting, or integrating through other software. Third-party software examples include orchestrations tools or even business applications. Finally, NX-OS can be extended through its Linux foundation.

NX-OS runs as an application on top of a 64-bit Linux distribution from Wind River. Wind River is based on the Yocto project, which is focused on using Linux for embedded systems, for example a network device. The underlying foundation of Linux enables organizations to manage NX-OS devices in a similar fashion as they do Linux servers with Bash scripting, containers, or upgrades via YUM or RPM. Using Linux also makes NX-OS software modular and supports distributed multithreaded processing on symmetric multiprocessors (SMPs), Intel x64 multicore CPUs, and distributed line-card processors. Cisco NX-OS modular processes are instantiated on demand, each in a separate protected memory space. Thus, processes are started and system resources allocated only when a feature is enabled. The modular processes are governed by a real-time preemptive scheduler that helps ensure the timely processing of critical functions. Figure 3-3 depicts the relationship between the hardware, the Linux operating system, and NX-OS.

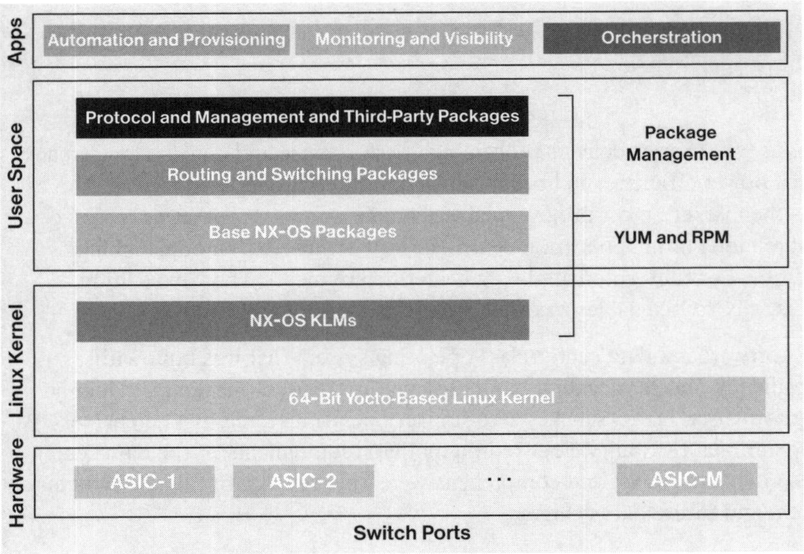

Figure 3-3 *Cisco Nexus Architecture*

Some Nexus 9K device support ACI with a simple software change. Currently all 9300 and 9300EX switches support ACI.

Cisco Application-Centric Infrastructure (ACI)

Cisco ACI is a comprehensive SDN-enabled data center network solution. ACI makes SDN easy by allowing the network to be application aware without complicated integrations or changing the application. ACI consists of three connected components, first a 40GB fabric enabled by Nexus 9000 hardware and second, the application policy infrastructure controller (APIC) that provides fabric automation and holistic policy management. A network policy model, which dynamically configures the fabric based on the application is the third component. Figure 3-4 depicts the three components of ACI.

The ACI fabric is built, using Nexus 9000 hardware configured in spine/leaf architecture. The fabric utilizes VXLAN as an overlay to provide layer 2 services across layer 3-connected leafs. Workloads in ACI can exist anywhere in the fabric and only be two hops away from any other host. In conjunction with the APIC controller, the fabric is managed as one large switch supporting separation of workload location and identity. ACI workloads can be connected, moved, or scaled to any leaf in the fabric. To optimize traffic across the fabric, ACI deploys an Anycast gateway, which configures every SVI (default gateway) for every VLAN simultaneously on every leaf, as shown in Figure 3-5.

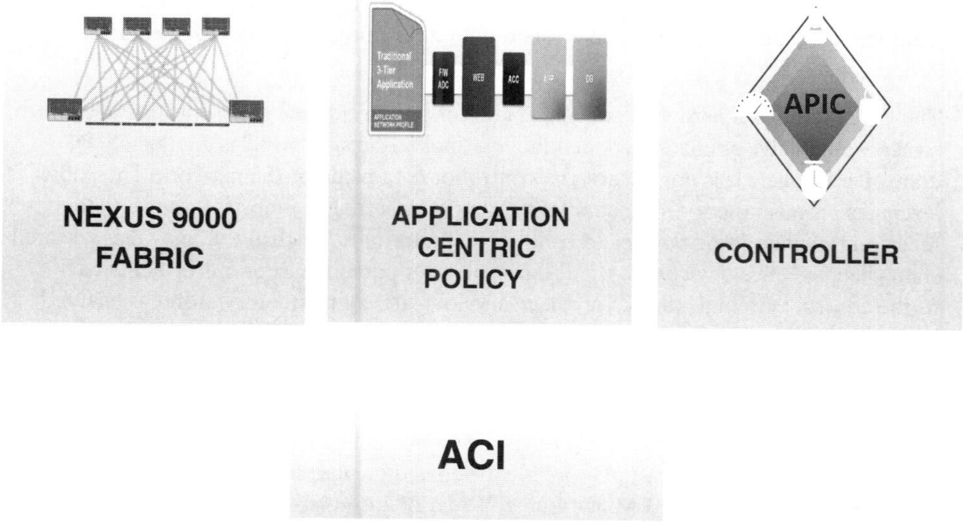

Figure 3-4 *ACI Building blocks*

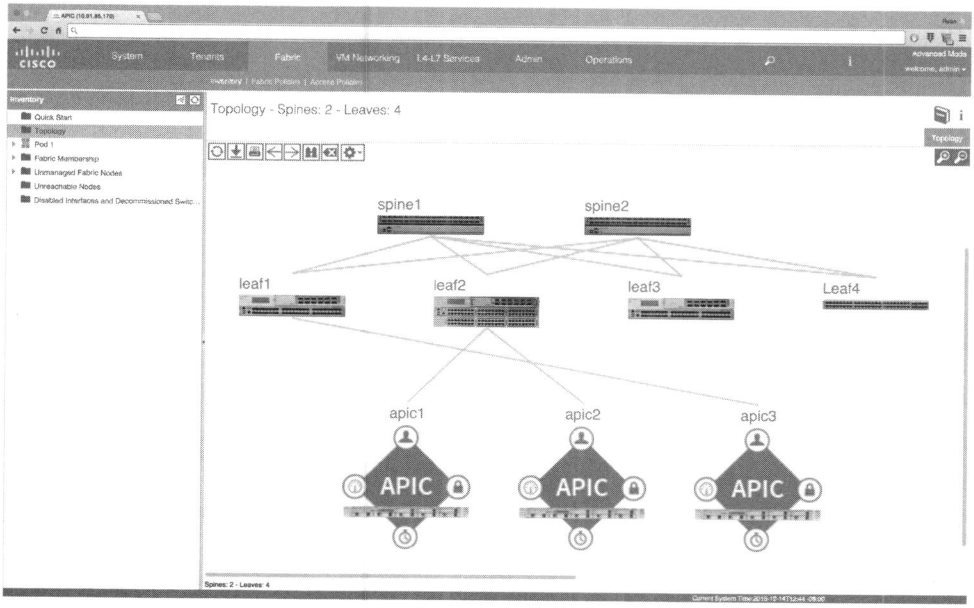

Figure 3-5 *ACI Fabric*

The APIC is the unifying point of automation and management for the ACI fabric. The APIC controller fully automates deployment and operations of the entire ACI fabric, including the IGP underlay and the VXLAN overlay. APIC fabric automation significantly reduces the time and effort required for initial fabric deployments and fabric maintenance.

The Cisco APIC is a hardware appliance, and for production environments, installed with either three or five appliances, depending on total fabric size. APIC is a unique SDN controller because it is not part of the control or data plane of the network. The APIC leverages promise theory for instantiating configuration of the fabric. Promise theory relies on the underlying devices to handle configuration state changes, known as "desired state changes." The devices are then responsible for passing exceptions or faults back to the control system. High-performance and low-latency traffic forwarding is ensured because packets are only processed in dedicated switching ASICs.

ACI policy simplifies complex network configuration with business centric connectivity rules. ACI policy is built using end point groups (EPG) (see Figure 3-6), contracts, and application network profiles (ANP). EPGs are simple collections of servers, applications, or VLANs that share policy. EPGs are identified and created by IP address, VLAN, VXLAN, physical port, or VM attributes. When ACI is integrated into a hypervisor management system, for example OpenStack or vSphere, the EPG is populated and consumed by the virtual machine administrator.

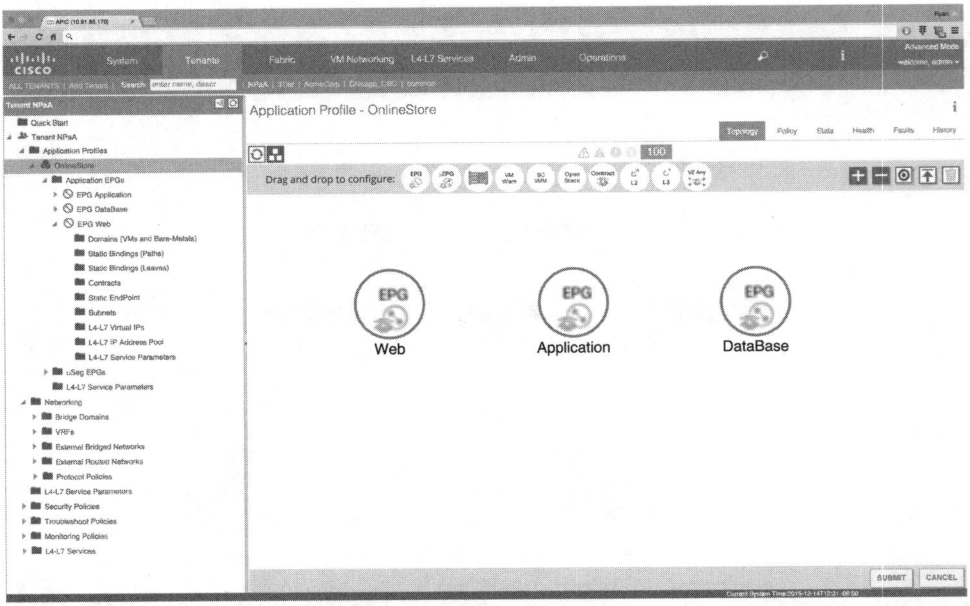

Figure 3-6 *EPG for a Three-tier Application*

ACI contracts connect EPGs. ACI is a white-list security model, and communication must be explicitly defined for hosts to communicate. Network configuration, for example, QoS and ACLs, lives in the contract in addition to service graphs which introduce layer 4 through layer 7 network services (see Figure 3-7). Service graphs switch or route traffic to either a physical or virtual devices and dynamically configure the device based on setting in the contract.

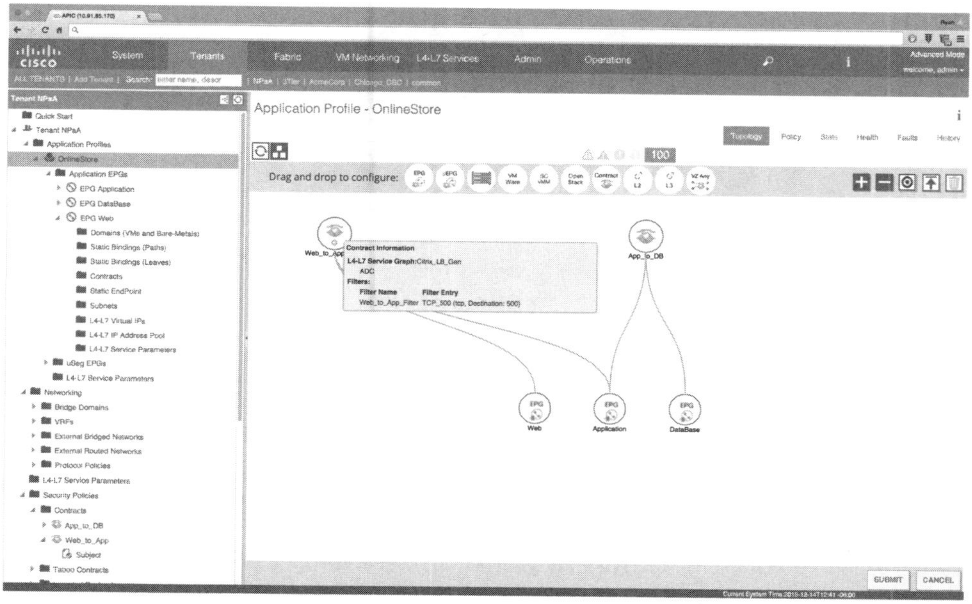

Figure 3-7 *EPG for a Three-tier Application with Contracts*

An Application Network Profile (ANP) is a collection of EPGs and contracts that define an Application. ANPs are the logical representation of an application and its interdependencies in the network fabric. Application Network Profiles are modeled in a way that matches the way that applications are designed and deployed.

The APIC controllers dynamically instantiate ACI policy across the fabric. The fabric in ACI is stateless and allows any port to accept or change any configuration. Configurations (policy) are instantiated to a leaf when the application is identified through an EPG. In the event the application moves, scales, or is removed, the fabric automatically reconfigures the fabric. Network layers 4 through 7 services are also stateless and dynamically configured through ACI policy (see Figure 3-8).

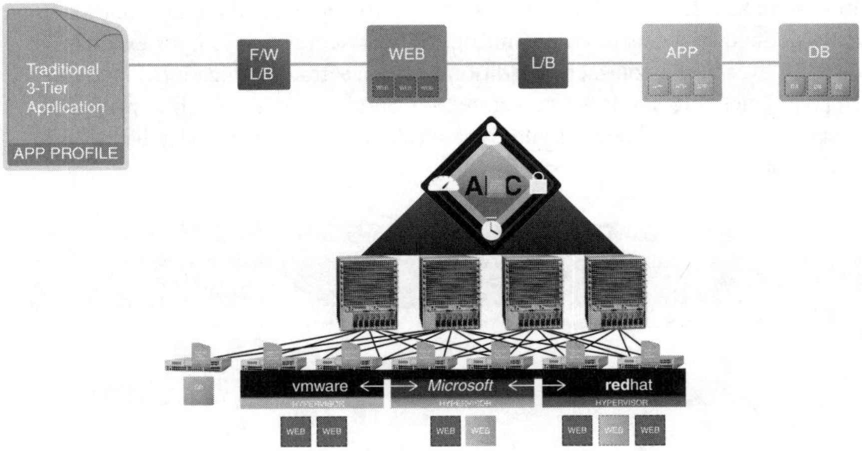

Figure 3-8 *ACI Instantiate Policy in a Stateless Fabric*

Nexus Data Broker

Cisco Nexus Data Broker is a simple, scalable, and cost-effective solution to monitor, capture, or analyze high-volume and business-critical traffic. It replaces traditional purpose-built matrix switches with one or more Cisco Nexus 3000 or Nexus 9000 Series Switches that can be interconnected to build a scalable network tap and Cisco Switched Port Analyzer (SPAN) aggregation infrastructure. This infrastructure supports 1, 10, 25, 40, 50, and 100 Gbps connectivity and supports NDB controlled ports and traditional Ethernet ports on the same switch allowing the matrix network to simultaneously support an out-of-band network.

Nexus Data Broker switches connect traffic from ingress ports connected to a production data center network to egress ports connected to network analysis tools, for example, Wireshark, security analytics, or data-capture devices. Ingress data can come from configured SPAN ports in the production data center or from dedicated optical taps. Nexus Data Broker supports 1 to 1, many to 1 and many to many replication with or without traffic filters. It is managed by the Nexus Data Broker Server, which features an easy-to-use GUI and a RESTful interface. The Nexus Data Broker Server runs as a virtual machine or in smaller installations directly on a Nexus 9000 switch.

Figure 3-9 depicts an example deployment of Data Broker, using both SPAN ports and optical taps.

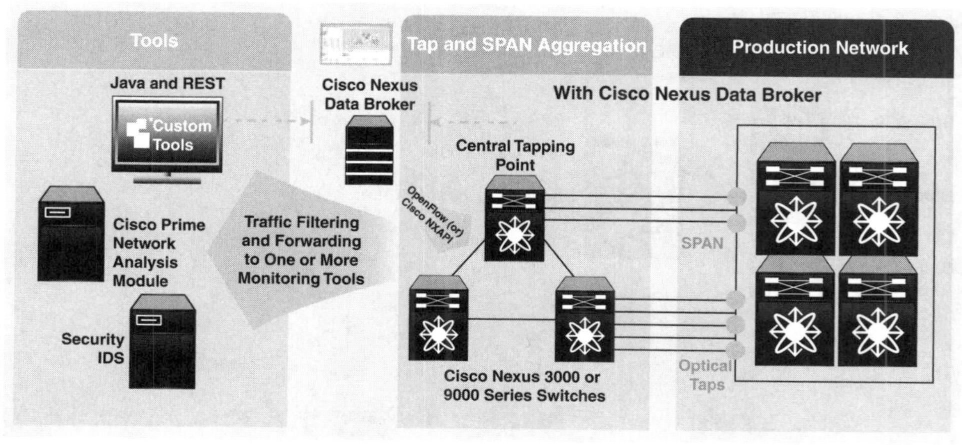

Figure 3-9 *Nexus Data broker Architecture*

Note Nexus Data Broker can be paired with a Cisco Netflow Generation Appliance to generate Netflow data from the data center.

Note Nexus Data Broker's RESTful API is not covered in this text. Documentation for the API can be found on the NDB Server at https://{IP Address}:8443/swagger.

Use Case—Nexus Data Broker

An organization needs to automate capturing and filters traffic from specific applications in the data center. The Nexus 9500 and 9300 are leveraged as the Data Broker matrix switches. Interfaces from the matrix switches are permanently connected to every production top of rack (TOR) switch, providing 20Gb of monitored traffic. (See Figure 3-10). A network administrator, using the NDB RESTful API and a Python script, dynamically configures SPAN and optical taps in the production network to replicate traffic to the NDB ports. The same Python script also configures NDB to send the replicated traffic to Wireshark for analysis. When the capture is complete, the network administrator runs a Python script to tear down the tap.

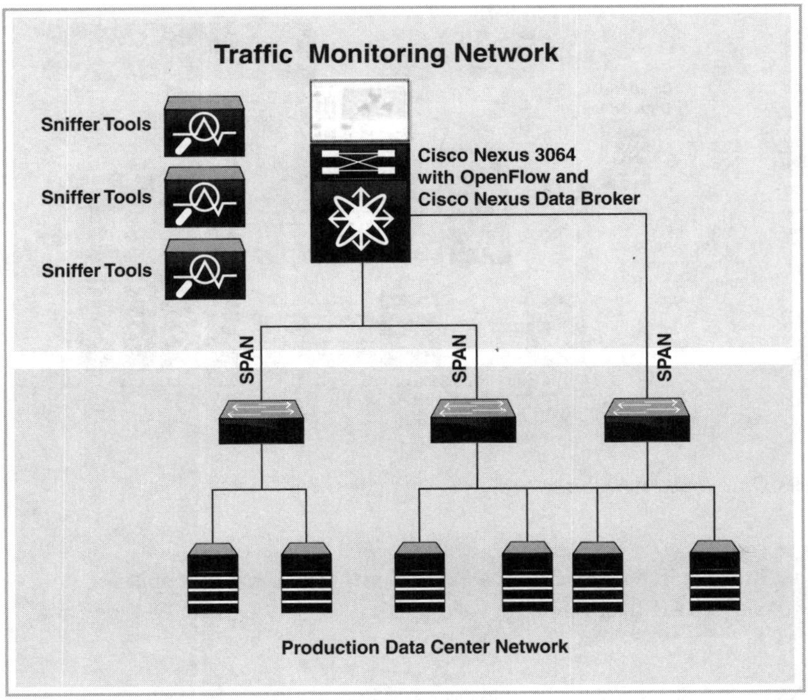

Figure 3-10 *Nexus Data Broker Architecture*

Evolution of Data Center Network Architecture

Cisco Nexus 9000 supports traditional network architecture based on layer 2 technologies, for example, STP and VPC and the next evolution of network architecture, which is based on layer 3 protocols and overlays. The combination of layer 3 protocols and an overlay enables network architecture to support modern applications, are more resilient, and offer better performance than traditional network architecture.

These next-generation data center fabrics are based on spine-to-leaf architecture where every leaf is connected to every spine; however, leafs are not connected to each other, and spines are not connected to each other. Every host in a spine/leaf architecture is two hops away from every other host facilitating modern N-tier applications. N-tier applications, defined as breaking large applications into smaller components, significantly increase the amount of east-west data center traffic. To make the most of the architecture, spine/leaf fabrics are built on a layer 3 foundation and an overlay that provides layer 2 services to the leafs. Figure 3-11 depicts a common spine/leaf architecture using the Nexus 9K.

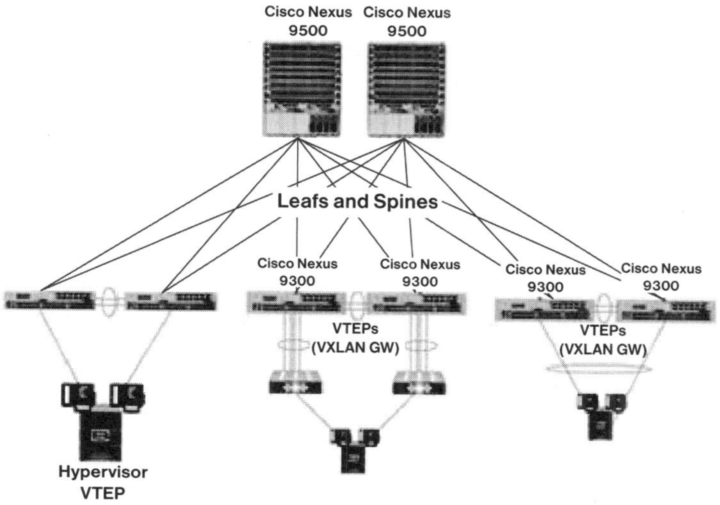

Figure 3-11 *Next-generation Data Center Fabric*

Layer 3 spine/leaf fabrics provide more resiliency, better performance, and better scalability then networks built using layer 2 protocols. Layer 2 networks are very hard to troubleshoot and monitor, and are prone to failure. (See "What's wrong with layer 2-based architecture" below.) Layer 3 spine/leaf fabrics utilize highly resilient layer 3 routing protocols that very quickly adapt to link and switch failure. A failure of a spine device only reduces the available fabric bandwidth and in most cases does not impact traffic forwarding. Failure of a leaf device can disrupt hosts connected to that device. However, dual-connected hosts paired with multi-chassis aggregate Ethernet (vPC) can reduce or eliminate traffic-forwarding issues. Spine/leaf fabrics provide better performance by leveraging all available links with Equal Cost Multiple Path (ECMP) or in the case of ACI, intelligently routing traffic across multiple links using flowlet switching. Finally, spine/leaf fabrics offer scalability, where access ports are increased by adding leaf nodes, and adding spines increases bandwidth. The modular nature of spine/leaf architecture enables a mismatch of access switches to adopt the latest and greatest hardware-based features. Layer 3 data center fabrics require an overlay protocol to provide layer 2 VLANs across the data center. The VXLAN overlay protocol provides layer 2 adjacency over layer 3 links in a data center fabric.

What's wrong with L2-based network architecture? Traditional data center networks with three-tier architecture are built using layer 2 protocols including Spanning Tree Protocol, Virtual Topology System or hot standby redundancy protocol, and so on. This architecture has many problems related to how modern applications communicate, the network, network performance, and network resiliency.

Traditional applications are built and delivered as large monolithic distributions. The size and complexity of these applications made them very difficult to deploy and operate. Modern applications are broken up into smaller components called tiers, often referred to as *n*-tiered applications. Breaking applications into tiers allows application components to be deployed, patched, and scaled individually, based on the needs of the application. The shift from large distributions (monolithic) to *n*-tier applications has significantly changed data center network traffic flows. Traffic flows for *n*-tiered applications are now mostly east-west as the tiers of the application exchange data and a perfect match for spine/leaf network architecture. Traditional three-tier network architecture built using L2-based protocols is optimized for applications that communicate north-south.

L2-based network architecture is hard to troubleshoot and monitor and is prone to failure. Any network component within a L2 domain is also in the same failure domain. A failure domain is an expectation of what else can fail in the event that any other component in the domain fails. The failure could be as simple as a link failure, which can cause the entire data center network to reconverge and temporarily stop forwarding traffic or to a failed component of or in the network, which must be discovered and removed before the network returns to normal operation. Spine/leaf data center networks are built on top of layer 3 networks, which limit the fault domain to a single link in the data center. In the event of failure in a layer 3-based network, the nonimpacted parts of the network continue to forward traffic, and in most cases, single network component failure will not have any impact on the application.

Troubleshooting large L2 networks is very difficult due the complexity of the spanning tree protocol (STP). When a spanning tree network stops or incorrectly forwards packets, the distributed nature of the environment, teamed up with the number of moving parts in STP, do little to isolate the issues. As a result, spanning tree networks have no systematic troubleshooting procedures. Troubleshooting quickly gets reduced to random trial and error, often physically disconnecting redundant links. Spanning tree networks require careful planning to organize the multiple components, for example root bridges and ports. Small changes in the environment, for example, adding a switch, can have major impacts to the overall architecture and cause unknown and foreseen issues. More recent enhancements to Spanning Tree, for example, root guard or BPDU Guard, limit the impact of network changes. However, the enhancements add to the overall complexity of the solution and require more processes that can fail.

STP-based networks are also prone to a "soft" failure because of the nature of STP itself, where the network fails and stops forwarding traffic, and yet does not fail enough to reconverge. This type of failure is common with network operating system bugs or flapping links. These types of errors usually result in large-scale instability, requiring the restart or reboot of large number of network devices.

Monitoring STP networks is also very difficult. Switches in STP communicate with each other via bridge protocol data units (BPDUs). BPDUs are sent every couple of seconds from every switch on every interface. Switches, depending on their STP configuration, accept or ignore the BDPU. There are also different types of BPDUs. Monitoring BPDUs technically has the capability to alert of pending or even specific failures; however, due to the number of BPDU collections issues, and complexity contained within the BPDU, this is not done in practice. Most organizations monitor the switch by its IP address and maybe logs. However, neither of these directly monitor STP. Moreover, troubleshooting the BPDU is very difficult because it could come from anywhere in the network, and the data of the BPDU identifies devices by MAC address.

Another difficultly with layer 2 networks is monitoring a communication path. The designed layer 2 path can automatically change, be very hard to predict, or be different on a per-VLAN basis. To understand a path through a layer 2 network, an administrator must understand, hop-by-hop, where the traffic should go—versus where it did go. This involves dissecting STP blocked ports and MAC address tables. In many cases, troubleshooting an issues related to path is useless because the path that caused the issue is no longer the current path, with no way to go back in time and little indication of a reconvergence. In contrast, a layer 3 network path is well defined, easy to troubleshoot, and easy to monitor.

Finally, layer 2 networks have a number of security concerns. Modern networks require a "whitelist" model where communication between any two hosts must be explicitly defined. Whitelisting a network is very difficult, if not impossible in a layer 2 environments. The private VLAN feature is excellent at restricting all communications between hosts; however, due to the east-west nature of traffic, is no longer acceptable. Whitelisting a network is best accomplished via layer 3 stateless access control lists (ACL). ACLs block an address or better yet, a group of addresses, from commutating where the IP address(s) uniquely identify an application. In the event something requires quarantine, a simple ACL can isolate a machine or even reroute it to a remediation server.

There are two types of network engineers: those who have experienced spanning tree failure and those whot are about to!

Note VXLAN is a standards-based overlay protocol designed for a next-generation data center (see Figure 3-12). VXLAN is a MAC in UDP encapsulation that adds 8 bytes to the original frame. VXLAN virtualization supports multitenancy with a 24-bit VXLAN identifier, which can also extend the number of allowed VLANs.

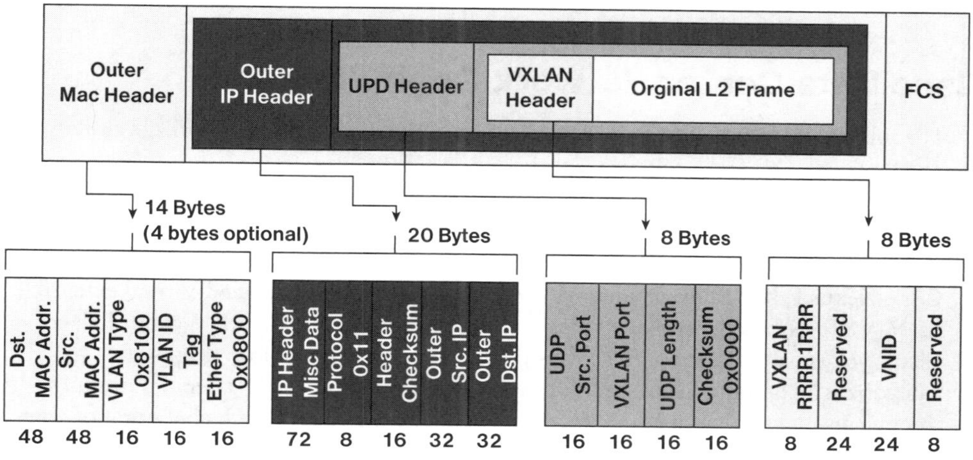

Figure 3-12 *VXLAN Packet*

VXLAN-based fabrics forward packets with host-based reachability information stored in the leaf and/or the spine. First-generation VXLAN operated without a control plane with a flood and learn model. Flood and learn forwards broadcasts, unknown unicast, and multicast traffic (otherwise known as BUM traffic) wrapped in a multicast packet and flooded to all leaf nodes in the fabric. Once the destination host responds to the flooded packet forwarding information for that host is stored on the leaf. Flood and learn is great at building host-based reachability but is inefficient. Second-generation VXLAN leverages a control plane built with multi-protocol BGP with eVPN.

VXLAN with eVPN builds a host-based reachability database on the spines. BUM traffic is flooded via a multicast; however, once a host is learned, the leaf distributes reachability information via MP-BGP to the spines. The spines operate as BGP route reflectors (proxy), eliminating the need for leafs to maintain iBGP relationships and provides a host-reachability database. A leaf will first check the destination against a locally maintained database and if a match is not found, forwards a query to the spines. If the spine is updated on the destination, reachability information will be forwarded to the leaf.

VXLAN provides optimal traffic forwarding and separates location and identity of hosts connected to the fabric. Dynamic host-based reachability information enables workload mobility where any host can be connected or moved to any port within the fabric. VXLAN provides optimal forwarding, using Anycast gateways, which build logical SVI interfaces on every leaf, ensuring hosts do not traverse the fabric for their default gateway.

Next-generation data center fabrics can be built and managed with programmability tools, traditional box-by-box CLI or with a controller. A key component of Next-generation data centers are network controllers. Controllers automate deployment, operations, and troubleshooting of the interior gateway protocol (OSPF, IS-IS) or the VXLAN overlay or both. Introducing a controller to the network provides a layer of abstraction and a single programmability interface. Cisco controllers include Nexus Fabric Manager (NFM), Virtual Topology System (VTS), and Cisco ACI (APIC).

Cisco Data Center Network Controllers

The following sections will address some of the Cisco data center network controllers in greater detail.

Nexus Fabric Manager

Cisco Nexus Fabric Manager automatically implements a self-managed Virtual extensible LAN (VXLAN-based) topology incorporating an Ethernet VPN (EVPN) control plane. Cisco Nexus Fabric Manager discovers the fabric's physical topology, learns and categorizes all points of connectivity, and delivers control to the IT operation teams through a simplified point-and-click, web-based interface. Full switch configurations are automatically built, pushed, and managed on the individual switches, based on simplified user requests, with no need for the user to interact with the command-line interface (CLI).

NFM features a Northbound RESTful API for programmability and integration. To date, NFM supports devices in the 9K family.

Virtual Topology System (VTS)

The Cisco Virtual Topology System (VTS) is an open, standards-based overlay management and provisioning system for VXLAN in data center networks. It automates VXLAN fabric provisioning but has no IGP management. VTS supports BGP eVPN VXLAN deployments across all VXLAN-enabled Cisco switches, including the 5, 6, 7, 8, and 9K in addition to other vendor products. VTS is best used in conjunction with an interior gateway protocol (IGP) management and provisioning tool, for example Cisco Prime Infrastructure. VTS offers an open RESTful API, enabling programmability and Cloud integrations.

Cisco ACI

Cisco ACI is a best-in-class data center fabric solution that simplifies the network and network services with application-based policy. The APIC controller provides a GUI interface to deploy, operate, and troubleshoot the network. APIC automates deployment of the underlay (IS-IS) and VXLAN and manages application policy. ACI policy defines infrastructure configuration per application, which is dynamically instantiated as needed to the fabric. ACI reduces operational complexity and enables the network to add value to application delivery in Cloud operational models. ACI is built exclusively on Nexus 9000 hardware, which runs dedicated ACI software. Table 3-1 summarizes Cisco's Data Center Network controllers and their capabilities.

Table 3-1 *Cisco Controller Comparison*

Controller	IGP Automation	VXLAN Automation	Policy	Multivendor Switch Hardware	API
ACI	Yes	Yes	Yes	No	RESTful
NFM	Yes	Yes	No	No	RESTful
VTS	No	Yes	No	Yes	RESTful

Note The APIs for NFM and VTS are not covered in this text; however, the fundamental skills covered in Chapter 2 apply to their use. Documentation for the NFM API will be released soon, and the VTS API is found at VTS: http://www.cisco.com/c/dam/en/us/td/docs/net_mgmt/virtual_topology_system/2_0/api/Cisco_VTS_2_0_API_Doc.pdf.

Summary

Cisco's Data Center networking portfolio offers market leading products to build traditional and next-generation data centers. Cisco offers choice of ASIC, choice of architecture, and choice of controller for organizations of all types to solve their specific networking challenges and enhance their business using the network. Cisco's focus on programmability and integration is represented with feature-rich and easy-to-use APIs and SDKs that span across the entire networking portfolio. The following chapters discuss how Cisco's data center products are deployed and operated, using programmability and automation toolsets.

Chapter 4

On-Box Programmability and Automation with Cisco Nexus NX-OS

Cisco NX-OS Software is a data center-class operating system built with modularity, resiliency, and serviceability. Cisco NX-OS helps ensure continuous availability and sets the standard for mission-critical data center environments. The self-healing and highly modular design of Cisco NX-OS makes zero-impact operations a reality and enables exceptional operational flexibility. Focused on the requirements of the data center, Cisco NX-OS provides a robust and comprehensive feature set that fulfills the switching and storage networking needs of present and future data centers. Open NX-OS is a technical strategy that unlocks the potential of the Nexus 9000 platform with open interfaces, integrated automation, and application extensibility.

Open NX-OS Automation—Bootstrap and Provisioning

NX-OS software features built-in switch provisioning with a Cisco power on auto provisioning (POAP) or iPXE boot. POAP can significantly reduce the time involved with new data center-switch deployments and switch replacement by automatically deploying NX-OS and applying an initial configuration.

Cisco POAP

POAP automates the provisioning of fresh out-of-the-box Nexus devices. When a POAP devices boots and does not find a startup configuration, the device enters POAP mode. POAP will first search a USB drive, followed by a network location for a POAP configuration script. POAP configuration scripts detail where the switch can obtain provisioning information.

Note Not all NX-OS releases support USB boot. Check the release notes.

A POAP network process sends a DHCP request for IP and provisioning information from a DHCP server. The DHCP response must include IP address of a local TFTP script server and the name of the POAP script. The switch will download the POAP configuration script. The configuration script enables the switch to download and install the appropriate software image and configuration file from the configuration server. Image and configuration can utilize SCP, HTTP, FTP, TFTP, or SFTP. However, reliable and secure transport protocols are preferred. Figure 4-1 illustrates the components required to use POAP.

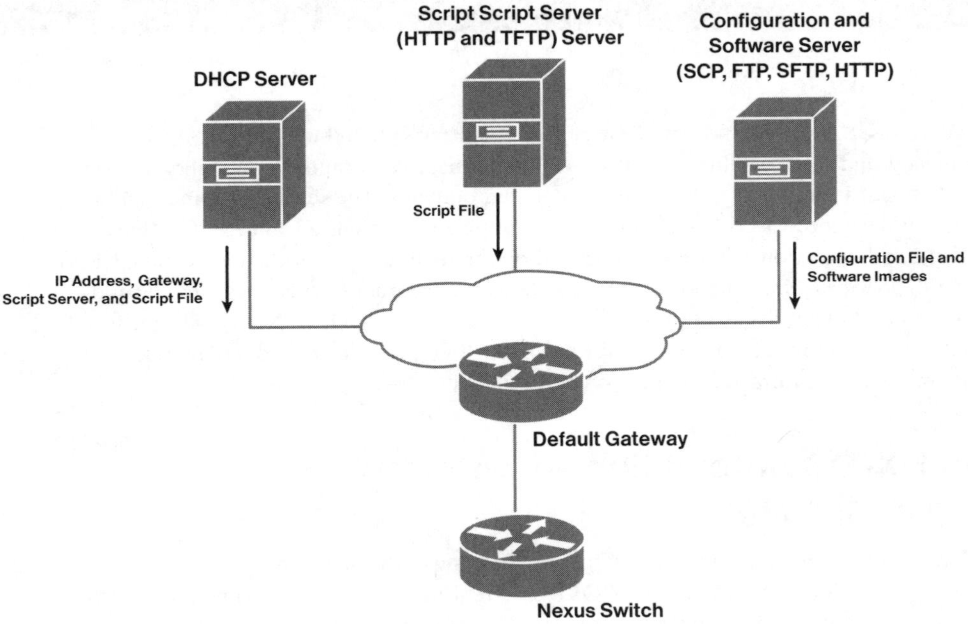

Figure 4-1 *POAP required components*

POAP can utilize any standard DHCP server, including Cisco IOS and dhcpd. DHCP option 66 or 150 instructs the POAP process where to find its TFTP server (use 66 for a single TFTP server or option 150 for multiple) and option 67 pushes the name of the file that is the configuration script.

The following example shows the IOS DHCP configuration for POAP.

```
ip dhcp pool POAP-Pool
 network 10.1.5.0 255.255.255.0
 default-router 10.1.5.1
 dns-server 8.8.8.8
```

```
domain-name cisco.com
option 66 ascii 10.1.5.100 #tftp server address
option 67 ascii poap.py #POAP script
```

DHCP services from Linux commonly use dhcpd, the following example shows dhcpd.conf for POAP.

```
group {
   filename "/poap.py";
   next-server 10.1.5.100; #tftp server address
   option tftp-server-name "10.1.5.100";
   option bootfile-name "/poap.py"; #POAP script
}
```

The configuration script is a Python or Cisco TCL file and must be located on the TFTP or HTTP server as defined in the DHCP options. In some cases, the DHCP and TFTP service on the same server. A sample script is located at:

https://github.com/datacenter/nexus9000/tree/master/nx-os/poap

The configuration script starts with Python variables that must be modified. All data is a Python string and must be contained in quotes. The following example shows the poap.py configuration data.

```
# system and kickstart images, configuration: location on server (src) and
target (dst)
n9k_image_version        = "7.0.3.I2.2a" # this must match your code version
image_dir_src            = "/home/admin"  #Even if it's the home directory!
ftp_image_dir_src_root   = image_dir_src
tftp_image_dir_src_root  = image_dir_src
n9k_system_image_src     = "nxos.7.0.3.I2.2a.bin"
#config_file_src          = "/tftpboot/conf"
config_file_src          = "/home/admin/blank" #use an existing NX-OS configuration
image_dir_dst            = "bootflash:poap"
system_image_dst         = n9k_system_image_src
config_file_dst          = "volatile:poap.cfg"
md5sum_ext_src           = "md5"
# Required space on /bootflash (for config and system images)
required_space           = 350000

# copy protocol to download images and config
protocol                 = "scp" # protocol to use to download images/config

# Host name and user credentials
username                 = "admin" # server account
ftp_username             = "admin" # server account
password                 = "cisco" # password
hostname                 = "10.1.1.1" # ip address of ftp/scp/http/sftp server
```

```
# vrf info
vrf = "management"
if os.environ.has_key('POAP_VRF'):
    vrf=os.environ['POAP_VRF']

Future down the file set the switch identification type.
config_file_type        = "serial_number"
```

The POAP script will instructs the switch to download the switch image and configuration. The previous example is configured to use SCP.

Note Use an existing NX-OS configuration to ensure perfect formatting!

Note POAP configuration scripts are authenticated using a MD5 hash in the POAP.py file. The MD5 hash is located in second line of the file under #md5sum= and must be recalculated every time the file is changed. To recalculate the MD5 hash, run the following *single* command on a Linux machine.

```
f=poap.py ; cat $f | sed '/^#md5sum/d' > $f.md5 ; sed -i
"s/^#md5sum=.*/#md5sum=\"$(md5sum $f.md5 | sed 's/ .*//')\"/" $f
```

This command is referenced in the sample poap.py file.

POAP will validate both the NX-OS image and the poap.py file with an MD5 hash located in a file with the same name and an .md5 extension. The configuration line in poap.py sets the extension.

```
md5sum_ext_src          = "md5"
```

To create the md5 files, redirect the output of md5sum:

```
md5sum poap.py > poap.py.md5 - ok

md5sum nxos.7.0.3.I2.2a.bin >> nxos.7.0.3.I2.2a.bin.md5
```

POAP loads a specific configuration based on the location of a switch, (CDP, LLDP) or on a per-switch basis by serial number. The name of the configuration file is dictated by the poap.py line "config_file_src." The POAP script will look for a file with this name, with the serial number as an extension. This file must exist on the configuration server. The following is an example file for a switch with the serial number of SAL15492HSH.

```
blank. SAL15492HSH
```

The entire POAP process, including errors, is logged to the switch's boot flash directory. The log files are time stamped. However, unless the hardware clock on the switch is accurate, the timestamp will be wrong.

The POAP process concludes when the switch reboots with the supplied configuration.

Note POAP files can be tested by running the script locally with "python poap.py".

Cisco Ignite

Cisco Ignite is a graphical tool to update software and apply configurations using POAP. Ignite is located at https://github.com/datacenter/ignite. Ignite can be cloned and installed on any Linux server, or the GitHub repository offers an easy to use OVA.

Using Ignite

Ignite (Figure 4-2) supports building topologies by adding spine, leafs, and core routers to the graph. All links must be modified to reflect the actual port for Ignite auto discovery to correctly identify and apply configuration to the switch.

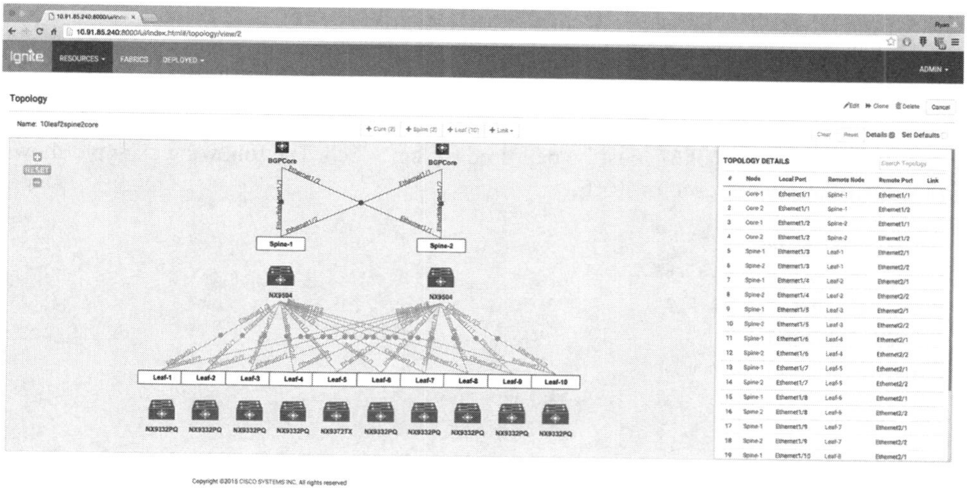

Figure 4-2 *Cisco Ignite*

Building a topology also involves templating a configuration. Any valid NX-OS configuration can be applied with Ignite through configlets. Configets are snippets of NX-OS code or Python scripts to apply a more advanced configuration. Once a valid configuration is submitted, Ignite waits for a POAP-enabled switch to access the server for a configuration.

The Ignite project is evolving very quickly. The latest GitHub clone includes a "Getting Started Guide" in the /docs directory with step-by-step documentation.

NX-OS iPXE

iPXE is an open-source, pre-boot execution tool. It is derived from PXE boot and supports modern file transport protocols. iPXE supports downloading Cisco secured NX-OS software via HTTP over with either IPv4 or IPv6. Similar to POAP, iPXE utilizes DHCP for initial boot up and server location; however, iPXE can be used after a configuration is stored on the switch.

By default, a Nexus 9000 switch will boot Linux via an NX-OS image located in bootflash. The Nexus 9000 boots from the standard Linux boot loader, named GRUB. GRUB is responsible for system control until the Linux kernel loads. The boot process can be changed either by the NX-OS command, "boot order," or by manual boot interruption. To manually interrupt the boot process, enter a **Ctrl+b** within three seconds of power on. Boot interruption will display the menu in the following example.

```
Please choose a bootloader shell:
1). GRUB shell
2). PXE shell
Enter your choice:
```

The command **boot order pxe bootflash** configures GRUB to boot to iPXE. If IPXE fails the switch will boot from bootflash.

Similar to POAP, DHCP 67 must be delivered to the switch. The following example shows IOS DHCP configuration for iPXE.

```
ip dhcp pool ipxe-Pool
 network 10.1.5.0 255.255.255.0
 default-router 10.1.5.1
 dns-server 8.8.8.8
 domain-name cisco.com
option 67 ascii http://10.91.85.240/nxos.7.0.3.I2.1a.bin
```

Bash

Cisco Nexus 9000 can be extended and managed via BASH. The Bash shell is a powerful command line processor and is the default shell on most Linux and Mac systems. It is also available for Windows OS. Bash supports scripting in the form of a series of Linux commands to automate a task. Bash on the Nexus platform allows the network administrator to manage the switch similar to Linux systems, including operations, troubleshooting, and scripting.

The Bash shell is found on modem Mac or Linux platforms via the "terminal." To access BASH on Nexus, the BASH feature must be enabled.

```
switch(config)# feature bash-shell
```

```
Accessing the BASH shell from enable mode.
```

```
switch# run bash
bash-4.2$
```

Bash Scripting

Bash scripting is a simple yet powerful tool to automate Linux environments. A Bash script is interpreted line-by-line by the Bash shell. Bash files must have execute permissions and should have a .sh extension. Bash scripts run a list of standard commands but often require connecting multiple commands to parse text and make changes.

Bash Variables, Conditions, and Loops

Similar to Python, Bash supports variables, conditions, and flow control.

To create a Bash variable, assign a string to a variable name. Bash variables are typed as strings but can be treated as a number. Spaces in variable declaration are not allowed. The following output declares the variable "v", assigns the value "hello world."

```
v="hello world"
echo $v
hello world
```

The output leverages the BASH command "echo" to print the output of v. The $ symbol requests the value of v. By default, Bash has a number of built-in variables. The built-in variables are automatically set when the shell starts and are very useful in writing Bash scripts. With the exception of the $PATH, built-in variables are not commonly changed. Common built-in Bash variables are listed in Table 4-1.

Table 4-1 *Common Built-In Bash Variables*

$PATH	Working path
$PWD	Current directory
$HOME	Users Home directory
$RANDOM	Generate a random number

Note Use the command "set" to see all Bash variables.

Bash supports passing parameters into a script. Passed parameters are listed after the script name and are represented in the script as positional variables. The value of positional variables is referenced with $(*parameter number*) for example $1.

The following example shows Bash command-line arguments are variables.

```
bash-4.2$ touch simplebash.sh
bash-4.2$ chmod +x simplebash.sh
bash-4.2$ echo '#!/bin/bash' > simplebash.sh
bash-4.2$ echo echo The first input is \$1 and the second is \$2 >> simplebash.sh
bash-4.2$./simplebash.sh Hello Cisco
The first input is Hello and the second is Cisco
```

The previous example first creates a file called simplebash.sh, and then uses chmod to set execute permissions. Lines three and four use ">" and ">>" echo commands as text into the file, where ">" replaces everything in the file with the text and and ">>" appends the file. The backslashes in line four escape the $ character to insert a $1 into the file instead of the value of the variable 1. Finally, the command is run using "./". Dot/slash specifies to run the script from the current directory.

Bash Arithmetic

Bash variables are strings; however, they can be declared as integers. The following commands set the variables V1 and V2 with numbers, but they are stored as strings. The command "echo $V1+$V2" does not add the values and instead prints the string, including the literal symbol "+"

```
bash-4.2$ V1=10
bash-4.2$ V2=5
bash-4.2$ echo $V1+$V2
10+5
```

The **BASH** command "declare –" can initialize or convert a variable to an integer.

The following output declares the variable "result" as an integer and calculates a number.

```
bash-4.2$ int1=12
bash-4.2$ int2=5
bash-4.2$ declare -i result
bash-4.2$ result=int1*int2
bash-4.2$ echo $result
60
```

As an alternative to the "declare" command, double parentheses signal Bash to treat the variables as integers.

The following output adds the values using double parentheses.

```
bash-4.2$ V1=10
bash-4.2$ V2=5
bash-4.2$ echo $(($V1+$V2))
15
```

Bash supports common arithmetic operations including addition, subtraction, multiplication, and division.

Bash Conditions and Flow Control

Bash conditions and flow control introduce logic and looping to Bash scripts.

Bash if/then/else statements compare two or more values and executes a command.

The following example shows a simple BASH if statement.

```
bash-4.2$ if [ "Cisco" = "Cisco" ];
> then
> echo True
> else
> echo false
> fi
True
```

The condition in the previous example compares if the string "Cisco" is equal to another string of "Cisco," and if true, prints the word "True." The **fi** command signals Bash that the conditional block has ended. The example leverages a Bash condition in the interactive shell. "If" statements saved in a script are on a single line and require the use of a semicolon as shown in the following example.

```
if [ "Cisco" = "Cisco" ];  then echo True; else echo false; fi
```

Bash if statements evaluate the expression using the **test** command. The **test** command requires brackets and supports both string and integer operators. Table 4-2 defines common BASH operators.

Table 4-2 *Bash Operators*

Operator	Description	Type
eq	Equal to	Integer
ne	Not equal to	Integer
gt	Greater than	Integer
ge	Greater than or equal to	Integer
lt	Less than	Integer

(Continued)

Table 4-2 *Continued*

Operator	Description	Type
le	Less than or equal to	Integer
= or ==	Equal to	String
<	Less than	String
>	Greater than	String
–z	Is null (or empty)	String
–n	Is not null (not empty)	String

Bash if statements support else-if with "elif" and can be nested.

Case is another Bash conditional and is good at evaluating multiple options. Case statements are a cleaner alternative than nested ifs. The following example leverages the case statement to evaluate a variable against multiple options.

```
bash-4.2$ cat simplecase.sh
#!/bin/bash

case "$1" in

1) echo one ;;

2) echo two ;;

3) echo three ;;

esac

bash-4.2$./simplecase.sh 2
two
```

The case statement in the previous example compares the first input argument against the string values 1, 2, and 3. Case statements can match multiple patterns with a |, as shown in the following example.

```
bash-3.2$ cat simplecase.sh
#!/bin/bash

case "$1" in

1 | [Oo][Nn][Ee] ) echo 1 ;;
```

```
2 | [Tt][wW][Oo] ) echo 2 ;;

3 | [Tt][Hh][Rr][Ee][Ee] ) echo 3 ;;

esac

bash-3.2$ ./simplecase.sh oNe
1
bash-3.2$ ./simplecase.sh THRee
3
bash-3.2$
```

The previous example utilizes the case statement to match on the number, that is, 1, 2, or 3, of the word one, two, or three in any case.

Bash flow control tools include for and while loops. By default, BASH for loops iterate a string using a blank space as a separator, as shown in the following example.

```
#!/bin/bash
for i in $1;
    do
    echo $i
done

bash-3.2$ ./simplefor.sh 'This is FUN'
This
is
fun
```

The previous example inputs a string, in this case "This is fun," and loops for every word the string.

In some cases, we need a loop for to perform something a number of times. The Linux **seq** command can be used in a for loop, as shown in the following example.

```
bash-3.2$ cat simplefor2.sh
#!/bin/bash
for i in 'seq 5';
    do
    echo i equals $i
done

bash-3.2$ ./simplefor2.sh
i equals 1
i equals 2
i equals 3
i equals 4
i equals 5
```

Bash while loops run code 0 or more times. Initiating and using a counter variable is a common use of while loops, as shown in the following example.

```
bash-3.2$ cat simplewhile.sh
#!/bin/bash
         counter=0
         while [  $counter -lt 5 ]; do
             echo The counter is $counter
             let counter=counter+1
         done

bash-3.2$ ./simplewhile.sh
The counter is 0
The counter is 1
The counter is 2
The counter is 3
The counter is 4
```

Bash Redirection and Pipes

A Linux program normally will take input from the keyboard and will output any results or errors to the screen. This is referred to as standard input (stdin), standard output (stdout), and standard error (stderr), respectively. Bash redirection allows the user to change or redirect the in and outs of the application.

A user complains that an application stops working from time to time. Ping is used to troubleshoot the issue; however, it is not very efficient to sit and watch it for 7–10 days. We can redirect the output of ping by using the redirection command >.

```
ping www.yahoo.com > somefile.txt
```

The Bash shell will create the file "somefile.txt" and store the results in the file.

Note Use of the >> redirector will append an existing file. For example,

```
ping www.yahoo.com >> somefile.txt
```

The following example shows the contents on somefile.txt:

```
PING yahoo.com (98.138.253.109): 56 data bytes
64 bytes from 98.138.253.109: icmp_seq=0 ttl=48 time=41.837 ms
64 bytes from 98.138.253.109: icmp_seq=1 ttl=48 time=42.385 ms
From 192.168.5.5 icmp_seq=2 Destination Host Unreachable
64 bytes from 98.138.253.109: icmp_seq=10 ttl=48 time=42.385 ms
```

Over time, this file will become very large and difficult to use. Bash pipes send the output of the first process into the input of the second. Bash pipes and the grep tool are very useful to parse large files. Grep is a powerful text searching utility that matches text, using regular expressions. The following example searches the output of somefile.txt for the word unreachable:

```
cat somefile.txt | grep -e "unreachable"
bash-4.2$
```

The grep search for "unreachable" in the previous example does not return any results because regular expression searches are case sensitive. Use **–i** to ignore case, as shown in the following example/

```
cat somefile.txt | grep -i -e "Destination Host Unreachable"
From 192.168.5.5 icmp_seq=2 Destination Host Unreachable
bash-4.2$
```

In the previous example, the output displays that the term "Destination Host Unreachable" is present in the file but does not offer any context. "–A" and "–B" will display the lines before and after the search term, respectively.

```
cat somefile.txt | grep -i -A 2 -B 2 -e "Destination Host Unreachable"


64 bytes from 98.138.253.109: icmp_seq=0 ttl=48 time=41.837 ms
64 bytes from 98.138.253.109: icmp_seq=1 ttl=48 time=42.385 ms
From 10.91.64.1 icmp_seq=3 Destination Host Unreachable
64 bytes from 98.138.253.109: icmp_seq=4 ttl=48 time=42.385 ms
```

To deal with multiple instances of the match use **grep –n** to display line numbers, as shown in the following example.

```
cat somefile.txt | grep -i -n -A 2 -B 2 -e "Destination Host Unreachable"


3:64 bytes from 98.138.253.109: icmp_seq=0 ttl=48 time=41.837 ms
4:64 bytes from 98.138.253.109: icmp_seq=1 ttl=48 time=42.385 ms
5:From 10.91.64.1 icmp_seq=3 Destination Host Unreachable
6:64 bytes from 98.138.253.109: icmp_seq=4 ttl=48 time=42.385 ms
```

Standard input is normally from the keyboard; however, Bash allows input redirection with the < command. The following example takes a text file, named numbers.txt, and uses the Linux sort command and input redirection to sort the numbers from smallest to largest.

```
bash-3.2$ cat numbers.txt
5
2
4
1
3
```

```
bash-3.2$ sort < numbers.txt
1
2
3
4
5
```

Note The input redirection in the examples “sort < number.txt” is used as a simple example and is not required.

Working with Text in Bash

Bash scripting usually involves working with text, and Bash provides a number of tools to search and manipulate it. The most popular tools are grep (covered in the previous section), Awk, and Sed.

Sed is a text Stream Editor and is useful for searching for and manipulating text. Sed inputs a stream of text, either a line or an entire file. Sed uses a common syntax of a regular expression pattern followed by an action. Available actions include “d” for delete, “p” for print, and the most common sed tool is “s” for substitution. All actions leverage a slash as a delimiter.

```
bash-4.2$ cat somefile.txt
I love networking

bash-4.2$ cat somefile.txt | sed s/networking/"Cisco networking"/
I love Cisco networking
```

The previous example pipes the output of somefile.txt, and uses sed to replace “networking” with “Cisco networking.” Sed s (substitution) locates what text is delimited in the first set of / / and replaces it with the text in the second block of / /. This command does not change the file.

Sed supports regular expressions, which are very useful to parse a file and make changes to a file.

```
bash-4.2$ cat somefile.txt
I love networking
dns server 192.168.4.5
ntp server 192.168.5.5
AAA server 192.168.6.5
whocares server 192.168.7.5
```

Somefile.txt in the previous example has three different addresses for network services. The following example will use sed and regex expression metacharacter "." to standardize on a single server. The "." matches any single character.

```
bash-4.2$ cat somefile.txt | sed s/192.168...5/192.168.10.5/
I love networking
dns server 192.168.10.5
ntp server 192.168.10.5
AAA server 192.168.10.5
whocares server 192.168.10.5
```

Sed can use any regex, including brackets. In the following example [4–6] is used to only change the DNS, NTP, and AAA server address in somefile.txt.

```
bash-4.2$ cat somefile.txt | sed s/192.168.[4-6].5/192.168.10.5/
I love networking
dns server 192.168.10.5
ntp server 192.168.10.5
AAA server 192.168.10.5
whocares server 192.168.7.5
```

The previous example changes the network services address but also prints the first and last line. The following example uses a second | and grep to match lines with a "10" in them and further parse the output.

```
bash-4.2$ cat somefile.txt | sed s/192.168.[4-6].5/192.168.10.5/ | grep 10
dns server 192.168.10.5
ntp server 192.168.10.5
AAA server 192.168.10.5
```

A common use for sed is to remove markup tags from HTML or XML. The following example leverages sed to remove the XML tags from books.xml.

```
bash-4.2$ cat book.xml
<book id="1000">
      <author>Douglas, Adams</author>
      <title>Hitchhiker's Guide to the Galaxy</title>
      <price>24.95</price>
</book>

bash-4.2$ sed 's/<[^>]*>//g' book.xml

      Douglas, Adams
      Hitchhiker's Guide to the Galaxy
      24.95
```

The previous example replaces any tag with a blank space. The sed command "sed 's/<[^>]*>//g'" says match anything between XML tags.

The "g" command replaces all occurrences of the tag.

Let's say we just want the title. XML tagging is helpful to find the data we need. However, XML tagging is not very human readable. To get just the title, use a combination of commands:

```
bash-4.2$ grep -e "<author>" book.xml | sed 's/<[^>]*>//g'


      Douglas, Adams
```

The previous example uses **grep** to find lines with the word "**<author>**" and sends it to **sed** to remove the tags. Notice the output has a number of spaces before the text. Sed to the rescue!

The following example shows sed piped to sed to remove the blank spaces.

```
bash-4.2$ grep -e "<author>" book.xml | sed 's/<[^>]*>//g' | sed "s/ //g"
Douglas,Adams
```

The **sed** command **sed "s/ //g"** removes all the spaces. The following example uses **sed** with **regex** to remove spaces before the first word.

```
Bash-4.2$ grep -e "<author>" book.xml | sed 's/<[^>]*>//g' | sed -e 's/^[ \t]*//'
Douglas, Adams
```

The sed command "sed -e 's/^[\t]*//'" says match the beginning of the line (^) with a tab and zero or more characters.

Awk

Awk is a very powerful text processor that excels in parsing and displaying text. Awk is a language unto itself that supports variables, conditions, and loops. Awk is particularly useful when working with text that is preformatted in delimited data, for example, a table or JSON. The basic syntax of Awk matches a pattern and performs an action.

```
Pattern {action}
```

Given the file tab-delimited awkme.txt:

```
bash-3.2$ cat awkme.txt
Model           type      access      RU       type
9372tx     leaf      48       1       Cu
9372px     leaf      48       1       SFP
9396tx     leaf      48       2       Cu
9396px     leaf      48       2       SFP
```

```
93128          leaf     96     3     Cu
93120          leaf     96     2     Cu
9332          leaf     32     1     QSFP
```

Aawk, using the default delimiter of white space, can print the file, similar to the cat command as shown in the following example.

```
ash-3.2$ awk '{ print }' awkme.txt
Model          type     access     RU     type
9372tx     leaf     48     1     Cu
9372px     leaf     48     1     SFP
9396tx     leaf     48     2     Cu
9396px     leaf     48     2     SFP
93128          leaf     96     3     Cu
93120          leaf     96     2     Cu
9332          leaf     32     1     QSFP
```

The previous example matches the entire file and leverages the awk print action to print it. Notice the awk command is encased in ' '.

In most cases we ask awk to match a pattern and only print the match. The following instructs awk to match lines that contain px (case sensitive) and print:

```
bash-3.2$ awk '/px/ { print }' awkme.txt
9372px     leaf     48     1     SFP
9396px     leaf     48     2     SFP
```

The awk has a number of built in variables. Any columns in the file are referenced by $column_number.

The following awk match and print columns one, three, and five:

```
bash-3.2$ awk '/px/ { print $1,$3,$5}' awkme.txt
9372px 48 SFP
9396px 48 SFP
```

> **Note** Most Linux distributions include built-in documentation called **man**. Man, short for manual, provides detailed usage instructions. To use man, type man, followed by the command in question. For example, "man awk." Man pages can be long and uses the output modifier "less" to view page by page and "/" to search.

Bash on Nexus 9000

Nexus devices feature the **vsh** command to run NX-OS cli commands from the Bash shell. Configuration changes are only allowed through the **vsh** command. By default, Bash shell access is available to users in the net-admin or DevOps roles. Text-based output can be searched or manipulated with standard Linux tools. Vsh has no state, meaning commands are not persistent from one command to subsequent commands. The following output will fail:

```
vsh -c configure terminal
vsh -c interface e1/1
vsh -c ip address 1.1.1.1 255.255.255.0
```

The following output demonstrates the correct usage of the **vsh** command:

```
bash-4.2$ vsh -c "configure t ; interface ethernet1/1 ; no switchport ; ip address
1.1.1.1 255.255.255.0"
```

Vsh can be used for NX-OS show commands:

```
bash-4.2$ vsh -c "show ip interface brief"
IP Interface Status for VRF "default"(1)
Interface              IP Address       Interface Status
Lo0                    10.1.1.1         protocol-up/link-up/admin-up
Eth1/25                192.168.1.1      protocol-up/link-up/admin-up
Eth1/26                192.168.1.9      protocol-up/link-up/admin-up
```

The output of the **vsh** command can be parsed with standard linux tools, for example grep, sed, and awk:

```
vsh -c 'show interface'| grep "Ethernet1..* is up"
Ethernet1/1 is up
Ethernet1/26 is up
```

This example leverages grep and a regex of "Ethernet1..*. ..*" matches any character, followed by zero or more of any character. The following is the same, only using sed.

```
vsh -c 'show interface'| sed -n '/Ethernet1..* is up/p'
vsh -c 'show interface' | grep -n "input errors"
```

The following output shows interface parsed awk:

```
bash-4.2$ vsh -c 'sh interface brief' | awk '/up/ { print $1,$7 }'
mgmt0
Eth1/25 40G(D)
Eth1/26 40G(D)
Lo0
```

The output shows only up interfaces and their port speed.

Nexus 9000 supports common Linux network tools, for example ifconfig, Tcpdump, ethtool to manage and monitor the switch. Access to this and other tools allows administrators to manage the switch in a similar fashion to their Linux environment.

ifconfig

ifconfig is a common Linux tool to manage network interfaces. It is most often used to check interface status, take an interface up or down, or assign network addresses. NX-OS supports ifconfig to check and change interface status. NX-OS ifconfig is restricted from assigning an IP address or other changes that may conflict with the CLI. ifconfig requires root access, and this must be run in conjunction with the sudo command.

By default the ifconfig tool will display information about any up interface on the system, as shown in the following output. The "–a" option will display information about all interfaces and passing a specific interface will highlight a specific interface.

```
bash-4.2$ sudo ifconfig Eth1-26
Eth1-26   Link encap:Ethernet  HWaddr f8:c2:88:23:b0:c3
          inet addr:192.168.1.9  Bcast:192.168.1.11  Mask:255.255.255.252
          UP BROADCAST RUNNING MULTICAST  MTU:1500  Metric:1
          RX packets:176562 errors:0 dropped:137477 overruns:0 frame:0
          TX packets:73583 errors:0 dropped:0 overruns:0 carrier:0
          collisions:0 txqueuelen:100
          RX bytes:10120309 (9.6 MiB)  TX bytes:6644923 (6.3 MiB)
```

The output in the above example displays the IP information, the MAC address, and traffic statistics. Notice the output syntax of the interface, Eth1-26 is different than NX-OS's Eth1/26. To change the interface status, follow the command with up|down. This is will translate to shut or no shut in the CLI:

```
sudo ifconfig Eth1-26 down
interface Ethernet1/26
  ip address 192.168.1.9/30
  ip ospf network point-to-point
  ip router ospf 1 area 0.0.0.0
  ip pim sparse-mode
  shutdown
```

Tcpdump

Tcpdump is a popular Linux tool to capture and display IP packet headers. By default, Tcpdump will capture the first 96 bytes of a packet, however this is configurable. **Tcpdump** requires root access. The -i parameter captures traffic on a specific interface:

```
bash-4.2$ sudo Tcpdump -i Eth1-26
Tcpdump: verbose output suppressed, use -v or -vv for full protocol decode
listening on Eth1-26, link-type EN10MB (Ethernet), capture size 65535 bytes
18:16:22.904037 STP 802.1w, Rapid STP, Flags [Learn, Forward], bridge-id
8001.f8:c2:88:90:cf:17.8035, length 43
18:16:24.807971 IP 192.168.1.9 > 224.0.0.13: PIMv2, Hello, length 30
```

Control-C breaks Tcpdump and returns to a user prompt.

Tcpdump's console output is useful for quick troubleshooting; however, in most cases, we need to save the output for off-box analysis. **Tcpdump** output files are readable by Wireshark and other network analysis tools:

```
bash-4.2$ sudo Tcpdump -i Eth1-26 -w eth126.cap
```

Use control-C to break Tcpdump and return to the prompt. Unless changed, the file will be saved to the home directory of the user, in this case admin. Use SCP or SFTP to transfer the file.

Note To use an SCP or SFTP client, the SCP and SFTP servers must be enabled in NX-OS.

```
spine1(config)# feature scp-server
spine1(config)# feature sftp-server
```

Tcpdump support easy to use filters to limit the capture. Filters can be tied together for more specific data. Table 4-3 lists commonly used Tcpdump filters. Table 4-4 lists commonly used Tcpdump options.

Table 4-3 *Tcpdump Filters*

Filter	Usage
host	host 192.168.1.1
net	net 192.168.1.0/24
port	port 80
src	src 192.168.1.1
dst	dst 192.168.1.1
src dst	src or dst
tcp	tcp
udp	uUdp
icmp	icmp
src port	src port 80
dst port	dst port 80
and	tcp and src port 80
or	tcp or src port 80
not	tcp not src port 80

Table 4-4 *Common Tcpdump Options*

Option	Description
-D	List all available interfaces
-cX	Capture X packets
-e	Capture Ethernet headers
-q	Quiet the output
-vvv	Verbose output

ethtool

ethtool in NX-OS can be used to display statistics about the front panel Ethernet interfaces.

The following example captures statistics from interface Ethernet1-26 and uses grep to display counters with data (nonzero).

```
bash-4.2$ ethtool -S Eth1-26 | grep .*[^0]$
NIC statistics:
     admin_status: 1
     oper_status: 1
     reset_counter: 636
     rx_bit_rate1: 336
     tx_bit_rate1: 128
     rx_bit_rate2: 248
     tx_bit_rate2: 128
     rx_multicast_pkts: 186505
     rx_broadcast_pkts: 472
     rx_input_pkts: 186977
     rx_bytes_input_pkts: 14172461
     tx_multicast_pkts: 74928
     tx_broadcast_pkts: 1271
     tx_output_pkts: 76199
     tx_bytes_output_pkts: 7261951
```

Run a Bash Script at Startup

Linux boots at a specific run level, which in part defines what processes or applications that are started at boot. Run level 1 is single user (considered a safe mode), where only the bare minimum processes start. Run level 3, the default for Nexus devices, is a normal boot without a GUI. The init level is specified in the /etc/inittab file. Applications are launched from scripts located in the /etc/init.d directory, and the script must have execute permissions. Which applications are initiated in what run levels are controlled by the files in /etc/rc(run level).d directory, for example rc3.d. The rc directories should only be changed via the chkconfig utility.

```
bash-4.2$ cd /etc/init.d/
bash-4.2$ sudo touch hello_world.sh
bash-4.2$ sudo chmod +x hello_world.sh
bash-4.2$ sudo touch hello_world
bash-4.2$ sudo chmod +x hello_world
```

The previous output creates two files, hello_world.sh and hello_world. The application hello_world.sh writes "hello world" and the date to /tmp/hello_world. The chkconfig script hello_world works with the hello_world.sh application. The following examples detail the hello_world.sh and hello_world files.

```
bash-4.2$ cat hello_world.sh
PIDFILE=/tmp/hello_world.pid
#PIDFILE holds the process id and is used to stop and check status

OUTPUTFILE=/tmp/hello_world


echo $$ > $PIDFILE
rm -f $OUTPUTFILE
#endless loop to write date and hello world to a file
while true
do
    echo $(date) >> $OUTPUTFILE
    echo 'Hello World' >> $OUTPUTFILE
    sleep 10
done
```

The following example shows the hello_world file.

```
bash-4.2$ cat hello_world
#!/bin/bash
#
# hello Trivial "hello world" example Third Party App
#
# chkconfig: 2345 15 85
# description: Trivial example Third Party App
#
### BEGIN INIT INFO
# Provides: hello_world
# Required-Start: $local_fs $remote_fs $network $named
# Required-Stop: $local_fs $remote_fs $network
# Description: Trivial example Third Party App
### END INIT INFO
```

```
PIDFILE=/tmp/hello_world.pid

# See how we were called.
case "$1" in
start)
    /etc/init.d/hello_world.sh &
    RETVAL=$?
;;
stop)
    kill -9 'cat $PIDFILE'
    RETVAL=$?
;;
status)
    ps -p 'cat $PIDFILE'
    RETVAL=$?
;;
restart|force-reload|reload)
    kill -9 'cat $PIDFILE'
    /etc/init.d/hello_world.sh &
    RETVAL=$?
;;
*)
echo $"Usage: $prog {start|stop|status|restart|force-reload}"
RETVAL=2
esac

exit $RETVAL
```

Note Detailed syntax of the chkconfig file is outside of the scope of this book.

Once the files are installed on the system, chkconfig is used to control the application.

Add the script:

```
bash-4.2$ sudo chkconfig --add hello_world
```

Configure script to start at run level 3:

```
bash-4.2$ sudo chkconfig --level 3 hello_world
```

Using **chkconfig** for verification:

```
bash-4.2$ sudo chkconfig --list hello_world
hello_world     0:off   1:off   2:on    3:on    4:on    5:on    6:off
```

The following example lists that hello_world starts on levels 2–5.

The chkconfig script can be used to manually manipulate the service:

```
bash-4.2$ sudo /etc/init.d/hello_world stop
bash-4.2$ sudo /etc/init.d/hello_world start
bash-4.2$ sudo /etc/init.d/hello_world status
  PID TTY          TIME CMD
10740 pts/2    00:00:00 hello_world
bash-4.2$
```

Bash Example—Configure NTP Servers at boot

This example bash script runs at boot and reconfigures the NX-OS NTP server configuration on boot. This example configures NTP, based on static data but could be easily modified to update any configuration with dynamic data from an IP connected source.

The following example shows the **boot_config.sh** command:

```
bash-4.2$ cat /etc/init.d/boot_config.sh
update_ntp()
{
        sleep 3
        NTP=$(vsh -c "show ntp peers" | awk 'NR>3 { print $1 }') #AWK decode in
the following note

        vsh -c " config t ; no ntp server $NTP"
        vsh -c " config t ; ntp server 192.168.1.1 "
}

update_ntp &
```

Note (The AWK syntax **awk 'NR>3 { print $1 }'**) says match the rows greater than 3 and print column 1.

The previous example leverages vsh to discover the current NTP server and replace it with a static address, and demonstrates a BASH function.

Linux Containers (LXC)

Nexus NX-OS supports Linux containers (LXC) to provide a decoupled and protected space to execute commands, customize the Linux environment, and install third-party applications. Containers virtualize a Linux application environment and thus protect resources from third-party processes. Container virtualization is more efficient than standard hypervisors (ESXi, HyperV, KVM) because the host and guest share the kernel and do not duplicate shared functions. Linux namespaces (IPC, UTS, mount, PID, network, and user) uniquely identify and isolate containers from each other and the host. A list of Linux namespaces and their descriptions are shown in Table 4-5.

Table 4-5 *Linux LCX Namespace*

Namespace	Description
User	User IDs
PID	Process ID
Network	Network ID (address)
UTS	Hostname ID
Mount	File system ID
IPC	Interprocess communication ID

Containers in NX-OS are considered a virtual service. The **virtual-service** commands are used to install, upgrade, and destroy containers:

```
switch# virtual-service ?
  connect     Request a virtual service shell
  install     Add a virtual service to install database
  move        Move a virtual service log or core files
  reset       Virtualization reset commands
  uninstall   Remove a virtual service from the install database
  upgrade     Upgrade a virtual service package to a different version
```

The **list** command displays all virtual services running on the switch:

```
switch# show virtual-service list

Virtual Service List:

Name                    Status             Package Name
-----------------------------------------------------------------------
guestshell+             Activated          guestshell.ova
```

The **virtual-service** command is used to connect to the console of the container:

```
switch# virtual-service connect name guestshell+ console
```

To exit the login shell, enter Ctrl-C three times.

NX-OS ships with a Linux container called the guest shell. Guestshells are recommended when using third-party agents, for example, Puppet and Nexus Data Broker. NX-OS guestshells are a CentOS 7 Linux image preloaded with popular tools including:

- yum, pip
- net-tools
- Tcpdump
- ifconfig
- ethtool
- Python

By default, an LXC container is limited to 1% of CPU, 200mb of memory and 200mb of storage but can be increased to use up to 3.8 GB of RAM and 2 GB of storage. CPU is limited to 1% only during times of contention; if the CPU is not taxed, the container CPU usage is not limited.

The Nexus 3000 and 9300 have Intel i3 dual-core 2.5-GHz, CPU, 16GB of RAM and 64GB SSD drives. The Nexus 9500 has two supervisor options creativity named Supervisor A and Supervisor B.

- Supervisor A has Intel E5-2403 (4-core, 1.8-GHz) CPU, with 16 GB of RAM and 64-GB SSD drive, and Supervisor B features 6-core, 2.2-GHz x86 CPU, with 24 GB of RAM and 256-GB SSD drive.

From within the Guest Shell, the network admin has the following capabilities:

- Access to the network over Linux network interfaces.
- Access to Cisco Nexus 9000 bootflash.
- Access to Cisco Nexus 9000 volatile tmpfs.
- Access to Cisco Nexus 9000 CLI.
- Access to Cisco NX-API REST.
- The ability to install and run python scripts.
- The ability to install and run 32-bit and 64-bit Linux applications.

A Guestshell has access to all network interfaces, access to bootflash and volatile storage, and access to CLI. NX-OS Guestshells can run prepackaged OVAs for example Nexus Data Broker or Puppet agent, Python interpreters or blank Linux environments. NX-OS Guestshell supports 32- and 64-bit applications.

NX-OS automatically creates guest shells with the command **run guestshell**:

```
leaf1# run guestshell
[guestshell@guestshell ~]$
```

Optionally an application can be launched as a CLI parameter with "run Guestshell":

```
leaf1# run guestshell python /bootflash/helloWorld.py
```

Guestshell supports running NX-OS commands with the **dohost** command. The CLI syntax must be contained in double quotes:

```
[guestshell@guestshell ~]$ dohost "show run"
```

Guestshell commands can be piped to Linux tools like grep to narrow down the results.

```
[guestshell@guestshell ~]$ dohost "show run" | grep interface
```

Network Access in Guestshell

Guestshell has access to all front panel ports and all VRFs in NX-OS; however network settings may not be modified:

```
[guestshell@guestshell ~]$ ifconfig | grep -A 7 Vlan100
Vlan100: flags=4163<UP,BROADCAST,RUNNING,MULTICAST>  mtu 1500
        inet 192.168.100.5  netmask 255.255.255.0  broadcast 192.168.100.255
        ether f8:c2:88:90:b6:4f  txqueuelen 100  (Ethernet)
        RX packets 0  bytes 0 (0.0 B)
        RX errors 0  dropped 0  overruns 0  frame 0
        TX packets 2  bytes 84 (84.0 B)
        TX errors 0  dropped 0 overruns 0  carrier 0  collisions 0
```

By default, a guestshell is in the default VRF but can be changed. The command **chvrf** is used to change the VRF in the guestshell:

```
[guestshell@guestshell ~]$ chvrf management
[guestshell@guestshell ~]$ ifconfig
eth1: flags=4163<UP,BROADCAST,RUNNING,MULTICAST>  mtu 1500
        inet 10.1.1.183  netmask 255.255.255.128  broadcast 10.1.1.255
        ether f8:c2:88:90:b6:48  txqueuelen 1000  (Ethernet)
        RX packets 14043817  bytes 2458426247 (2.2 GiB)
        RX errors 0  dropped 0  overruns 0  frame 0
        TX packets 499018  bytes 64185936 (61.2 MiB)
        TX errors 0  dropped 0 overruns 0  carrier 0  collisions 0
```

'chvrf' can be used with a single command, similar to NX-OS:

```
[guestshell@guestshell ~]$ chvrf default ping 192.168.100.5
PING 192.168.100.5 (192.168.100.5) 56(84) bytes of data.
64 bytes from 192.168.100.5: icmp_seq=1 ttl=59 time=0.031 ms
```

DNS settings are not utilized from NX-OS and must be manually configured in Guestshell. Similar to Linux systems, Guestshell DNS is configured in /etc/resolv.conf:

```
 [guestshell@guestshell ~]$ cat /etc/resolv.conf
nameserver 192.168.0.50
domain cisco.com
```

Installing Applications in Guestshell

NX-OS Guestshell supports running third-party applications. Application can be installed manually or using Yum (preferred). The default repository is the CentOS-base configured in /etc/yum.repos.d/CentOS-Base.repo.

By default, Linux containers in NX-OS are limited to running Cisco digital signed packages, however this policy can be modified to run unsigned OVA packages.

Change Package signing security by using:

```
leaf1(config-virt-serv-global)# signing level ?
  cisco     Allow only Cisco signed packages
  none      Most restrictive, don't allow package installation
  unsigned  Least restrictive, allow unsigned and all signing methods

leaf1(config-virt-serv-global)# signing level unsigned
```

By default the main partition in the Guestshell are very small and will most likely need to be resized.

To increase disk space on the Guestshell to 2GB, use:

```
switch# guestshell resize rootfs 2000
```

Guestshells support 32- or 64-bit applications; however, by default, 32-bit support is not enabled. To support 32-bit applications, glibc.i686 must be installed via yum:

```
sudo chvrf management yum -y install glibc.i686


output suppressed…


Installed:
  glibc.i686 0:2.17-106.el7_2.1


Dependency Installed:
  nss-softokn-freebl.i686 0:3.16.2.3-13.el7_1


Dependency Updated:
  glibc.x86_64 0:2.17-106.el7_2.1
glibc-common.x86_64 0:2.17-106.el7_2.1
```

To install glibc.i686, Yum found and resolved the dependent applications.

Puppet Agent Installation in Guestshell

Puppet is a popular automation engine used by many organizations. Puppet automates deployment to common configuration across any number of devices. A Puppet system requires a Puppet master server and puppet agents installed on the local servers. NX-OS supports installing a Puppet agent in a Guestshell.

To Install Puppet agent in a Guestshell:

```
[Optionally change the vrf]
 sudo chvrf management
Enable the Puppet repository
sudo yum install http://yum.puppetlabs.com/puppetlabs-release-pc1-cisco-wrlinux-5.
noarch.rpm
Install Puppet agent
sudo yum install puppet-agent
Check puppet agent status
sudo systemctl status puppet
```

NMap Installation in Guestshell

Nmap is a popular network mapping and security tool. It is very useful for testing firewalls, network services, and mapping a network. Nmap can be installed and utilized within a Guestshell.

To Install NMAP in a Guestshell:

```
sudo chvrf management
sudo yum install nmap
nmap -p 22 10.1.1.195
Nmap output
Starting Nmap 6.40 ( http://nmap.org ) at 2016-01-05 19:53 UTC
Host is up (0.000034s latency).
PORT   STATE  SERVICE
22/tcp closed ssh

Nmap done: 1 IP address (1 host up) scanned in 0.07 seconds
```

Embedded Nexus Data Broker

The Nexus Data Broker management software can optionally run in a NX-OS container.

To Install NDB to 9300:

1. Download Nexus Data Broker software from Cisco.com
2. Unzip the file
3. Upload the OVA to the switch:

```
ndb1000-sw-app-emb-k9-2.2.0.ova
```

4. Install the OVA to the switch:

```
switch# configure terminal
switch(config)# virtual-service data_broker
```

5. Activate the image:

```
switch(config-virt-serv)# activate
```

6. Connect to NDB:

```
https://<ip address>/8443:monitor
Default username and password - admin/admin
```

Nexus Embedded Event Manager

Embedded event manager (EEM) monitors a network device for predefined system events, for example, syslog messages, hardware issues, or CLI input, and can tie the event to a user-defined action. EEM is a system automation tool that has been embedded in Cisco devices for some time; however, Nexus adds the capability to define a Python script as an action. EEM and on-box Python scripting offer powerful and easy-to-use tools for advanced network automation. Tables 4-6 and 4-7 list the available EEM events and actions.

Table 4-6 *NX-OS System Events*

cli	gold	Online-Insertion-Removal
counter	memory	policy-default
fanabsent	module	Power over budget
fanbad	module-failure	snmp.
fib	neighbor-discovery	storm-control
syslog	sysmgr	Tag
temperature	test	Track

Note Not all events are supported on every platform.

EEM supports the actions in action statements shown in Table 4-7:

Table 4-7 *Actions in Action Statements Supported by EEM*

Execute a Python Script	Execute any CLI	Update a Counter
Log an exception	Force shutdown of a module	Reload the device.
Generate syslog message	Generate Call Home event	Generate SNMP notification
Shut down specified modules because the power is over budget		

EEM Policy, the combination of an event and action, are configured from the CLI.

The following example shows simple EEM.

```
event manager applet test1
  event cli match "copy running-config startup-config"
  action 1 cli copy running-config bootflash:/current_config.txt
  action 2 syslog msg Configuration saved and copied to bootflash
  action 3 event-default
```

This example leverages EEM, saves a copy of the running config on bootflash, and writes a message to syslog.

> **Note** Use the following to tie a Python script to EEM.
>
> ```
> action 1 cli python bootflash:somepython.py
> ```

> **Note** "Event-default" is required as the last action because we want to allow the CLI command. Without "event-default," the CLI command will be blocked.

EEM Variables

EEM supports creating and using environment variables. Variables are convenient when working with dynamic data and can be set, using Python or BASH vsh scripts.

EEM variable are set though the NX-OS command line:

```
event manager environment some_server "192.168.1.1"
```

EEM variable set via vsh in a BASH script:

```
run bash eem_date=$(date) ; vsh -c "configure t ; event manager environment
todays_date '$eem_date' "
```

To verify and EEM policy, use the command:

```
show event manager events action-log
```

EEM and Python integration will be demonstrated in the next section.

On-box Python Scripting

Cisco Nexus 9000 offers a built in Python interpreter to execute both interactive and non-interactive scripts. On-Box Python is a powerful network automation tool to automate configurations, EEM actions, or other functions. The following output demonstrates accessing the Nexus interactive interpreter.

```
switch# python
Python 2.7.5 (default, Oct  8 2013, 23:59:43)
```

```
[GCC 4.6.3] on linux2
Type "help", "copyright", "credits" or "license" for more information.
>>>
```

Note By default, at the time of this writing, 9k NX-OS ships with Python 2.7.5.

NX-OS ships with the standard Python and Cisco specific libraries. Cisco libraries enable interaction with NX-OS and include "cli" for cli-like interaction and "cisco" for direct object interaction. The following example demonstrates importing the cli library.

```
>>> from cli import *
>>> dir (cli)
['__builtins__', '__doc__', '__file__', '__name__', '__package__', 'cli',
'cli_syntax_error', 'clid', 'clip', 'cmd_exec_error', 'data_type_error', 'json',
'shlex', 'structured_output_not_supported_error', 'subprocess', 'unexpected_
error', 'xmltodict']
>>>

Cisco Library import

>>> import cisco
>>> help(cisco)
NAME
    cisco

FILE
    /isan/python/scripts/cisco/__init__.py

PACKAGE CONTENTS
    acl
    bgp
    buffer_depth_monitor
    check_port_discards
    cisco_secret
    feature
    history
    interface
    ipaddress
    key
    line_parser
    mac_address_table
    nxcli
    ospf
    routemap
    routes
```

```
section_parser
ssh
system
tacacs
transfer
vlan
vrf
```

Using the NX-OS Python CLI Library

The Python programming language uses three APIs that can execute CLI commands. The APIs are available from the Python CLI module.

These APIs are listed in the following table. You need to enable the APIs with the **from cli import** * command. The arguments for these APIs are strings of CLI commands. To execute a CLI command through the Python interpreter, you enter the CLI command as an argument string of one of the APIs listed in Table 4-8.

Table 4-8 *NS-OS CLI API*

CLI Command APIs

API	Description
cli() Example: string = cli ("cli-command")	Returns the raw output of CLI commands, including control/ special characters.
	Note The interactive Python interpreter prints control/special characters 'escaped'. A carriage return is printed as '\n' and gives results that might be difficult to read. The clip() API gives results that are more readable.
clid() Example: json_string = clid ("cli-command")	For CLI commands that support XML, this API returns JSON output. This API can be useful when searching the output of show commands.
	Note An exception is thrown when XML is not used.
clip() Example: clip ("cli-command")	Prints the output of the CLI command directly to stdout and returns nothing to Python.
	Note clip ("cli-command") is equivalent to r = cli("cli-command") print r

When two or more commands are run individually, the state is not persistent from one command to subsequent commands.

In the following example, the second command fails because the state from the first command does not persist for the second command:

```
>>> cli("conf t") >>> cli("interface eth4/1")
```

When two or more commands are run together, the state is persistent from one command to subsequent commands.

In the following example, the second command is successful because the state persists for the second and third commands:

```
>>> cli("conf t ; interface eth4/1 ; shut")
```

Using NX-OS Cisco Python Library

Nexus 9000 NX-OS 7.0 and higher provides a Cisco Python package that enables access to many core network device modules, such as interfaces, VLANs, VRFs, ACLs, and routes. You can display the details of the Cisco Python package by entering the **help()** command. To obtain additional information about the classes and methods in a module, you can run the help command for a specific module. For example, **help(*cisco.vrf*)**displays the properties of the cisco.vrf module, as shown in the following example:

```
>>> help(cisco.vrf)


    class VRF(__builtin__.object)
     |  Use this object to create/delete a VRF on the switch, add/remove
interfaces
     |  to a VRF or simply just to check if a VRF exists.
     |
     |  Methods defined here:
     |
     |  __init__(self, vrf)
     |      Initializes a VRF object with the specified VRF name or ID and returns
     |      the new object.
     |
     |      Arguments:
     |          vrf: VRF name (string) or the VRF ID (int). If the VRF is
specified
     |              as an integer only VRF values corresponding to an existing VRF
     |              will be accepted because it is not possible to create a VRF
     |              using an ID.
     |
     |      Example:
     |          a. v = VRF('management')
     |          b. v = VRF(2)
     |
```

```
 |      Returns: VRF object on success
 |
 |  add_interface(self, if_name, **args)
 |      Sets the specified interface's VRF membership to this VRF.
 |
 |      Arguments:
 |          if_name: A string specifying the interface name
 |
 |      Optional Arguments:

 |              interface's VRF membership.
 |
 |      Returns: True on success
 |
 |      Example:
 |          v = VRF('floor1')
 |          v.create()
 |          v.add_interface('Ethernet 1/1')
 |
 |  create(self, **args)
 |      Creates the VRF
 |
 |      Arguments: None
 |
 |      Optional Arguments:
 |          no: A boolean, set to true to delete the VRF
 |
 |      Example:
 |          v = VRF('floor1')
 |          v.create()
 |
 |      Returns: True on success
:
```

```
Example - Using the Cisco API to set interface IP address

>>> x = cisco.Interface("Ethernet1/2")
>>> x.set_description("hello")
True
>>> x.set_ipaddress("2.1.1.1 255.255.255.0")
True
>>>
```

Non-Interactive Python

Python scripts can be saved and executed in NX-OS. Scripts must be saved in the /bootflash directory. The following output creates some simple Python and demonstrates running a Python script in NX-OS.

```
run bash
cd /bootflash
touch some_python.py          #create a file
echo 'print "Hello World" > some_python.py'   #Python code to print hello world
exit          #exit bash
switch# python some_python.py
Hello World
switch#
```

Saved Python scripts can be tied to EEM or NX-OS scheduler. NX-OS scheduler schedules a Python script to run at a certain time or be repeated. NX-OS scheduler is a feature and must be enabled.

Enable Feature:

```
switch#(config) feature schedule
```

Schedule configuration:

```
scheduler job name schedule_some_python
python bootflash:/some_python.py
end-job

scheduler schedule name schedule_some_python


scheduler schedule name my_schedule
  job name schedule_some_python
  time start 2015:11:27:19:09 repeat 0:0:10
```

Cisco or CLI Package?

The CLI and Cisco modules are equivalent in driving configuration to NX-OS; however, in most cases, the Cisco module will be easier to use. The CLI module is very useful when the Cisco module does not cover a configuration object or the configuration already exists.

On-Box Python—Use Cases and Examples

The Cisco command "reload in" is a popular failsafe when working with configuration. Reload in will automatically reload a Cisco device after a configurable amount of time. It is very useful when working with remote boxes because if a configuration change is made that disables access to the device, the device will reload to startup configuration and restore access. By default, NX-OS on the 9k does not have a reload in command, however a simple python script can replicate its functionality.

Reload_in Pseudocode

Step 1. Input number of minutes, or optionally if the configuration should be saved or canceled from user.

Step 2. Cancel script if input is not correct

Step 3. Determine current time

Step 4. Add users input in minutes to current time

Step 5. Enable scheduler feature

Step 6. Option—Save Configuration

Step 7. Use CLI to schedule reload

Step 8. Option—Cancel reload

```
### Start with documentation!


# Written by Ryan Tischer @ Cisco -  @ryantischer
# Designed to run on Nexus 9000 swtich
# script replicates IOS "reload in" command to schedule reloads
# leverages scheduler feature in NXOS

#Usage Documentation -

#copy/save script in bootflash/scripts folder on swtich
#from NXOS CLI type "source reloadin.py [options]
#options...
#       - number of minutes until reload
#       - "save" to save configuration before reload.  Must be used as second
option behine minutes
#       - "cancel" cancel reload

Usages Examples

#Examples
# source reloadin.py 20 - schedules a reload in 20 minutes
# source reloadin.py 20 save - schedules a reload in 20 minutes and saves the
config
# source reloadin.py cancel - cancels current reloadin command.
```

```
#imports - datatime for current time, cli for access to the cli and sys for
input
# variables


import datetime
from cli import cli
import sys
#get the number of inputed arguments

numArg = len(sys.argv)

#check input for cancelation

if sys.argv[1] == "cancel":

        schedCLIjob = 'conf t ; no scheduler job name reloadinCommand5657373'
        schedCLItime = 'conf t ; no scheduler schedule name
        reloadinCommand5657373'
        print "Canceling reload"

#check number of args and if first one is a int
elif numArg <= 3:
        try:    #python error handling

                requestTime = int(sys.argv[1])
        except:
                print "Enter a integer for time"
                sys.exit() #bail out if input is wrong  #exit if input is
                incorrect

        now = datetime.datetime.now()  #get the current time
        actionTime = now + datetime.timedelta(minutes = requestTime)  #set
        the reload time
        reloadTime = str(actionTime) # reload time in a string
        reloadTime=reloadTime[11:-10]

#Build CLI command with unique schedule name
        schedCLIjob = 'conf t ; scheduler job name reloadinCommand5657373 ;
        reload ; exit'
        schedCLItime = 'conf t ; scheduler schedule name
        reloadinCommand5657373 ; time start ' + reloadTime + ' repeat 48:00 ;
        end '

#save configuration
        if numArg == 3 and sys.argv[2] == "save".lower():
                cli('copy running-config startup-config')
                print "Saving config before reload"
```

```
#print script output
        print "current time on the switch is " + str(now)
        print "reload scheduled at " + reloadTime

#run the CLI
cli('conf t ; feature scheduler')




#schedule the job
try:
        cli(schedCLIjob)
except:
        print "operation failed..did you cancel a job that was not there?"
        sys.exit()


cli(schedCLItime)
print "Operation success"
```

EEM Neighbor Discovery

This example leverages a python script from the EEM syslog event.

The EEM configuration is straightforward:

```
event manager applet CDP_Helper
  event syslog pattern "IF_UP"
  action 1 cli source cdp_neighbor.py
```

The EEM syslog event will wait for a syslog message with the pattern IF_UP and when observed, runs the python script cdp_neighbor.py.

The cdp_neighbor.py python script leverages cli and clid to get cdp data from the switch and use it as an interface description.

```
#import libraries
from cli import *
import json

#get cdp data as json
cdp_data = clid('show cdp neigh')

#format the json
cdp_data_json=json.loads(cdp_data)
```

```
#The cdp output was nice enough to give how many neighbors are connected
num_neighbors=cdp_data_json["neigh_count"]
#num neighbors is used for the loop, however we need to account for 0
num_neighbors = int(num_neighbors)-1

counter=0 #init a counter variable

#compare counter to num neighbors
while counter < num_neighbors:

   #d[number] gets relevant data from cdp_data_json
   d1=cdp_data_json["TABLE_cdp_neighbor_brief_info"]["ROW_cdp_neighbor_brief_
   info"][counter]["platform_id"]
   d2=cdp_data_json["TABLE_cdp_neighbor_brief_info"]["ROW_cdp_neighbor_brief_
   info"][counter]["device_id"]
   d3=cdp_data_json["TABLE_cdp_neighbor_brief_info"]["ROW_cdp_neighbor_brief_
   info"][counter]["intf_id"]

#create the NX-OS cli command
cliCommand = "conf t ;  interface " + d3 + " ; description Connected device is a "
+ d1 + " named " + d2

#run the cli command
            cli(cliCommand )

     #add to the counter
            counter = counter + 1
```

The following shows the **cdp_neighbor.py** output:

```
interface Ethernet1/2
  description Connected device is a cisco WS-C2960S-48TS-L named oob_Switch
```

The following shows the raw data from json.dumps:

```
print (json.dumps(cdp_data_json, indent=4))
{
    "neigh_count": "3",
    "TABLE_cdp_neighbor_brief_info": {
        "ROW_cdp_neighbor_brief_info": [
            {
                "platform_id": "cisco WS-C2960S-48TS-L",
                "intf_id": "mgmt0",
                "capability": [
                    "switch",
                    "IGMP_cnd_filtering"
                ],
```

```
                    "ttl": "166",
                    "ifindex": "83886080",
                    "port_id": "GigabitEthernet1/0/27",
                    "device_id": "Switch"
                },
                {
                    "platform_id": "N9K-C9504",
                    "intf_id": "Ethernet1/49",
                    "capability": [
                        "router",
                        "switch",
                        "Supports-STP-Dispute"
                    ],
                    "ttl": "158",
                    "ifindex": "436232192",
                    "port_id": "Ethernet1/1",
                    "device_id": "Spine2(FOX1830GW5Y)"
                },
                {
                    "platform_id": "N9K-C9332PQ",
                    "intf_id": "Ethernet1/53",
                    "capability": [
                        "router",
                        "switch",
                        "Supports-STP-Dispute"
                    ],
                    "ttl": "158",
                    "ifindex": "436234240",
                    "port_id": "Ethernet1/26",
                    "device_id": "spine1(SAL18391KGF)"
                }
            ]
        }
    }
```


Note For more examples, check out Cisco's Data Center page on Github.com located at https://github.com/datacenter

Summary

Modern data center networks, powered by NX-OS, enable agile and consistent network deployment and operations. Modern consumers have demanding performance and reliability application expectations that traditional network management tools do not meet. Using industry standard tools, NX-OS open interfaces transform the network from simple transport to a dynamic and critical infrastructure component to ensure positive application experiences. NX-OS automated provisioning enables network administrators to quickly deploy data center networks and reduce time to value. On-box Python or Bash scripting enables the network to react to network or outside events to maximize a user's application experience. The next chapter focuses off-box programmability with NX-API and infrastructure automation tools.

Chapter 5

Off-Box Programmability and Automation with Cisco Nexus NX-OS

Off-box programmability and automation are tools that run outside of the network equipment. Off-box programmability allows the network to be managed holistically or as part of an automation or orchestration solution. Off-box programmability provides a pathway for the network to be leveraged in Cloud operational models.

Off-box Cisco Nexus solutions include an API, named NX-API, that provides full configuration and monitoring of the switch. Additionally, NX-OS supports next-generation automation tools, including Puppet, Chef, and Ansible. NX-API serves as the interface that enables Nexus solutions to participate in continuous integration/continuous delivery software development methodologies, include DevOps.

Nexus NX-API

NX-API is a RESTful API that provides full access to the switch over HTTP/HTTPS. NX-API is supported on all 9k/3k platforms, with limited support on legacy Nexus. It supports either a CLI method, in which CLI commands are passed over the API, or an object model in which objects, for example border gateway protocol configuration is directly managed. Any configurations, including **show** commands, are supported in CLI-based NX-API; however, only specific objects are supported.

NX-API Transport

NX-API uses HTTP/HTTPS as its transport. Commands or queries are encoded into the HTTP/HTTPS body. The NX-API backend uses the Nginx HTTP server. The Nginx process, and all of its child processes, are under Linux cgroup protection, where the CPU and memory usage is capped. If the Nginx memory usage exceeds the cgroup limitations, the Nginx process is restarted and restored.

NX-API Message Format

NX-API offer a choice of data formatting, including XML, JSON, and JSON Remote Procedure Call (RPC). In general, JSON-RPC will be easier to use because it calls a procedure, called a method, on the switch and supports passing parameters for the procedure directly in the payload. The following table illustrates how JSON and JSON-RPC send a **show interface brief** to NX-OS. As described, JSON-RPC calls the **cli** method with a parameter for the command, while the JSON formatted message must specify all details about the command and output.

JSON	JSON-RPC
{	{
"version": "1.0",	"jsonrpc": "2.0",
"type": "cli_show",	"method": "cli",
"chunk": "0",	"params": {
"sid": "1",	"cmd": "show interface brief",
"input": "show interface brief",	"version": 1
"output_format": "json"	},
}	

NX-API Security

NX-API supports HTTPS. All communication to the device is encrypted when you use HTTPS. NX-API is integrated into the authentication system on the device. Users must have appropriate accounts to access the device through NX-API. NX-API uses HTTP basic authentication. All requests must contain the username and password in the HTTP header.

NX-API provides a session-based cookie, **nxapi_auth**, when users first successfully authenticate. With the session cookie, the username and password are included in all subsequent NX-API requests that are sent to the device. The username and password are used with the session cookie to bypass performing the full authentication process again. If the session cookie is not included with subsequent requests, another session cookie is required and is provided by the authentication process. Avoiding unnecessary use of the authentication process helps to reduce the workload on the device.

A **nxapi_auth** cookie expires in 600 seconds (10 minutes). This value is fixed and cannot be adjusted.

NX-API is disabled by default and must be enabled in the CLI. NX-OS is enabled with an NX-OS **feature** command:

```
(config)# feature nxapi
```

NX-API Sandbox

NX-API includes a sandbox to build and test NX-API calls. The sandbox is a web front end that is accessed from a switch's base URL (Figure 5-1).

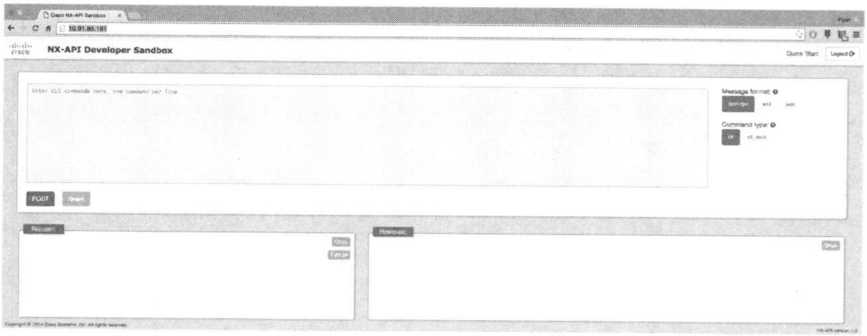

Figure 5-1 *NX-API Sandbox*

The NX-API sandbox accepts any NX-OS command (as shown in the top box of Figure 5-2) and converts it to formatted data to send to the switch. The formatting is specified as JSON-RPC, JSON, or XML. The POST button will send formatted data to the switch and return the formatted results.

Figure 5-2 *Show Interface in NX-API Sandbox*

The NX-API sandbox is very useful for understanding the exact data formatting used for both sending data to and receiving it from NX-API. The NX-API sandbox also includes a feature that automatically transforms the CLI input into a simple Python program. Use the (Python) button to convert the CLI command to Python. The following example demonstrates NX-API–generated Python code for the command **show interface ethernet1/1.**

```
import requests
import json

"""
Modify these please
"""
url='http://YOURIP/ins'
switchuser='USERID'
switchpassword='PASSWORD'

myheaders={'content-type':'application/json-rpc'}
payload=[
  {
    "jsonrpc": "2.0",
    "method": "cli",
    "params": {
      "cmd": "show interface ethernet1/1",
      "version": 1
    },
    "id": 1
  }
]
response=requests.post(url,data=json.dumps(payload),headers=myheaders,auth=
(switchuser,switchpassword)).json()
```

Note The NX-API sandbox leverages the Python requests library to send the CLI command to the switch.

To use the generated Python code, fill in the variables **url**, **switchuser**, and **switchpassword**, and run the program. The variables are strings that will require single or double quotes. In this case, the program ends with a **print** command to dump sorted and indented output to terminal. The following example demonstrates the completed variables, the final **print** command, and the output.

Note In Python single and double quotes are interchangeable; however consistency is required in the same expression.

```
url='http://192.168.1.1/ins'
switchuser='admin'
switchpassword='Cisco13579!'


print json.dumps(response, indent=4, sort_keys=True)

Truncated output of show_eth.py
{
    "id": 1,
    "jsonrpc": "2.0",
    "result": {
        "body": {
            "TABLE_interface": {
                "ROW_interface": {
                    "admin_state": "down",
                    "eth_autoneg": "on",
                    "eth_bw": 40000000,
                    "eth_clear_counters": "never",
                    "eth_coll": "0",
        "eth_hw_desc": "10000/40000 Ethernet",
        "interface": "Ethernet1/1",
                    "medium": "broadcast",
                    "share_state": "Dedicated",
                    "state": "down",
                    "state_rsn_desc": "XCVR not inserted"
                }
            }
        }
    }
}
```

Using NX-API in Python

NX-API can be leveraged from any language or interface, including Python, Ruby, Perl, or Postman. For reasons stated in Chapter 2, "Foundational Skills," Python is the preferred language to use with NX-API. Since NX-API is a RESTful service, the Python requests library is leveraged for communication. NX-API does not require any Cisco-specific Python libraries or SDKs.

NX-API supports sending either CLI or an object data model. In CLI mode NX-API expects formatted data (JSON-RPC preferred) with a **cmd** option. The **cmd** dictionary value holds the command to run. The following text demonstrates a CLI method to configure an IP address on an interface.

```
{
    "jsonrpc": "2.0",
    "method": "cli",
    "params": {
      "cmd": "ip address 2.2.2.2 255.255.255.0",
      "version": 1
      },
```

NX-API expects CLI commands in context, which is to say that any configuration changes will require configuration mode. The message in the following example will fail unless the **conf t** and **interface e1/1** commands are sent first. The following Python program demonstrates the CLI method for configuring an IP address on the device ethernet1/1.

Configuring an IP Address with Python and NX-API

The following example leverages NX-API to configure the IP address on ethernet1/1.

```
#import requests and json libraries
import requests
import json

"""
#Python variables with authentication data, http headers, and the payload.
"""
url='http://192.168.1.1/ins'
switchuser='admin'
switchpassword='Cisco'
myheaders={'content-type':'application/json-rpc'}

#the payload variable holds the commands to run against the switch.

payload=[
  {
    "jsonrpc": "2.0",
    "method": "cli",
    "params": {
      "cmd": "config t",
      "version": 1
    },
    "id": 1
  },
  {
    "jsonrpc": "2.0",
    "method": "cli",
    "params": {
```

```
            "cmd": "interface ethernet1/1",
            "version": 1
          },
          "id": 2
        },
        {
          "jsonrpc": "2.0",
          "method": "cli",
          "params": {
            "cmd": "ip address 2.2.2.2 255.255.255.0",
            "version": 1
          },
          "id": 3
        }
      ]

#Where the magic happens
  response = requests.post(url,data=json.dumps(payload), headers=myheaders,auth=
  (switchuser,switchpassword)).json()
```

As seen in the previous example, when the CLI method is used, the configuration data is stored in the variable **payload**, and runs a "**config t**" followed by the the CLI command to enter the interface and configure the IP address. The response variable leverages requests and HTTP POST to authenticate and push the configuration to the switch. Before the data is sent, **json.dumps** encodes the data.

Building applications with the NX-API CLI method involves sending and receiving data via the CLI method and using Python to parse and manipulate the text. Common string formatting commands or regular expressions can be used to efficiently send formatted text to the device. When JSON-RPC or JSON is used, any data sent to NX-API should be encoded with **json.dumps**.

NX-API REST: An Object-Oriented Data Model

In addition to CLI commands, NX-API supports an object-oriented data model, referred to as NX-API REST. Object data is native to the switch and therefore does not require a CLI parser or translator. Data models are easier to use, because they bypass the constraints of CLI-based programmability by requesting the state of an object. NX-API object configuration will require less string manipulation or NX-OS sequencing. A NX-OS object is a configuration of a specific feature, for example BGP or an interface. Not all available objects or configurations are yet available under the object model. Figure 5-3 illustrates the working with a configuration with CLI vs an object.

Note To learn what objects and currently available in NX-API, visit https://opennxos.cisco.com/.

```
{
 "l1PhysIf": {
  "attributes": {
   "addr": "2.2.2.2/24"
  }
 }
}
```

```
payload=[
 {
  "jsonrpc": "2.0",
  "method": "cli",
  "params": {
   "cmd": "configt",
   "version": 1
  },
  "id": 1
 },
 {
  "jsonrpc": "2.0",
  "method": "cli",
  "params": {
   "cmd": "interface ethernet1/1",
   "version": 1
  },
  "id": 2
 },
 {
  "jsonrpc": "2.0",
  "method": "cli",
  "params": {
   "cmd": "ip address 2.2.2.2 255.255.255.0",
   "version": 1
  },
  "id": 3
 }
]
```

Figure 5-3 *CLI vs Object Model*

In the Cisco NX-API REST object framework, the configuration and state information of the switch is stored in a hierarchical tree structure known as the management information tree (MIT), as shown in Figure 5-4. Each node in the MIT represents a managed object or group of objects. These objects are organized in a hierarchical way, creating logical object containers.

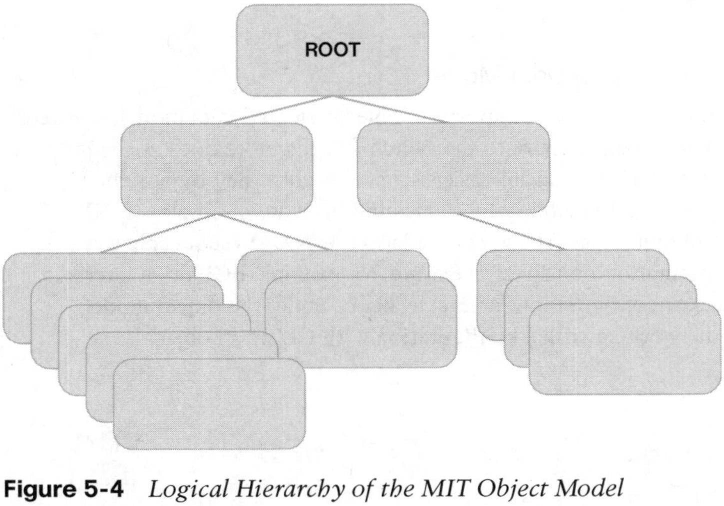

Figure 5-4 *Logical Hierarchy of the MIT Object Model*

NX-API objects use an information-model-based architecture in which the model describes all the information that can be controlled by a management process. Object instances are referred to as managed objects (MOs). Every managed object in the system can be identified by a unique distinguished name (DN). This approach allows the object to be referred to globally. An object's DN is the full path of the object specific to the device. The DN of ethernet1/27 on Nexus 9000 would be written as:

```
sys/intf/phys-[eth1/27]d
```

Objects in the MIT are part of a class, which represents the parent level structure for an object. Classes are generally used for queries on higher level data, for example an entire switch chassis.

Managed objects and classes are accessed by their DN, using standard HTTP verbs, including GET, POST, PUT, and DELETE. The URL format used can be represented as:

```
<switch ip >:/api/[mo|class]/[dn|class][:method].[xml|json]?{options}
```

The various building blocks of the preceding URL are as follows:

- **mo | class**: Indicatesd whether this is a managed object or class-level query
- **class**: Managed-object class (as specified in the information model) of the objects queried; the class name is represented
- **dn**: Distinguished name (unique hierarchical name of the object in the MIT tree) of the object queried
- **method**: Optional indication of the method being invoked on the object; applies only to HTTP POST requests
- **xml | json**: Encoding format
- **options**: Query options, filters, and arguments. Query options include **self** or **children** to define what data to query. For example "?query-target=self"

An Example URL to work with BGP would be:

```
http://192.168.0.1/api/mo/sys/bgp.json
```

NX-API REST Object Model Data

NX-API objects operate in forgiving mode, which means that missing attributes are substituted with default values that are maintained in the internal data management engine (DME). The DME validates and rejects incorrect attributes. Any changes from the API are atomic, which is to say that if any part of the configuration is bad, none of the configuration is applied. The API returns the configuration to its previous state, stops the API operation, and returns an error code.

NX-API features an on-box object store browser (Visore) to find and understand objects, as shown in Figure 5-5. The Visore browser is accessible at http://<switch IP>/visore.html.

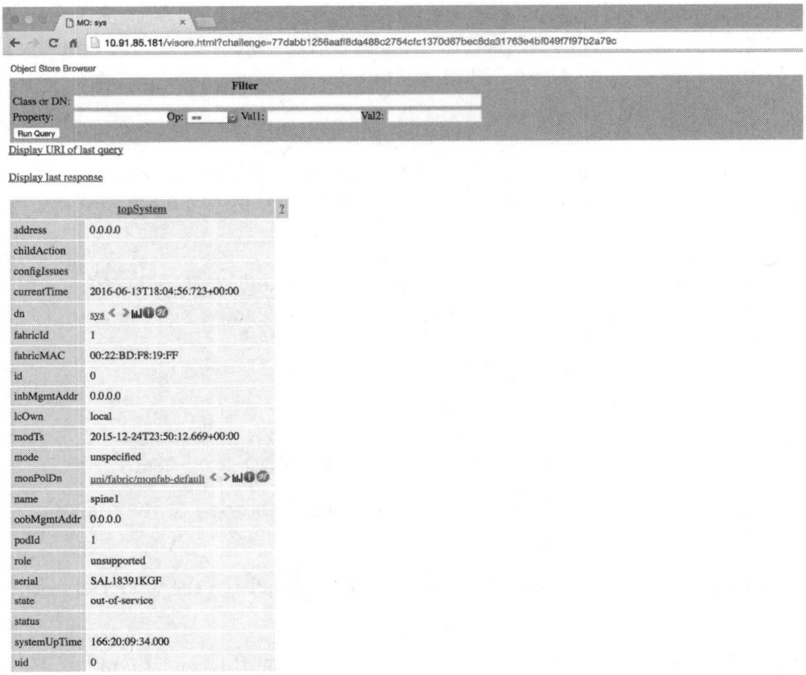

Figure 5-5 *Visore Browser*

The Visore browser is useful to ascertain data about an object, including DN and object attributes. The Visore browser displays real data queried from the switch. If an object is not configured in NX-OS, the Visore browser will not find/display any data.

> **Note** The Visore browser is reused from ACI.

The main functions of the Visore browser are provided by the two green arrows (< >) located on the **dn** line. The left arrow (<) displays the parent object where the right arrow (>) displays the object children.

As shown in Figure 5-5, the first page in Visore will display the class **topSystem**. In this case **topSystem** is a class and **sys** is the object created from the class. Using > will query child classes and objects of the switch. The interfaces are represented as in the

interfaceEntity class with the object DN of **sys/intf**. The > arrow on the **interfaceEntity** class displays the class of l1PhysIf and all the objects (interfaces) created from l1PhysIf. To get information about a desired interface, in Figure 5-6, ethernet1/25, (DN = sys/intf/phys-[eth1/25]) and click on the DN (consider creating a new tab).

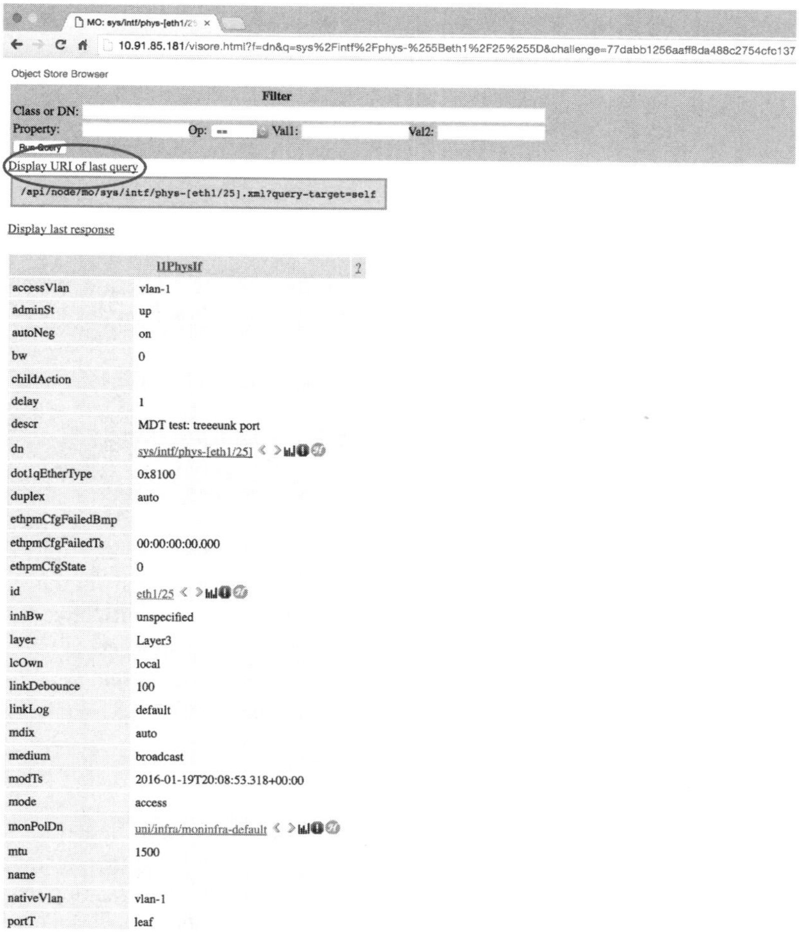

Figure 5-6 *ethernet1/25 in Visore*

Once the object is located, click **Display URI of last query** to display the URI data to access this object. This URI is

```
/api/node/mo/sys/intf/phys-[eth1/25].xml?query-target=self
```

Notice that this HTTP message requests a data exchange in XML; however this can be changed by replacing **.xml** with **.json**.

The URI is required to display or change the data from Python or Postman. Figure 5-7 depicts using Postman to query the interface object.

Figure 5-7 *Using Postman to Query Object Data from NX-API*

The URL in Figure 5-7 is **http://10.91.85.181/api/mo/sys/intf/phys-[eth1/25].json**, which consists of the switch's IP address and the URI captured from Visore. Postman displays the JSON formatted data in the bottom window.

Note This Postman example will require authentication. Postman authentication is covered later in this chapter.

Visore also features a filter to query the system for a specific class or DN. For example, to find all of the interface objects created from the **l1PhysIf** class, type **l1PhysIf** in the "Class or DN" search bar. Specific objects can be searched; for example **sys/intf/phys-[eth1/27]** displays the properties of the interface object. Property filters are used to find specific properties about a class or DN. For example, to search for interfaces that are currently up, search the class **l1PhysIf** with the property of **adminSt == up**.

Authenticating to NX-API (nxapi_auth cookie)

Before NX-API can be used in Python or Postman, it must be authenticated. NX-API leverages web tokens or cookies, which provide a very popular method for authenticating users to a web service. Web token authentication begins with the user authenticating to a system (most often with a username and password) and receiving a token. The token is sent from the server and stored on the client machine. The token is then sent with all subsequent requests; however, it has a limited lifespan. When the token expires, the session will have to be re-authenticated. In the case of NX-API, the token life time is 10 minutes.

Note—As seen in previous NX-API examples, authentication information can be passed inline using Python requests. This is perfect for simple applications or single-line use cases.

The URL for authentication is

```
http://<switch IP Address>/api/mo/aaaLogin.json
```

with JSON data formatted as follows.

```
{"aaaUser": {"attributes": {"name": "admin", "pwd": "Cisco"}}}
```

Figure 5-8 depicts leveraging Google Postman to successfully authenticate to a Nexus 9K.

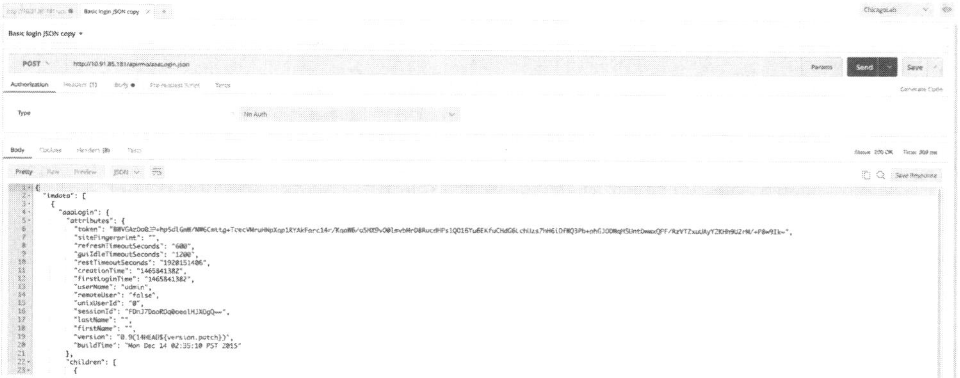

Figure 5-8 *Successful Postman Authentication*

Authenticating in Python is similar to authenticating in Postman; however the token or cookie is saved in a variable.

Step 1. Create two strings that hold the URL and the name/password information

```
auth_base_url = 'http://192.168.1.1/api/aaaLogin.json'
name_pass={"aaaUser": {"attributes": {"name": "admin", "pwd": "cisco"}}}
```

Step 2. Then use Python requests to dump JSON formatted data to the switch and store the response.

```
auth_response = requests.post(auth_base_url, json=name_pass, timeout = 5)
```

Upon successful authentication **auth_response** will hold data similar to the following ...

```
"imdata":[{"aaaLogin":{"attributes":{"token":"xQpLc42IdbXR
Wpv0tTCnb857F85N9qOg7RWGcdAuv3BcOwYHsW4t8boebDqcltsa05KSO
Gg9YKQnpc1Lhmm2NU45iraH5CQHGzN4BogXE9i3fM6NABZsWOvEfY/GuS/
GsPheaajan9VaIXznfJvYOJzNazKWpZXa0qfITd8OGAY=",
```


The token is stored in the dictionary key **token** with the data of the actual token.

Step 3. The JSON formatted data needs to be massaged to retrieve the token. To do this, first decode the JSON data

```
auth = json.loads(auth_response.text)
```

Step 4. Next get the token and store it in a new string. In this case the variable **auth_token** holds the token.

```
login_attributes = auth['imdata'][0]['aaaLogin']['attributes']
auth_token = login_attributes['token']
```

Note that in this example the string **login_attributes** slims the data down for clarity. Alternatively the **auth_token** could be found with the following:

```
auth_token = auth['imdata'][0]['aaaLogin']['attributes']['token']
NX-API requires token authentication in JSON formatted data as follows
{'APIC-Cookie': "TOKEN"}
```

To create this, build a new Python dictionary and insert **auth_token** as follows

```
cookies = {}
cookies['APIC-Cookie'] = auth_token
```

Finally, the token is captured and formatted so it can be used in subsequent http calls.

```
url='http://192.168.1.1/api/mo/sys/intf/phys-[eth1/25].json'
response = requests.post(url, cookies=cookies, json=payload)
```

Changing NX-API Objects Data via Postman

Modifying data with NX-API objects involves using a URL for the object (learned from Visore) and JSON formatted data. To modify the description of an Ethernet interface (object), use the following procedure.

The URL for the ethernet1/25 object is:

```
http://10.91.85.181/api/mo/sys/intf/phys-[eth1/25].json
```

To change the interface description, send JSON formatted payload data as follows.

```
{
  "l1PhysIf": {
    "attributes": {
      "descr": "Some Interface Description"
    }
  }
}
```

The JSON formatted payload is ascertained from either a Postman HTTP GET for the interface object or from Visore. To retrieve data from Postman, send an HTTP GET to the interface object. It will return data as follows:

```
{
  "totalCount": "1",
  "imdata": [
    {
      "l1PhysIf": {
        "attributes": {
          "accessVlan": "vlan-1",
          "adminSt": "up",
          "autoNeg": "on",
          "bw": "0",
          "childAction": "",
          "delay": "1",
          "descr": ""
          "dn": "sys/intf/phys-[eth1/25]",
          <Data Truncated>
```

Sending the Postman response data back to the switch will require editing (Figure 5-9), specifically removing **totalCount**, **imdata**, and the {} characters that encase the data. For example, to change the interface description attribute, the data would have to be formatted as follows.

```
{
  "l1PhysIf": {
    "attributes": {
      "descr": "Some Interface Description"
    }
  }
  }
```

Note Use an online JSON formatting tool, such as the one at http://www.jsoneditoronline.org/, to make sure JSON formatting is correct.

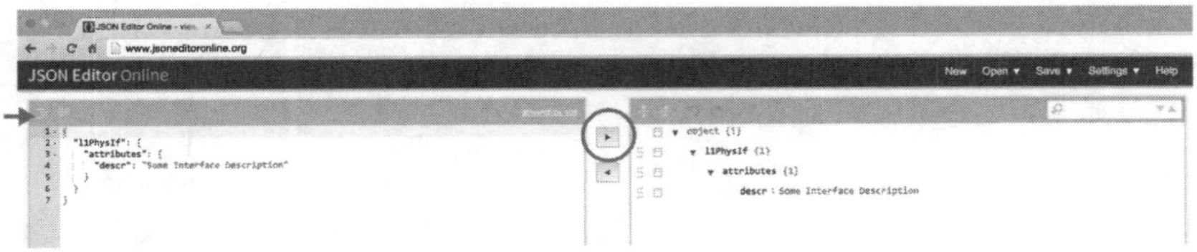

Figure 5-9 *www.JSONEditOnline.org*

Modifying NX-API Objects Data via Python

The use of Python, with the requests library, is the easiest way to modify NX-API objects. The following example sets an interface description.

```
#import requests and json libraries
import requests
import json

#the payload variable holds the object data.

payload ={
  "l1PhysIf": {
    "attributes": {
      "descr": "Some Interface Description"
    }
  }
}

#login switch and get authentication cookie (nxapi_auth)
#broken out for clarity

auth_base_url = 'http://192.168.1.1/api/aaaLogin.json'
name_pass={"aaaUser": {"attributes": {"name": "admin", "pwd": "cisco"}}}
#use requests to post username and password for auth token
auth_response = requests.post(auth_base_url, json=name_pass, timeout = 5)

#format response in json
auth = json.loads(auth_response.text)
```

```
#Get the token
login_attributes = auth['imdata'][0]['aaaLogin']['attributes']
auth_token = login_attributes['token']

#Create the cookie
cookies = {}
cookies['APIC-Cookie'] = auth_token

#end authentication

#Where the magic happens
url='http://192.168.1.1/api/mo/sys/intf/phys-[eth1/25].json'
   response = requests.post(url, cookies=cookies, json=payload)
```

The following example demonstrates configuring interface descriptions from CDP data. It uses NX-API with CLI to capture the CDP data and NX-API objects to configure the interface. (The source code is located on the book's GitHub account.)

```
#!/usr/bin/python
import requests
import json
import re

"""
Modify these please
"""
url='http://192.168.0.1/ins'
switchuser='admin'
switchpassword='Cisco'
switch='192.168.0.1'

myheaders={'content-type':'application/json'}
payload={
  "ins_api": {
    "version": "1.0",
    "type": "cli_show",
    "chunk": "0",
    "sid": "1",
    "input": "show cdp n",
    "output_format": "json"
  }
}
```

```
response = requests.post(url,data=json.dumps(payload), headers=myheaders,auth=
(switchuser,switchpassword)).json()

num_neigh= response['ins_api']['outputs']['output']['body']['neigh_count']

counter=0 #init a counter variable

#compare counter to num neighbors
while counter < num_neigh:

#Get the data to set the interface description

d1=response['ins_api']['outputs']['output']['body']["TABLE_cdp_neighbor_brief_
info"]["R
W_cdp_neighbor_brief_info"][counter]["platform_id"]

d2=response['ins_api']['outputs']['output']['body']["TABLE_cdp_neighbor_brief_
info"]["R
W_cdp_neighbor_brief_info"][counter]["device_id"]

d3=response['ins_api']['outputs']['output']['body']["TABLE_cdp_neighbor_brief_
info"]["R
W_cdp_neighbor_brief_info"][counter]["intf_id"]

  Interface_Description = "description Connected device is a " + d1 + " named " +
d2

#Create the interface object
  payload ={
    "l1PhysIf": {
      "attributes": {
        "descr": Interface_Description
      }
    }
  }

  #Increment the counter
  counter = counter + 1
#login switch and get authentication cookie (nxapi_auth)
#broken out for clarity

  auth_base_url = 'http://' + switch + '/api/mo/aaaLogin.json'
  name_pass={"aaaUser": {"attributes": {"name": switchuser, "pwd":
switchpassword}}}
```

```
#use requests to post username and password for auth_token
  auth_response = requests.post(auth_base_url, json=name_pass, timeout = 5)

#format response in json
  auth = json.loads(auth_response.text)

  #Get the token
  login_attributes = auth['imdata'][0]['aaaLogin']['attributes']
  auth_token = login_attributes['token']

  #Create the cookie
  cookies = {}
  cookies['APIC-Cookie'] = auth_token

#end authentication



#build the interface for the object URL
#Show CDP outputs interface as full name, object is first 3 chars followed by int
num
#the following lines fix this.

  if d3 != 'mgmt0': #do not set cdp on management port
    #first grab the first 3 chars and lowercase
    interface_format = str.lower(str(d3[:3]))
    #then grab the interface number
    interface_num = re.search(r'[[1-9]/[1-9]*', d3)
    #now combine the strings
    interface = interface_format + str(interface_num.group(0))
    #set URL
    url='http://' + switch + '/api/mo/sys/intf/phys-[' + interface + '].json'
    #send it
      response = requests.post(url, cookies=cookies, json=payload)
```

NX-API Event Subscription

When an API query is performed, there is an option to create a subscription to any future changes that may occur during your active API session in the results of that query. When any MO is created, changed, or deleted because of a user- or system-initiated action, an event is generated. If that event changes the results of an active subscribed query, the NX-OS switch generates a push notification to the API client that created the subscription.

The API subscription feature uses the WebSocket protocol (RFC 6455) to implement a two-way connection with the API client through which the API can send unsolicited notification messages to the client. To establish this notification channel, you must first open a WebSocket connection with the API object. WebSockets are not available with /ins API calls. Only a single WebSocket connection is needed to support multiple query subscriptions with multiple NX-API-REST instances. The WebSocket connection is dependent on the API session connection and closes when the API session ends.

To create a subscription to a query, perform the query with the option **?subscription=yes.** This example creates a subscription to a query of the **aaaUser** class in the JSON format:

```
GET https://192.0.20.123/api/class/aaaUser.json?subscription=yes
```

The query response contains a subscription identifier, **subscriptionId**, that one can use to refresh the subscription and to identify future notifications from this subscription.

To continue to receive event notifications, you must periodically refresh each subscription during your API session. To refresh a subscription, send an HTTP GET message to the API method **subscriptionRefresh** with the parameter id equal to the **subscriptionId**, as shown in this example:

```
GET https://<IP_Address>/api/subscriptionRefresh.json?id=18374686771712622593
```

The following example leverages the Python library websocket to open a WebSocket to a Nexus 9K. It subscribes to the ethernet1/26 object. Websocket is best installed using PIP. To install websocket with PIP, use **pip install websocket.**

```
#WebSoc.py:
#Use at your own risk
#Contact @ryantischer

#!/usr/bin/python
__author__ = 'Ryan Tischer'

import requests
import re
import json
import websocket

#login switch and get authentication cookie (nxapi_auth)
#broken out for clarity
"""
Modify these please
"""
switchuser='admin'
switchpassword='Cisco13579!'
switch='10.91.85.181'
```

```
auth_base_url = 'http://' + switch + '/api/mo/aaaLogin.json'
name_pass={"aaaUser": {"attributes": {"name": switchuser, "pwd":
switchpassword}}}
#use requests to post username and password for auth token
auth_response = requests.post(auth_base_url, json=name_pass, timeout = 5)

#format response in json
auth = json.loads(auth_response.text)

  #Get the token
login_attributes = auth['imdata'][0]['aaaLogin']['attributes']
auth_token = login_attributes['token']

  #Create the cookie
cookies = {}
cookies['APIC-Cookie'] = auth_token

#end authentication

websocket.enableTrace(True)
# websocket.enableTrace(True) enables websocket debugging

#Create the websocket to the Nexus
websURL = ("ws://" + switch + "/socket%s" % (cookies["APIC-Cookie"],))
ws = websocket.WebSocket()
print websURL
ws.connect(websURL)
# is a string substitution.  The final url is ws://192.168.1.1/thesub

response = requests.get("http://" + switch + "/api/mo/sys/intf/phys-
eth1/26].json?subscription=yes", cookies=cookies)

data = response.json()
print data["subscriptionId"]
#print the subscription ID for use for receiving data and refresh

#listen for updates
while True:
    print ws.recv()
```

This program waits until a change to the MO of ethernet1/26, which in this case was a new interface description. The final line prints the output to the screen, as follows.

```
{"subscriptionId":["18374686853317001217"],"imdata":[{"l1PhysIf":{"attributes":
{"childAction":"","descr":"Some New Description","dn":"sys/intf/phys-
[eth1/26]","modTs":"2016-06-03T15:15:55.504+00:00","rn":"","status":"modified"}}}]}
```

NX-OS subscriptions are an extremely powerful tool to monitor objects. A typical use case is monitoring an interface for changes during a troubleshooting session.

NXTool Kit

NXTool Kit is an open source Python library that greatly simplifies writing Python programs for NX-OS based devices. NXTool Kit enables configuration of NX-API objects using a simplified Python libraries. NXTool Kit libraries encapsulate complex Python programming, for example, authentication or configures, and provides simplified Python calls. The toolkit must be installed into a Python environment. The NXTool kit is best installed through GitHub using the following command.

```
bash-3.2$ git clone https://github.com/datacenter/nxtoolkit.git
```

Git will clone NXTool kit the currently directory; however it does not install the libraries. The following is an example of a successful git clone of NXTool kit.

```
Cloning into 'nxtoolkit'...
remote: Counting objects: 157, done.
remote: Total 157 (delta 0), reused 0 (delta 0), pack-reused 157
Receiving objects: 100% (157/157), 231.83 KiB | 0 bytes/s, done.
Resolving deltas: 100% (100/100), done.
Checking connectivity... done.
  bash-3.2$
```

An install tool is included with NXTool kit. To install NXTool kit run the install using **sudo**:

```
bash-3.2$ cd nxtoolkit
  bash-3.2$ sudo python setup.py install
```

NXTool Kit documentation, including sample applications, is located at opennxos.cisco .com, which maintains active links to the Cisco data center GitHub repository.

To use NXTool Kit, the library must be imported in Python:

```
import nxtoolkit.nxtoolkit as NX
```

Alternatively, to import the entire library use:

```
from nxtoolkit.nxtoolkit import *
```

Using NXTool Kit

Similar to NX-API, the first step in using the NXTool Kit is authenticating to the switch. NXTool Kit provides a class named Session that can be used to grab and capture an authentication token, as shown in the following example.

```
#Create the variables to hold data
username='admin'
password='Cisco'
```

```
url='http://192.168.1.1/'

#create a variable named mySession to invoke the NX.Session class.

mySession = NX.Session(url, username, password)

#do the login
  mySession.login()
```

Subsequent NXTook Kit commands will require passing this session variable.

Once authenticated, NXTool Kit can drive any object-based configuration to the device. The following example enables the NX-OS BGP feature.

```
# Create a variable name myFeature by invoking the NX Feature class.
The authentication data from mySession must be passed in.
myFeature = NX.Feature(mySession)
#Enable BGP
myFeature.enable('BGP')
#Push the configuration to the device
  resp = mySession.push_to_switch(myFeature.get_url(), myFeature.get_json())
```

In this case, the **resp** variable holds the results of the command; the value 200 specifies HTTP success.

```
>>> print resp
  <Response [200]>
```

Note Consider using the following code to ensure that the configuration was pushed to the switch:

```
if not resp.ok:
    print('%% Error: Could not push configuration to Switch')
      print(resp.text)
```

The statement **if not resp.ok code** generates an error message if the authentication was invalid.

```
%% Error: Could not push configuration to Switch
   {"imdata":[{"error":{"attributes":{"code":"403","text":"Need a valid webtoken
   cookie (named APIC-Cookie) or a signed request with signature in the cookie APIC-
   Request-Signature for all REST API requests"}}}]}
```

Python **dir** and **help** commands help navigate the NXTool Kit library.

```
>>> dir(NX)
['ARP', 'AaaAaa', 'AaaProviderRef', 'AaaRadius', 'AaaRadiusProvider', 'AaaRole',
'AaaTacacs', 'AaaTacacsProvider', 'AaaTacacsProviderGroup', 'AaaUser',
'AaaUserRole', 'AccessList', 'AsPath', 'BGPAdvPrefix', 'BGPDomain', 'BGPDomainAF',
```

```
'BGPPeer', 'BGPPeerAF', 'BGPSession',
(output truncated)
  >>>
```

NXTool Kit BGP Configuration

The following example creates a BGP configuration using NXTool Kit.

```
#!/usr/bin/python
__author__ = 'Ryan Tischer'

#FILENAME.py: Description of program or code.
#Use at your own risk
#Contact @ryantischer

#import NXtoolkit as NX
import nxtoolkit.nxtoolkit as NX

#Switch authentication

username='admin'
password='Cisco'
url='http://192.168.1.1/'

mySession = NX.Session(url, username, password)
mySession.login()
#end switch authentication

#enable BGP feature; use Mysession to authenticate to switch
myFeature = NX.Feature(mySession)
myFeature.enable('BGP')

#push the configuration to the switch
resp = mySession.push_to_switch(myFeature.get_url(), myFeature.get_json())

#check if configuration push was successful
if not resp.ok:
    print('%% Error: Could not push configuration to Switch')
    #print(resp.text)

#BGP Configuration

#Create BGP router with AS 20
bgpSession = NX.BGPSession("50")

bgpDom= NX.BGPDomain("default")
bgpDom.set_router_id("192.168.1.1")
```

```
#create BGP peer
bgpPeer = NX.BGPPeer("10.0.0.1", bgpDom)
bgpPeer.set_remote_as("1")
bgpDom.add_peer(bgpPeer)

bgpPeerAf = NX.BGPPeerAF('ipv4-ucast', bgpPeer)

#create another BGP peer
bgpPeer = NX.BGPPeer("192.168.100.100", bgpDom)
bgpPeer.set_remote_as("2")
bgpPeer.add_af(bgpPeerAf)
bgpDom.add_peer(bgpPeer)

bgpDomAf = NX.BGPDomainAF('ipv4-ucast', bgpDom)

advPrefix = NX.BGPAdvPrefix("192.168.0.1/32", bgpDomAf)
bgpDomAf.add_adv_prefix(advPrefix)

#add configuration to the object.
bgpDom.add_af(bgpDomAf)
bgpSession.add_domain(bgpDom)

#print bgpSession.get_url(bgpSession)
#print bgpSession.get_json()
#send configuration to the switch
  resp = mySession.push_to_switch(bgpSession.get_url(bgpSession),

                                  bgpSession.get_json())
```

The following example depicts the BGP configuration delivered from NXTool Kit.

```
feature bgp

router bgp 50
  router-id 192.168.1.1
  address-family ipv4 unicast
    network 192.168.0.1/32
  neighbor 10.0.0.1
    remote-as 1
    description 10.0.0.1
    address-family ipv4 unicast
  neighbor 192.168.100.100
    remote-as 2
    description 192.168.100.100
      address-family ipv4 unicast
```

The following example depicts in JSON formatting the BGP object that was sent from NXTool Kit.


```
{
  "bgpEntity": {
    "attributes": {},
    "children": [
      {
        "bgpInst": {
          "attributes": {
            "asn": "20"
          },
          "children": [
            {
              "bgpDom": {
                "attributes": {
                  "name": "default",
                  "rtrId": "10.0.0.14"
                },
                "children": [
                  {
                    "bgpPeer": {
                      "attributes": {
                        "asn": "1",
                        "name": "10.0.0.1",
                        "addr": "10.0.0.1"
                      },
                      "children": [
                        {
                          "bgpPeerAf": {
                            "attributes": {
                              "type": "ipv4-ucast",
                              "name": "ipv4-ucast"
                            },
                            "children": []
                          }
                        }
                      ]
                    }
                  },{
                    "bgpPeer": {
                      "attributes": {
                        "asn": "2",
                        "name": "192.168.45.25",
                        "addr": "192.168.45.25"
                      },
```

```
                "children": [
                  {
                    "bgpPeerAf": {
                      "attributes": {
                        "type": "ipv4-ucast",
                        "name": "ipv4-ucast"
                      },
                      "children": []
                    }
                  }
                ]
              }
            }, {
              "bgpDomAf": {
                "attributes": {
                  "type": "ipv4-ucast",
                  "name": "ipv4-ucast"
                },
                "children": [
                  {
                    "bgpAdvPrefix": {
                      "attributes": {
                        "addr": "10.0.0.11/32"
                      },
                      "children": []
                      }}]}}]}}]}}]}}
```

Automation and DevOps Tools

Automation tools push consistent configuration across any number of devices. Sometimes referred to as configuration management tools, they are very common with server, application, and DevOps teams because application delivery environments (servers, OS, etc.) can be quickly deployed or changed. Traditionally automation tools did not have connections to network hardware, forcing manual or over-simplified network configurations. NX-OS support many of the popular automation tools.

Automation tools, such as Puppet, Chef, Ansible, and SaltStack, support pushing a configuration to NX-OS devices. Some automation tools, for example Puppet and Chef, require an agent on the device. The agent is responsible for translating configuration details into a device-specific configuration. NX-OS agents are installed in the base Linux OS, or as a best practice as a container (Guestshell). Installation of the puppet agent is covered in Chapter 4, "Working with Cisco Nexus On-Box Programmability." Agentless tools, for example Ansible and Salt, leverage a device-specific API (NX-API) or Secure Shell Protocol (SSH) and do not require installation of an agent. Agentless tools are often quicker to deploy; however, they may have more operational complexity.

Puppet

The Puppet software package, developed by Puppet Labs, is an automation toolset for managing infrastructure such as servers and network devices. Puppet enforces a state or configuration of a device by pushing configurations from a central server, and it comes in both an open source and more fully featured enterprise version.

Puppet components include a puppet agent that runs on the managed device (node) and a puppet master (server) that typically runs on a separate dedicated server and serves multiple devices. Puppet agents periodically connect to the puppet master, which sends a configuration request, referred as a manifest, to the agent. The agent reconciles this manifest with the current state of the node and updates state, based on differences.

Figure 5-10 details the relationship of the puppet master and nodes.

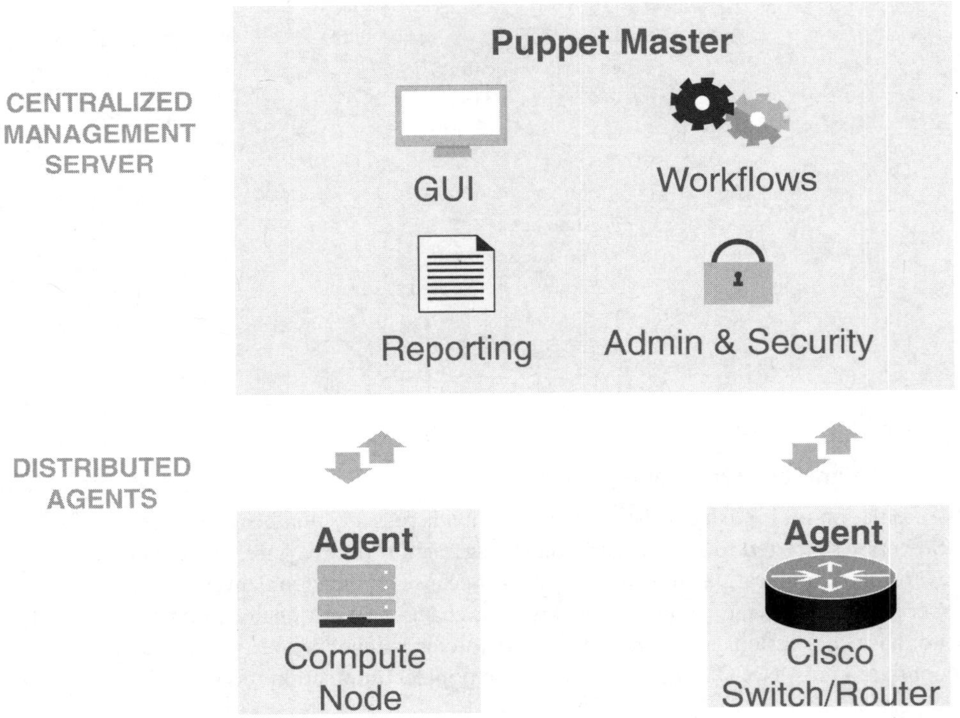

Figure 5-10 *Puppet Overview*

A puppet manifest is a collection of property definitions for setting the state on the device. The details for checking and setting these property states are abstracted so that a manifest can be used for more than one operating system or platform. Manifests are commonly used for defining configuration settings, but they can also be used to install software packages, copy files, and start services. The following example pushes a NTP configuration to Redhat or Ubuntu systems.

```
case $operatingsystem {
  centos, redhat: { $service_name = 'ntpd' }
  debian, ubuntu: { $service_name = 'ntp' }
}

package { 'ntp':
  ensure => installed,
}

service { 'ntp':
  name      => $service_name,
  ensure    => running,
  enable    => true,
  subscribe => File['ntp.conf'],
}

file { 'ntp.conf':
  path    => '/etc/ntp.conf',
  ensure  => file,
  require => Package['ntp'],
  source  => "puppet:///modules/ntp/ntp.conf",
  # This source file would be located on the Puppet master at
  # /etc/puppetlabs/code/modules/ntp/files/ntp.conf
}
```

The sample code shown in Example 5-11 will check if the NTP service is installed, running, and configured from the file on the puppet master server. The line **source => "puppet:///modules/ntp/ntp.conf"** specifies the configuration file.

Using Puppet

The puppet master server (or service) is a single interface for manifest creation and management through a defined workflow. The workflow follows the following steps, and is shown in Figure 5-11:

1. Administrator connects to the puppet master to define the devices and create manifests.
2. Puppet supports running simulations to better understand how the manifest will affect the device (optional).
3. Puppet compares the running configuration to the desired configuration and if necessary makes changes. The puppet master connects to the puppet agent either at prescheduled (every 5 minutes) intervals or on demand.
4. Puppet reports back to the administrator.

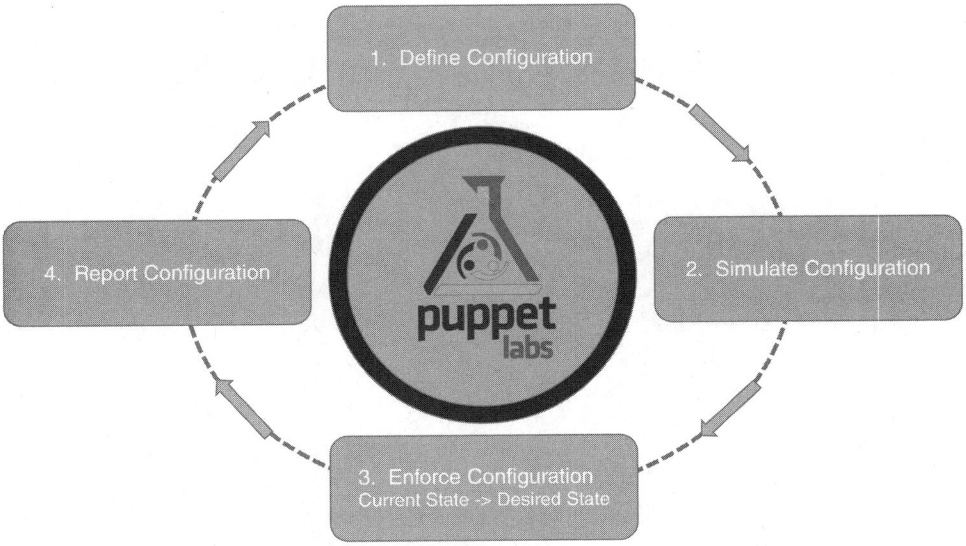

Figure 5-11 *Puppet Workflow*

Puppet and Nexus 9000

Cisco Nexus supports configuration management with Puppet. Puppet cannot speak directly to NX-OS and requires a puppet agent running on the switch. The agent is installed in a Guestshell to prevent the agent from impacting the switch's CPU. Working together, Puppet and Nexus enable agile and consistent network configuration delivery and integration with application and DevOps teams. The Nexus puppet agent allows DevOps team to build the network into existing workflows and use network infrastructure to enhance application delivery.

Note Installation of the puppet agent in NX-OS is covered in Chapter 4.

To manage Cisco Nexus 9000, the Puppet master server requires installation of the ciscopuppet agent module. The module is downloaded from Puppet's software repository, called Puppet forge.

To install ciscopuppet use:

```
puppetserver$ puppet module install puppetlabs-ciscopuppet
```

To verify the ciscopuppet installation, use:

```
root@puppetmaster:~ # puppet module list
/etc/puppetlabs/code/environments/production/modules
   ├── puppetlabs-ciscopuppet (v1.1.0)
```

The ciscopuppet module supports any NX-OS configuration through a CLI tool or a feature-specific configuration through types, which are listed in Table 5-1. If available, a feature-specific type will be easier to use.

Table 5-1 *Available Cisco Configurations in Puppet*

cisco_command_config	cisco_bgp	cisco_bgp_af
cisco_bgp_neighbor	cisco_bgp_neighbor_af	cisco_interface
cisco_interface_ospf	cisco_ospf	cisco_ospf_vrf
cisco_snmp_community	cisco_snmp_group	cisco_snmp_server
cisco_snmp_user	cisco_tacacs_server	cisco_tacacs_server_host
cisco_vlan	cisco_vrf	cisco_vtp

The command_**config type** enables Puppet to send any CLI configuration to a Nexus 9000. The following example uses **command_config** to drive an IP address and interface description to an Ethernet interface.

```
class ciscopuppet::demo_command_config {

  cisco_command_config { 'Ethernet1/1':
    command => "
      interface ethernet1/1
        description configured by puppet
        ip address 192.168.1.1/24
      "}
```

When available, a feature-specific type uses a predefined format to drive a configuration. In most cases the predefined format will result in fewer issues and will be easier to use. The following example defines the OSPF type

```
class ciscopuppet::demo_ospf {
  cisco_ospf { 'Sample':
    ensure => present,
  }
  $md_password = '046E1803362E595C260E0B240619050A2D'
  cisco_interface_ospf { 'Ethernet1/1 Sample':
    ensure                          => present,
    area                            => 200,
    cost                            => '200',
    hello_interval                  => 'default',
    dead_interval                   => '200',
    message_digest                  => true,
    message_digest_key_id           => 30,
    message_digest_algorithm_type   => md5,
```

```
message_digest_encryption_type => cisco_type_7,
message_digest_password        => $md_password,
passive_interface              => true,
}
```

Additional documentation on ciscopuppet, including example site.pp and NX-OS manifests, can be found at:

https://opennxos.cisco.com/public/codeshop/cisco-puppet-module/

https://forge.puppetlabs.com/puppetlabs/ciscopuppet

Note Puppet recently announced a module for automating the deployment of VXLAN with MP-BGP. More details are available at https://puppet.com/blog/networking-industry-first-puppet-orchestrated-vxlan-fabricAnsible.

Ansible is an agentless automation tool that pushes consistent configurations to parts of a network infrastructure, such as servers, operating systems, and network hardware. Ansible is agentless and thus leverages SSH or RESTful APIs to connect and configure devices.

Ansible requires a management server and a device configuration template, referred to as a playbook. Ansible management servers are extremely lightweight and in some cases may be run on simple servers or personal computers. The management server holds the the Ansible playbook files.

Ansible configurations files, including the playbook, are formatted using yet another mark-up language (YAML). YAML formatting focuses on human readability and is structured (similar to JSON) with key | value pairs. The following output shows an example of a YAML file.

```
books:
    - Hitchhikers guide to the Galaxy
    - A Short History of nearly everything
    - Monster Hunter International
    - World War Z
    ...
```

The key is **books** and the values are the book titles.

Ansible's main configuration file is the playbook, which defines what configurations are pushed to the device. The configurations can detail deployment directives, including application installation. For example, a playbook could define that the Ngnix web server should be installed and that the web server should handle a Ansible-pushed web page.

Note Ansible examples are located on their GitHub site, https://github.com/ansible/ansible-examples.

Ansible playbooks work in conjunction with an inventory file. The inventory file details which devices are under Ansible's control. The following output shows an example of a host inventory file:

```
 [MYwebserver]
10.1.1.1
10.1.1.2
  webapp01
```

The heading **[MYwebsever]** is user defined; however it must match what is configured in the playbook.

Ansible and Nexus 9000

Ansible can drive configurations to Nexus 9000 devices. The integration leverages NX-API; however, it requires Cisco-specific modules on the Ansible management server. To install Cisco modules on an Ansible management server, use:

```
sudo pip install pycsco
  git clone https://github.com/jedelman8/nxos-ansible.git
```

The GitHub repo includes a sample playbook. The following example shows an Ansible playbook for Nexus 9000.

```
---

- name: sample playbook
  hosts: n9k1

  tasks:

    - name: default interfaces
      nxos_interface: interface={{ item }} state=default host={{ inventory_
hostname }}
      with_items:
        - Ethernet1/1
        - Ethernet2/1

    # Ensure an interface is a Layer 3 port and that it has the proper description
    - name: config interface
      nxos_interface: interface=Ethernet1/1 description='Configured by Ansible'
mode=layer3 host={{ inventory_hostname }}
```

```
    # Admin down an interface
    - nxos_interface: interface=Ethernet2/1 admin_state=down host={{ inventory_
hostname }}
```

The data in the **hosts** key must match the heading in the inventory file.

More details, including videos and specific installation instructions, can be found at:

https://opennxos.cisco.com/public/api/ansible/

Summary

NX-OS and the Nexus 9000 feature a number of tools to extend and automate configuring the network. Using NX-API, the network can be leveraged to automate configurations, streamline troubleshooting, or integrate directly into the application. NX-API objects allow the developer to completely bypass the constraints of CLI and speak in the native language of the device. Finally, NX-OS devices support popular automation engines and may be manipulated like operating systems to integrate into DevOps workflows.

Resources

https://docs.puppetlabs.com/puppet/latest/reference/lang_summary.html

Chapter 6

Network Programmability with Cisco ACI

Cisco ACI is a next generation, software defined, data center network solution. ACI automates network deployments and operations, freeing network engineers and managers from mundane but complex, network tasks. ACI is an open system, featuring a robust API to network programmability and integrations.

One of the major innovations of ACI is the policy model. Policy provides an abstracted configuration or state of the network on a per-application basis. The abstracted configuration greatly simplifies Cloud integration and programmability by suppressing the complex details the network and centrally managing configurations. Abstraction enables policy administrators to utilize network features with minimal concern of the underlying infrastructure. A key differentiator of ACI is the policy invokes network hardware ASICs to provide network features, for example, access control lists and quality of service with line-rate, deterministic traffic forwarding. In the event of network issues or capacity limitations, ACI provides user consumable feedback, in the form of health scores, to alert administrators or an orchestration engine of the *impact* of the issue.

Note The impact of a network issue is much more important than the issue itself. Modern network architecture can handle node failure (total or partial), link failure, and a number of other issues with minimal, if any, application disruption. For example, failure of a link degrades available bandwidth; however, the application will continue as normal. Impact describes the issue in context, specifically to the application owner. Conversely, when the context of a failure is lost, any network issues are assumed to have the maximum negative impact to the application.

Cisco ACI Automation

The Cisco ACI fabric is a highly scalable, high-performance, leaf-and-spine architecture powered by virtual extensible LAN (VXLAN). VXLAN is a next-generation overlay (MAC-UDP) that provides layer 2 connectivity over layer 3 links. VXLAN can be deployed and operated with traditional CLI. However, due to increased complexity associated with overlay networking, a VXLAN automation tool is highly recommended. The controller in ACI, referred to as the application policy interface controller (APIC), fully automates VXLAN deployment and operations with the zero-touch fabric. ACI zero-touch fabric removes all user input and the complexity of deploying and managing a VXLAN-based data center network.

ACI zero-touch fabric, automatically configures the underlay (IS-IS) and the VXLAN overlay, including:

- Layer 3 interfaces with /30 prefixes
- IS-IS IGP
- Subnets to advertise in IS-IS
- IS-IS passive loopbacks
- IS-IS peers
- Tunes routing timers
- Multicast routing
- VRFs
- Verify cabling and neighbors.
- VXLAN overlay
- VLAN-to-VXLAN maps

ACI hardware, once racked and cabled, only requires a couple of minutes to discover and deploy the fabric. Fabric discovery uses LLDP between the Nexus 9K switch and the APIC. Day two administrative tasks, for example, managing SVIs, VRFs, and VLANs, are also automated within the fabric. ACI zero-touch fabric significantly reduces opportunities for outages due to network administrator issues or misconfiguration (chair-to-keyboard errors) when deploying VXLAN-based fabrics (Figure 6-1).

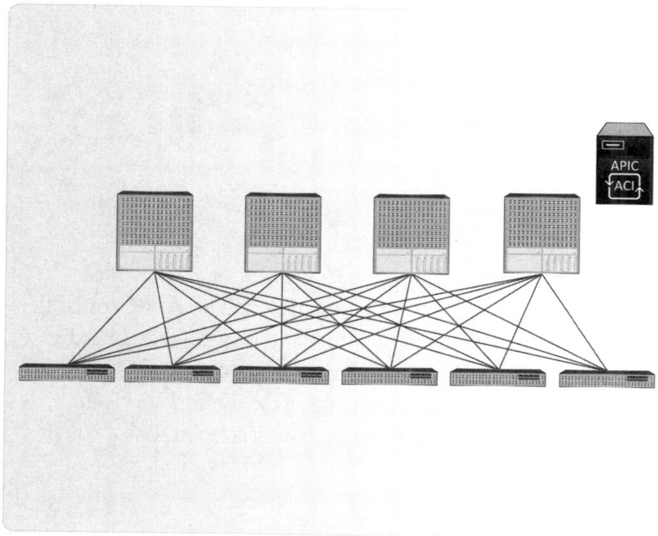

Figure 6-1 *ACI Fabric*

ACI Policy Instantiation

ACI policy dynamically configures network infrastructure through an abstracted and simplified language. Policy allows network administrators, on a per-application basis, to define exactly how the network should respond when an application appears in the environment. The abstracted nature of policy enables a network administrator to define smart network configurations and the application owners to consume the policy. ACI policy changes the consumption model of networking, allowing application owners the freedom to deploy applications anywhere, anytime, and at any scale without directly involving network administrators.

ACI policy is built using end-point groups (EPG) and contracts. EPGs are a collection of servers, virtual machines, or applications that share policy. Applications are dynamically placed in a single EPG with "pick-off" parameters that include VLAN, IP address, VMware attributes, or physical port. All network configurations (policy) is contained within the contract.

ACI contracts define how EPGs communicate with each other. Contracts contain the network features, including ACLs, QoS, and Layer 4-7 services to define how devices in a pair of EPGs connect. Contracts are built in one direction only to define a provider/consumer relationship between EPGs. For example, a database can provide TCP port 1522 for a consumer web service. Contracts contain filters, which define specific IP connectivity, most commonly TCP ports. Contracts and filters enable a whitelist security model that explicitly defines how applications communicate and reduces attack vectors in an environment. Contracts are ACI objects that can be reused across multiple sets of EPGs. Figure 6-2 depicts an example EPG/contract configuration for a three-tier application.

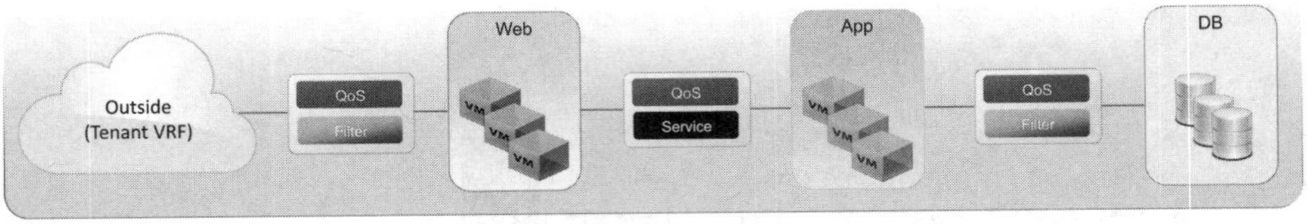

Figure 6-2 *ACI EPG and Contracts*

Together EPGs and contracts create an application network profile, or ANP, which defines total network and services configuration for an application. The APIC controller automatically instantiates the ANP's components across the stateless, physical hardware when the workload is matched in an EPG. In the event the application moves, scales, or goes away, the APIC controller automatically changes the network and services configuration. Figure 6-3 depicts an abstracted ANP being instantiated across a stateless infrastructure.

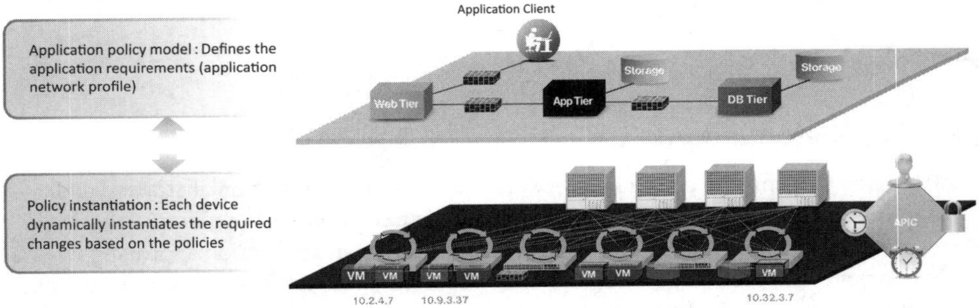

Figure 6-3 *ACI Policy Instantiation Across a Stateless Infrastructure*

A Bit More Python

A best practice for network programmability is to leverage virtual environments and Python exception handling. Exception handling is precoding how errors are handled. Exception handling provides a better user experience and easier application troubleshooting by providing human-readable feedback when an error occurs. Virtual environments enable a developer to write software without the constraints of existing environment attributes, such has installed libraries and Python versions. Additionally, virtual environments are easy to package and ship to other servers.

Virtualenv

The Python tool virtualenv creates discrete virtual environments for Python projects. Virtual environments allow Python projects to be reusable and portable by dictating specific library and version requirements. Virtual environments can be used in PyCharm or command-line environments. Python virtualenv is installed from PIP with pip install virtualenv. The following example demonstrates installation of virtualenv on a Mac or Linux system.

```
bash-3.2$pip install virtualenv
Downloading/unpacking virtualenv
  Downloading virtualenv-14.0.5-py2.py3-none-any.whl (1.8MB): 1.8MB downloaded
Installing collected packages: virtualenv
Successfully installed virtualenv
Cleaning up...
bash-3.2$
```

Once installed, virtual environments must be created. Creating a virtual environment builds a directory that holds the necessary files to build the environment. Consider creating a directory to hold all of your virtual environments. In the following example, we create and then enter a folder named "env." The **virtualenv** command followed by **aci_project** creates a directory (virtual environment) and installs PIP, setup tools, and wheel.

```
bash-3.2$ mkdir env
bash-3.2$ cd env
bash-3.2$ virtualenv aci_project
New python executable in /Users/ryantischer/env/aci_project/bin/python
Installing setuptools, pip, wheel...done.
bash-3.2$ ls
aci_project
bash-3.2$
```

Virtual environments can be customized with specific Python versions. As shown in the following example, the **-p** switch builds a virtual environment named aci_project1 with Python 2.6.

```
bash-3.2$ virtualenv -p /usr/bin/python2.6 aci_project1
Running virtualenv with interpreter /usr/bin/python2.6
New python executable in /Users/ryantischer/env/aci_project1/bin/python2.6
Also creating executable in /Users/ryantischer/env/aci_project1/bin/python
Installing setuptools, pip, wheel...done.
bash-3.2$
```

Use **activate** and **deactivate** to access and exit a virtual environment, as shown in the following example. Both activate and deactivate scripts are located in the virtual environment folder. The activate script requires the Linux command "source" to preserve environment variables.

```
bash-3.2$ source aci_project1/bin/activate
(aci_project1) bash-3.2$ python --version
Python 2.6.9
 (aci_project1) bash-3.2$ deactivate
bash-3.2$
```

The example starts with running (source) a script named "activate" located in the newly created virtual environment. Once in the virtual environment, the prompt changes to include the name of the environment. The **deactivate** command exits the environment.

Python libraries can be installed into active virtual environments using the PIP tool, as shown in the following example.

```
(aci_project) bash-3.2$ pip install requests
Collecting requests
  Using cached requests-2.9.1-py2.py3-none-any.whl
Installing collected packages: requests
Successfully installed requests-2.9.1
(aci_project) bash-3.2$

(aci_project) bash-3.2$ pip install websocket
Collecting websocket
  Downloading websocket-0.2.1.tar.gz (195kB)
    100% |████████████████████████████████| 196kB 335kB/s
Collecting gevent (from websocket)
  Downloading gevent-1.0.2-cp27-none-macosx_10_10_x86_64.whl (337kB)
    100% |████████████████████████████████| 339kB 691kB/s
Collecting greenlet (from websocket)
  Downloading greenlet-0.4.9.tar.gz (54kB)
    100% |████████████████████████████████| 57kB 2.6MB/s
Building wheels for collected packages: websocket, greenlet
  Running setup.py bdist_wheel for websocket ... done
  Stored in directory: /Users/ryantischer/Library/Caches/pip/wheels/d2/a6/fd/
  da345b9aee6fbc3a3cc49ba5b1859b0314eaa7abf51b99f209
  Running setup.py bdist_wheel for greenlet ... done
  Stored in directory: /Users/ryantischer/Library/Caches/pip/wheels/08/9c/52/3d8ee
  766d654c43b131dcc954f255f8c6270bef617da0ac3e6
Successfully built websocket greenlet
Installing collected packages: greenlet, gevent, websocket
Successfully installed gevent-1.0.2 greenlet-0.4.9 websocket-0.2.1
```

Python applications created within this environment would use and thus require requests and websocket to function. Virtual environments can be frozen to document what libraries or requirements are required. The following example freeze the active project.

```
(aci_project) bash-3.2$ pip freeze
gevent==1.0.2
greenlet==0.4.9
requests==2.9.1
websocket==0.2.1
wheel==0.26.0
(aci_project) bash-3.2$
```

The output of PIP freeze details the requirements for the Python application. This output is commonly saved to file for reuse. The following example freezes the environment and saves the output to requirements.txt.

```
(aci_project) bash-3.2$ pip freeze > requirements.txt
(aci_project) bash-3.2$ ls
aci_project          aci_project1          requirements.txt
(aci_project) bash-3.2$ cat requirements.txt
gevent==1.0.2
greenlet==0.4.9
requests==2.9.1
websocket==0.2.1
wheel==0.26.0
(aci_project) bash-3.2$
```

The requirements.txt file is used to recreate and share the virtual environment: The following example creates a new project called "new_project" and installs the required libraries from the requirements.txt file.

```
(new_project) bash-3.2$ pip install -r requirements.txt
Collecting gevent==1.0.2 (from -r requirements.txt (line 1))
  Using cached gevent-1.0.2-cp27-none-macosx_10_10_x86_64.whl
Collecting greenlet==0.4.9 (from -r requirements.txt (line 2))
Collecting requests==2.9.1 (from -r requirements.txt (line 3))
  Using cached requests-2.9.1-py2.py3-none-any.whl
Collecting websocket==0.2.1 (from -r requirements.txt (line 4))
Requirement already satisfied (use --upgrade to upgrade): wheel==0.26.0 in
./new_project/lib/python2.7/site-packages (from -r requirements.txt (line 5))
Installing collected packages: greenlet, gevent, requests, websocket
Successfully installed gevent-1.0.2 greenlet-0.4.9 requests-2.9.1 websocket-0.2.1

(new_project) bash-3.2$ pip list
gevent (1.0.2)
greenlet (0.4.9)
pip (8.0.2)
requests (2.9.1)
setuptools (19.6.2)
websocket (0.2.1)
wheel (0.26.0)
(new_project) bash-3.2$
```

Note PIP list displays the libraries installed in the virtualenv.

Virtualenv in PyCharm

Virtualenv is installed by default in PyCharm and supports different Python interpreters (versions) and library installations.

1. Open the Settings dialog box, and then open the **Project Interpreters** page.
2. Click the sprocket next to **Project Interpreter** field, and choose the option **Create VirtualEnv.**
3. Create a virtualenv with custom specifications.

Figure 6-4 depicts building a virtualenv in Pycharm.

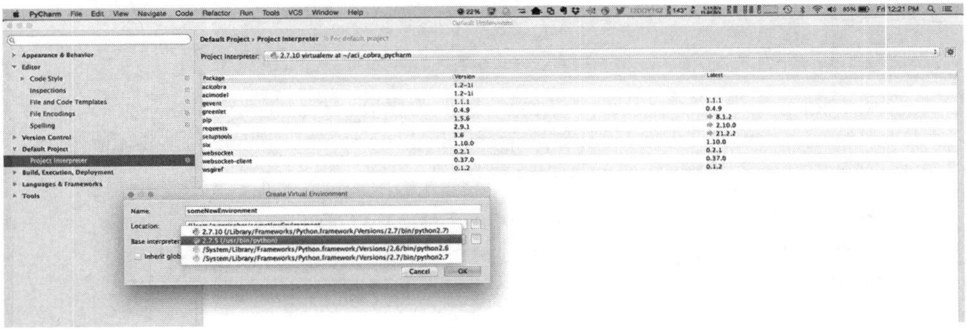

Figure 6-4 *Building a Virtualenv in Pycharm*

Python Exceptions Handling

Exception handling is highly recommended in any software development effort. It provides a better experience for the user and better reporting of issues, which helps the developer troubleshoot production issues. Exception handling instructs the application how to respond when something within the application does not work correctly. When and where to implement exception handling is up to the developer. However, as a general guideline, any time the application requires input or output to another system or user, the action is best wrapped in exception handling.

Python exceptions throw errors in a traceback statement. Traceback statements are normally printed to signal exactly what happened.

This application leverages requests to perform an HTTP GET to cisco.com. There is an error in the value of the URL variable.

```
#!/usr/bin/python
__author__ = 'Ryan Tischer'


import requests


url=' ://www.cisco.com'


r=requests.get(url)
print r
```

The following is the output of this application:

```
/Library/Frameworks/Python.framework/Versions/2.7/bin/python2.7 /Users/
ryantischer/PycharmProjects/NPaA/Python_exceptions.py
Traceback (most recent call last):
  File "/Users/ryantischer/PycharmProjects/NPaA/Python_exceptions.py", line 8, in
  <module>
    r=requests.get(url)
  File "/Library/Python/2.7/site-packages/requests/api.py", line 69, in get
    return request('get', url, params=params, **kwargs)
  File "/Library/Python/2.7/site-packages/requests/api.py", line 50, in request
    response = session.request(method=method, url=url, **kwargs)
  File "/Library/Python/2.7/site-packages/requests/sessions.py", line 468, in
  request
    resp = self.send(prep, **send_kwargs)
  File "/Library/Python/2.7/site-packages/requests/sessions.py", line 570, in send
    adapter = self.get_adapter(url=request.url)
  File "/Library/Python/2.7/site-packages/requests/sessions.py", line 644, in
  get_adapter
    raise InvalidSchema("No connection adapters were found for '%s'" % url)
requests.exceptions.InvalidSchema: No connection adapters were found for
' ://www.cisco.com'
```

This output is not user friendly and offers an impression that the application is not working correctly. The Python statements "try" and "except" work together to handle issues within applications. The try statement requires indentation and runs command contained within the block. In the event anything throws an exception, the exception is compared against statements in except block. The following examples leverages Python "try:" to access a URL via the requests library In this case the line **r=requests.get(url)** has an issue (missing the "http"), and the interpreter moves to syntax under except. In this case, **except:** with no specific exception is a catch-all.

```
#!/usr/bin/python
__author__ = 'Ryan Tischer'

import requests

url='://www.cisco.com'

try:
    r=requests.get(url)
    print r

except:
    print("something went wrong")
```

The output of this example is as follows.

```
something went wrong

Process finished with exit code 0
```

Python exceptions can be specifically called out. The output from the previous example demonstrates how requests throws an exception because of an invalid URL. A best practice to build exception handling for common issues, for example connection timeouts or invalid user input. The following example demonstrates a specific requests exception for an invalid URL, which requests calls an "InvalidSchema":

```
#!/usr/bin/python
__author__ = 'Ryan Tischer'

import requests

url=':/www.cisco.com'

try:
    r=requests.get(url)
    print r

except requests.exceptions.InvalidSchema:
    print("invalid URL")

except:
    print("something went wrong")
```

Output:

```
invalid URL
Process finished with exit code 0
```

Note Exception handling is specific to each Python module and should be documented in the library itself or online. Best practice when using the requests library is to build exceptions for timeout and redirects. Use "requests.exceptions.Timeout" and "requests.exceptions.TooManyRedirects."

ACI Fundamentals

The APIC controller serves as an unified interface for the ACI fabric. The all interactions with the APIC leverage a RESTful API that, as depicted in Figure 6-5, can be accessed by tools provide by Cisco, such as the default GUI, or third party applications, for example, Cisco CloudCenter or Python scripts. The single RESTful interface provides uniformity of both the RESTful call and the provided data.

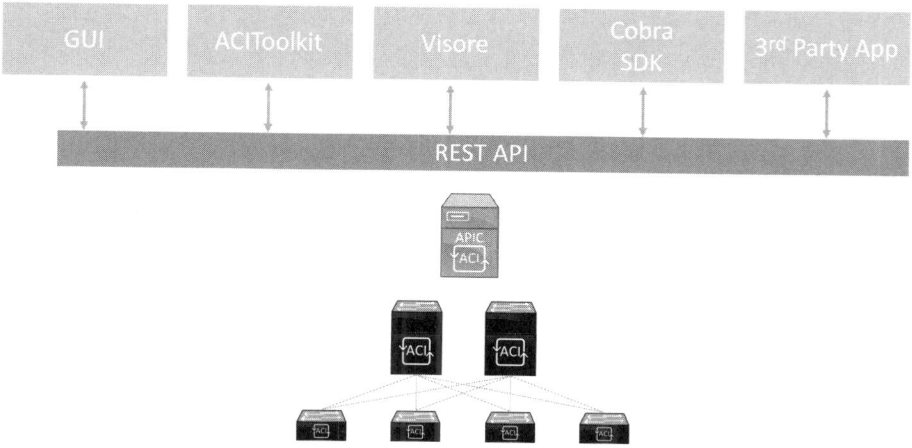

Figure 6-5 *ACI Programmability Architecture*

ACI Management Information Model

All physical and logical components in the ACI fabric are represented as a managed object (MO). MOs contain the abstraction of the administrative state and the operational state of a component. An MO can represent a physical object, such as a switch or adapter, or a logical object, such as a policy or fault. Some MOs are created automatically by the fabric (for example, power supply objects, and fan objects).

MOs are organized in a hierarchical management information tree (MIT). The hierarchical structure starts at the top (root) and contains parent and child nodes, as shown in Figure 6-6. Each node in this tree is an MO, and each object in the ACI fabric has a unique distinguished name (DN) that describes the object and its place in the tree.

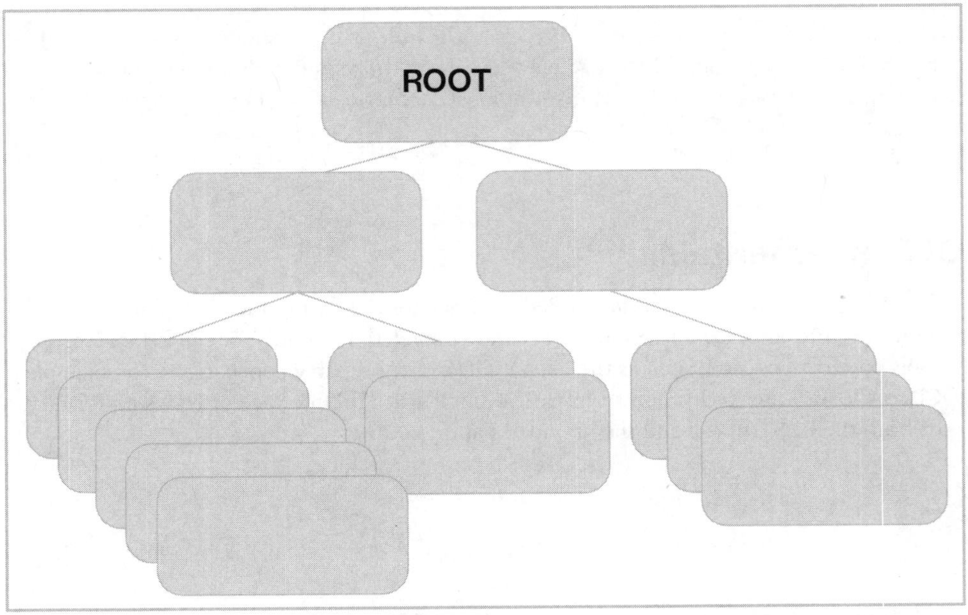

Figure 6-6 *API MIT*

ACI Object Naming

ACI objects can be located by their distinguished name (DN), relative name (RN), or custom tags.

The DN is the full path for the object where the RN is relative to another object. In most cases, the DN will be more consistent.

The DN contains a sequence of RNs.

topology/pod-1/node-103/sys/br-[eth1/16]/rsbrConf

DN provides a fully qualified path for fabport-1 from the top of the object tree to the object, as shown in Figure 6-7. The DN specifies the exact managed object on which the API call is operating. < dn ="sys/ch/lcslot-1/lc/fabport-1" />

Each object in ACI has statistics, faults, and a health score associated with it. Statistics are collected specific to the object and the type of object. For example, an interface would include bytes in/out or dropped packets. Faults include critical to informational objet events, for example, up/down for the object. ACI faults move throughout a life cycle from initial observation to cleared.

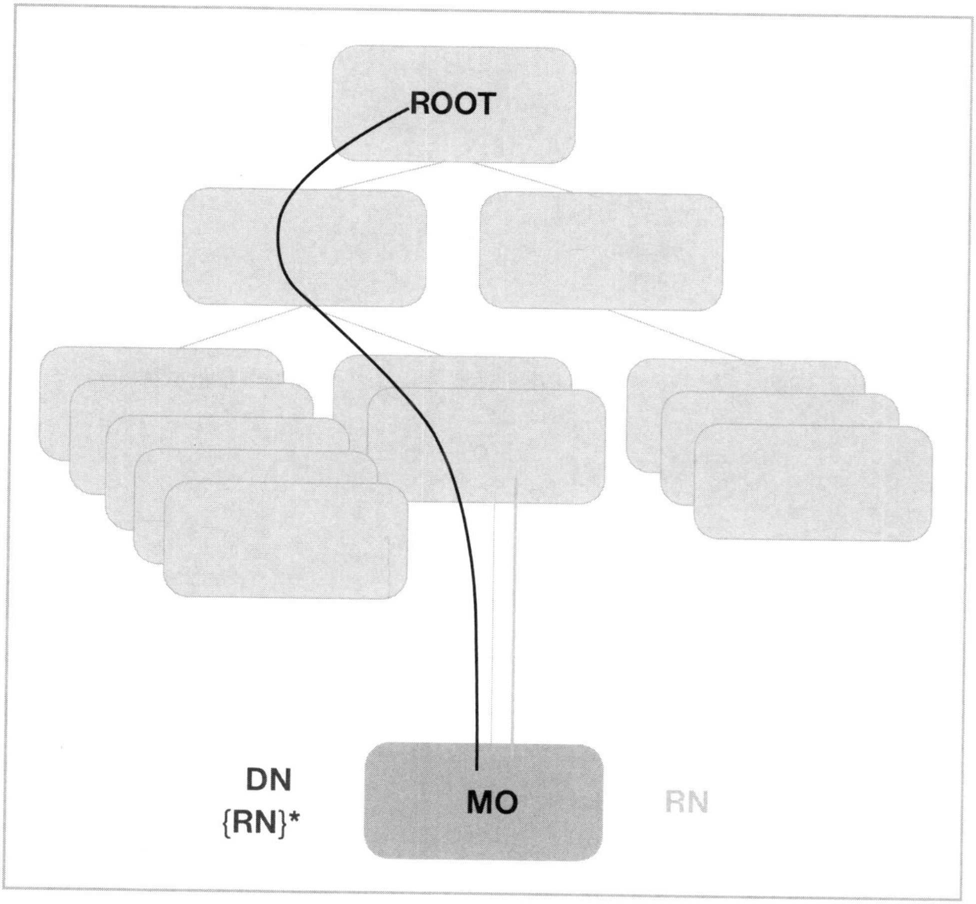

Figure 6-7 *API MIT*

Fault Lifecycle

APIC fault MOs are stateful, and a fault is raised by the APIC transitions through more than one state during its lifecycle. In addition, the severity of a fault may change due to its persistence over time, so a change in state may also entail a change in severity.

Only one instance of a given fault MO can exist on each parent MO. If the same fault occurs again while the fault MO is active, the APIC increments the number of occurrences. Figure 6-8 depicts a common fault lifecycle after a fault is detected.

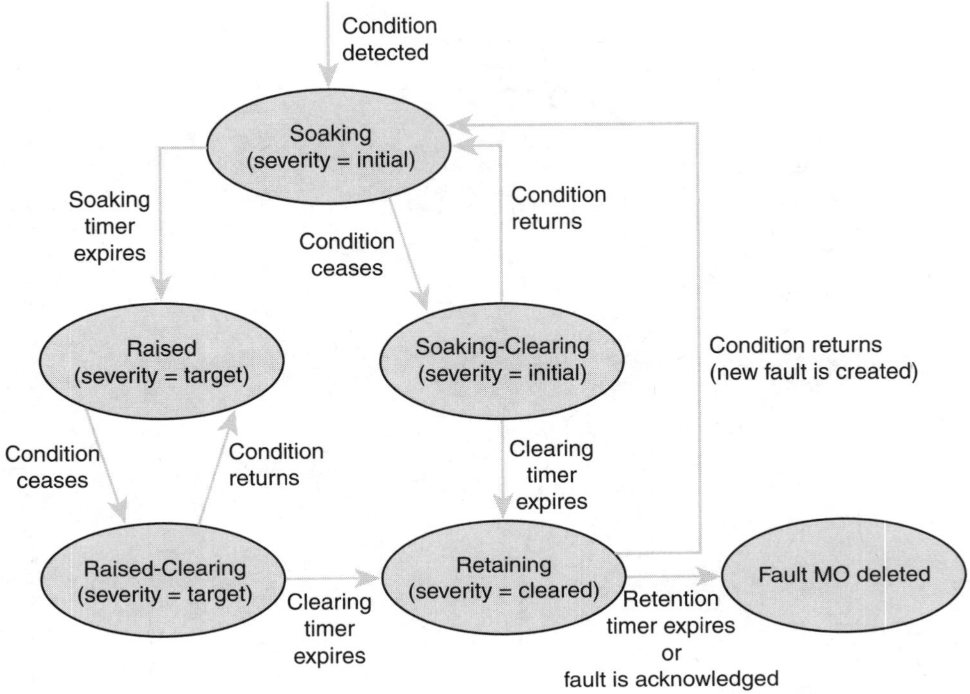

Figure 6-8 *Fault Life Cycle*

The characteristics of each state are as follows:

- Soaking—A fault MO is created when a fault condition is detected. The initial state is soaking, and the initial severity is specified by the fault policy for the fault class. Because some faults are important only if they persist over a period of time, a soaking interval begins, as specified by the fault policy. During the soaking interval, the system observes whether the fault condition persists or whether it is alleviated and reoccurs one or more times. When the soaking interval expires, the next state depends on whether the fault condition remains.
- Soaking-Clearing—If the fault condition is alleviated by the end of the soaking interval, the fault MO enters the soaking-clearing state, retaining its initial severity. A clearing interval begins. If the fault condition returns during the clearing interval, the fault MO returns to the soaking state. If the fault condition does not return during the clearing interval, the fault MO enters the retaining state.
- Raised—If the fault condition persists when the soaking interval expires, the fault MO enters the raised state. Because a persistent fault may be more serious than a transient fault, the fault is assigned a new severity, the target severity. The target severity is specified by the fault policy for the fault class. The fault remains in the raised state at the target severity until the fault condition is alleviated.

- Raised-Clearing—When the fault condition of a raised fault is alleviated, the fault MO enters the raised-clearing state. The severity remains at the target severity, and a clearing interval begins. If the fault condition returns during the clearing interval, the fault MO returns to the raised state.
- Retaining—When the fault condition is absent for the duration of the clearing interval in either the raised-clearing or soaking-clearing state, the fault MO enters the retaining state with the severity level cleared. A retention interval begins, during which the fault MO is retained for a length of time specified in the fault policy. This interval ensures that the fault reaches the attention of an administrator even if the condition that caused the fault has been alleviated, and that the fault is not deleted prematurely. If the fault condition reoccurs during the retention interval, a new fault MO is created in the soaking state. If the fault condition has not returned before the retention interval expires, or if the fault is acknowledged by the user, the fault MO is deleted.

Whenever a lifecycle transition occurs, the system automatically creates a fault record object to log it. Fault records are never modified after they are created, and they are deleted only when their number exceeds the maximum value specified in the fault retention policy.

Fault Severity

The fault severity is an estimate of the impact of the fault condition on the capability of the system to provide service.

A fault raised by the system can transition through more than one severity during its lifecycle. The following fault severities are listed in decreasing order of severity:

- Critical—A service-affecting condition that requires immediate corrective action. For example, this severity level could indicate that the managed object is out of service and its capability must be restored.
- Major—A service-affecting condition that requires urgent corrective action. For example, this severity could indicate a severe degradation in the capability of the managed object and that its full capability must be restored.
- Minor—A non-service-affecting fault condition that requires corrective action to prevent a more serious fault from occurring. For example, this severity level could indicate that the detected alarm condition is not currently degrading the capacity of the managed object.
- Warning—A potential or impending service-affecting fault that currently has no significant effects in the system. Action should be taken to further diagnose, if necessary, and correct the problem to prevent it from becoming a more serious service-affecting fault.

- Info—A basic notification or informational message, possibly independently insignificant.
- Cleared—A notification that the condition that caused the fault has been resolved and the fault has been cleared.

ACI Health scores provide a summary indication of an object health as a score from 0 to 100, determined by calculating the scores of all contributing elements and factors weighted by their impact on the overall health.

ACI Health Scores

The APIC combines faults, network statistics, and other data to calculate a health score. Health scores provide a real-world summary of a user's experience on a per-application basis and provide actionable data that can be tied to automation systems for self-healing networking and an overall better application experience. Health scores are presented from 0 to 100, where 0 means total system failure and 100 is optimal. Health scores can be aggregated for a variety of areas such as for the infrastructure, applications, or services.

ACI fabric health information is available for the following views of the system:

- Application—Application-level health scores aggregate scores from supporting components to determine application-specific experience.
- System—aggregation of system-wide health, including pod health scores, tenant health scores, system fault counts by domain and type, and the APIC cluster health state.
- Tenant—aggregation of health scores for a tenant, including performance data for objects, such as applications and EPGs that are specific to a tenant, and tenant-wide fault counts by domain and type.
- Managed object—health score policies for managed objects (MOs), which includes their dependent and related MOs. These policies can be customized by an administrator.

ACI Programmability

Cisco ACI features a robust RESTful API for application integrations, configurations, and monitoring. The API accepts and returns HTTP or HTTPS messages with JSON or XML documents and is compatible with most modern programming languages. The API operates in forgiving mode, which means that missing attributes are substituted with default values (if applicable) that are maintained in the internal data management engine (DME). The DME validates and rejects incorrect attributes. The API is also atomic. If multiple MOs are being configured (for example, virtual NICs), and any of the MOs cannot be configured, the API stops its operation. It returns the configuration to its prior state, stops the current API operation, and returns an error code. Figure 6-9 displays DME actions from API input.

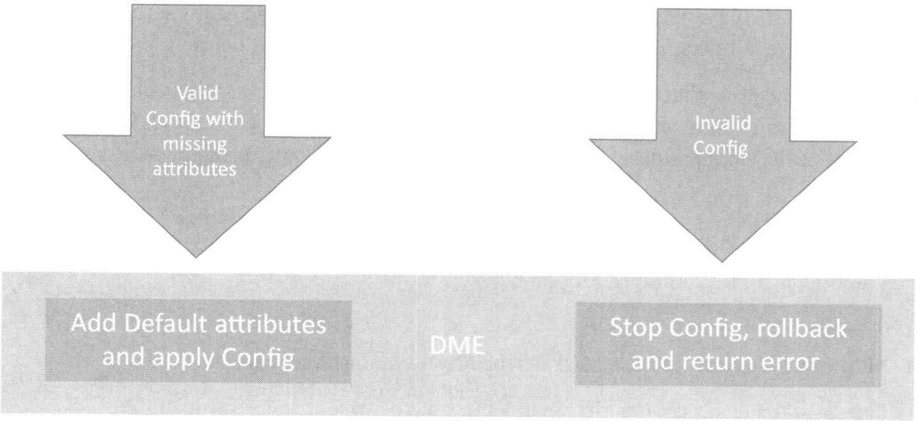

Figure 6-9 *Forgiving Mode and Atomic Modes*

The API serves as the single interface for all ACI interactions, including the default GUI and Cloud orchestration tools, for example CliQr or UCS Director. The APIC is responsible for all endpoint communication, such as state updates; users cannot communicate directly to endpoints. In this way, developers are relieved from understanding the complexity of the network and can focus on application specific configurations.

The API model includes these programmatic entities:

- Classes—Templates that define the properties and states of objects in the management information tree. APIC classes start with "fv": for example "fvTenant"

  A Class contains a list of properties to define how the objects created from the class can be used.

  Class fv:BD

```
Class ID:1887
Class Label: Bridge Domain
Encrypted: false - Exportable: true - Persistent: true - Configurable: true
Write Access: [admin, tenant-connectivity-l2]
Read Access: [admin, nw-svc-device, nw-svc-policy, tenant-connectivity-l2,
tenant-connectivity-mgmt,
tenant-epg, tenant-ext-connectivity-l2, tenant-network-profile, tenant-
protocol-l2, tenant-protocol-l3]
Creatable/Deletable: yes (see Container Mos for details)
Semantic Scope: EPG
Semantic Scope Evaluation Rule: Explicit
Monitoring Policy Source: Explicit
Monitoring Flags : [ IsObservable: true, HasStats: true, HasFaults: true,
HasHealth: true ]
```

NOTE – An ACI bridge domain is a unique layer 2-forwarding domain that contains one or more subnets. Each bridge domain must be linked to a context.

The above details that the class fv:BD is both read and writable, what roles can read and write to it, its monitoring capabilities, and other details. This data is located in the on-APIC documentation at http://{APIC IP Address}/doc/html/.

> **Note** Reminder—A class is a template or framework for how to create an object and what methods (actions) can be run on that object.

- Methods—Actions that the API performs on one or more objects.
- Types—Object properties that map values to the object state (for example, equipmentPresence).

A typical request comes into the DME and is placed in the translator queue in first-in, first-out (FIFO) order. The translator gets the request from the queue, interprets the request, and performs an authorization check. After the request is confirmed, the translator updates the MIT. This complete operation is done in a single transaction.

Invoking the API

You can invoke an API function by sending an HTTP or HTTPS POST, GET, or DELETE message to the APIC. The HTML body of the POST message contains a JSON or XML data structure that describes an MO or an API method. The HTML body of the response message contains a JSON or XML structure that contains requested data, confirmation of a requested action, or error information. Figures 6-10 and 6-11 depict URL formatting for reading, creating, or updating MOs using APIC's RESTful API.

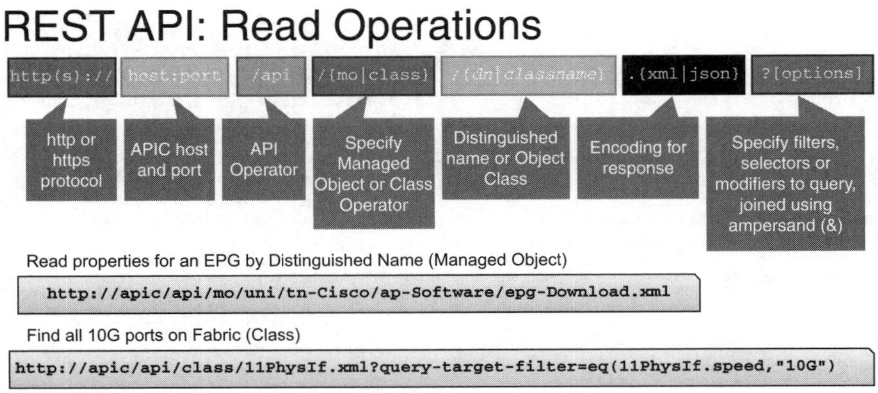

Figure 6-10 *API Read Operations*

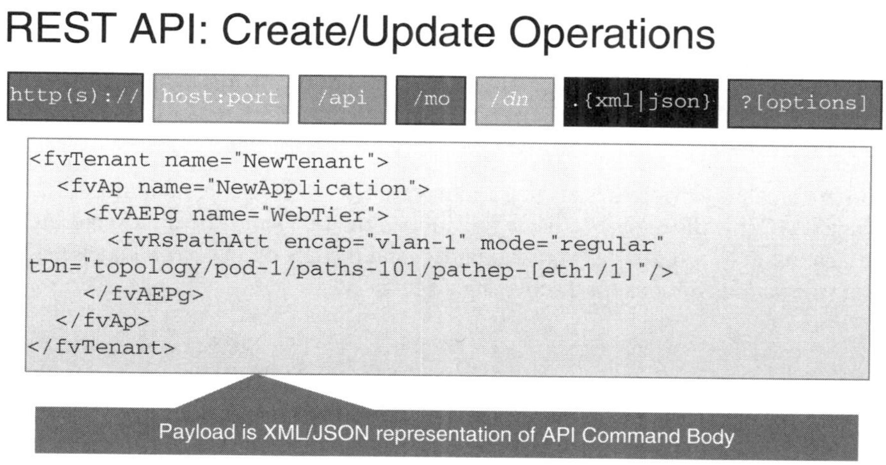

Figure 6-11 *API Write Operations*

Note Guidelines for Composing the API Command Body:

- The data structure does not need to represent the entire set of attributes and elements of the target MO or method, but it must provide at minimum set of properties or parameters necessary to identify the MO and to execute the command, not including properties or parameters that are incorporated into the URI.
- In the data structure, the colon after the package name is omitted from class names and method names. For example, in the data structure for an MO of class zzz:Object, label the class element as zzzObject.
- Although the JSON specification allows unordered elements, the APIC REST API requires that the JSON "attributes" element precede the "children" array or other elements.
- If an XML data structure contains no children or subtrees, the object element can be self-closing.
- The API is case sensitive. When sending an API command, with "api" in the URL, the maximum size of the HTML body for the API POST command is 1 MB. When uploading a device package file, with "ppi" in the URL, the maximum size of the HTML body for the POST command is 10 MB.

The ACI RESTful API can be accessed with or without a Cisco specific library. The API supports transmitting raw JSON or XML data using standard tools, for example, Python requests or Google Postman. ACI programmability without the SDK is lightweight and more portable but often requires parsing text and recreating the wheel for common tasks such as authentication.

APIC programmability involves managing and monitoring MOs, classes, and methods. To manage a MO, the distinguished name (position in the MIT) must be discovered. ACI provides a number of tools to discover and understand the DN of an object. Figure 6-12 represents the various options for discovering a MO in ACI.

Figure 6-12 *DN Discovery Tools*

GUI

The HTML APIC GUI leverages APIC RESTful API, and the managed object is contained within the URL. For example, when managing a bridge domain named VLAN10 in the NPaA_Book Tenant the URL is https://10.1.1.1./#bTenants:NPaA_Book|uni/tn-NPaA_Book/BD-vlan10.

Additionally the GUI has a debug mode that displays both the managed object and the class name. Debug mode must be enabled from under admin. Debug data is displayed in a blue bar at the bottom of the page, and looks similar to the following:

```
Current Screen:insieme.stromboli.layout.Tab [fv:infoBD:center:b ] | Current
Mo:insieme.stromboli.model.def.fvBD [uni/tn-NPaA_Book/BD-vlan10 ]
```

APIC Object Save-as

The APIC GUI allows any object and optionally any children of that object to be downloaded in either XML or JSON formatting. To use object save-as right click on any object in the APIC and choose "save-as". This data is useful to understand the DN or configuration parameters of an object. The downloaded data can also be used to POST configurations directly from the GUI. Figure 6-13 demonstrates object save-as in the APIC.

The Data from APIC will be in a single line and is very difficult to read. Consider using a JSON formatting tool, for example, http://www.jsoneditoronline.org/.

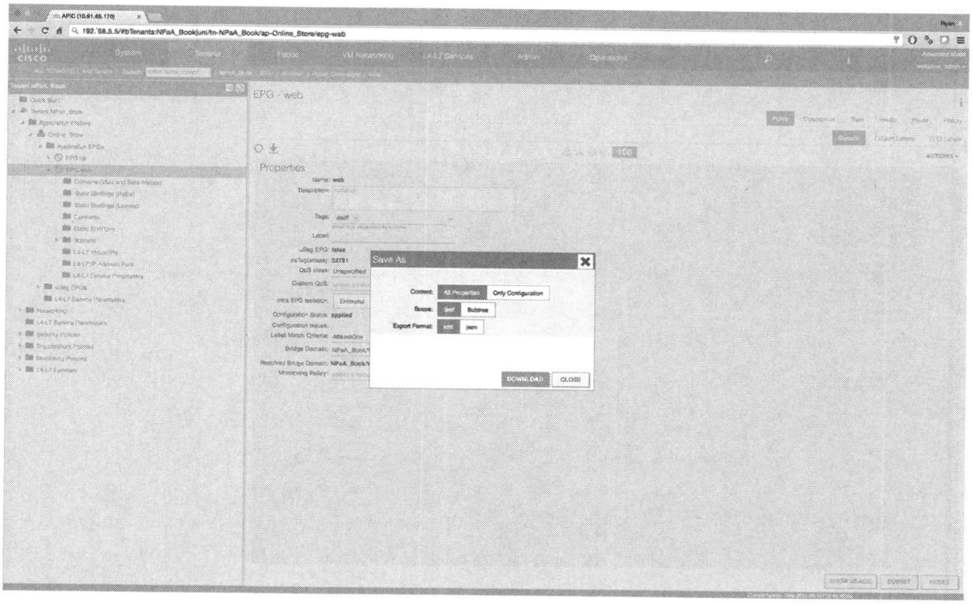

Figure 6-13 *Download JSON Formatted Data from the APIC*

The data in Figure 6-14 displays an EPG object named "web" with a DN as "uni/tn-NPaA_Book/ap-Online_Store/epg-web" This object could be modified, however in this example only the label match criteria is located within the object. The subtree (children) objects associated with the EPG contain more configuration data, such as bridge domain association.

Downloading object data from the APIC displays static information and can be difficult to trace. APIC's API inspector is much easier to use.

APIC API Inspector

Cisco APIC features the API inspector tool. API inspector is a real-time, web-based tool that monitors the connection between the GUI and the REST API. API inspector is very useful to understand exactly what happens with a GUI configuration or object monitoring.

API inspector is launched from the upper right corner of the APIC, under the {Welcome, *login user*}. Figure 6-15 demonstrates launching API inspector.

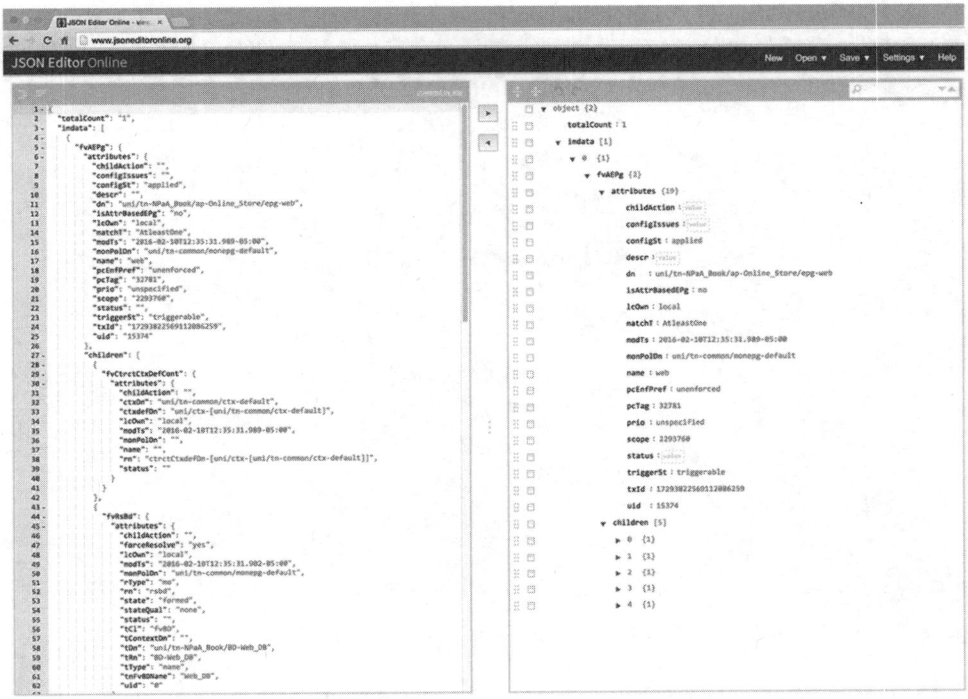

Figure 6-14 *JSON Formatted Data from the APIC*

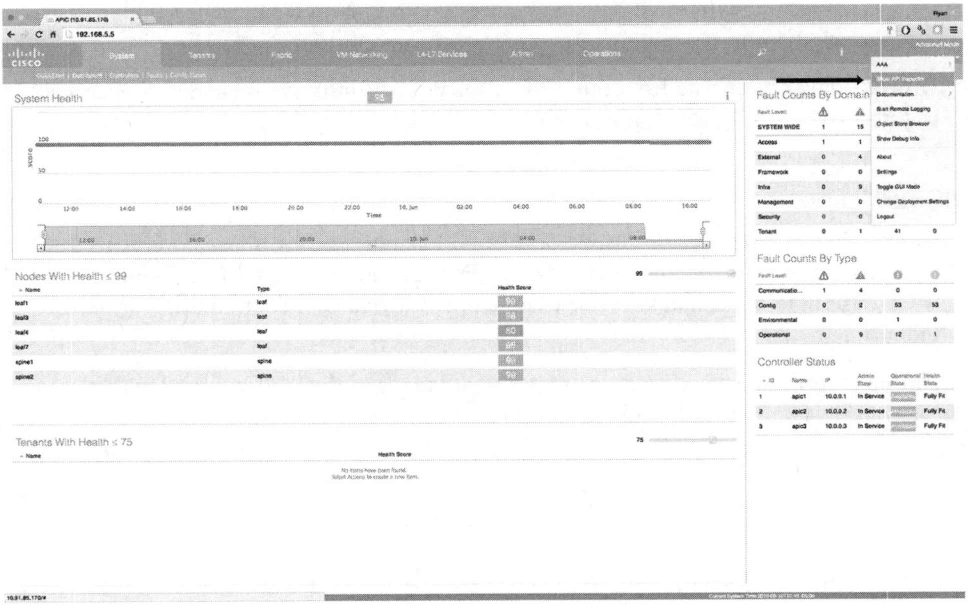

Figure 6-15 *Launch API Inspector*

Most pages in the APIC GUI display dynamic data, such as health scores, which are auto-refreshed from the RESTful API. The API call and the data will fill the API inspector screen within a short time period. Figure 6-16 depicts common API inspector data.

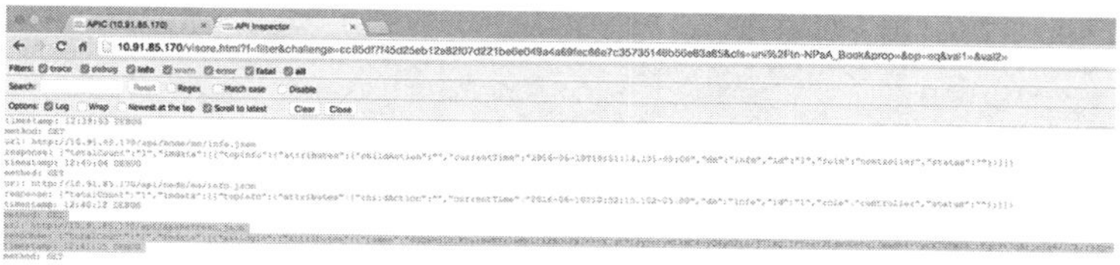

Figure 6-16 *PS070616*

Movement or a query of an object in the GUI will be displayed as a DEBUG message presented in four discrete (sometimes very long) lines. Both the URL data and the response are JSON formatted. Table 6-1 breaks down the data discovered from API inspector.

Table 6-1 *API Inspector Data*

method: GET	HTTP Verb
url: https://10.91.85.170/api/aaaRefresh.json	URL with DN
response:	JSON formatted response
timestamp: 14:48:32 DEBUG	Timestamp and level

Note Unchecking "Scroll to latest" works similar to a pause button.

ACI inspector has both built-in and custom filters to help find specific entries. The built-in filters can specify verbosity levels and by default are set to the most verbose. The custom filter supports a standard text-based search or any regex expression.

The regular expression in Figure 6-17 is "[Hh]ealth" which searches for the word "health" with or without a capital "h."

Figure 6-17 *API Inspector with Regex*

APIC Object Store Browser (Visore)

APIC features a visual object browser, referred to a Visore. Visore is used to understand the DN or class name of managed objects in ACI. Visore is accessed from an APIC controller http://"APIC IP address"/visore.html. Figure 6-18 depicts the Visore browser.

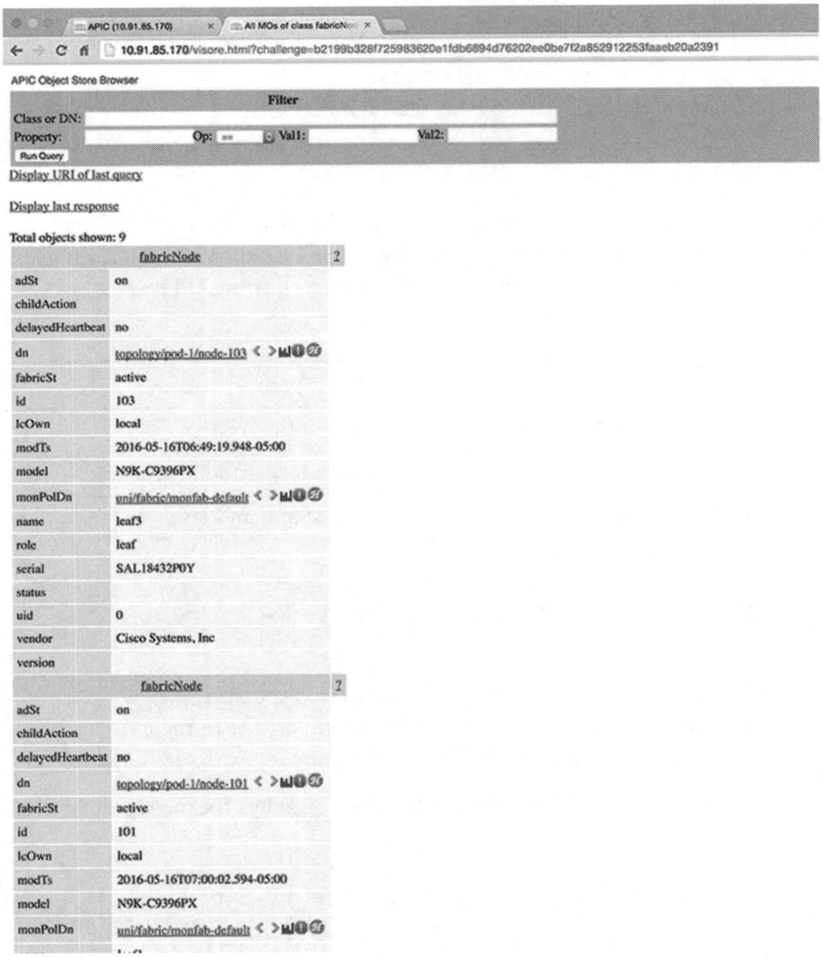

Figure 6-18 *APIC Visore*

The main function of Visore is the filter, which searches for class or DN information. If the DN is understood from API inspector or GUI debug, for example uni/tn-NPaA_Book, the DN can be inputted directly into the search bar. If the DN is not understood, searching for the class, for example, FvTenant will return all tenants configured on the system. Visore returns the properties of the object along with its relationship to other objects. Figure 6-19 depicts Visore output for the NPaA_Book tenant object.

fvBD	?
arpFlood	no
bcastP	225.0.235.192
childAction	
descr	
dn	uni/tn-NPaA_Book/BD-vlan10
epMoveDetectMode	
lcOwn	local
limitIpLearnToSubnets	no
llAddr	::
mac	00:22:BD:F8:19:FF
modTs	2016-02-12T13:44:35.195-05:00
monPolDn	uni/tn-common/monepg-default
mtu	inherit
multiDstPktAct	bd-flood
name	vlan10
ownerKey	
ownerTag	
pcTag	49162
scope	2293760
seg	15794150
status	
uid	15374

Figure 6-19 *APIC Visore data*

When an object or class is displayed in Visore, the complete query for the URI and the XML formatted data can be found by using the “Display URI of last query” and “Display last response” buttons. The URI can be used to create API calls from Python or Postman. Figure 6-20 depicts the output from these options.

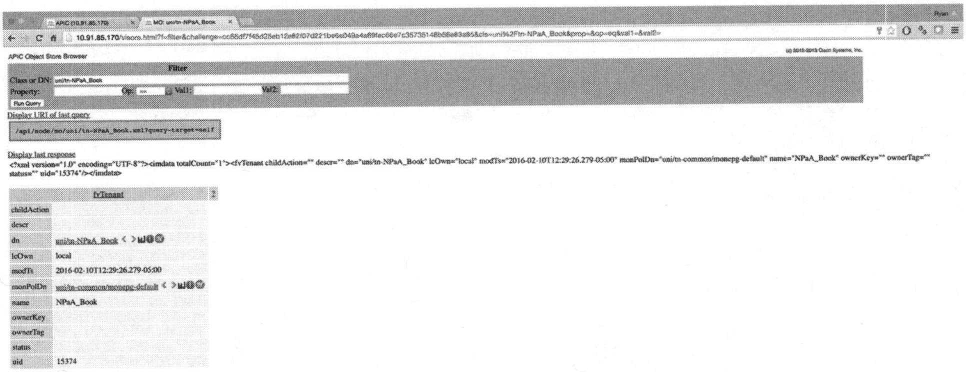

Figure 6-20 *Output of API Call Options*

Visore is useful to understand the data, including stats, faults, and health for an object. The links at the end of the DN line will return any stats, faults, and health (respectively) for an object and the URI for querying the data. The green < > is used as a MIT browser by moving to any parent object (<) or child objects (>). Figure 6-21 depicts the stats, faults, and health options in Visore.

Figure 6-21 *Links at the End of the DN Line*

The “?” located to the right of the object name recalls the on APIC object documentation. The documentation details the class including a diagram of where the object sits in the MIT. Figure 6-22 is very useful in both programmability projects and day-to-day ACI administration.

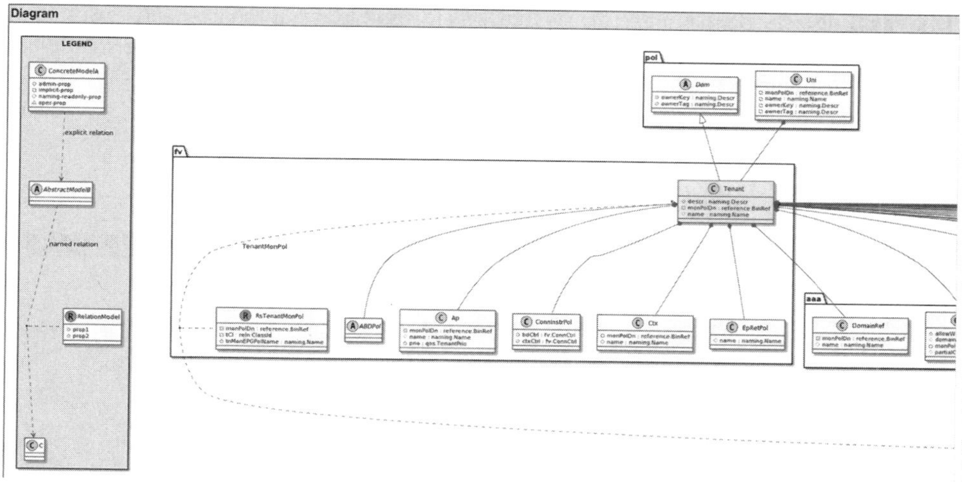

Figure 6-22 *APIC Documentation Object Diagrams*

APIC API Authentication

The APIC API requires username and password authentication. Upon successful authentication, the API returns a data structure that includes a session timeout period in seconds and a token that represents the session. The token is also returned as a cookie in the HTTP response header. To maintain your session, you must send login refresh messages to the API if no other messages are sent for a period longer than the session timeout period. The token changes each time that the session is refreshed.

The default session timeout period is 300 seconds or 5 minutes.

JSON formatted authentication to an APIC requires an APIC login method. The method is accessed with https://(*APIC IP ADDRESS*)/api/aaa{method name}.json.

> **Note** Use .xml for XML formatted methods.

APIC available authentication methods are available for login, logout, and refresh.

- **aaaLogin**—Sent as a POST message, this method logs in a user and opens a session. The message body contains an aaa:User object with the name and password attributes, and the response contains a session token and cookie. If multiple AAA login domains are configured, you must prepend the user's name with apic:domain.

  ```
  {"aaaUser": {"attributes": {"name": "USERNAME", "pwd": "PASSWORD"}}}
  ```

- **aaaRefresh**—Sent as a GET message with no message body or as a POST message with the aaaLogin message body, this method resets the session timer. The response contains a new session token and cookie.

- **aaaLogout—**Sent as a POST message, this method logs out the user and closes the session. The message body contains an aaa:User object with the name attribute. The response contains an empty data structure.

```
{"aaaUser": {"attributes": {"name": "USERNAME", "pwd": "PASSWORD"}}}
```

Figure 6-23 demonstrates successful authentication to the APIC.

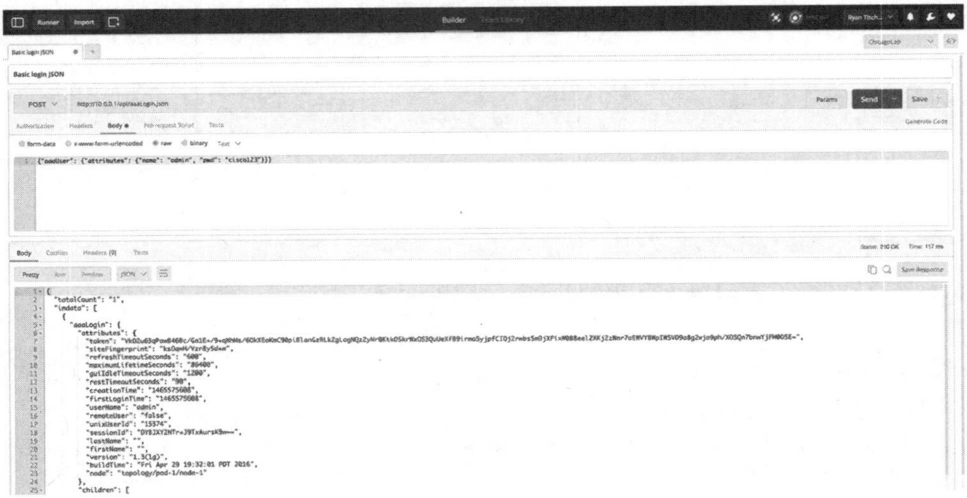

Figure 6-23 *Using Postman to Authenticate to APIC*

Once successfully authenticated, subsequent Postman calls use this session.

Using Python to Authenticate to APIC

The following code logins into the APIC and saves the token in a Python dictionary variable named cookies:

```
#!/usr/bin/python
__author__ = 'Ryan Tischer'

#Contact @ryantischer

import requests
import json
```

```
#set variablesâ
apic = "10.1.1.1"
username= "admin"
password="cisco13579"
#Login into APIC and get a cookie


#build base url
base_url = 'http://' + apic + '/api/aaaLogin.json'
print base_url
# create credentials structure
name_pwd = {"aaaUser": {"attributes": {"name": "username", "pwd":
password"}}}
name_pwd["aaaUser"]["attributes"]["pwd"] = password
name_pwd["aaaUser"]["attributes"]["name"] = username
print name_pwd

# log in to API, get cookie
try:
    post_response = requests.post(base_url, json=name_pwd, timeout = 5)
except requests.exceptions.RequestException as e:
    print "Error with http connection  Your error is around... "
    print e
    sys.exit()

# get token from login response structure
auth = json.loads(post_response.text)
try:
    login_attributes = auth['imdata'][0]['aaaLogin']['attributes']
except:
    print "Authentication error"
    sys.exit()
auth_token = login_attributes['token']

# create cookie array from token
cookies = {}
cookies['APIC-Cookie'] = auth_token
print cookies
```

Output from Example 6-20

http://10.91.85.170/api/aaaLogin.json

```
{'aaaUser': {'attributes': {'pwd': 'cisco13579', 'name': 'admin'}}}
{'APIC-Cookie': u'rVXD99O9AN55IawnVxFsuhj5y65qxDx0Y2xwNky52HqfeRTiDp5mMH6GEbiZAMk
LhdkrV4XU3e2/4P3CSsYTjIPSTOQKbuE343KskorHjG3rq3Rq7ffG+cfkKv2w7RShvfQn0XpleaQmyH/
F8qWH/AO+6WYRQskpkp+5p4HSDHQ='}
```

The data in the cookie variable is the auth_token and used as a requests parameter.

```
requests.post(workingUrl, cookies=cookies, json=workingData)
```

Using Postman to Automate APIC Configurations

Postman can leverage APIC's API to test, manage, and monitor APIC. Postman is ideal for testing the APIC API and understanding a specific URL, formatted payload, or formatted response. It can also be used to drive and automate configurations when more complex Python is not available.

> **Note** Postman supports collections, which are a library of API calls with data. Collections are downloaded directly from the Postman website or as a text file. The author's personal Postman collection is available under the book's GitHub site located at http://github.com/ryantischer
>
> To learn more about Postman collections, see https://www.getpostman.com/docs/collections.

Using Postman

Using Google Postman involves the following:

1. Input URL
2. Configure HTTP verb
3. (Optional) if using a HTTP verb (POST…creating or changing a configuration) configuring formatted data

Figure 6-24 is configured to http POST the URL https://10.1.1.1/api/mo/uni.xml with the XML formatted data as "<fvTenant name="Some_New_Tenant"/>". This creates a new tenant named "Some_New_Tenant" from the class fvTenant.

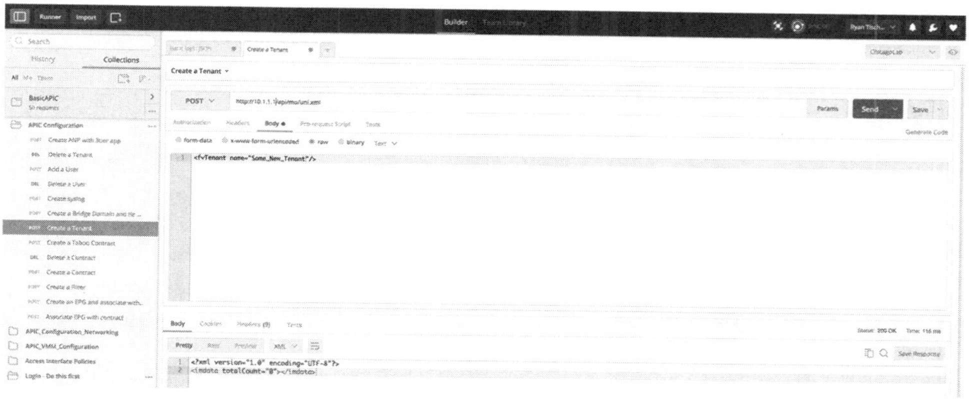

Figure 6-24 *Create a Tenant Using Postman*

Creating New Postman Calls

Any of the DN discovery tools discussed previously can be used to create Postman calls; however, API inspector is by far the easiest. The output of API inspector details the required Postman inputs.

Navigating the system faults page produced the following data in API inspector:

```
method: GET

url: https://10.91.85.170/api/node/class/faultSummary.json?order-by=faultSummary
.severity|desc&page=0&page-size=15
```

The data that details the http verb is GET and the URL to get the data is "https://10.91.85.170/api/node/class/faultSummary.json?order-by=faultSummary .severity|desc&page=0&page-size=15".

This URL asks for the fault summary formatted in JSON and sets query ordering and display parameters. The query ordering and display parameters are optional (remove everything after the term "JSON").

Figure 6-25 depicts using Postman to display a Fault Summary from APIC.

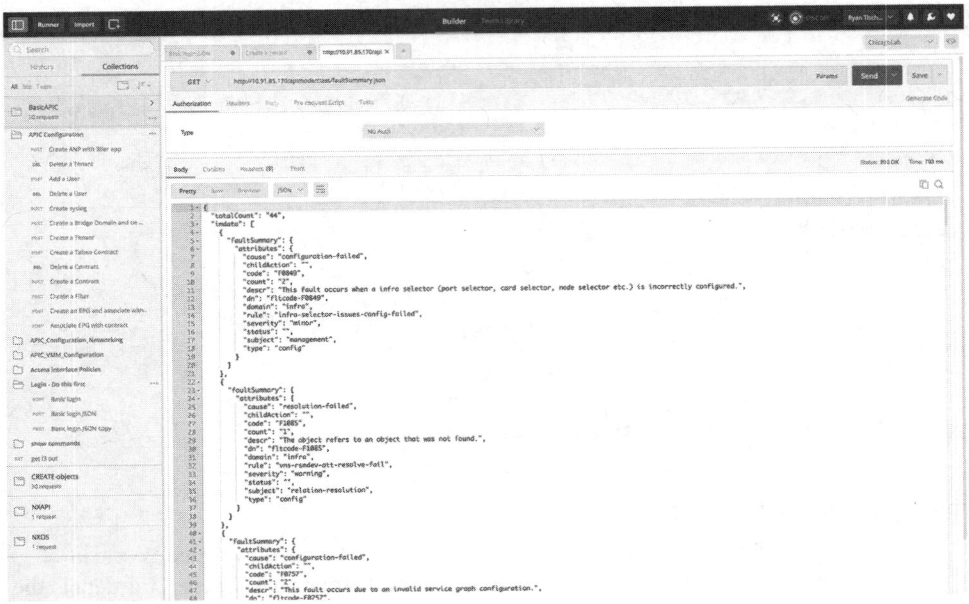

Figure 6-25 *Postman Configuration to Display System Faults*

Postman returns the following (truncated) data:

```
{
  "totalCount": "29",
  "imdata": [
    {
      "faultSummary": {
        "attributes": {
          "cause": "resolution-failed",
          "childAction": "",
          "code": "F1128",
          "count": "1",
          "descr": "The object refers to an object that was not found.",
          "dn": "fltcode-F1128",
          "domain": "infra",
          "rule": "vz-rs-subj-graph-att-resolve-fail",
          "severity": "warning",
          "status": "",
          "subject": "relation-resolution",
          "type": "config"
        }
      }
    },
```

Posting configurations works in much the same way but requires formatting data in the HTTP body. Choose “Body” and “raw” in Postman after http POST is configured.

The following example demonstrates using API inspector to post a configuration via Postman. API inspector produced the following data.

```
method: POST
url: https://10.91.85.170/api/node/mo/uni/tn-NPaA_Book/BD-DB_vlan100.json

payload{"fvBD":{"attributes":{"dn":"uni/tn-NPaA_Book/BD-DB_vlan100","mac":"00:22:
BD:F8:19:FF","name":"DB_vlan100","rn":"BD-DB_vlan100","status":"created"},
"children":[]}}
```

The following example, shown in Figure 6-26, creates a bridge domain named BD_vlan100 from the API inspector data. The payload is JSON formatted data that can be cut and pasted into Postman.

Note Use a JSON formatting tool, for example, http://www.jsoneditoronline.org/ to make the data easier on the eyes.

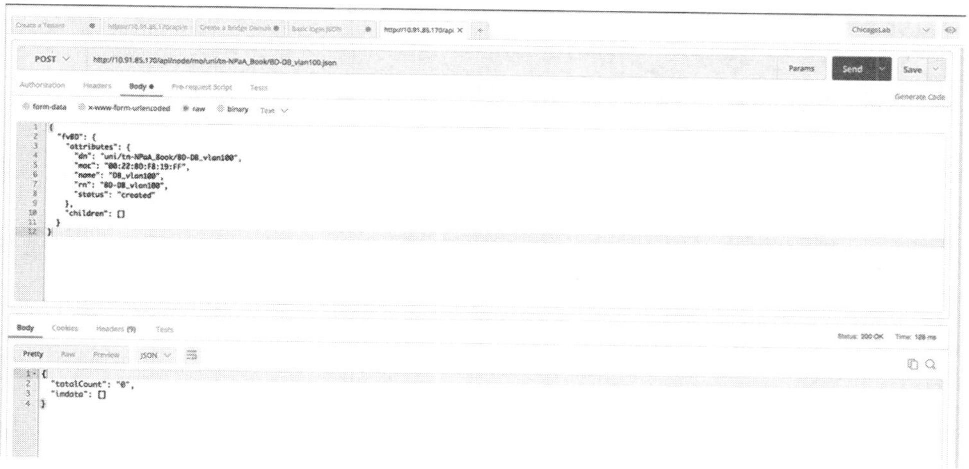

Figure 6-26 *API Inspector Payload in Google Postman*

Programmability Using the APIC RESTful API

Writing software using the RESTful API involves using Python request, JSON and optionally regex to send and receive formatted data. Standard Python string parsing and manipulation is used to build payloads to send to the APIC. The following example creates a bridge domain named vlan1000 in the NPaA_book tenant.

The URL to POST to APIC is https://10.1.1.1/api/node/mo/uni/tn-NPaA_Book/BD-bd_vlan1000.json.

With a payload of ...

```
{
  "fvBD": {
    "attributes": {
      "dn": "uni/tn-NPaA_Book/BD-bd_vlan1000",
      "mac": "00:22:BD:F8:19:FF",
      "name": "bd_vlan1000",
      "rn": "BD-bd_vlan1000",
      "status": "created"
    },
    "children": []
  }
}
```

The payload is JSON data that fits into a Python dictionary.

```
>>> payload={
...    "fvBD": {
...      "attributes": {
...        "dn": "uni/tn-NPaA_Book/BD-bd_vlan1000",
...        "mac": "00:22:BD:F8:19:FF",
...        "name": "bd_vlan1000",
...        "rn": "BD-bd_vlan1000",
...        "status": "created"
...      },
...      "children": []
...    }
... }
>>>

>>> print payload
{'fvBD': {'attributes': {'dn': 'uni/tn-NPaA_Book/BD-bd_vlan1000', 'status':
'created', 'mac': '00:22:BD:F8:19:FF', 'name': 'bd_vlan1000', 'rn':
'BD-bd_vlan1000'}, 'children': []}}
```

Because the Python data is in a dictionary, it can be accessed by a key using [ ] with the key in double quotes.

```
>>> print payload["fvBD"]["attributes"]["dn"]
uni/tn-NPaA_Book/BD-bd_vlan1000
>>>
```

The data can also be changed by key. For example, to change the VLAN to 2000:

```
>>> payload["fvBD"]["attributes"]["dn"] = "uni/tn-NPaA_Book/BD-bd_vlan2000"

>>> print payload["fvBD"]["attributes"]["dn"]
uni/tn-NPaA_Book/BD-bd_vlan2000
>>>
```

In order to change the VLAN, the other attributes will have to be changed including the URL.

The following example leverages APIC RESTful API to assign an interface to an EPG.

```
__author__ = 'ryantischer'
#!/usr/bin/env python
#
# Written by Ryan Tischer @ Cisco


#Script configures a physical port in an EPG for a bare metal server
#Assumes the physical port is configured under fabric \ access policies


#Requires sys, json and requests.
#Requires http enabled on the APIC.  Optionally can configure TLS1.1/1.2 on script
server for https and will require
#changing base_url and workingURL to https


# To enable http on APIC...


#On the menu bar, FABRIC -> Fabric Policies -> Pod Policies -> Policies ->
Communication
#Under Communication, click the default policy
#In the Work pane, enable HTTP and disable HTTPS


#NOTE:  Configuration is atomic, if it fails for whatever reason, the entire
configuration fails.


#usage Can be run by opening this file and directly editing the variables.
Optionally command line arguments can be
#used.  If command line arguments are used the script only checks for correct
number of arguments.  --help prints help
```

```
import json
import requests
import sys

numArg = len(sys.argv)
if numArg == 1:
    #Vars to be filled out.  Can be switched to sys agrv
    apic = "10.1.1.1"
    username = "admin"
    password = "cisco123"
    apicTenant = "skywalker"
    apicANP = "OnlineStore"
    apicEPG = "web"
    apicVlan = "1"
    apicPOD = "pod-1"
    apicSwitch = "101"
    apicPort = "eth1/1"

elif numArg == 2 and sys.argv[numArg-1] == "--help":

    print " usage: python build_port.py apic username password tenant ANP epg vlan
    POD switch port"
    print " example: python build_port.py 10.1.1.1 admin cisco123 tenant1 2Tierapp
    DBservers 1 pod-1 101 eth1/1"
    print " help found with --help"
    print""
    sys.exit() #bail out

elif numArg == 11:
    apic = sys.argv[1]
    username = sys.argv[2]
    password = sys.argv[3]
    apicTenant = sys.argv[4]
    apicANP = sys.argv[5]
    apicEPG = sys.argv[6]
    apicVlan = sys.argv[7]
    apicPOD = sys.argv[8]
    apicSwitch = sys.argv[9]
    apicPort = sys.argv[10]

else:
    print "You did something wrong.  Read below and try again"
    print " usage: build_port.py apicip username password tenant ANP epg vlan POD
    switch port"
    print " example: build_port.py 10.91.85.170 admin cisco123 tenant1 2Tierapp
    DBservers 1 pod-1 101 eth1/1"
    sys.exit() #bail out
```

```
#Login into APIC and get a cookie

#build base url
base_url = 'http://' + apic + '/api/aaaLogin.json'

# create credentials structure
name_pwd = {"aaaUser": {"attributes": {"name": "username", "pwd": "password"}}}
name_pwd["aaaUser"]["attributes"]["pwd"] = password
name_pwd["aaaUser"]["attributes"]["name"] = username


# log in to API, get cookie
try:
    post_response = requests.post(base_url, json=name_pwd, timeout = 5)
except requests.exceptions.RequestException as e:
    print "Error with http connection  Your error is around... "
    print e
    sys.exit()

# get token from login response structure
auth = json.loads(post_response.text)
try:
    login_attributes = auth['imdata'][0]['aaaLogin']['attributes']
except:
    print "Authentication error"
    sys.exit()
auth_token = login_attributes['token']

# create cookie array from token
cookies = {}
cookies['APIC-Cookie'] = auth_token

#once we have the cookie we can make changes

#build dict to send to apic
workingUrl =  "http://" + apic + "/api/node/mo/uni/tn-" + apicTenant + "/ap-" +
apicANP + "/epg-" + apicEPG + ".json"
workingData = {"fvRsPathAtt":{"attributes":{"encap":"vlan-","instrImedcy":
"immediate","tDn":"topology/pod-1/paths-101/pathep-[eth1/1]","status":"created"},
"children":[]}}
workingData["fvRsPathAtt"]["attributes"]["encap"] = "vlan-" + apicVlan
workingData["fvRsPathAtt"]["attributes"]["tDn"] = "topology/" + apicPOD +
"/paths-" + apicSwitch + "/pathep-[" +apicPort + "]"
```

```
#create the static port in egp
try:
    post_response = requests.post(workingUrl, cookies=cookies, json=workingData)
    print "http code = " + str(post_response)
    print "http code 400 will show up if configuration is already present"
    print ""
    print "data send to APIC..."
    print json.dumps(workingData, sort_keys=True, indent=4)
    print ""
    print "URL = " + workingUrl
except requests.exceptions.RequestException as e:
    # This saves the exception in the var e.  This is useful to tell the user what
    happened.
    print "something went wrong with sending json to APIC. Your issue is around"
    print e
    sys.exit()
```

ACI Event Subscription

When an API query is performed, there is an option to create a subscription to any future changes in the results of that query that occur during your active API session. When any MO is created, changed, or deleted because of a user- or system-initiated action, an event is generated. If that event changes the results of an active subscribed query, ACI generates a push notification to the API client that created the subscription.

The API subscription feature uses the WebSocket protocol (RFC 6455) to implement a two-way connection with the API client through which the API can send unsolicited notification messages to the client. To establish this notification channel, you must first open a WebSocket connection with the API object. Only a single WebSocket connection is needed to support multiple query subscriptions with multiple NX-API-REST instances. The WebSocket connection is dependent on an API session connection and closes when the API session ends.

To create a subscription to a query, perform the query with the option **?subscription=yes**. This example creates a subscription to a query of the aaaUser class in the JSON format:

```
GET https://192.0.20.123/api/class/aaaUser.json?subscription=yes
```

The query response contains a subscription identifier, subscriptionId, which one can use to refresh the subscription and to identify future notifications from this subscription.

To continue to receive event notifications, you must periodically refresh each subscription during your API session. To refresh a subscription, send an HTTP GET message to the API method subscriptionRefresh with the parameter id equal to the subscriptionId as in this example:

```
GET https://<IP_Address>/api/subscriptionRefresh.json?id=18374686771712622593
```

The following example program leverages event subscription to monitor a layer 3 out. In the event the managed object changes, the APIC will send data to the program. This program will run until stopped by the user.

```
#Use at your own risk
#Contact @ryantischer

#!/usr/bin/python
__author__ = 'Ryan Tischer'

import requests
import re
import json
import websocket

#login swtich and get authentication cookie (nxapi_auth)
#broken out for clarity
"""
Modify these please
"""
APICuser='admin'
APICpassword='cisco'
APIC='192.168.10.10'

auth_base_url = 'http://' + APIC + '/api/mo/aaaLogin.json'
name_pass={"aaaUser": {"attributes": {"name": APICuser, "pwd": APICpassword}}}
#use requests to post username and password for auth token
auth_response = requests.post(auth_base_url, json=name_pass, timeout = 5)


#format response in json
auth = json.loads(auth_response.text)

  #Get the token
login_attributes = auth['imdata'][0]['aaaLogin']['attributes']
auth_token = login_attributes['token']

  #Create the cookie
cookies = {}
cookies['APIC-Cookie'] = auth_token

#end authentication

websocket.enableTrace(True)
# websocket.enableTrace(True) enables websocket debugging
```

```
#Create the websocket to the nexus
websURL = ("ws://" + APIC + "/socket%s" % (cookies["APIC-Cookie"],))
ws = websocket.WebSocket()
ws.connect(websURL)
# is a string substitution.  The final url is ws://192.168.1.1/socketMchQEw3Kl

response = requests.get("http://" + APIC + "/api/node/mo/uni/tn-Routing_Demo/
out-outer_ospf.json?subscription=yes?query-target=subtree", cookies=cookies)
data = response.json()
print data["subscriptionId"]
#print the subscription ID for use for receiving data and refresh

#listen for updates
while True:
    print ws.recv()


**** end program
```

The output of this application after the description is changed is

```
72057770148560897
{"subscriptionId":["72057770148560897"],"imdata":[{"l3extOut":{"attributes":
{"childAction":"","descr":"Some New description","dn":"uni/tn-Routing_Demo/
out-router_ospf","modTs":"2016-06-03T12:09:21.647-05:00","rn":"","status":
"modified"}}}]}
```

Cobra SDK

The Cisco APIC Python SDK, referred to as Cobra, enables developers and network administrators to write software to interact with APIC. The SDK leverages the RESTful API and due to built-in functionally is easier to use.

Note Documentation for the SDK is located on Cisco DevNet at https://developer.cisco.com/media/apicDcPythonAPI_v0.1/index.html. Documentation on APIC objects is located on the APIC http://{APIC IP}/doc/html/index.html.

Cobra is two installable .egg files. .egg files are a standard method to distribute complex Python packages. The .egg files must be installed in the main Python environment or, as a best practice, in a virtual environment. The .egg files are downloaded directly from the APIC and are specific to the APIC version. For example, the following .egg files are compatible with APIC 1.2_1i.

```
acimodel-1.2_1i-py2.7.egg
acicobra-1.2_1i-py2.7.egg
```

The .egg files are downloaded from

http://{APIC IP}//cobra/_downloads/

Install .egg files with easy_install. Easy_install is an installation tool bundled with setup tools. Setup tools are available for all major operating systems and provided by default on modern Linux and Mac systems. The following example depicts the creation of a new virtualenv named "aci_cobra" and the installation of the cobra SDK.

Note The ACI Cobra .egg must be installed first!

```
bash-3.2$ virtualenv aci_cobra
New python executable in /Users/ryantischer/aci_cobra/bin/python
Installing setuptools, pip, wheel...done.
bash-3.2$ source aci_cobra/bin/activate
(aci_cobra) bash-3.2$ pip freeze
wheel==0.26.0
(aci_cobra) bash-3.2$ easy_install -Z /Users/ryantischer/Downloads/acicobra-
1.2_1i-py2.7.egg
Processing acicobra-1.2_1i-py2.7.egg
creating /Users/ryantischer/aci_cobra/lib/python2.7/site-packages/acicobra-1.2_
1i-py2.7.egg
Extracting acicobra-1.2_1i-py2.7.egg to /Users/ryantischer/aci_cobra/lib/
python2.7/site-packages
Adding acicobra 1.2-1i to easy-install.pth file

Installed /Users/ryantischer/aci_cobra/lib/python2.7/site-packages/acicobra-
1.2_1i-py2.7.egg
Processing dependencies for acicobra===1.2-1i
Searching for requests
Reading https://pypi.python.org/simple/requests/
Best match: requests 2.9.1
Downloading https://pypi.python.org/packages/source/r/requests/requests-2.9.1.tar
.gz#md5=0b7f480d19012ec52bab78292efd976d
Processing requests-2.9.1.tar.gz
Writing /var/folders/vy/wvsxv52j03qfcjktm1w4yy2m0000gn/T/easy_install-JDzghM/
requests-2.9.1/setup.cfg
Running requests-2.9.1/setup.py -q bdist_egg --dist-dir /var/folders/vy/wvsxv52j03
qfcjktm1w4yy2m0000gn/T/easy_install-JDzghM/requests-2.9.1/egg-dist-tmp-ZLNwEb
creating /Users/ryantischer/aci_cobra/lib/python2.7/site-packages/requests-2.9.1-
py2.7.egg
Extracting requests-2.9.1-py2.7.egg to /Users/ryantischer/aci_cobra/lib/python2.7/
site-packages
Adding requests 2.9.1 to easy-install.pth file

Installed /Users/ryantischer/aci_cobra/lib/python2.7/site-packages/requests-2.9.
1-py2.7.egg
```

```
Finished processing dependencies for acicobra===1.2-1i
(aci_cobra) bash-3.2$ easy_install -Z /Users/ryantischer/Downloads/acimodel-
1.2_1i-py2.7.egg
Processing acimodel-1.2_1i-py2.7.egg
creating /Users/ryantischer/aci_cobra/lib/python2.7/site-packages/acimodel-1.2_1i-
py2.7.egg
Extracting acimodel-1.2_1i-py2.7.egg to /Users/ryantischer/aci_cobra/lib/
python2.7/site-packages
Adding acimodel 1.2-1i to easy-install.pth file

Installed /Users/ryantischer/aci_cobra/lib/python2.7/site-packages/acimodel-
1.2_1i-py2.7.egg
Processing dependencies for acimodel===1.2-1i
Finished processing dependencies for acimodel===1.2-1i
(aci_cobra) bash-3.2$ pip freeze
acicobra===1.2-1i
acimodel===1.2-1i
requests==2.9.1
wheel==0.26.0
(aci_cobra) bash-3.2$
```

The Cobra .egg files require Python requests and automatically resolve the dependency.

ACI Cobra SDK contains a series of modules to work with ACI. Modules cover most tasks including authentication and direct object manipulation. Table 6-2 details the various modules available in the Cobra SDK.

Table 6-2 *Cobra SDK Modules*

Naming Module	Create and parse object names. Collect information about the object. Uses RN or DN.
Session Module	Authentication to the APIC
Request Module	The request module handles configuration and queries to the APIC including: Create, delete, or update a managed object (MO) Call a method within an MO Run a query on a MO
Services Module	Create and manage L4-L7 services
Access Module	Manage network endpoints
Managed Object (MO) Module	Work directly with MOs

Using APIC Cobra

The first step is to import the required libraries. If possible, best practice dictates that only the required libraries are imported into Python. This uses the Python code of from X import Y, as seen in the previous example **from cobra.mit.access import MoDirectory**.

This imports the specific module for MoDirectory and allows reference without its fully-qualified name. MoDirectory can then be directly accessed, for example, moDir = MoDirectory(loginSession).

Alternatively, the entire library can be imported with:

```
import cobra.mit.access
import cobra.mit.request
import cobra.mit.session
import cobra.model.fv
```

However, the library must be specifically referenced by its fully-qualified name, for example:

```
fvTenant = cobra.model.fv.Tenant(polUni, 'NPaA_Book')
```

The SDK includes two libraries, cobra.mit and cobra.model (MIT and MODEL). MIT contains methods to work with the APIC, while MODEL is a direct reference to the MIT. Model is used to directly build, create, or modify ACI objects. The two libraries work together. For example, MODEL builds the object, and a MIT method instantiates it.

Similar to direct accessing the RESTful API, the authentication to the APIC is required. Authentication with Cobra is considerably easier, as shown in the following example.

```
#!/usr/bin/python

import requests

from cobra.mit.access import MoDirectory
from cobra.mit.session import LoginSession

#Contact @ryantischer

apicUrl = 'http://10.1.1.1'
loginSession = LoginSession(apicUrl, 'admin', 'cisco')
moDir = MoDirectory(loginSession)
moDir.login()

# Use the connected moDir queries and configuration...
moDir.logout()
```

The line "loginSession = LoginSession(apicUrl, 'admin', 'cisco')" stores authentication information. The authentication information is referenced in the next line by the variable loginSession. The final line completes the login.

Working with Objects

Building software using Cobra involves creating, monitoring, or manipulating ACI objects. Use cobra.model.*class.object* to directly configure an object. Child objects must be referenced by their parent. For example, to create a tenant, the universe object (uni) must be referenced.

```
import cobra.model.fv
import cobra.model.pol

polUni = cobra.model.pol.Uni('')
fvTenant = cobra.model.fv.Tenant(polUni, 'NPaA_Book')
```

The Python variable "fvTenant" builds a tenant object 'NPaA_Book' under the universe (uni). The variable polUni references the parent object Uni and is referenced in fvTenant. The DN of object is uni/tn-NPaA_Book.

Any child objects under the tenant are unique and required a reference to the parent object. For example, to create a bridge domain under the tenant NPaA_Book would require:

```
fvBD = cobra.model.fv.BD(fvTenant, mac=u'00:22:BD:F8:19:FF', name=u'vlan1500')
```

This string is added to the tTenant configuration object.

Object creation from the models must be committed using cobra.mit.request. ConfigRequest(). Configuration commits are atomic (all-or-nothing) and use a single http POST:

```
import cobra.mit.request
c = cobra.mit.request.ConfigRequest() #create a variable "c"
c.addMo(fvTenant)
md.commit(c)
```

To create a managed object or configurations to existing objects, for example a tenant, objects can be "looked up" or queried. Objects can be queried by DN or class. Class queries support filters to find specific object information. Object query uses methods called "lookupByDN" or "lookupByClass" from MoDirectory found in cobra.mit.access and moDir = MoDirectory(loginSession)) as shown in the following example:

```
from cobra.mit.access import MoDirectory
moDir = MoDirectory(loginSession)

uniMo = moDir.lookupByDn('uni/tn-NPaA_Book')
print uniMo
Returns...

<cobra.modelimpl.pol.uni.Uni object at 0x102365690>
```

The output returns a reference to the managed object. This reference can then be used to create or modify the object or object underneath it.

Lookups by class return an array of objects of the class type. The following example leverages lookupByClass to query all tenants on an APIC.

```
from cobra.mit.access import MoDirectory
moDir = MoDirectory(loginSession)


uniMo = moDir.lookupByClass('fv.Tenant')
print uniMo
Returns…
[<cobra.modelimpl.fv.tenant.Tenant object at 0x10ad88190>, <cobra.modelimpl.
fv.tenant.Tenant object at 0x10ad88290>, <cobra.modelimpl.fv.tenant.Tenant object
at 0x10ad88390>, <cobra.modelimpl.fv.tenant.Tenant object at 0x10ad88490>,
```

Filters on the lookupByClass method narrow down the results to specific objects. The following code leverages lookupByClass with a filter name of "NPaA_Book."

```
uniMo = moDir.lookupByClass('fv.Tenant', propFilter='eq(fvTenant.name,
"NPaA_Book")')
print uniMo
Returns…
[<cobra.modelimpl.fv.tenant.Tenant object at 0x10f33a5d0>]
```

The variable uniMO can now be leveraged to create a child object under the tenant object, for example fvBD = cobra.model.fv.BD(uniMo). The following code creates a bridge domain named vlan10. The code uses lookupByDN to find the parent object (tenant).

```
#import required libraries
import cobra.mit
from cobra.mit.access import MoDirectory
from cobra.mit.session import LoginSession
import cobra.mit.request
from cobra.model.fv import BD

#authenticate to the APIC
apicUrl = 'http://10.91.85.170'
loginSession = LoginSession(apicUrl, 'admin', 'cisco13579')
moDir = MoDirectory(loginSession)
moDir.login()

#Do the lookup
uniMo = moDir.lookupByDn('uni/tn-NPaP_Book')
```

```
#Create a local object
fvTenantMo = BD(uniMo, 'vlan10')

#commit the local object to the APIC
commit = cobra.mit.request.ConfigRequest()
commit.addMo(fvTenantMo)
moDir.commit(commit)
```

Querying an object connects to the APIC are returns data on that object. In some cases, querying can be avoided and the object can be created locally with cobra.model.x. Both a query and local insanitation build the same object. However, local is faster and will use fewer resources.

Example Cobra SDK—Creating a Complete Tenant Configuration

The following example is from Cisco Devnet located at https://developer.cisco.com/media/apicDcPythonAPI_v0.1/api-examples/index.html. This code uses Cobra to build an ACI tenant complete with bridge domains and EPGs.

```
!/usr/bin/env python


# Import access classes
from cobra.mit.access import MoDirectory
from cobra.mit.session import LoginSession
from cobra.mit.request import ConfigRequest

# Import model classes
from cobra.model.fvns import VlanInstP, EncapBlk
from cobra.model.infra import RsVlanNs
from cobra.model.fv import Tenant, Ctx, BD, RsCtx, Ap, AEPg, RsBd, RsDomAtt
from cobra.model.vmm import DomP, UsrAccP, CtrlrP, RsAcc


# Policy information
VMM_DOMAIN_INFO = {'name': "mininet",
                   'ctrlrs': [{'name': 'vcenter1', 'ip': '192.0.20.3',
                               'scope': 'vm'}],
                   'usrs': [{'name': 'admin', 'usr': 'administrator',
                             'pwd': 'pa$$word1'}],
                   'namespace': {'name': 'VlanRange', 'from': 'vlan-100',
                                 'to': 'vlan-200'}
                  }

TENANT_INFO = [{'name': 'ExampleCorp',
                'pvn': 'pvn1',
```

```
                'bd': 'bd1',
                'ap': [{'name': 'OnlineStore',
                        'epgs': [{'name': 'app'},
                                 {'name': 'web'},
                                 {'name': 'db'},
                                ]
                       },
                      ]
               }
              ]

def main(host, port, user, password):

    # CONNECT TO APIC
    print('Initializing connection to APIC...')
    apicUrl = 'http://%s:%d' % (host, port)
    moDir = MoDirectory(LoginSession(apicUrl, user, password))
    moDir.login()

    # Get the top level Policy Universe Directory
    uniMo = moDir.lookupByDn('uni')
    uniInfraMo = moDir.lookupByDn('uni/infra')

    # Create Vlan Namespace
    nsInfo = VMM_DOMAIN_INFO['namespace']
    print "Creating namespace %s.." % (nsInfo['name'])
    fvnsVlanInstPMo = VlanInstP(uniInfraMo, nsInfo['name'], 'dynamic')
    #fvnsArgs = {'from': nsInfo['from'], 'to': nsInfo['to']}
    EncapBlk(fvnsVlanInstPMo, nsInfo['from'], nsInfo['to'], name=nsInfo['name'])

    nsCfg = ConfigRequest()
    nsCfg.addMo(fvnsVlanInstPMo)
    moDir.commit(nsCfg)

    # Create VMM Domain
    print('Creating VMM domain...')

    vmmpVMwareProvPMo = moDir.lookupByDn('uni/vmmp-VMware')
    vmmDomPMo = DomP(vmmpVMwareProvPMo, VMM_DOMAIN_INFO['name'])

    vmmUsrMo = []
    for usrp in VMM_DOMAIN_INFO['usrs']:
        usrMo = UsrAccP(vmmDomPMo, usrp['name'], usr=usrp['usr'],
                        pwd=usrp['pwd'])
        vmmUsrMo.append(usrMo)
```

```
    # Create Controllers under domain
    for ctrlr in VMM_DOMAIN_INFO['ctrlrs']:
        vmmCtrlrMo = CtrlrP(vmmDomPMo, ctrlr['name'], scope=ctrlr['scope'],
                            hostOrIp=ctrlr['ip'])
        # Associate Ctrlr to UserP
        RsAcc(vmmCtrlrMo, tDn=vmmUsrMo[0].dn)

    # Associate Domain to Namespace
    RsVlanNs(vmmDomPMo, tDn=fvnsVlanInstPMo.dn)

    vmmCfg = ConfigRequest()
    vmmCfg.addMo(vmmDomPMo)
    moDir.commit(vmmCfg)
    print "VMM Domain Creation Completed."

    print "Starting Tenant Creation.."
    for tenant in TENANT_INFO:
        print "Creating tenant %s.." % (tenant['name'])
        fvTenantMo = Tenant(uniMo, tenant['name'])

        # Create Private Network
        Ctx(fvTenantMo, tenant['pvn'])

        # Create Bridge Domain
        fvBDMo = BD(fvTenantMo, name=tenant['bd'])

        # Create association to private network
        RsCtx(fvBDMo, tnFvCtxName=tenant['pvn'])

        # Create Application Profile
        for app in tenant['ap']:
            print 'Creating Application Profile: %s' % app['name']
            fvApMo = Ap(fvTenantMo, app['name'])

            # Create EPGs
            for epg in app['epgs']:

                print "Creating EPG: %s..." % (epg['name'])
                fvAEPgMo = AEPg(fvApMo, epg['name'])

                # Associate EPG to Bridge Domain
                RsBd(fvAEPgMo, tnFvBDName=tenant['bd'])
                # Associate EPG to VMM Domain
                RsDomAtt(fvAEPgMo, vmmDomPMo.dn)
```

```
        # Commit each tenant seperately
        tenantCfg = ConfigRequest()
        tenantCfg.addMo(fvTenantMo)
        moDir.commit(tenantCfg)
    print('All done!')

if __name__ == '__main__':
    from argparse import ArgumentParser
    parser = ArgumentParser("Tenant creation script")
    parser.add_argument('-d', '--host', help='APIC host name or IP',
                        required=True)
    parser.add_argument('-e', '--port', help='server port', type=int,
                        default=80)
    parser.add_argument('-p', '--password', help='user password',
                        required=True)
    parser.add_argument('-u', '--user', help='user name', required=True)
    args = parser.parse_args()

    main(args.host, args.port, args.user, args.password)
```

APIC REST Python Adapter (Arya)

APIC REST Python Adapter is a tool to convert APIC objects directly into Cobra-based Python code. It is open source and supports either XML or JSON. Arya is often a first step in using Cobra because it does not validate the output. It will, however, will require reworking the code before deployment. Arya can be used in "file mode" where JSON and XML files are passed to Arya or in a real-time mode using AryaLogger that starts a simple server on a Mac or Linux machine and uses APIC remote logging.

Arya and AryaLogger are available from Cisco's datacenter GitHub site at, https://github.com/datacenter/arya, or via a simple PIP install.

The preferred method to install AryaLogger is via PIP, which is shown in the following example.

```
bash-3.2$ virtualenv aci_Arya
New python executable in /Users/ryantischer/aci_Arya/bin/python
Installing setuptools, pip, wheel...done.

bash-3.2$ source aci_Arya/bin/activate

Arya requires the Cobra .egg files.
Arya
bash-3.2$ easy_install -Z /Users/ryantischer/Downloads/acicobra-1.2_1i-py2.7.egg
bash-3.2$ easy_install -Z /Users/ryantischer/Downloads/acimodel-1.2_1i-py2.7.egg
```

Now install AryaLogger. The pip install will also install Arya and SimpleAciUiLogServer.

```
(aci_Arya) bash-3.2$ pip install AryaLogger
Collecting AryaLogger
Collecting SimpleAciUiLogServer>=1.1.3 (from AryaLogger)
  Using cached SimpleAciUiLogServer-1.1.3-py2.py3-none-any.whl
Collecting arya>=1.1.4 (from AryaLogger)
  Using cached arya-1.1.5-py2-none-any.whl
Requirement already satisfied (use --upgrade to upgrade): acicobra in ./aci_Arya/
lib/python2.7/site-packages/acicobra-1.2_1i-py2.7.egg (from AryaLogger)
Requirement already satisfied (use --upgrade to upgrade): setuptools in ./aci_
Arya/lib/python2.7/site-packages (from acicobra->AryaLogger)
Requirement already satisfied (use --upgrade to upgrade): requests in ./aci_Arya/
lib/python2.7/site-packages/requests-2.9.1-py2.7.egg (from acicobra->AryaLogger)
Installing collected packages: SimpleAciUiLogServer, arya, AryaLogger
Successfully installed AryaLogger-1.1.7 SimpleAciUiLogServer-1.1.3 arya-1.1.5
(aci_Arya) bash-3.2$
```

Arya can be installed standalone for "file-mode":

```
bash-3.2$ pip install arya
Downloading/unpacking arya
  Downloading arya-1.1.5-py2-none-any.whl
Installing collected packages: arya
Successfully installed arya
Cleaning up...
bash-3.2$
```

Using AryaLogger

AryaLogger starts a simple server and accepts APIC remote logging commands. APIC will require access to ports 8987 or 8443 (secure) and any local firewalls may require configuration. AryaLogger communication encryption must match APIC GUI encryption. For example, if HTTP is enabled and leveraged on the APIC GUI, Arya must use HTTP.

When AryaLogger starts, it will display the server address that must be configured on the APIC, as demonstrated below.

serving at:

http://10.9.68.106:8987/apiinspector

https://10.9.68.106:8443/apiinspector

This address must be configured as a remote logging source. This setting is located under the "Welcome, {username} tab. Figure 6-27 depicts APIC configuration to use ARYA.

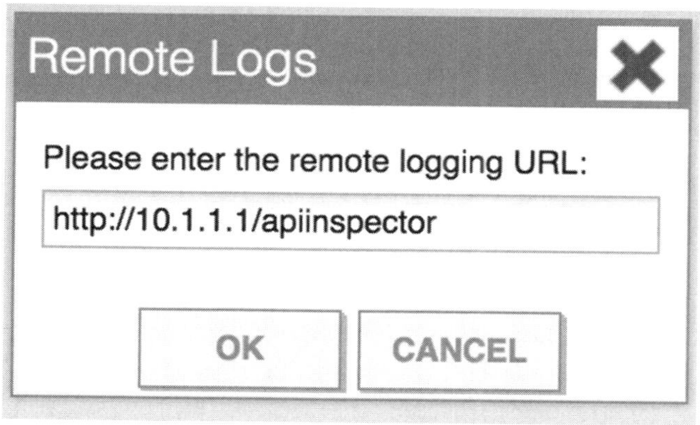

Figure 6-27 *Configure Remote Logging to AryaLogger*

Once configured, navigating through the APIC GUI will generate Cobra-enabled Python code, the correct URL, and the JSON payload.

```
POST URL: http://10.1.1.1/api/node/mo/uni/tn-NPaA_Book/BD-vlan1500.json
POST Payload:

{"fvBD":{"attributes":{"dn":"uni/tn-NPaA_Book/BD-vlan1500","mac":"00:22:BD:F8:19:
FF","name":"vlan1500","rn":"BD-vlan1500","status":"created"},"children":[]}}

SDK:

    polUni = cobra.model.pol.Uni('')
    fvTenant = cobra.model.fv.Tenant(polUni, 'NPaA_Book')
    fvBD = cobra.model.fv.BD(fvTenant, mac=u'00:22:BD:F8:19:FF', name=u'vlan1500')

    c = cobra.mit.request.ConfigRequest()
    c.addMo(fvTenant)
    md.commit(c)
```

This code can be cut and pasted into a working Python script.

Alternately, the "file-mode" of Arya will generate a complete Python script. The XML file is generated from APIC GUI using "save-as":

```
(aci_ayra) bash-3.2$ arya -f /Downloads/BD-vlan1500.xml

#!/usr/bin/env python
'''
Autogenerated code using arya
```

```
Original Object Document Input:
<?xml version="1.0" encoding="UTF-8"?><imdata totalCount="1"><fvBD arpFlood="no"
bcastP="225.0.173.160" childAction="" descr="" dn="uni/tn-NPaA_Book/BD-vlan1500"
epMoveDetectMode="" lcOwn="local" limitIpLearnToSubnets="no" llAddr="::"
mac="00:22:BD:F8:19:FF" modTs="2016-02-16T07:49:31.809-06:00" monPolDn="uni/
tn-common/monepg-default" mtu="inherit" multiDstPktAct="bd-flood" name="vlan1500"
ownerKey="" ownerTag="" pcTag="32782" scope="2293760" seg="16383905" status=""
uid="15374" unicastRoute="yes" unkMacUcastAct="proxy" unkMcastAct="flood"
vmac="not-applicable"/></imdata>
'''
raise RuntimeError('Please review the auto generated code before ' +
                    'executing the output. Some placeholders will ' +
                    'need to be changed')

# list of packages that should be imported for this code to work
import cobra.mit.access
import cobra.mit.request
import cobra.mit.session
import cobra.model.fv
import cobra.model.pol
from cobra.internal.codec.xmlcodec import toXMLStr

# log into an APIC and create a directory object
ls = cobra.mit.session.LoginSession('https://1.1.1.1', 'admin', 'password')
md = cobra.mit.access.MoDirectory(ls)
md.login()

# the top level object on which operations will be made
polUni = cobra.model.pol.Uni('')
fvTenant = cobra.model.fv.Tenant(polUni, 'NPaA_Book')

# build the request using cobra syntax
fvBD = cobra.model.fv.BD(fvTenant, multiDstPktAct='bd-flood', seg='16383905',
unicastRoute='yes', unkMcastAct='flood', descr='', llAddr='::', vmac='not-
applicable', bcastP='225.0.173.160', mac='00:22:BD:F8:19:FF', epMoveDetectMode='',
ownerTag='', ownerKey='', name='vlan1500', unkMacUcastAct='proxy', arpFlood='no',
limitIpLearnToSubnets='no', mtu='inherit', pcTag='32782')



# commit the generated code to APIC
print toXMLStr(fvTenant)
c = cobra.mit.request.ConfigRequest()
c.addMo(fvTenant)
md.commit(c)

(aci_ayra) bash-3.2$
```

The line "ls = cobra.mit.session.LoginSession("https://1.1.1.1", "admin", "password")" will have to be changed to reflect the actual URL, username, and password of the APIC.

In some cases, the XML code that comes from Arya is too verbose and contains information that the ACI/DME will not accept. Some tags will have to be removed. The error will show up after the request commit. In this case, the following XML made the previous example work:

```
fvBD = cobra.model.fv.BD(fvTenant, multiDstPktAct='bd-flood',
unicastRoute='yes', unkMcastAct='flood', descr='', llAddr='::', vmac='not-
applicable', mac='00:22:BD:F8:19:FF', epMoveDetectMode='', ownerTag='',
ownerKey='', name='vlan1500', unkMacUcastAct='proxy', arpFlood='no',
limitIpLearnToSubnets='no')
```

Note Check out WebArya, which is a simple web-enabled Arya server. Webarya is located at https://github.com/datacenter/webarya.

APIC Automation with UCS Director

UCS Director (UCS-D) is a data center automation tool for Cisco UCS, multivendor storage, and ACI network configurations. It is a key component of Cloud operational models because it provides a layer of abstraction between the hardware and an orchestration tool. UCS-D simplifies integration into the orchestration layer by masking the complexity of the infrastructure (firmware, interfaces status, etc.). This avoids teaching the orchestrator about the infrastructure, which greatly decreases the effort involved in scripting workflows.

UCS Director ships with over 150 tasks to drive common ACI configurations. Tasks include common configurations for example managing tenants, EPGs, and contracts. Tasks are connected together to form custom workflows that automate complete application deployments that include network, storage, and server resources. UCS-D workflows are built in an intuitive drag-and-drop interface, referred to the workflow designer, and are the easiest way to programmatically manage ACI. Figure 6-28 portrays a sample UCS Director workflow.

UCS-D workflows are presented in self-service catalogs. UCS-D self-service catalogs automate network, server, and storage for fast and consistent application delivery.

Self-service catalogs are the most important component of a Cloud operational model. They provide the user interface to create and manage technology services but do so in business language. Self-service catalogs can offer simple services, for example, infrastructure as a service or platform as a service, or extend into IT as a service, offering everything from mobile phones HR services.

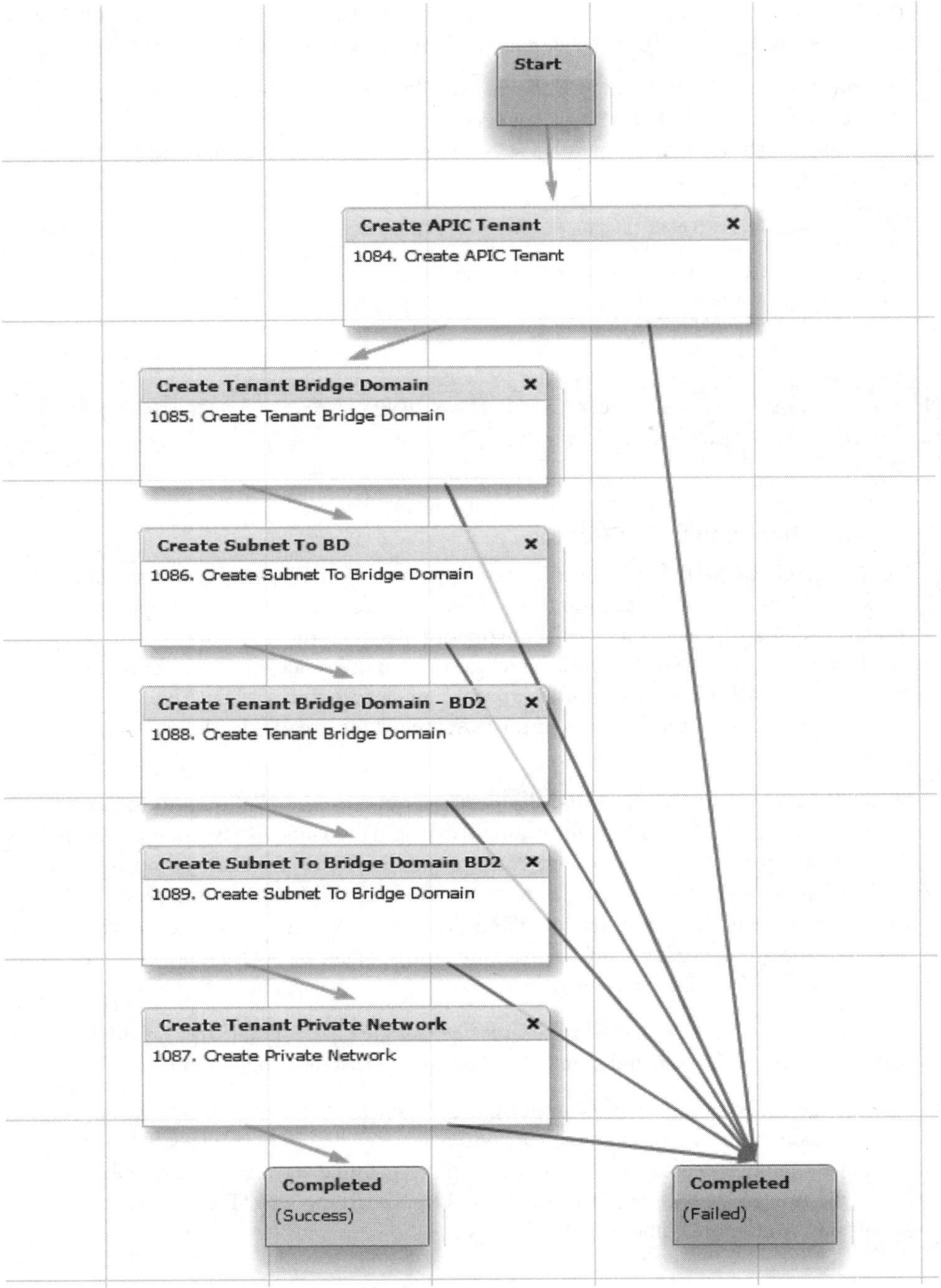

Figure 6-28 *Custom APIC Workflow*

Note The self-service catalog featured in UCS-D is focused on providing infrastructure as a service (IaaS) and is meant to be consumed by IT professionals. Cisco's Prime Service Catalog is a full-featured self-service catalog, offering information technology as a service (ITaaS). ITaaS encompasses all things technology related, including applications, phones, and other services.

Summary

Cisco ACI is a next-generation, software-defined, data center network solution that, via open interfaces, can drive network programmability and automation. ACI out-of-the-box automation quickly deploys a scalable and resilient VXLAN-based fabric. Programmability, via the APIC controller, enables network, application, or DevOps engineers to quickly and consistently provision or modify the network to meet the needs of an ever-changing application landscape. ACI programmability is open, allowing anyone to utilize the network and easy to use with the RESTful API or Cobra SDK. The API on the APIC allows integration to Cloud automation or orchestration tools enabling the network to enhance application delivery.

Chapter 7

On-Box Automation and Operations Tools

Automation for daily tasks is something that most network engineers rely on to handle their daily workload. However, there are many network engineers under the impression that new software or management tools with a steep learning curve must be purchased in order to accomplish such automation. This leads to automation tools often times getting overlooked or put aside. Other common drivers for not using automation tools are due to budget restraints, varying skill sets, and unfamiliarity with the different tools that are available. The good news is that there are many automation tools natively available on most Cisco IOS platforms. For instance, on most Cisco Catalyst switches, there are tools built into the operating system's command line interface (CLI) that allow the programmability of these devices automatically. This allows for the automation of large number of common tasks. For example, a network engineer could build a set of custom templates or macros that would apply various configuration parameters to particular ports on a switch, based on the types of devices that are connected to those specific ports. This chapter will cover the following on-box automation tools in greater detail:

- Auto SmartPorts
- AutoConf
- Auto Security
- AutoQoS
- Smart Call Home
- Tcl Shell
- Embedded Event Manager (EEM)

Note For brevity, all configuration examples and outputs in this chapter are displayed in IOS only. IOS XE and IOS XR outputs are not included in this chapter.

Automated Port Profiling

These types of automation tools are especially important when it comes to scale. Imagine a network team that handles an entire enterprise campus LAN. Commonly, there are only a select few network engineers who have access to the network switches and are authorized to make any configuration changes. These engineers are usually very busy and have a finite amount of time to work on daily moves, additions, and changes (MACs). From a business perspective, this greatly hinders the capability of being able to fluidly and dynamically move users around an office environment. For example, a user moves from one department to another and takes their IP phone with them. This would result in a network engineer having to get involved and reprogram the switch port that the user is going to be connecting to. Often, these users are moved by a help desk team without notifying the network engineering team of the move. If the new port wasn't properly provisioned prior to the user moving, then the user may not be able to connect to the network and perform their job.

There are many settings that need to be applied to a switch port in order for an IP phone to operate properly. Some of the more common switch port settings for an IP phone are:

- Power over Ethernet (PoE) settings
- Voice VLAN configuration
- Quality of Service (QoS) settings
- Data VLAN configuration
- Speed/Duplex settings

The following sections of this chapter will cover some of the simple, yet powerful tools that are included within most of the Cisco Catalyst switches. These are tools, available today, that can automate many configuration tasks, reduce downtime, and increase agility.

AutoSmart Ports

AutoSmart Ports (ASP) are an IOS tool that allows you to consolidate many of the necessary port settings for various device types into an automated process that can be applied to a single port or a series of ports. AutoSmart ports use a macro-based mechanism that commonly uses CDP and LLDP to discover the physical device type that is connected to a switch port. Once the device type is determined, the switch will then check to see if a corresponding macro is defined that matches the specific device type that was connected. If the device type is known and there is a macro definition for it, the switch will then automatically provision the port, based on the settings defined in the macro. This will significantly reduce the amount of time needed to establish connectivity to users who move around the environment or for new users who are being brought on board for the first time. Figure 7-1 outlines the process for what happens when a Cisco IP phone device is connected to a Catalyst switch while AutoSmart Ports are enabled.

Note AutoSmart Ports are available in IOS 12.2(55)SE or later.

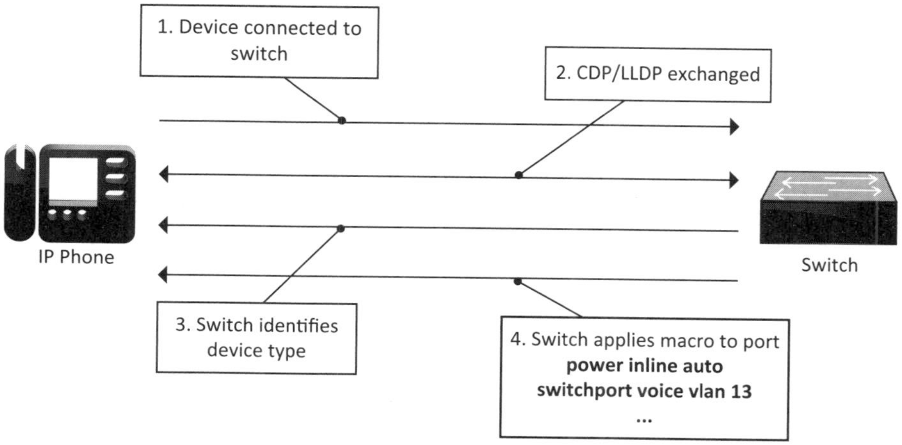

Figure 7-1 *AutoSmart Port discovery process for Cisco IP phone*

One of the main advantages of AutoSmart ports is that the switches contain predefined macros that can be modified to suit your environment. In addition, you can also customize those predefined macros to include all the necessary parameters for your specific environment. Table 7-1 shows a list of some of the predefined device-specific macros that are available in most Cisco Catalyst switches.

Table 7-1 *Device Specific Macros and Descriptions*

Macro Name	Macro Description
access-point	Auto configuration information for the autonomous access point
ip-camera	Auto configuration information for the video surveillance camera
lightweight-ap	Auto configuration information for the lightweight access point
media-player	Auto configuration information for the digital media player
Phone	Auto configuration information for the phone device
Router	Auto configuration information for the router device
Switch	Auto configuration information for the switch device

Enabling AutoSmart Ports on a Cisco Catalyst Switch

In order to enable AutoSmart Ports on a Cisco Catalyst switch, you must follow the steps illustrated in the following example. Another key advantage of this specific automation tool is that it takes a single command to enable to macro functionality.

```
Switch> enable
Switch# configure terminal
Enter configuration commands, one per line.  End with CNTL/Z.
Switch(config)# macro auto global processing
Switch(config)# end
Switch#
```

Occasionally, predefined macros contain most of the desired settings that are needed without requiring any modification to the macro. In some cases, however, customizing a macro to fit your needs is a better alternative. Customized macros are commonly deployed when more granular configurations are required. For example, a customized macro may be one that not only changes voice and data VLANs, but can also be used to configure quality of service (QoS) settings and other various options. The following example lists the default settings of the Cisco IP phone macro. This can be seen with the **show macro auto device phone** command.

```
Switch# show macro auto device phone
Device:phone
Default Macro:CISCO_PHONE_AUTO_SMARTPORT
Current Macro:CISCO_PHONE_AUTO_SMARTPORT
Configurable Parameters:ACCESS_VLAN VOICE_VLAN
Defaults Parameters:ACCESS_VLAN=1 VOICE_VLAN=2
Current Parameters:ACCESS_VLAN=1 VOICE_VLAN=2
```

Note To view the entire list of predefined macros that are available in a Cisco Catalyst switch, issue the **show shell functions** command.

The following output illustrates the configuration steps that are necessary to customize and trigger a predefined macro. In this example, the macro, when applied, will change the voice and data VLANs for a port when Cisco IP phone is connected.

```
Switch# configure terminal
Switch(config)# macro auto execute CISCO_PHONE_EVENT builtin CISCO_PHONE_AUTO_
SMARTPORT ACCESS_VLAN=11 VOICE_VLAN=13
Switch(config)# macro auto global processing
Switch(config)# exit
```

To verify this macro is properly modified with the new VLAN assignments, issue the **show shell triggers** command from the EXEC prompt of the CLI. The following snippet shows the output from the **show shell triggers** command.

```
Switch# show shell triggers

User defined triggers
---------------------
Built-in triggers
-----------------
Trigger Id: CISCO_PHONE_EVENT
Trigger description: Event for ip-phone macro
Trigger environment: ACCESS_VLAN=11 VOICE_VLAN=13
Trigger mapping function: CISCO_PHONE_AUTO_SMARTPORT
```

```
Other common event triggers that can be viewed and modified are:
Trigger Id: CISCO_ROUTER_EVENT
Trigger Id: CISCO_SWITCH_EVENT
Trigger Id: CISCO_WIRELESS_AP_EVENT
Trigger Id: CISCO_WIRELESS_LIGHTWEIGHT_AP_EVENT
```

In certain cases, the device you connect to the switch may not be able to use CDP or LLDP to identify itself to the switch. In these instances, you can create a custom macro that uses a BASH-like language syntax. Another interesting use case utilizes the MAC address OUI to identify and properly configure various devices on the switch. The following example shows a custom macro for a printer, using the MAC address OUI as a classifier.

```
Switch(config)# macro auto mac-address-group OUI_PRINTER_PORT
 oui list 0000AA
 exit

Switch(config)# macro auto execute OUI_PRINTER_PORT  {
 if [[ $LINKUP -eq YES ]]
  then conf t
  interface $INTERFACE
  description OUI_PRINTER_PORT macro
  switchport
  switchport mode access
  switchport access vlan data_vlan
  power inline never
  spanning-tree portfast
  exit
  end
 fi
 if [[ $LINKUP -eq NO ]]
  then conf t
  interface $INTERFACE
   switchport access vlan data_vlan
   no spanning-tree portfast
   no description
   exit
  end
 fi
}
```

AutoSmart Ports are a great start to automating specific tasks when it comes to managing your campus LAN. It should be noted that even though AutoSmart Ports are not the most granular way to automate port configurations based on device, it is still a very powerful solution to help reduce some of the more arduous tasks that relate to day-to-day moves, additions, and changes (MACs).

Note For more information on AutoSmart Ports, please visit the following link: www.cisco.com/go/SmartOperations/

AutoConf

Similar to AutoSmart Ports, AutoConf is used to automate various functions within a Cisco Catalyst switch. However, unlike AutoSmart Ports, AutoConf is a template-based solution that is more granular and user friendly. Although these features accomplish similar outcomes, the configurations are applied in a different manner. Interface templates are configured and applied to a specific port or range of ports much like AutoSmart Ports. Table 7-2 lists some of the available predefined interface templates within a Cisco Catalyst switch.

Note AutoConf is available in IOS 15.2(2)E and IOS-XE 3.6 or later.

Table 7-2 *AutoConf Interface Templates and Descriptions*

Template Name	Template Description
AP_INTERFACE_TEMPLATE	Wireless access point interface template
DMP_INTERFACE_TEMPLATE	Digital media player interface template
IP_CAMERA_INTERFACE_TEMPLATE	IP camera interface template
IP_PHONE_INTERFACE_TEMPLATE	IP phone interface template
LAP_INTERFACE_TEMPLATE	Lightweight access point interface template
MSP_CAMERA_INTERFACE_TEMPLATE	Multiservices platform camera interface template
MSP_VC_INTERFACE_TEMPLATE	Multiservices platform VC interface template
PRINTER_INTERFACE_TEMPLATE	Printer interface template
ROUTER_INTERFACE_TEMPLATE	Router interface template
SWITCH_INTERFACE_TEMPLATE	Switch interface template
TP_INTERFACE_TEMPLATE	Telepresence interface template

Some of the key benefits of using templates are as follows:

- Simpler configuration and management than AutoSmart Port macros.
- All interface templates are customizable.
- Templates take up less room in the configuration file than AutoSmart Port macros.
- Template updates apply to all interfaces subscribing to the template.
- Templates can be per session or per port.

The following output shows an example of the built-in IP Phone template by issuing the **show template interface source built-in IP_PHONE_INTERFACE_TEMPLATE** command.

```
Switch# show template interface source built-in IP_PHONE_INTERFACE_TEMPLATE

Template Name        : IP_PHONE_INTERFACE_TEMPLATE
Modified             : No
Template Definition :
 spanning-tree portfast
 spanning-tree bpduguard enable
 switchport mode access
 switchport block unicast
 switchport port-security maximum 3
 switchport port-security maximum 2 vlan access
 switchport port-security violation restrict
 switchport port-security aging time 2
 switchport port-security aging type inactivity
 switchport port-security
 storm-control broadcast level pps 1k
 storm-control multicast level pps 2k
 storm-control action trap
 mls qos trust cos
 service-policy input AUTOCONF-SRND4-CISCOPHONE-POLICY
 ip dhcp snooping limit rate 15
 load-interval 30
 srr-queue bandwidth share 1 30 35 5
 priority-queue out
```

Note To see a list of all the built-in interface templates, issue the **show template interface source built-in all** command.

Below is a list of some of the common key points to keep in mind about AutoConf Templates:

- By default, all templates automatically use VLAN 1. This includes any access VLAN, voice VLAN, and native VLAN in regard to trunk ports.
- Templates applied to interfaces are not shown in running configuration. In order to see the configuration applied to an interface, issue the **show derived-config interface <interface>** command.
- EtherChannel interfaces do not support AutoConf interface templates.
- Once AutoConf is enabled globally, it is applied to all interfaces by default. To disable AutoConf on a per-interface basis, issue the **access-session inherit disable autoconf** command.

- The template configuration itself does not show up in the running configuration unless the template is modified. For example, the access VLAN is changed from the default value of VLAN 1.
- All template configuration settings applied to an interface are removed once the device is disconnected from the switch port.

Enabling AutoConf on a Cisco Catalyst Switch

To enable AutoConf, the **autoconf enable** command must be issued from the global configuration mode. The following example illustrates the steps on how to enable AutoConf globally on a Cisco Catalyst Switch.

```
Switch> enable
Switch# configure terminal
Enter configuration commands, one per line.  End with CNTL/Z.
Switch(config)# autoconf enable
Switch(config)# end
Switch#
```

AutoConf is now enabled globally on the Catalyst Switch. To verify AutoConf is working properly, a Cisco IP phone is connected into interface GigabitEthernet0/1 on the Catalyst switch. As displayed in the following output, once the phone is connected, AutoConf will apply the IP_PHONE_INTERFACE_TEMPLATE to the interface.

```
Switch# show template binding target gigabitEthernet0/1

Interface Templates
===================
Interface: Gi0/1

Method              Source              Template-Name
------                  ------                  -------------
dynamic             Built-in              IP_PHONE_INTERFACE_TEMPLATE


Service Templates
=================
Interface: Gi0/1

Session             Source              Template-Name
-------                 ------                  ------------
```

Based on the previous output, the IP_PHONE_INTERFACE_TEMPLATE was successfully applied to the GigabitEthernet0/1 interface.

Note In general, to see the details of what settings are applied to an interface once a device is connected, issue the **show derived-config interface <interface_name>** command.

Notice that the applied template does not show up in the running configuration of the Catalyst switch. The following snippet shows the output of the **show running-config interface gigabitEthernet0/1** command, illustrating that the interface template is hidden in the running configuration.

```
Switch# show running-config interface gigabitEthernet0/1
Building configuration...

Current configuration : 36 bytes
!
interface GigabitEthernet0/1
end
```

To see the details of what settings were applied to the GigabitEthernet0/1 interface when the Cisco IP phone was connected, issue the **show derived-config interface gigabitEthernet0/1** command as shown in the following output.

```
Switch# show derived-config interface gigabitEthernet0/1
Building configuration...

Derived configuration : 669 bytes
!
interface GigabitEthernet0/1
 switchport mode access
 switchport block unicast
 switchport port-security maximum 3
 switchport port-security maximum 2 vlan access
 switchport port-security violation restrict
 switchport port-security aging time 2
 switchport port-security aging type inactivity
 switchport port-security
 load-interval 30
 srr-queue bandwidth share 1 30 35 5
 priority-queue out
 mls qos trust cos
 storm-control broadcast level pps 1k
 storm-control multicast level pps 2k
 storm-control action trap
 spanning-tree portfast
 spanning-tree bpduguard enable
```

```
 service-policy input AUTOCONF-SRND4-CISCOPHONE-POLICY
 ip dhcp snooping limit rate 15

Switch#
```

Modifying a Built-in Template

Commonly, built-in templates need to be modified to fit the desired configuration model of the environment. Modification of a built-in template allows for the flexibility of having a customized template, based on settings that align with the business needs. The following example lists the steps necessary to modify the built-in IP_PHONE_INTERFACE_TEMPLATE. These configuration steps will change the voice and data VLANs from the default of VLAN 1 to VLANs 11 and 13, respectively, and will add a custom description to the template.

```
Switch> enable
Switch# configure terminal
Enter configuration commands, one per line.  End with CNTL/Z.
Switch(config)# template IP_PHONE_INTERFACE_TEMPLATE
Switch(config-template)# switchport access vlan 11
Switch(config-template)# switchport voice vlan 13
Switch(config-template)# description CUSTOM_IP_PHONE_INTERFACE_TEMPLATE
Switch(config-template)# end
Switch#
```

To display the configuration changes made to the template, issue the **show template interface source built-in IP_PHONE_INTERFACE_TEMPLATE** command as shown in the following output.

```
Switch# show template interface source built-in IP_PHONE_INTERFACE_TEMPLATE
Building configuration...

Template Name        : IP_PHONE_INTERFACE_TEMPLATE
Modified             : Yes
Template Definition :
 spanning-tree portfast
 spanning-tree bpduguard enable
 switchport access vlan 11
 switchport mode access
 switchport block unicast
 switchport voice vlan 13
 switchport port-security maximum 3
 switchport port-security maximum 2 vlan access
 switchport port-security violation restrict
 switchport port-security aging time 2
 switchport port-security aging type inactivity
```

```
 switchport port-security
 storm-control broadcast level pps 1k
 storm-control multicast level pps 2k
 storm-control action trap
 mls qos trust cos
 service-policy input AUTOCONF-SRND4-CISCOPHONE-POLICY
 ip dhcp snooping limit rate 15
 load-interval 30
 description CUSTOM_IP_PHONE_INTERFACE_TEMPLATE
 srr-queue bandwidth share 1 30 35 5
 priority-queue out
!
end

Switch#
```

Once an AutoConf template has been modified, the template will now be visible in the running configuration of the Catalyst switch. The following snippet illustrates that the template is now present in the output of the **show running-config** command.

```
Switch# show running-config
Building configuration...
! Output omitted for brevity
!
autoconf enable
!
template IP_PHONE_INTERFACE_TEMPLATE
 spanning-tree portfast
 spanning-tree bpduguard enable
 switchport access vlan 11
 switchport mode access
 switchport block unicast
 switchport voice vlan 13
 switchport port-security maximum 3
 switchport port-security maximum 2 vlan access
 switchport port-security violation restrict
 switchport port-security aging time 2
 switchport port-security aging type inactivity
 switchport port-security
 storm-control broadcast level pps 1k
 storm-control multicast level pps 2k
 storm-control action trap
 mls qos trust cos
 service-policy input AUTOCONF-SRND4-CISCOPHONE-POLICY
 ip dhcp snooping limit rate 15
 load-interval 30
```

```
 description CUSTOM_IP_PHONE_INTERFACE_TEMPLATE
 srr-queue bandwidth share 1 30 35 5
 priority-queue out
!
! Output omitted for brevity
```

Note Even though the template is now visible in the running-config, it still does not list the configuration under the interface(s) that it is applied to.

Although the IP_PHONE_INTERFACE_TEMPLATE is modified and applied, the configuration is still hidden from the interface in the running-config. In order to see the customized configuration that is applied to the interface, the **show derived-config interface gigabitEthernet0/1** command must be used again. The following output shows the modified template that is applied to the gigabitEthernet0/1 interface.

```
Switch# show derived-config interface gigabitEthernet0/1
Building configuration...

!
interface GigabitEthernet0/1
 description CUSTOM_IP_PHONE_INTERFACE_TEMPLATE
 switchport access vlan 11
 switchport mode access
 switchport block unicast
 switchport voice vlan 13
 switchport port-security maximum 3
 switchport port-security maximum 2 vlan access
 switchport port-security violation restrict
 switchport port-security aging time 2
 switchport port-security aging type inactivity
 switchport port-security
 load-interval 30
 srr-queue bandwidth share 1 30 35 5
 priority-queue out
 mls qos trust cos
 storm-control broadcast level pps 1k
 storm-control multicast level pps 2k
 storm-control action trap
 spanning-tree portfast
 spanning-tree bpduguard enable
 service-policy input AUTOCONF-SRND4-CISCOPHONE-POLICY
 ip dhcp snooping limit rate 15
end

Switch#
```

AutoConf is a feature that not only eases the burden of device management and configuration, it also allows for a zero-touch deployment model of commonly connected devices. AutoConf is often used in campus LANs as well as remote branch office deployments. Most organizations enforce a standard when it comes to the type of devices in their environment. Even though make, model, and form factors may differ, AutoConf can assist in reducing the manual configuration tasks needed to deploy different device types such as computers, printers, IP phones, IP cameras, and so forth. If a device supports both AutoConf and AutoSmart ports, it is recommended to use AutoConf first, then AutoSmart ports. However, using both features together could cause undesired results.

Note For more information on AutoConf templates, please visit: http://www.cisco.com/c/en/us/td/docs/ios-xml/ios/ibns/configuration/15-e/ibns-15-e-book/ibns-autoconf.html

Auto Security

Cisco Auto Security is a feature that, when applied, automatically configures some of the most common baseline campus switching security features. Some of these features include:

- DHCP snooping
- Dynamic ARP inspection (DAI)
- Port Security

DHCP Snooping is a security feature that is designed to protect internally trusted DHCP servers and clients in your environment. DHCP Snooping works by verifying DHCP messages are received from only trusted DHCP servers within your campus environment. All messages from untrusted devices can be filtered or rate-limited, based on the desired configuration parameters. This security mechanism is to keep untrusted hosts from generating DHCP messages that could negatively impact your network. These DHCP messages can be malicious in nature or simply be the product of a misconfiguration. For example, a host computer has a DHCP server feature inadvertently turned on and is providing an unrouteable, incorrect IP address range to various devices in the environment. This will result in end hosts not being able to talk to the rest of the network. However, receiving a DHCP lease from any rogue server could be very problematic even if the IP address ranges are valid in your environment.

When enabled, the DHCP snooping feature keeps track of all devices sending and receiving DHCP messages. This information is stored in a table called the DHCP binding database. When DHCP messages are determined to be legitimate, they are processed normally. If for some reason the intercepted DHCP messages do not meet the proper criteria, the packets are discarded. This helps to protect your environment from DHCP snooping attacks.

Dynamic ARP inspection (DAI) is a feature that is used to prevent address resolution protocol (ARP) spoofing attacks. An ARP spoofing attack is when someone maliciously injects a duplicate MAC address onto a LAN in an attempt to redirect traffic to an alternate destination. DAI uses the DHCP binding database to verify that there is a valid layer 2 MAC address to layer 3 IP address binding before allowing any traffic to be forwarded on the segment. If it is determined that there is not such a valid mapping, the invalid ARP packets are discarded.

Port Security is a security feature that protects the network by setting dynamic or hard MAC address limits on specific switch ports. For example, the following list provides some of the Port Security features that are available in Catalyst switches.

- Secure ports, based on statically assigned MAC addresses
- Secure ports, based on dynamically learned MAC addresses
- Limit dynamically learned MAC addresses—helps prevent CAM table flooding attacks
- Shut down port when violation occurs
- Restrict port and send SNMP trap when violation occurs

Enabling Auto Security on a Cisco Catalyst Switch

The following example illustrates how to enable Auto Security on a Catalyst switch with a single command.

```
Switch> enable
Switch# configure terminal
Enter configuration commands, one per line.  End with CNTL/Z.
Switch(config)# auto security
Switch(config)# end
```

To verify what interfaces the Auto Security configuration has been applied to, issue the **show auto security** command shown in the following output.

```
Switch# show auto security
Auto Security is Enabled globally

AutoSecurity is Enabled on below interface(s):
--------------------------------------------
   GigabitEthernet0/1

Switch#
```

Because GigabitEthernet0/1 is configured as an access port, the following snippet illustrates the configuration that is visible in the running-config under that specific interface.

```
Switch# show running-config interface GigabitEthernet0/1
Building configuration...
```

```
Current configuration : 85 bytes
!
interface GigabitEthernet0/1
 auto security-port host
 spanning-tree portfast
end

Switch#
```

In order to see the specific configuration that has been automatically applied to the Catalyst switch the **show auto security configuration** command must be issued. The following output depicts the steps necessary to verify the Auto Security configuration.

```
Switch# show auto security configuration
%AutoSecurity provides a single CLI config 'auto security'
 to enable Base-line security Features like
 DHCP snooping, ARP inspection and  Port-Security

Auto Security CLIs applied globally:
---------------------------------
ip dhcp snooping
ip dhcp snooping vlan 2-1005
no ip dhcp snooping information option
ip arp inspection vlan 2-1005
ip arp inspection validate src-mac dst-mac ip


Auto Security CLIs applied on Access Port:
----------------------------------------
switchport port-security maximum 2
switchport port-security maximum 1 vlan access
switchport port-security maximum 1 vlan voice
switchport port-security violation restrict
switchport port-security aging time 2
switchport port-security aging type inactivity
switchport port-security
ip arp inspection limit rate 100
ip dhcp snooping limit rate 100


Auto Security CLIs applied on Trunk Port:
--------------------------------------
ip dhcp snooping trust
ip arp inspection trust
switchport port-security maximum 100
```

```
switchport port-security violation restrict
switchport port-security

Switch#
```

As seen from the above configuration, Auto Security enables an entire baseline of security features on the Catalyst switch. All of these security features and settings have been streamlined into a single command. This automates the deployment of these features, which makes it easier to secure the campus LAN environment.

Note Although many First-Hop Security features have been available in various IOS versions for some time, the Auto Security feature is available in IOS XE 3.6.0E and IOS 15.2(2)E and later.

For more information on Auto Security, please visit: http://www.cisco.com/c/en/us/td/docs/switches/lan/catalyst4500/XE3-6-0E/15-22E/configuration/guide/xe-360-config/auto_sec.pdf

Quality of Service for Campus Architectures

Quality of Service (QoS) is an integral part of any campus environment. QoS allows for the prioritization of specific traffic flows as they traverse over the campus network. For example, it may be desirable to allow voice and video traffic to have priority over bulk FTP traffic during a time of network congestion. One of the most common reasons that QoS is not deployed is due to its complexity. This section will discuss some different ways to automate the deployment of QoS for LAN devices.

Note A base understanding of QoS is assumed. QoS fundamentals are not covered in this chapter. To become more familiar with QoS and its components, please visit: www.cisco.com/go/qos

AutoQoS on Campus LAN Devices

As campus networks continue to grow, more emphasis is being put on the LAN. Today, it is becoming even more important to capitalize on the available LAN bandwidth as much as possible. Often, campus networks are designed with a specific set of goals in mind. For example, the following list are some of the more common business drivers and use cases that put demand on the campus LAN infrastructure:

- Gigabit Ethernet to the desktop
- Campus video communications
- Voice and IP phones

Alternatively, there are some other use cases that are beginning to be more prevalent in enterprise networks. These different, but not uncommon use cases are increasing the demand for connectivity in the LAN:

- Wayfinding devices
- Digital signage
- HVAC systems
- Manufacturing/industrial networks
- Building lighting

All of the above use cases are putting increased demand on the network and, by default, demand on the network engineering team.

Enabling AutoQoS on a Cisco Catalyst Switch

To enable AutoQoS, the following configuration steps must be followed:

Step 1. Enable AutoQoS globally

Step 2. Enable AutoQoS settings under interface

AutoQoS is enabled globally in the following example on the Catalyst switch by issuing the **auto qos global compact** command from the global configuration prompt. Once the feature is enabled globally, it can be verified with the **show auto qos** command.

```
Switch# configure terminal
Enter configuration commands, one per line.  End with CNTL/Z.
Switch(config)# auto qos global compact
Switch(config)# end
Switch# show auto qos

AutoQoS not enabled on any interface

Switch#
```

As you can see from the output of the **show auto qos** command in the following code snippet, there are no interfaces currently configured with any AutoQoS parameters. Once AutoQoS is enabled globally, you must then specify the interface configuration settings. For example, see the following output that illustrates how to enable the AutoQoS settings under a Gigabit Ethernet interface of a Catalyst switch. The configuration shown is for a Cisco IP phone.

```
Switch# configure terminal
Enter configuration commands, one per line.  End with CNTL/Z.
Switch(config)# interface GigabitEthernet0/1
```

```
Switch(config-if)# auto qos voip cisco-phone
Switch(config-if)# end
Switch#
```

Now that AutoQoS is enabled globally and there is an interface with AutoQoS settings applied to it, the **show auto qos** command is re-issued to verify the configuration as shown in the following snippet. Based on the output of the **show auto qos** command, we see that there is a difference in the information displayed as opposed to output shown previously. When AutoQoS is enabled under the GigabitEthernet0/1 interface, it now includes the interface configuration in the show command.

```
Switch# show auto qos
GigabitEthernet0/1
auto qos voip cisco-phone

Switch#
```

In order to display the actual QoS settings that get applied to the GigabitEthernet0/1 interface when a Cisco IP phone is connected, the **show auto qos interface GigabitEthernet0/1 configuration** command must be issued. The following snippet shows that based on the output of this command, there is an ingress policy named AUTOQOS-PPM-SRND4-CISCOPHONE-POLICY that is applied to the GigabitEthernet0/1 interface. The output also shows that the outbound egress priority queue is enabled and that the interface has been set to automatically trust the DSCP markings from the Cisco IP phone.

```
Switch# show auto qos interface GigabitEthernet0/1 configuration
GigabitEthernet0/1
auto qos voip cisco-phone
Ingress Policy: AUTOQOS-PPM-SRND4-CISCOPHONE-POLICY
Egress Priority Queue: enabled
The port is mapped to qset : 1
Trust device: cisco-phone
```

Next, to further validate the settings within the AUTOQOS-PPM-SRND4-CISCOPHONE-POLICY that is applied to the GigabitEthernet0/1 interface, we issue the show policy-map AUTOQOS-PPM-SRND4-CISCOPHONE-POLICY command as shown in the following output.

```
Switch# show policy-map AUTOQOS-PPM-SRND4-CISCOPHONE-POLICY
  Policy Map AUTOQOS-PPM-SRND4-CISCOPHONE-POLICY
    Class AUTOQOS_PPM_VOIP_DATA_CLASS
      set dscp ef
      police 128000 8000 exceed-action policed-dscp-transmit
    Class AUTOQOS_PPM_VOIP_SIGNAL_CLASS
      set dscp cs3
      police 32000 8000 exceed-action policed-dscp-transmit
```

```
    Class AUTOQOS_PPM_DEFAULT_CLASS
      set dscp default
      police 10000000 8000 exceed-action policed-dscp-transmit
Switch#
```

Based on the previous output, we can see that the following parameters have been set in the QoS policy-map applied to the GigabitEthernet0/1 interface on the Catalyst switch:

- Voice data packets are being marked with the DSCP value of EF (46)
- Policing of the VOIP_DATA_CLASS is set to 128Kbps
- Call signaling packets are being marked with the DSCP value of CS3
- Policing of the VOIP_SIGNAL_CLASS is set to 32Kbps
- All other packets are being marked with DSCP value of DEFAULT (0)
- Policing of the DEFAULT_CLASS is set to 10Mbps

The following snippet illustrates the output of the **show auto qos voip cisco-phone configuration** command, which is an alternate way of displaying the AutoQoS configuration that will be applied to an interface when a Cisco IP phone is connected. This command will also display the DSCP/CoS markings, queuing strategy, and associated thresholds settings that will be applied.

```
Switch# show auto qos cisco-phone configuration
Traffic(DSCP / COS)          IngressQ-Threshold    EgressQ-Threshold
---------------------------------------------------------------------
VoIP(46/5)                          N/A - N/A              01 - 01
Signaling(24/3)                     N/A - N/A              03 - 01
Best-Effort(00/0)                   N/A - N/A              02 - 01
```

All of the QoS settings mentioned above were deployed by issuing only two commands: the **auto qos global compact** global command and the **auto qos voip cisco-phone** interface command. We can begin to see how powerful tools like AutoQoS can be in a campus environment, eEspecially with hundreds to thousands of connected host devices. The following section of this chapter will cover deploying AutoQoS in the campus WAN environment.

AutoQoS on Campus WAN Devices

The best practice in general from a QoS perspective is to mark the traffic closest to the source and carry those markings across your LAN and WAN end-to-end. The biggest reason for this is so that end users and applications have a consistent experience. Marking and prioritizing traffic on the LAN is just one step in a bigger QoS design. Using AutoQoS for the WAN, you can simplify the steps needed to achieve that end-to-end user and application experience. Figure 7-2 illustrates the high level end-to-end QoS design model from an IP phone in one location to an IP phone in another location.

Note Although we will not discuss AutoQoS for WAN in depth in this chapter, the purpose of this section is to inform the readers that there are tools for AutoQoS on Cisco routers.

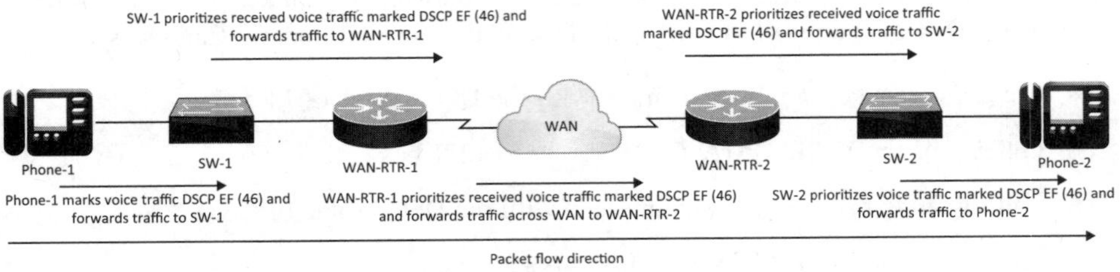

Figure 7-2 *End-to-end QoS example*

As you can see based on Figure 7-2, the QoS markings are kept intact from source to destination across the campus LAN and WAN networks. In this specific case, voice data traffic from Phone-1 to Phone-2 is marked with DSCP EF (46), and those markings are honored on a hop-by-hop basis across the entire network. This is called per-hop behavior (PHB).

Enabling AutoQoS on a Cisco ISR Router

The following example lists the steps that are necessary to enable AutoQoS for the WAN on a Cisco ISR router.

```
Router# configure terminal
Router(config)# interface FastEthernet0/1
Router(config-if)# auto qos voip
Router(config-if)# end
Router#
```

One of the convenient things about AutoQoS for the WAN is that by enabling it on one of the interfaces of the router, it automatically enables the feature globally. Furthermore, it applies all the QoS policy-maps and other settings automatically. The following snippet illustrates an example output of the **show auto qos** command from a Cisco ISR router, illustrating what features AutoQoS will automatically activate when the feature is enabled.

```
Router# show auto qos
 !
 policy-map AutoQoS-Policy-UnTrust
  class AutoQoS-VoIP-RTP-UnTrust
   priority percent 70
   set dscp ef
  class AutoQoS-VoIP-Control-UnTrust
   bandwidth percent 5
```

```
   set dscp af31
  class AutoQoS-VoIP-Remark
   set dscp default
  class class-default
   fair-queue
 !
 class-map match-any AutoQoS-VoIP-Remark
  match ip dscp ef
  match ip dscp cs3
  match ip dscp af31
 !
 class-map match-any AutoQoS-VoIP-Control-UnTrust
  match access-group name AutoQoS-VoIP-Control
 !
 class-map match-any AutoQoS-VoIP-RTP-UnTrust
  match protocol rtp audio
  match access-group name AutoQoS-VoIP-RTCP
 !
 ip access-list extended AutoQoS-VoIP-RTCP
  permit udp any any range 16384 32767 (6 matches)
 !
 ip access-list extended AutoQoS-VoIP-Control
  permit tcp any any eq 1720
  permit tcp any any range 11000 11999
  permit udp any any eq 2427
  permit tcp any any eq 2428
  permit tcp any any range 2000 2002
  permit udp any any eq 1719
  permit udp any any eq 5060
 !
 rmon event 33333 log trap AutoQoS description "AutoQoS SNMP traps for Voice
Drops" owner AutoQoS
 rmon alarm 33333 cbQosCMDropBitRate.34.14175073 30 absolute rising-threshold
1 33333 falling-threshold 0 owner AutoQoS

FastEthernet0/1 -
 !
 interface FastEthernet0/1
  service-policy output AutoQoS-Policy-UnTrust
```

Note AutoQoS for the WAN is platform dependent. To learn more about AutoQoS for WAN and what platforms the feature is supported on, please visit: http://www.cisco.com/c/en/us/products/ios-nx-os-software/autoqos/index.html

AutoQoS, in conjunction with some of the other automation mechanisms discussed earlier in the Automatic Port Profiling section of this chapter, can start to build a very robust and powerful tool set. This tool set can help network engineers ease the operational complexity of managing a constantly changing campus network environment. Chapter 8 "Network Automation Tools for Campus Environments" will highlight another tool set known as the application policy infrastructure controller enterprise module (APIC-EM). APIC-EM offers a wide variety of features that include tools to assist in configuring and automating quality of service in campus environments. We will also discuss some future APIC-EM applications.

Automating Management and Monitoring Tasks

This section will discuss a very robust set of tools that are built-in to many Cisco devices such as:

- Smart Call Home
- Tcl Shell
- Embedded Event Manager (EEM)

These tools are designed to make life a bit easier for the network operations staff by leveraging on-box automation.

Smart Call Home

Cisco's Smart Call Home is a feature that is built into a large number of Cisco devices that allows the devices to automatically reach out to Cisco TAC when there is an issue in your campus environment. Smart Call Home can report a wide variety of different events. For example:

- Generic online diagnostics (GOLD)
- Syslog events
- Environment events and alarms
- Inventory and configuration
- Field notices
- Product security incident response team (PSIRT) notifications

There are three primary ways that Smart Call Home can collect this information from the IOS: Alert Groups and Profiles, collecting show commands, and interaction with the CLI. This information is sent via one of three different transport modes: HTTP(S) direct, HTTP(S) via a transport gateway, or via email through a transport gateway. A transport gateway is a device that securely forwards Call Home messages that are sourced from devices within the network. The information that is gathered and sent to Cisco TAC is then stored in a database within Cisco's data centers. Once the information is collected and stored in the database, you will be able to view the information from a web portal where you can manage all your devices. Smart Call Home allows TAC to do multiple things with the collected information:

- Automatically create TAC service requests, based on issues with the device(s)
- Notify the Cisco partner should they need to be contacted
- Notify the device owner that there is something going on with the device(s)

This helps make your business more proactive, rather than reactive. An example of Smart Call Home would be if you have a Catalyst 4500 series switch and one of the power supplies failed in the middle of the night. Instead of having to wake up, open a TAC case, and upload the serial number of the switch and the configuration and go through troubleshooting steps, the switch would have used Smart Call Home to contact TAC and upload all the necessary information and a TAC case would have already been opened automatically. In turn, an RMA could be issued automatically for the failed part. This drastically reduces the amount of time and effort engineers have to spend, going through the motions of all the steps mentioned above in order to get a replacement power supply and bring the network back to 100 percent. In addition to this, there is an anonymous reporting feature that allows Cisco to receive minimal error and health information from various devices.

There are six basic steps to enable Cisco's Smart Call Home feature. Those steps are as follows:

- Enable Call Home
- Configure contact email address
- Activate CiscoTAC-1 profile
- Set transport mode
- Install security certificate
- Send a Call Home inventory to start the registration process

Enabling Smart Call Home on an Cisco Catalyst Switch

The following example depicts the process for setting up Smart Call Home on a Catalyst switch.

```
Switch# configure terminal
Switch(config)# service call-home
Switch(config)# call-home
Switch(cfg-call-home)# contact-email-addr neteng@yourcompany.com
Switch(cfg-call-home)# profile CiscoTAC-1
Switch(cfg-call-home-profile)# active
Switch(cfg-call-home-profile)# destination transport-method http
Switch(cfg-call-home-profile)# exit
```

```
Switch(cfg-call-home)# exit
Switch(config)# crypto pki trustpoint cisco
Switch(ca-trustpoint)# enrollment terminal
Switch(ca-trustpoint)# revocation-check crl none
Switch(ca-trustpoint)# exit
Switch(config)# crypto pki authenticate cisco

Enter the base 64 encoded CA certificate.
End with a blank line or the word "quit" on a line by itself

-----BEGIN CERTIFICATE-----
MIICPDCCAaUCEDyRMcsf9tAbDpq40ES/Er4wDQYJKoZIhvcNAQEFBQAwXzELMAkG
A1UEBhMCVVMxFzAVBgNVBAoTDlZlcmlTaWduLCBJbmMuMTcwNQYDVQQLEy5DbGFz
cyAzIFB1YmxpYyBQcmltYXJ5IENlcnRpZmljYXRpb24gQXV0aG9yaXR5MB4XDTk2
MDEyOTAwMDAwMFoXDTI4MDgwMjIzNTk1OVowXzELMAkGA1UEBhMCVVMxFzAVBgNV
BAoTDlZlcmlTaWduLCBJbmMuMTcwNQYDVQQLEy5DbGFzcyAzIFB1YmxpYyBQcmlt
YXJ5IENlcnRpZmljYXRpb24gQXV0aG9yaXR5MIGfMA0GCSqGSIb3DQEBAQUAA4GN
ADCBiQKBgQDJXFme8huKARS0EN8EQNvjV69qRUCPhAwL0TPZ2RHP7gJYHyX3KqhE
BarsAx94f56TuZoAqiN91qyFomNFx3InzPRMxnVx0jnvT0Lwdd8KkMaOIG+YD/is
I19wKTakyYbnsZogy1Olhec9vn2a/iRFM9x2Fe0PonFkTGUugWhFpwIDAQABMA0G
CSqGSIb3DQEBBQUAA4GBABByUqkFFBkyCEHwxWsKzH4PIRnN5GfcX6kb5sroc50i
2JhucwNhkcV8sEVAbkSdjbCxlnRhLQ2pRdKkkirWmnWXbj9T/UWZYB2oK0z5XqcJ
2HUw19JlYD1n1khVdWk/kfVIC0dpImmClr7JyDiGSnoscxlIaU5rfGW/D/xwzoiQ
-----END CERTIFICATE---
-----BEGIN CERTIFICATE-----
MIIE0DCCBDmgAwIBAgIQJQzo4DBhLp8rifcFTXz4/TANBgkqhkiG9w0BAQUFADBfMQswCQ
YDVQQGEwJVUzEXMBUGA1UEChMOVmVyaVNpZ24sIEluYy4xNzA1BgNVBAsTLkNsYXNzID
Mg
UHVibGljIFByaW1hcnkgQ2VydGlmaWNhdGlvbiBBdXRob3JpdHkwHhcNMDYxMTA4MDAwMD
AwWhcNMjExMTA3MjM1OTU5WjCByjELMAkGA1UEBhMCVVMxFzAVBgNVBAoTDlZlcmlTa
Wdu
LCBJbmMuMR8wHQYDVQQLExZWZXJpU2lnbiBUcnVzdCBOZXR3b3JrMTowOAYDVQQLEzEo
Yy
kgMjAwNiBWZXJpU2lnbiwgSW5jLiAtIEZvciBhdXRob3JpemVkIHVzZSBvbmx5MUUwQwYD
VQQDEzxWZXJpU2lnbiBDbGFzcyAzIFB1YmxpYyBQcmltYXJ5IENlcnRpZmljYXRpb24gQX
V0aG9yaXR5IC0gRzUwggEiMA0GCSqGSIb3DQEBAQUAA4IBDwAwggEKAoIBAQCvJAgIKXo1
nmAMqudLO07cfLw8RRy7K+D+KQL5VwijZIUVJ/XxrcgxiV0i6CqqpkKzj/i5Vbext0uz/o
9+B1fs70PbZmIVYc9gDaTY3vjgw2IIPVQT60nKWVSFJuUrjxuf6/WhkcIzSdhDY2pSS9KP
6HBRTdGJaXvHcPaz3BJ023tdS1bTlr8Vd6Gw9KIl8q8ckmcY5fQGBO+QueQA5N06tRn/Ar
r0PO7gi+s3i+z016zy9vA9r911kTMZHRxAy3QkGSGT2RT+rCpSx4/VBEnkjWNHiDxpg8v+
R70rfk/Fla4OndTRQ8Bnc+MUCH7lP59zuDMKz10/NIeWiu5T6CUVAgMBAAGjggGbMIIBlz
APBgNVHRMBAf8EBTADAQH/MDEGA1UdHwQqMCgwJqAkoCKGIGh0dHA6Ly9jcmwudmVya
XNp
Z24uY29tL3BjYTMuY3JsMA4GA1UdDwEB/wQEAwIBBjA9BgNVHSAENjA0MDIGBFUdIAAwKj
AoBggrBgEFBQcCARYcaHR0cHM6Ly93d3cudmVyaXNpZ24uY29tL2NwczAdBgNVHQ4EFgQU
f9Nlp8Ld7LvwMAnzQzn6Aq8zMTMwbQYIKwYBBQUHAQwEYTBfoV2gWzBZMFcwVRYJaW1h
```

```
Z2
UvZ2lmMCEwHzAHBgUrDgMCGgQUj+XTGoasjY5rw8+AatRIGCx7GS4wJRYjaHR0cDovL2xv
Z28udmVyaXNpZ24uY29tL3ZzbG9nby5naWYwNAYIKwYBBQUHAQEEKDAmMCQGCCsGAQU
FBz
ABhhhodHRwOi8vb2NzcC52ZXJpc2lnbi5jb20wPgYDVR0lBDcwNQYIKwYBBQUHAwEGCCsG
AQUFBwMCBggrBgEFBQcDAwYJYIZIAYb4QgQBBgpghkgBhvhFAQgBMA0GCSqGSIb3DQEBB
Q
UAA4GBABMC3fjohgDyWvj4IAxZiGIHzs73Tvm7WaGY5eE43U68ZhjTresY8g3JbT5KlCDD
PLq9ZVTGr0SzEK0saz6r1we2uIFjxfleLuUqZ87NMwwq14lWAyMfs77oOghZtOxFNfeKW/
9mz1Cvxm1XjRl4t7mi0VfqH5pLr7rJjhJ+xr3/

<snip> <Full certificate is issued from link in the Smart Call Home Quick Start
Guide> <snip>

quit
Certificate has the following attributes:
       Fingerprint MD5: EF5AF133 EFF1CDBB 5102EE12 144B96C4
      Fingerprint SHA1: A1DB6393 916F17E4 18550940 0415C702 40B0AE6B

% Do you accept this certificate? [yes/no]: yes
Trustpoint CA certificate accepted.
% Certificate successfully imported

Switch(config)# end
Switch# copy running-config startup-config
```

Note To obtain the proper certificate to paste into the call configuration, please visit the following link to get the Smart Call Home user guide for your model of equipment: http://www.cisco.com/en/US/docs/switches/lan/smart_call_home/user_guides/SCH_Ch6.pdf#G1039385

Once you complete the certificate import process, you must then initiate a call home to begin the registration process for the device. Before we begin the call home process, we will enable the **debug event manager action cli** command as the following snippet depicts. This will show the steps that the call-home feature is taking. It is important to remember that call-home uses embedded event manager (EEM) to function. The following example also shows the **call-home** command that is used to initiate the call-home and registration process on a Cisco Catalyst switch.

```
Switch# debug event manager action cli
Debug EEM action cli debugging is on
Switch# call-home send alert-group inventory profile CiscoTAC-1
Sending inventory info call-home message ...
Please wait. This may take some time ...
```

```
Switch#
Dec  7 22:48:38.089: %HA_EM-6-LOG: callhome : DEBUG(cli_lib) : : CTL : cli_open
called.
Dec  7 22:48:38.089: %HA_EM-6-LOG: callhome : DEBUG(cli_lib) : : OUT : Switch>
Dec  7 22:48:38.089: %HA_EM-6-LOG: callhome : DEBUG(cli_lib) : : IN  :
Switch>enable
Dec  7 22:48:38.099: %HA_EM-6-LOG: callhome : DEBUG(cli_lib) : : OUT : Switch#
Dec  7 22:48:38.099: %HA_EM-6-LOG: callhome : DEBUG(cli_lib) : : IN  : Switch#show
version
Dec  7 22:48:38.120: %HA_EM-6-LOG: callhome : DEBUG(cli_lib) : : OUT : Cisco IOS
Software, C3560CX Software (C3560CX-UNIVERSALK9-M), Version 15.2(3)E, RELEASE
SOFTWARE (fc4)
Dec  7 22:48:38.120: %HA_EM-6-LOG: callhome : DEBUG(cli_lib) : : OUT : Technical
Support: http://www.cisco.com/techsupport
Dec  7 22:48:38.120: %HA_EM-6-LOG: callhome : DEBUG(cli_lib) : : OUT :
Copyright (c) 1986-2014 by Cisco Systems, Inc.
Dec  7 22:48:38.120: %HA_EM-6-LOG: callhome : DEBUG(cli_lib) : : OUT : Compiled
Sun 07-Dec-14 13:15 by prod_rel_team
Dec  7 22:48:38.120: %HA_EM-6-LOG: callhome : DEBUG(c
Translating "tools.cisco.com"… domain server (X.X.X.X)li_lib) : : OUT :
Dec  7 22:48:38.120: %HA_EM-6-LOG: callhome : DEBUG(cli_lib) : : OUT : ROM:
Bootstrap program is C2960X boot loader
Dec  7 22:48:38.120: %HA_EM-6-LOG: callhome : DEBUG(cli_lib) : : OUT : BOOTLDR:
C3560CX Boot Loader (C3560CX-HBOOT-M) Version 15.2(3r)E1, RELEASE SOFTWARE (fc1)
Dec  7 22:48:38.120: %HA_EM-6-LOG: callhome : DEBUG(cli_lib) : : OUT :
Dec  7 22:48:38.120: %HA_EM-6-LOG: callhome : DEBUG(cli_lib) : : OUT : Switch
uptime is 1 day, 6 hours, 9 minutes
Dec  7 22:48:38.120 [OK]
i: %HA_EM-6-LOG: callhome : DEBUG(cli_lib) : : OUT : System returned to ROM by
power-on
Dec  7 22:48:38.120: %HA_EM-6-LOG: callhome : DEBUG(cli_lib) : : OUT : System
restarted at 16:38:44 UTC Sun Dec 6 2015
Dec  7 22:48:38.120: %HA_EM-6-LOG: callhome : DEBUG(cli_lib) : : OUT : System
image file is "flash:/c3560cx-universalk9-mz.152-3.E/c3560cx-universalk9-mz
.152-3.E.bin"
Dec  7 22:48:38.120: %HA_EM-6-LOG: callhome : DEBUG(cli_lib) : : OUT : Last reload
reason: power-on
Dec  7 22:48:38.120: %HA_EM-6-LOG: callhome : DEBUG(cli_lib) : : OUT :
Dec  7 22:48:38.120: %HA_EM-6-LOG: callhome : DEBUG(cli_lib) : : OUT :
Dec  7 22:48:38.120: %HA_EM-6-LOG: callhome : DEBUG(cli_lib) : : OUT :
Dec  7 22:48:38.120: %HA_EM-6-LOG: callhome : DEBUG(cli_lib) : : OUT : This
product contains cryptographic features and is subject to United
Dec  7 22:48:38.120: %HA_EM-6-LOG: callhome : DEBUG(cli_lib) : : OUT : States and
local country laws governing import, export, transfer and
Dec  7 22:48:38.120: %HA_EM-6-LOG: callhome : DEBUG(cli_lib) : : OUT : use.
Delivery of Cisco cryptographic products does not imply
Dec  7 22:48:38.120: %HA_EM-6-LOG: callhome : DEBUG(cli_lib) : : OUT : third-party
authority to import, export, distribute or use encryption.
Dec  7 22:48:38.120: %HA_EM-6-LOG: callhome : DEBUG(cli_lib) : : CTL : 20+ lines
read from cli, debug output truncated
```

```
Dec  7 22:48:38.620: %HA_EM-6-LOG: callhome : DEBUG(cli_lib) : : IN  : Switch#show
inventory oid
Dec  7 22:48:38.634: %HA_EM-6-LOG: callhome : DEBUG(cli_lib) : : OUT : NAME: "1",
DESCR: "WS-C3560CX-8PC-S"
Dec  7 22:48:38.638: %HA_EM-6-LOG: callhome : DEBUG(cli_lib) : : OUT : PID:
WS-C3560CX-8PC-S  , VID: V01  , SN: XXXXXXXXXXX
Dec  7 22:48:38.638: %HA_EM-6-LOG: callhome : DEBUG(cli_lib) : : OUT : OID:
1.3.6.1.4.1.9.12.3.1.3.1593
Dec  7 22:48:38.638: %HA_EM-6-LOG: callhome : DEBUG(cli_lib) : : OUT :
Dec  7 22:48:38.638: %HA_EM-6-LOG: callhome : DEBUG(cli_lib) : : OUT :
Dec  7 22:48:38.638: %HA_EM-6-LOG: callhome : DEBUG(cli_lib) : : OUT : Switch#
Dec  7 22:48:39.137: %HA_EM-6-LOG: callhome : DEBUG(cli_lib) : : IN  : Switch#show
env power
Dec  7 22:48:39.155: %HA_EM-6-LOG: callhome : DEBUG(cli_lib) : : OUT : SW  PID
Serial#    Status          Sys Pwr  PoE Pwr  Watts
Dec  7 22:48:39.155: %HA_EM-6-LOG: callhome : DEBUG(cli_lib) : : OUT : --  -------
-----------  ----------  ---------------  -------  -------  -----
Dec  7 22:48:39.155: %HA_EM-6-LOG: callhome : DEBUG(cli_lib) : : OUT :  1
Built-in                                     Good
Dec  7 22:48:39.155: %HA_EM-6-LOG: callhome : DEBUG(cli_lib) : : OUT :
Dec  7 22:48:39.155: %HA_EM-6-LOG: callhome : DEBUG(cli_lib) : : OUT : Switch#
Dec  7 22:48:39.658: %HA_EM-6-LOG: callhome : DEBUG(cli_lib) : : CTL : cli_close
called.
Dec  7 22:48:39.658:
Dec  7 22:48:39.658: tty is now going through its death sequence
Switch#
```

Now that this step is complete, an email will be sent to the email address used in the CiscoTAC-1 profile as shown in Figure 7-3. In this case, that email address is neteng@yourcompany.com. Once that email is received, to complete the registration process you must follow the directions in the email. You must also have a valid contract associated to the device you are trying to register to the Smart Call Home portal. Following the link will redirect you to the Smart Call Home Web Portal as shown in Figure 7-4. Once logged into the portal, the device registration process can be completed.

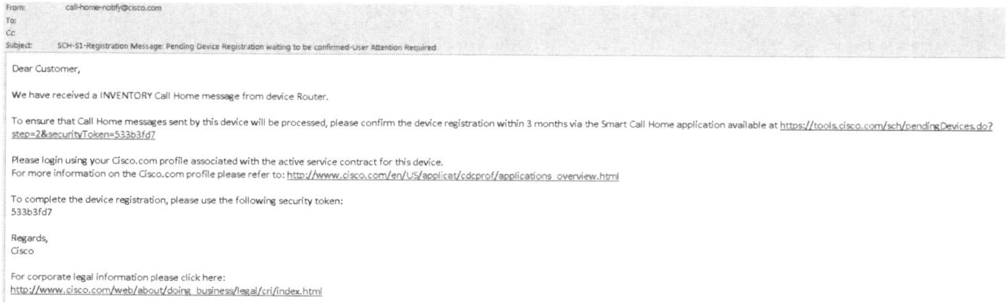
From: call-home-notify@cisco.com
To:
Cc:
Subject: SCH-S1-Registration Message: Pending Device Registration waiting to be confirmed-User Attention Required

Dear Customer,

We have received a INVENTORY Call Home message from device Router.

To ensure that Call Home messages sent by this device will be processed, please confirm the device registration within 3 months via the Smart Call Home application available at https://tools.cisco.com/sch/pendingDevices.do?step=2&securityToken=533b3fd7

Please login using your Cisco.com profile associated with the active service contract for this device.
For more information on the Cisco.com profile please refer to: http://www.cisco.com/en/US/applicat/cdcprof/applications_overview.html

To complete the device registration, please use the following security token:
533b3fd7

Regards,
Cisco

For corporate legal information please click here:
http://www.cisco.com/web/about/doing_business/legal/cri/index.html

Figure 7-3 *Email from Cisco Smart Call Home Tool*

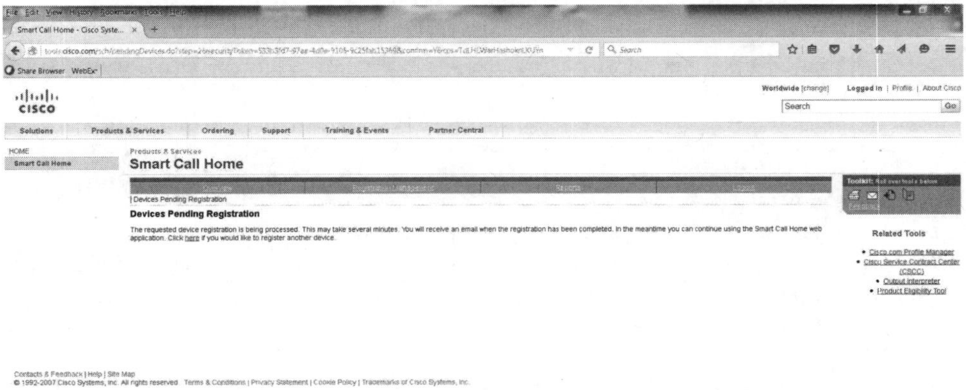

Figure 7-4 *Smart Call Home Web Portal*

To verify that Smart Call Home is running on your device, issue the **show call-home** command from the privileged exec prompt. The following snippet displays the output from the **show call-home** command on a Cisco Catalyst Switch. There are many different options that can be configured with Smart Call Home. The following alert groups are enabled automatically when configuring Smart Call Home with the **call-home send alert-group inventory profile CiscoTAC-1** command:

- Configuration
- Diagnostic
- Environment
- Inventory
- Syslog

```
Switch# show call-home
Current call home settings:
    call home feature : enable
    call home message's from address: Not yet set up
    call home message's reply-to address: Not yet set up

    vrf for call-home messages: Not yet set up

    contact person's email address: neteng@yourcompany.com

    contact person's phone number: Not yet set up
    street address: Not yet set up
    customer ID: Not yet set up
    contract ID: Not yet set up
    site ID: Not yet set up
```

```
    source ip address: Not yet set up
    source interface: Not yet set up
    Mail-server: Not yet set up
    Rate-limit: 20 message(s) per minute

Available alert groups:
    Keyword                  State   Description
    ------------------------ ------- ------------------------------
    configuration            Enable  configuration info
    diagnostic               Enable  diagnostic info
    environment              Enable  environmental info
    inventory                Enable  inventory info
    syslog                   Enable  syslog info

Profiles:
    Profile Name: CiscoTAC-1

Switch#
```

Note For more information on Smart Call Home, please visit: https://supportforums.cisco.com/community/4816/smart-call-home

Tcl Shell

Tcl Shell is a feature that is built into Cisco routers and switches that allows engineers to interact directly with the device by using various Tcl scripts. Tcl scripting has been around for quite some time and is a very useful scripting language. Tcl provides many ways to streamline different tasks that can help with day-to-day operations and monitoring of a network. Some of the following are tasks that can be automated by using these scripts:

- Verify IP and IPv6 reachability, using ping
- Verify IP and IPv6 reachability, using Traceroute
- Check interface statistics
- Retrieve SNMP information by accessing MIBs
- Send email messages containing CLI outputs from Tcl scripts

Most often, basic Tcl scripts are entered line by line within the Tcl shell, although, for some of the more advanced scripting methods, you can load the script into the flash of the device you are working on and execute the script from there. These scripts have to be in a specific Tcl format as shown in the following examples. The following example illustrates how to enter the Tcl shell on a Cisco router and execute a simple ping script.

```
Router# tclsh
Router(tcl)# foreach address {
+>(tcl)# 192.168.0.2
>(tcl)# 192.168.0.3
+>(tcl)# 192.168.0.4
+>(tcl)# 192.168.0.5
+>(tcl)# 192.168.0.6
+>(tcl)# } { ping $address
+>(tcl)# }
Type escape sequence to abort.
Sending 5, 64-byte ICMP Echos to 192.168.0.2, timeout is 2 seconds:
!!!!!
Success rate is 100 percent (5/5), round-trip min/avg/max = 4/4/4 ms
Type escape sequence to abort.
Sending 5, 64-byte ICMP Echos to 192.168.0.3, timeout is 2 seconds:

!!!!!
Success rate is 100 percent (5/5), round-trip min/avg/max = 4/4/4 ms
Type escape sequence to abort.
Sending 5, 64-byte ICMP Echos to 192.168.0.4, timeout is 2 seconds:
.....
Success rate is 0 percent (0/5)
Type escape sequence to abort.
Sending 5, 64-byte ICMP Echos to 192.168.0.5, timeout is 2 seconds:
!!!!!
Success rate is 100 percent (5/5), round-trip min/avg/max = 1/1/4 ms
Type escape sequence to abort.
Sending 5, 64-byte ICMP Echos to 192.168.0.6, timeout is 2 seconds:
!!!!!
Success rate is 100 percent (5/5), round-trip min/avg/max = 1/3/4 ms
Router(tcl)# tclquit
Router#
```

An alternate to entering the DNS node names or IP addresses in a line-by-line fashion, you can also enter some of the script commands on a single line within the Tcl shell. For instance, the following example shows a similar ping script to the one entered before, but now it is executed on the same line within the Tcl shell.

```
Router# tclsh
Router(tcl)# foreach address {192.168.0.2 192.168.0.3 192.168.0.4} {ping $address}

Type escape sequence to abort.
Sending 5, 64-byte ICMP Echos to 192.168.0.2, timeout is 2 seconds:
!!!!!
Success rate is 100 percent (5/5), round-trip min/avg/max = 4/4/4 ms
Type escape sequence to abort.
```

```
Sending 5, 64-byte ICMP Echos to 192.168.0.3, timeout is 2 seconds:
!!!!!
Success rate is 100 percent (5/5), round-trip min/avg/max = 4/4/4 ms
Type escape sequence to abort.
Sending 5, 64-byte ICMP Echos to 192.168.0.4, timeout is 2 seconds:
.....
Success rate is 0 percent (0/5)
Router(tcl)# tclquit
Router#
```

Note To abort a ping that is timing out while running a script, press and hold the CTRL+Shift keys and press the 6 key for each failing ping, then release all keys. This speeds up the script to keep processing past the node(s) that are not responding and does not stop the script from running.

To execute Tcl Scripts from the local flash memory, you would need to store the script in flash and then call the script by file name. Scripts can be stored on the device's local flash, USB flash, or compact flash. Tcl scripts can be transferred into the IOS File System (IFS) by using SCP, TFTP, FTP, or RCP. From a security perspective, SCP is preferred due to its use of SSH. To execute a locally stored script, the **source** command from within the Tcl shell prompt can be used. The following example illustrates the steps to call a script named *ping.tcl* from the local flash on a device. This script is an example of the same ping script that was shown earlier in this chapter.

Note The scripts that are stored locally to the device should be named in the following manner: filename.tcl

```
Router# tclsh
Router(tcl)# source flash:ping.tcl

Type escape sequence to abort.
Sending 5, 64-byte ICMP Echos to 192.168.0.2, timeout is 2 seconds:
!!!!!
Success rate is 100 percent (5/5), round-trip min/avg/max = 4/4/4 ms
Type escape sequence to abort.
Sending 5, 64-byte ICMP Echos to 192.168.0.3, timeout is 2 seconds:
!!!!!
Success rate is 100 percent (5/5), round-trip min/avg/max = 4/4/4 ms
Type escape sequence to abort.
Sending 5, 64-byte ICMP Echos to 192.168.0.4, timeout is 2 seconds:
.....
Success rate is 0 percent (0/5)
Router(tcl)# tclquit
Router#
```

Note The previous script that is stored locally in flash can also be executed by simply issuing the "tclsh flash:ping.tcl command.

Embedded Event Manager (EEM)

Embedded Event Manager (EEM) is a very flexible and powerful tool within Cisco IOS. EEM allows engineers to build software applets that can automate many tasks. EEM also derives some of its power from the fact that you can build custom scripts using Tcl so that they automatically execute, based on the output of an action or an event on a device. One of the main benefits of EEM is that it is all contained within the local device. There is no need to rely on an external scripting engine or monitoring device in most cases. Figure 7-5 illustrates some of the event detectors and how they interact with the IOS subsystem.

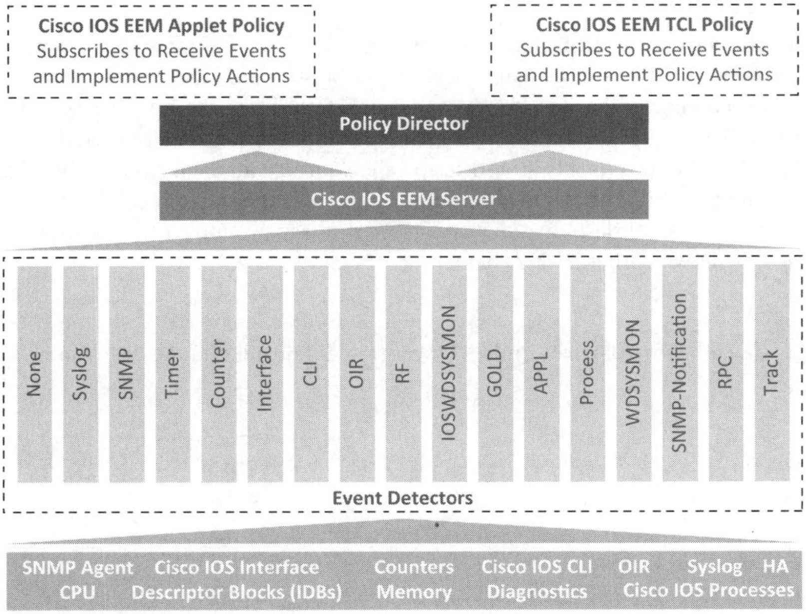

Figure 7-5 *EEM Event Detectors*

EEM Applets

EEM applets are comprised of multiple building blocks. In this chapter, we will focus on the two of the primary building blocks that make up EEM applets. Those building blocks are called events and actions. These EEM applets use a similar logic to the *if-then* statements found in some of the more common programming languages. For instance, *if* an event happens, *then* an action is taken. In the following example, we illustrate a very common EEM applet that is monitoring syslog messages on a router. This particular applet is looking for a specific syslog message, stating that the Loopback0 interface went down. The specific syslog message is matched using regular expressions. This is a very powerful and granular way of matching patterns. If this specific syslog pattern is matched (an event) at least once, then the following actions will be taken:

- The Loopback0 interface will be shutdown and brought back up (**shutdown**, then **no shutdown**)
- The router will generate a syslog message that says "I've fallen, and I can't get up!"
- An email message will be sent to the network administrator that includes the output of the **show interface loopback0** command.

```
event manager applet LOOP0
 event syslog pattern "Interface Loopback0.* down" period 1
 action 1.0 cli command "enable"
 action 2.0 cli command "config terminal"
 action 3.0 cli command "interface loopback0"
 action 4.0 cli command "shutdown"
 action 5.0 cli command "no shutdown"
 action 5.5 cli command "show interface loopback0"
 action 6.0 syslog msg "I've fallen, and I can't get up!"
 action 7.0 mail server 10.0.0.25 to neteng@yourcompany.com from
 no-reply@yourcompany.com subject "Loopback0 Issues!" body "The Loopback0
interface was
 bounced. Please monitor accordingly. "$_cli_result"
```

Note Remember to include the **enable** and **configure terminal** commands at the beginning of actions within your applet. This is necessary as the applet assumes you are in exec mode, not privileged exec or config mode. In addition, if you are using AAA command authorization, you will want to include the **event manager session cli username *username*** command. Otherwise, the CLI commands in the applet will fail. It is also good practice to use decimal labels similar to 1.0, 2.0, and so forth when building applets. This allows you to insert and action between other actions in the future. For example, 1.5 will allow you to insert an action between 1.0 and 2.0. Remember that labels are parsed as strings, which means 10.0 would come after 1.0, not 9.0.

Based on the output from the **debug event manager action cli**, you can see the actual actions taking place when the applet is running. The following example shows the applet being engaged when we issue the **shutdown** command on the Loopback0 interface. It also shows that there was an error when trying to connect to the SMTP server to send the email to the administrator. This is because the actual SMTP server we are using for this test is not configured. Notice that because we used the **$_cli_result** keyword in the configuration, it will include the output of any CLI commands that were issued in the applet. In this case, the output of the **show interface Loopback0** command will be included in the debug and the mail message.

```
Switch#
Switch# configure terminal
Enter configuration commands, one per line.  End with CNTL/Z.
Switch(config)# interface loopback0
Switch(config-if)# shutdown
Switch(config-if)#
Dec  6 17:21:59.214: %LINK-5-CHANGED: Interface Loopback0, changed state to
administratively down
Dec  6 17:21:59.217: %HA_EM-6-LOG: LOOP0 : DEBUG(cli_lib) : : CTL : cli_open
called.
Dec  6 17:21:59.221: %HA_EM-6-LOG: LOOP0 : DEBUG(cli_lib) : : OUT : Switch>
Dec  6 17:21:59.221: %HA_EM-6-LOG: LOOP0 : DEBUG(cli_lib) : : IN  : Switch>enable
Dec  6 17:21:59.231: %HA_EM-6-LOG: LOOP0 : DEBUG(cli_lib) : : OUT : Switch#
Dec  6 17:21:59.231: %HA_EM-6-LOG: LOOP0 : DEBUG(cli_lib) : : IN  : Switch#show
interface loopback0
Dec  6 17:21:59.252: %HA_EM-6-LOG: LOOP0 : DEBUG(cli_lib) : : OUT : Loopback0 is
administratively down, line protocol is down
Dec  6 17:21:59.252: %HA_EM-6-LOG: LOOP0 : DEBUG(cli_lib) : : OUT :   Hardware is
Loopback
Dec  6 17:21:59.252: %HA_EM-6-LOG: LOOP0 : DEBUG(cli_lib) : : OUT :   MTU 1514
bytes, BW 8000000 Kbit/sec, DLY 5000 usec,
Dec  6 17:21:59.252: %HA_EM-6-LOG: LOOP0 : DEBUG(cli_lib) : : OUT :
reliability 255/255, txload 1/255, rxload 1/255
Dec  6 17:21:59.252: %HA_EM-6-LOG: LOOP0 : DEBUG(cli_lib) : : OUT :
Encapsulation LOOPBACK, loopback not set
Dec  6 17:21:59.252: %HA_EM-6-LOG: LOOP0 : DEBUG(cli_lib) : : OUT :   Keepalive
set (10 sec)
Dec  6 17:21:59.252: %HA_EM-6-LOG: LOOP0 : DEBUG(cli_lib) : : OUT :   Last input
never, output never, output hang never
Dec  6 17:21:59.252: %HA_EM-6-LOG: LOOP0 : DEBUG(cli_lib) : : OUT :   Last
clearing of "show interface" counters never
Dec  6 17:21:59.252: %HA_EM-6-LOG: LOOP0 : DEBUG(cli_lib) : : OUT :   Input queue:
0/75/0/0 (size/max/drops/flushes); Total output drops: 0
Dec  6 17:21:59.252: %HA_EM-6-LOG: LOOP0 : DEBUG(cli_lib) : : OUT :   Queueing
strategy: fifo
Dec  6 17:21:59.252: %HA_EM-6-LOG: LOOP0 : DEBUG(cli_lib) : : OUT :   Output
queue: 0/0 (size/max)
Dec  6 17:21:59.252: %HA_EM-6-LOG: LOOP0 : DEBUG(cli_lib) : : OUT :   5 minute
input rate 0 bits/sec, 0 packets/sec
Dec  6 17:21:59.252: %HA_EM-6-LOG: LOOP0 : DEBUG(cli_lib) : : OUT :   5 minute
output rate 0 bits/sec, 0 packets/sec
Dec  6 17:21:59.252: %HA_EM-6-LOG: LOOP0 : DEBUG(cli_lib) : : OUT :      0 packets
input, 0 bytes, 0 no buffer
Dec  6 17:21:59.252: %HA_EM-6-LOG: LOOP0 : DEBUG(cli_lib) : : OUT :
Received 0 broadcasts (0 IP multicasts)
Dec  6 17:21:59.252: %HA_EM-6-LOG: LOOP0 : DEBUG(cli_lib) : : OUT :
0 runts, 0 giants, 0 throttles
Dec  6 17:21:59.252: %HA_EM-6-LOG: LOOP0 : DEBUG(cli_lib) : : OUT :      0 input
errors, 0 CRC, 0 frame, 0 overrun, 0 ignored, 0 abort
Dec  6 17:21:59.252: %HA_EM-6-LOG: LOOP0 : DEBUG(cli_lib) : : OUT :      0 packets
output, 0 bytes, 0 underruns
```

```
Dec  6 17:21:59.252: %HA_EM-6-LOG: LOOP0 : DEBUG(cli_lib) : : OUT :      0 output
errors, 0 collisions, 0 interface resets
Dec  6 17:21:59.252: %HA_EM-6-LOG: LOOP0 : DEBUG(cli_lib) : : OUT :      0 unknown
protocol drops
Dec  6 17:21:59.252: %HA_EM-6-LOG: LOOP0 : DEBUG(cli_lib) : : CTL : 20+ lines read
from cli, debug output truncated
Dec  6 17:21:59.252: %HA_EM-6-LOG: LOOP0 : DEBUG(cli_lib) : : IN  : Switch#config
terminal
Dec  6 17:21:59.266: %HA_EM-6-LOG: LOOP0 : DEBUG(cli_lib) : : OUT : Enter
configuration commands, one per line.  End with CNTL/Z.
Dec  6 17:21:59.266: %HA_EM-6-LOG: LOOP0 : DEBUG(cli_lib) : : OUT :
Switch(config)#
Dec  6 17:21:59.266: %HA_EM-6-LOG: LOOP0 : DEBUG(cli_lib) : : IN  :
Switch(config)#interface loopback0
Dec  6 17:21:59.277: %HA_EM-6-LOG: LOOP0 : DEBUG(cli_lib) : : OUT :
Switch(config-if)#
Dec  6 17:21:59.277: %HA_EM-6-LOG: LOOP0 : DEBUG(cli_lib) : : IN  :
Switch(config-if)#shutdown
Dec  6 17:21:59.287: %HA_EM-6-LOG: LOOP0 : DEBUG(cli_lib) : : OUT :
Switch(config-if)#
Dec  6 17:21:59.287: %HA_EM-6-LOG: LOOP0 : DEBUG(cli_lib) : : IN  :
Switch(config-if)#no shutdown
Dec  6 17:21:59.298: %HA_EM-6-LOG: LOOP0 : DEBUG(cli_lib) : : OUT :
Switch(config-if)#
Dec  6 17:21:59.298: %HA_EM-6-LOG: LOOP0: I've fallen and I can't get up!
Dec  6 17:22:01.293: %LINK-3-UPDOWN: Interface Loopback0, changed state to up
Dec  6 17:22:11.314: %HA_EM-3-FMPD_SMTP: Error occurred when sending mail to SMTP
server: 10.0.0.25 : error in connecting to SMTP server
Dec  6 17:22:11.314: %HA_EM-3-FMPD_ERROR: Error executing applet LOOP0 statement
7.0
Dec  6 17:22:11.314: %HA_EM-6-LOG: LOOP0 : DEBUG(cli_lib) : : CTL : cli_close
called.
```

Note For troubleshooting purposes, using the **debug event manager all** command will show all the outputs for the configured actions while the applet is being executed. For instance, it will show the same output as shown above but will include more details on all the other actions. To specifically troubleshoot the mail configuration and related error messages in an EEM Applet, the **debug event manager action mail** command is most useful as it filters out all the other unnecessary debug messages while you are trying to troubleshoot the mail configuration. This will allow you to focus on SMTP errors as shown in the previous example.

Another very useful aspect of EEM applets is that CLI patterns can be matched as an event. This means that when certain commands are entered into the router via CLI, they can trigger an EEM event within an applet. Then the configured actions will take place as a result of the CLI pattern being matched. The following example uses another common

EEM applet to match the CLI pattern "wr mem". Once the applet is triggered, the following actions will be invoked:

- The router will generate a syslog message that says "Configuration File Changed!"
- The startup-config will be copied to a TFTP server.
- Generate a syslog message stating that the configuration has been successfully saved.

```
event manager environment filename Router.cfg
event manager environment tftpserver tftp://10.1.200.29/
event manager applet BACKUP-CONFIG
 event cli pattern "write mem.*" sync yes
 action 1.0 cli command "enable"
 action 2.0 cli command "configure terminal"
 action 3.0 cli command "file prompt quiet"
 action 4.0 cli command "end"
 action 5.0 cli command "copy start $tftpserver$filename"
 action 6.0 cli command "configure terminal"
 action 7.0 cli command "no file prompt quiet"
 action 8.0 syslog priority informational msg "Configuration File Changed! TFTP
backup successful."
```

Note The **file prompt quiet** command disables the IOS confirmation mechanism that asks you to confirm your actions.

Note The priority and facility of the Syslog messages can be changed to fit your environment's alerting structure. For example, we used informational in the previous example.

As seen in the previous examples there are multiple ways to call out specific EEM environment values. The first example illustrated that you can use a single line to configure the mail environment and send messages with CLI output results. Using the event manager environment variables shown in the second example, you can statically set different settings that you can call on from multiple actions instead of calling them out individually on a single line. Although you can create custom names and values that are arbitrary and can be set to anything, it is good practice to use common and descriptive variables. Table 7-3 lists some of the most commonly used email variables in EEM.

Table 7-3 *Common EEM Email Variables*

EEM Variable	Description	Example
_email_server	SMTP server IP address or DNS name	10.0.0.25 or MAILSVR01
_email_to	Email address to send email to	neteng@yourcompany.com
_email_from	Email address of sending party	no-reply@yourcompany.com
_email_cc	Email address of additional email receivers	helpdesk@yourcompany.com

EEM and Tcl Scripts

Using an EEM applet to call Tcl scripts is another very powerful aspect of EEM. We have covered multiple ways to use EEM applets. In this section, we will discuss how to call a Tcl script from an EEM applet. The previous sections on EEM showed multiple ways of executing actions, based on the automatic detection of specific events when they are happening. This example shows how to manually execute an EEM applet that will, in turn, execute a Tcl script that is locally stored in the device's flash memory.

It is important to understand that there are many different ways to use EEM and that manually triggered applets are also a very useful tool. The following example depicts an EEM script that is configured with the **event none** command. This means that there is no automatic event that the applet is monitoring and that this applet will only run when it is triggered manually. To manually run an EEM applet, the **event manager run** command must be used as illustrated in second output.

```
event manager applet Ping
 event none
 action 1.0 cli command "enable"
 action 1.1 cli command "tclsh flash:/ping.tcl"
```

```
Router# event manager run Ping
Router#
Dec  6 19:32:16.564: %HA_EM-6-LOG: Ping : DEBUG(cli_lib) : : CTL : cli_open
called.
Dec  6 19:32:16.564: %HA_EM-6-LOG: Ping : DEBUG(cli_lib) : : OUT : Router>
Dec  6 19:32:16.568: %HA_EM-6-LOG: Ping : DEBUG(cli_lib) : : IN  : Router>enable
Dec  6 19:32:16.578: %HA_EM-6-LOG: Ping : DEBUG(cli_lib) : : OUT : Router#
Dec  6 19:32:16.578: %HA_EM-6-LOG: Ping : DEBUG(cli_lib) : : IN  : Router#tclsh
flash:/ping.tcl
Dec  6 19:32:16.711: %HA_EM-6-LOG: Ping : DEBUG(cli_lib) : : OUT : Type escape
sequence to abort.
Dec  6 19:32:16.711: %HA_EM-6-LOG: Ping : DEBUG(cli_lib) : : OUT : Sending 5,
100-byte ICMP Echos to 192.168.0.2, timeout is 2 seconds:
Dec  6 19:32:16.711: %HA_EM-6-LOG: Ping : DEBUG(cli_lib) : : OUT : !!!!!
Dec  6 19:32:16.711: %HA_EM-6-LOG: Ping : DEBUG(cli_lib) : : OUT : Success rate is
100 percent (5/5), round-trip min/avg/max = 1/1/4 ms
Dec  6 19:32:16.711: %HA_EM-6-LOG: Ping : DEBUG(cli_lib) : : OUT : Type escape
sequence to abort.
```

```
Dec  6 19:32:16.711: %HA_EM-6-LOG: Ping : DEBUG(cli_lib) : : OUT : Sending 5,
100-byte ICMP Echos to 192.168.0.3, timeout is 2 seconds:
Dec  6 19:32:16.711: %HA_EM-6-LOG: Ping : DEBUG(cli_lib) : : OUT : !!!!!
Dec  6 19:32:16.711: %HA_EM-6-LOG: Ping : DEBUG(cli_lib) : : OUT : Success rate is
100 percent (5/5), round-trip min/avg/max = 1/1/1 ms
Dec  6 19:32:16.711: %HA_EM-6-LOG: Ping : DEBUG(cli_lib) : : OUT : Type escape
sequence to abort.
Dec  6 19:32:16.711: %HA_EM-6-LOG: Ping : DEBUG(cli_lib) : : OUT : Sending 5,
100-byte ICMP Echos to 192.168.0.4, timeout is 2 seconds:
Dec  6 19:32:16.711: %HA_EM-6-LOG: Ping : DEBUG(cli_lib) : : OUT : !!!!!
Dec  6 19:32:16.711: %HA_EM-6-LOG: Ping : DEBUG(cli_lib) : : OUT : Success rate is
100 percent (5/5), round-trip min/avg/max = 1/1/3 ms
Dec  6 19:32:16.711: %HA_EM-6-LOG: Ping : DEBUG(cli_lib) : : OUT : Type escape
sequence to abort.
Dec  6 19:32:16.711: %HA_EM-6-LOG: Ping : DEBUG(cli_lib) : : OUT : Sending 5,
100-byte ICMP Echos to 192.168.0.5, timeout is 2 seconds:
Dec  6 19:32:16.711: %HA_EM-6-LOG: Ping : DEBUG(cli_lib) : : OUT : !!!!!
Dec  6 19:32:16.711: %HA_EM-6-LOG: Ping : DEBUG(cli_lib) : : OUT : Success rate is
100 percent (5/5), round-trip min/avg/max = 1/1/4 ms
Dec  6 19:32:16.711: %HA_EM-6-LOG: Ping : DEBUG(cli_lib) : : OUT : Type escape
sequence to abort.
Dec  6 19:32:16.711: %HA_EM-6-LOG: Ping : DEBUG(cli_lib) : : OUT : Sending 5,
100-byte ICMP Echos to 192.168.0.6, timeout is 2 seconds:
Dec  6 19:32:16.711: %HA_EM-6-LOG: Ping : DEBUG(cli_lib) : : OUT : !!!!!
Dec  6 19:32:16.711: %HA_EM-6-LOG: Ping : DEBUG(cli_lib) : : OUT : Success rate is
100 percent (5/5), round-trip min/avg/max = 1/1/1 ms
Dec  6 19:32:16.711: %HA_EM-6-LOG: Ping : DEBUG(cli_lib) : : CTL : 20+ lines read
from cli, debug output truncated
Dec  6 19:32:16.711: %HA_EM-6-LOG: Ping : DEBUG(cli_lib) : : CTL : cli_close called.
```

For reference, see the following snippet for the exact content of the ping.tcl script used in the manually triggered EEM applet in the previous example. To see the contents of a TCL script that resides in flash, issue the **more** command followed by the file location and filename. The **more** command can be used to view all other text based files stored in the local flash as well.

```
Router# more flash:ping.tcl
foreach address {
192.168.0.2
192.168.0.3
192.168.0.4
192.168.0.5
192.168.0.6
} { ping $address}
```

EEM Summary

There are many ways to utilize EEM. From applets to scripting, the possibly use cases can only be limited by the engineer's imagination. EEM provides on-box monitoring of various different components based on a series of events. Once an event is detected, an action can take place. This helps make some of the network monitoring more proactive, rather than reactive. This can also reduce the load on the network and improve efficiency from the monitoring system because now the devices can simply report when there is something wrong instead of continually asking the devices if there is anything wrong.

Note For information on EEM and its robust features, please visit http://www.cisco.com/c/en/us/products/ios-nx-os-software/ios-embedded-event-manager-eem/index.html

Summary

By automating daily configuration tasks, you gain some of the following benefits:

- Increased agility
- Reduced Opex
- Lower overall TCO
- Streamlined management
- Reduction of human error
- Increased visibility

Keeping the above in mind, then adding the fact that many organizations are dealing with lean IT problems and high turnover, network engineers are being asked to do more with less. Utilizing some of the tools that were covered in this chapter can help alleviate some of the pressure put on IT staff by offloading some of the more tedious, time-consuming, and repetitive tasks. This will allow the network engineer to focus more on critical mission responsibilities like network design and growth planning.

Chapter 8

Network Automation Tools for Campus Environments

There are many network automation tools available these days. This chapter is going to focus on some of the more common automation tools that are available. Network automation for the campus is not unlike that of the data center environments in that the reasons to use automation are very similar. Some of the most obvious reasons are:

- Speed of change/agility/frequency of change
- Compliance/standardization
- Improve reliability by reducing human error
- Free-up resources for other projects/tasks
- Reduce complexity
- Decrease cost of failure
- Lower operational expenses

Often, businesses have a high frequency of change in their network environment, and of those changes, some can be extremely complex. When businesses have increased complexity in their network, the cost of something failing can be very high. Failure in a network doesn't necessarily mean a hardware or software component. According to the following report, found at http://roc.cs.berkeley.edu/papers/easy01.pdf, on average, 50–70% of network outages are caused by human beings. The causes for these outages can be from misconfigurations due to lack of understanding the complexity of a given network. While not all outages or failures can be avoided, there are tools that can assist in lowering the number of overall outages that are caused by human error or misconfigurations.

To start to automate a task, a few things must first be clearly defined. The following list provides some of the most important points to consider when getting ready to begin the automation of a task or procedure. Automation of tasks can take the load off of network operators by efficiently automating the repetitive day-to-day tasks that become arduous over time. This helps businesses with lean IT departments become more strategic, rather than transactional as it relates to freeing up cycles to focus on more pressing matters like network security and future design projects.

- What issue or task are you trying to solve or automate?
- What are all the process steps needed to accomplish the task?
- What are the technical steps needed to produce the desired outcome?
- What is the desired outcome of the task you are trying to automate?
- Did the change you automated execute or complete successfully?

Data Models and Supporting Protocols

The following section will cover some of the most common data models and tools and how they are leveraged in a programmatic approach. Those data models and tools are:

- Yet another next generation (YANG) modeling language
- Network configuration protocol (NETCONF)
- ConfD

YANG Data Models

SNMP is widely used for fault handling and monitoring. However, it is not often used for configuration changes. CLI scripting is used more often than other methods. YANG data models are an alternative to SNMP MIBs and are becoming the standard for data definition languages. YANG was defined in RFC 6020 and uses data models. Data models are used to describe whatever can be configured on a device, everything that can be monitored on a device, and all the administrative actions that can be executed on a device, such as resetting counters or rebooting the device. This includes all the notifications that the device is capable of generating. All of these variables can be represented within a YANG model. Data models are very powerful in that they create a uniform way to describe data, which can be beneficial across vendors' platforms. Data models allow network operators to configure, monitor, and interact with network devices holistically across the entire enterprise environment. YANG models use a tree structure. Within that structure, the models are constructed similar to that of an XML format and are built in modules. These modules are hierarchical in nature and contain all the different data and types that make up a YANG device model. YANG models make a clear distinction between configuration data and state information. The tree structure represents how to reach a specific element of the model. These elements can be either configurable or not configurable. Elements all have a defined type. For example, an interface can be configured to be on or off. But the interface state cannot be configured, for example, up or down. The following example illustrates a simple YANG module taken from RFC 6020.

```
container food {
  choice snack {
      case sports-arena {
          leaf pretzel {
              type empty;
          }
          leaf beer {
              type empty;
          }
      }
      case late-night {
          leaf chocolate {
              type enumeration {
                  enum dark;
                  enum milk;
                  enum first-available;
              }
          }
      }
  }
}
```

The output in the previous example can be read as follows: You have food. Of that food, you have a choice of snacks. In the case that you are in the sports arena, your snack choices are pretzels and beer. If it is late at night, your snack choices are two different types of chocolate. You can choose to have milk chocolate or dark chocolate, and if you are in a hurry and do not want to wait, you can have the first available chocolate whether it is milk chocolate or dark chocolate. To put this into more network-oriented terms, see the following example.

```
list interface {
     key "name";

     leaf name {
         type string;
     }
     leaf speed {
         type enumeration {
             enum 10m;
             enum 100m;
             enum auto;
         }
     }
     leaf observed-speed {
         type uint32;
         config false;
     }
}
```

The YANG model shown can be read as follows: You have a list of interfaces. Of the available interfaces, there is a specific interface that has three configurable speeds. Those speeds are 10Mbps, 100Mbps, and auto as listed in the leaf named "speed." The leaf named "observed-speed" cannot be configured due to the **config false** command. This is because as the leaf is named, the speeds in this leaf are what was auto-detected (observed); hence it is not a configurable leaf. This is because it represents the auto-detected value on the interface, not a configurable value.

NETCONF

NETCONF was defined in RFC 4741 and RFC 6241. NETCONFIG is an IETF standard protocol that uses the YANG data models to communicate with the various devices on the network. NETCONF runs over SSH, TLS, or simple object access protocol (SOAP). Some of the key differences between SNMP and NETCONF are listed in Table 8-1. One of the most important differences is that SNMP can't distinguish between configuration data and operational data, but NETCONF can. Another key differentiator is that NETCONF uses paths to describe resources, whereas SNMP uses Object Identifiers (OIDs). A NETCONF path can be similar to interfaces/interface/eth0, which is much more descriptive than what you would expect out of SNMP. Below is a list of some of the more common use cases for NETCONF:

- Collect the status of specific fields
- Change the configuration of specific fields
- Take administrative actions
- Send event notifications
- Backup and restore configurations
- Test configurations before finalizing the transaction

Table 8-1 *Differences between SNMP and NETCONF*

	SNMP	NETCONF
Standard	**IETF**	**IETF**
Resources	OIDs	Paths
Data models	Defined in MIBs	YANG Core Models
Data Modeling Language	SMI	YANG
Management Operations	SNMP	NETCONF
Encoding	BER	XML, YANG, JSON
Transport Stack	UDP	SSH/TCP

Transactions are all or nothing. There is no order of operations or sequencing within a transaction. That means it doesn't matter what order the configurations are done. It is completely arbitrary. Transactions are processed in the same order every time on every device. Transactions, when deployed, run in a parallel state and do not have any impact on each other.

The following example illustrates an example of a NETCONF element from RFC 4741. This NETCONF output can be read as follows: There is a list of users named users. In that list, there are the following individual users named root, Fred, and Barney.

```
<rpc-reply message-id="101"
       xmlns="urn:ietf:params:xml:ns:netconf:base:1.0">
    <data>
      <top xmlns="http://example.com/schema/1.2/config">
        <users>
          <user>
            <name>root</name>
          </user>
          <user>
            <name>fred</name>
          </user>
          <user>
            <name>barney</name>
          </user>
        </users>
      </top>
    </data>
  </rpc-reply>
```

An alternate way of looking at this type of NETCONF output is to simply look at it as though it were a shopping list. The following example illustrates an example of the shopping list concept. This can be read as follows: you have a group of beverages. Of these beverages, you have soft drinks and tea. The available soft drinks are either cola or root beer. Of the available tea, there is sweetened or unsweetened.

```
Beverages
    Soft Drinks
        Cola
        Root Beer
    Tea
        Sweetened
        Unsweetened
```

ConfD

Network operators today are looking for a way to manage their networks holistically, rather than managing it on a box-by-box basis. To do this, many network devices have northbound APIs that allow a management tool or suite of tools to interact with the devices across the network. This allows for service applications and device setup to be done uniformly across the campus environment. This type of automation introduces the concept of a transactional deployment model. In the transactional deployment model, network operators will deploy services or configurations to devices in an all-or-nothing fashion. For example, if a network operator was deploying quality of service (QoS) on a box-by-box basis, there are many configuration steps that would have to be completed for QoS to function properly. Class-maps must classify and match traffic, policy-maps must be configured and applied to interfaces, and so on. If one of these steps is missed, QoS will not function properly. With a transactional model, you can deploy all the steps needed to enable QoS on all devices simultaneously, and if for some reason the entire configuration isn't fully deployed, it can be rolled back entirely. This is a much cleaner and less error-prone way to deploy certain features. In the transactional model, there wouldn't be any partially configured features resident in the campus devices, and this ensures the integrity of the network as a whole. This also functionally makes your network act as a federated database, rather than a collection of separated devices.

Service applications can include things like VPN provisioning, QoS, firewall capabilities, and so forth. Device setup components can be things, such as configuration templates, scripts, and other device-specific operations. ConfD is a device-management framework that is very different that the traditional management tools. ConfD uses YANG data models to interact with various network devices. It can also use NETCONF among other things as a protocol to carry the different transactions to the equipment to be executed. Once you have a YANG model for a device, ConfD automatically will render all the management protocols that were mentioned earlier. For example, you will automatically have a WEB UI into the YANG model of the device without having to program anything. The YANG model also supplies the configuration database (CBD) (covered in the next section) schema so the structure of the fields is taken from the YANG model, as well. Table 8-2 compares some of the differences between ConfD and other traditional management tools.

Table 8-2 *Comparison between ConfD and Traditional Management Tools*

Traditional Management Tools	ConfD
SNMP Agents	Data Model Driven (YANG)
CLI	Any protocol
Feature lag of management tool	Execute transactions for desired features

ConfD has many different management protocols that can be used northbound to manage the product. Some of these protocols are seen in Figure 8-1. Those management protocols are:

- NETCONF
- SNMP v1, v2c, v3

- REST
- CLI
- WEB UI

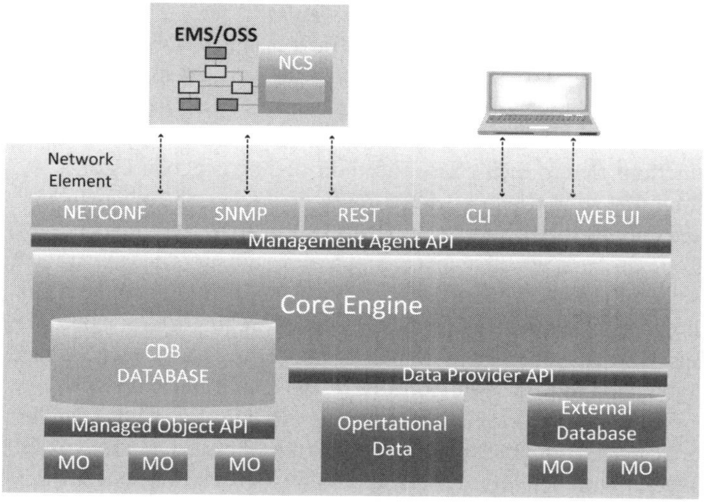

Figure 8-1 *ConfD Core Platform and Management APIs*

Some of the different components to ConfD are the Core Engine, CDB Database, Managed Object API and the Data Provider API. The CDB database is where the configurations are stored in the ConfD solution. The internal CDB database is optional and network operators can choose to have external databases for their configurations or use both internal and external databases to fit their needs. This may make sense if you have a number of legacy applications already using an external database. Most often, the internal CDB database is used.

Note You can also store alarms, performance data, internal state, and other items in the CDB database.

There are multiple components that comprise the ConfD core engine. Some of those components are as follows:

- Transaction management
- Session management/authentication
- Role-based access control (RBAC)
- Redundancy/replication for HA

- Event Logging/audit trails
- Validation syntax/semantic
- Rollback management
- Upgrades and downgrades

Once an operator has authenticated to ConfD, that operator is assigned one or more roles. These roles can dictate not only what the operator can see or not see, but what the operator can make changes to or what they can't make changes to. These roles can be very granular in nature. This gives the flexibility to have multiple tiers of operators that have job-specific functions tied to their roles. The audit trailing capabilities of ConfD allows for robust reporting on which operator configured what, the commands that were executed, where they were executed, and when. This is especially important when you have multiple operators responsible in a campus environment. The validation component of ConfD is one of the most important. It can validate that the syntax of the commands is indeed valid before they are sent to the devices. More importantly, because of the YANG data models, ConfD can verify the validity of specific variables with other variables. That means if you need to make sure portions of the configuration are unique throughout your environment, ConfD can verify that unique variable across your whole environment, such as duplicate IP addresses. Figure 8-2 illustrates how NETCONF uses YANG data models to interact with network devices and then talk back to management applications like ConfD.

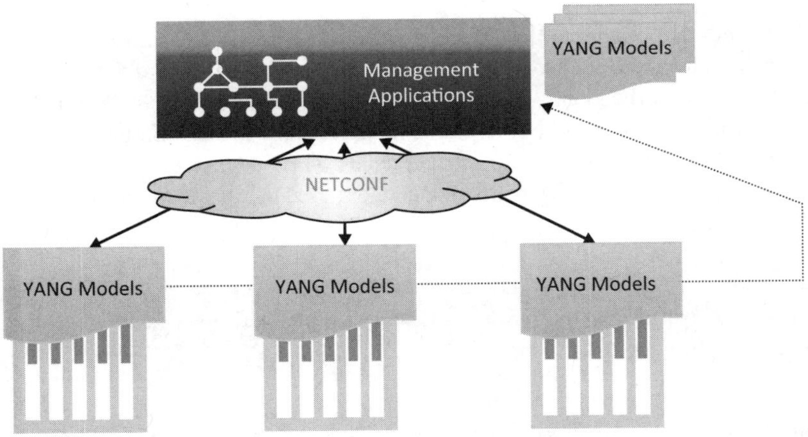

Figure 8-2 *NETCONF/YANG interfacing with management applications*

The rollback management function is another very useful component of ConfD. For instance, after a network operator authenticates to the ConfD system and gets a role assigned to them, the rollback management component will track all the transactions made by that operator within their current session and create rollback files in the event that the transactions need to be reverted back to a previous state. This creates a timeline of transactions that allows the operator to pick a point in time to rollback to.

ConfD is designed to make your devices more manageable, programmable, and compliant with the industry standards. ConfD enables multiple ways to interact with your campus devices such as NETCONF, SNMP, REST APIs, CLI, and Web user interfaces. A key benefit of ConfD is its ability to hide network complexity and provide useful northbound interfaces that humans and applications can use. Using ConfD can save you time when interacting with devices because it is data model driven. All the interfaces of the data models are automatically rendered and require no programming by default. It has a self-contained database, although you can have external databases and a variety of feature-rich APIs.

Application Policy Infrastructure Controller Enterprise Module (APIC-EM)

Application policy infrastructure controller enterprise module (APIC-EM) is a product that is designed to simplify network configuration and provisioning. APIC-EM brings SDN capabilities to the enterprise campus environment. This includes LAN, WAN, and access networks. Programmability and automation of these places in the network (PINs) help network operators respond more quickly to the pace of change in their environment. This also allows the network operators to streamline configuration changes and free up additional resources to deliver a more agile networking workforce that can be more readily available to help guide the design of the network in response to business growth. The following section covers APIC-EM and what the different components and use cases are for the product. Finally, this section discusses programmatic access leveraging RESTful APIs on APIC-EM, including examples in both Postman and Python.

APIC-EM Architecture

APIC-EM is a software-based network controller that has the ability to run on any x86 server. The APIC-EM software can be run as a virtual machine (VM) or as a standalone appliance. This is especially important when it comes to a disaster recovery (DR) or a highly available (HA) deployment. The APIC-EM software is an application-based platform that automates advanced configuration tasks by utilizing guided workflows and a user-friendly graphical user interface (GUI). One of the most important benefits of APIC-EM is that none of the users or network operators who use the APIC-EM software will need any programming skills whatsoever. The APIC-EM software offers integrated analytics, centralized policy management, and superior network abstraction. For network teams that are just starting to dip their toes into software-defined networking (SDN), APIC-EM offers an easy path to follow when approaching SDN. APIC-EM uses a policy-based architecture that allows the controller to automate provisioning of the campus infrastructure end to end, which in turn helps to increase the speed of deployment for enterprise applications and services. Some of the key benefits of APIC-EM software are as follows:

- Simplified configuration and provisioning
- Overall investment protection

- Open, programmable, and customizable
- Business policies and requirements are translated into network configurations.

The APIC-EM not only automates the network configurations, but it also has the capability to run compliance checks on the different network polices deployed across the entire campus network environment. APIC-EM works with currently deployed network infrastructure and does not require any network infrastructure replacements. This means that no new network hardware is needed to run APIC-EM. Programmability is a very important benefit of APIC-EM. The controller is highly programmable through open APIs and representational state transfer (REST). This allows for software developers to design and utilize customized network services and applications.

APIC-EM Applications

It was mentioned earlier that APIC-EM is an application-based software controller. What that means is that there are separate self-contained applications that run on the controller that accomplish different tasks or services as it pertains to the campus network environment. Below is a brief list of some of the applications that are available at the time of this writing on the APIC-EM software controller:

- Intelligent WAN (IWAN) Application
- Plug and Play (PnP) Application
- Path Trace Application

In the coming sections of this chapter, we will look a bit deeper into each of the APIC-EM applications mentioned in this section and some of the future roadmap applications.

Intelligent WAN (IWAN) Application

Cisco's Intelligent WAN (IWAN) product is getting a lot of attention these days. This is because of the high demand on network infrastructure because of the ever-growing amount of traffic and data that needs to be transferred between branches and other enterprise network locations. Below is a brief list of business-relevant applications and reasons that cause high demands on the campus WAN.

- Internet of things (sensors, cameras, connected buildings)
- Centralized data analytics
- Video and telepresence
- Mobility
- Guest access

The demands on the branches are growing at a significant pace, and as a direct result, users are suffering with network congestion, poor quality, and limited to no redundancy.

Often, the IT budgets are getting trimmed, and businesses are faced with having to do more with less. That's where IWAN can help. IWAN is an example of a software-defined WAN (SD-WAN) solution that can monitor all available WAN links and automatically utilize the best link available at any given time. IWAN is also application-aware, and this gives it the unique capability of ensuring the enterprise applications' performance over your WAN. It also addresses the redundancy and resiliency issues that most network environments have in their branch locations. This is achieved by having the ability to have a transport-independent WAN with diverse carriers and transport types. For example, you can have MPLS as one transport and Internet as another. Figure 8-3 illustrates an example of a typical hybrid IWAN deployment. Some of the benefits of this type of network design are:

- More control of routing
- Ability to create your own service level agreements (SLA)
- Single routing domain
- Active/active circuit utilization
- Increased resiliency

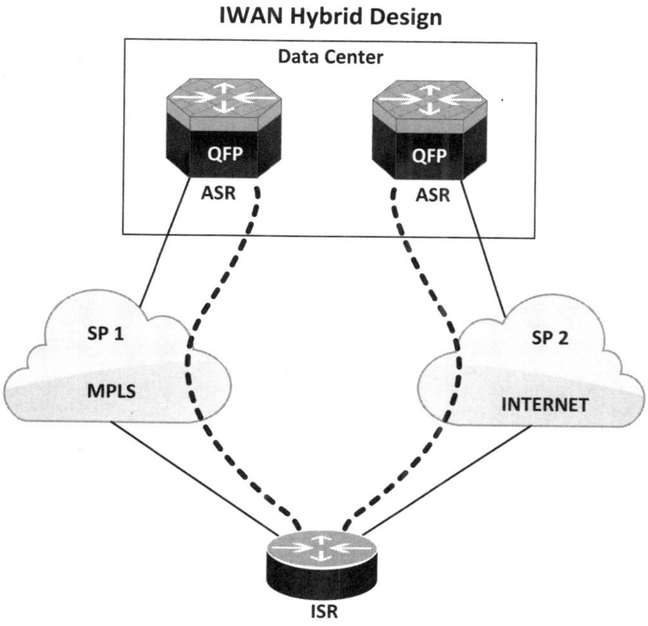

Figure 8-3 *Typical hybrid IWAN design*

The APIC-EM IWAN application offers the necessary tools to automate and configure IWAN. This gives a very prescriptive approach to the IWAN deployment. The IWAN application is built off of the Cisco Validated Designs (CVDs) for IWAN. This means it is specifically designed to work in such a way that by using deployment tools in the IWAN application, it is guaranteed that you are deploying IWAN in a best practice-validated design that is supported by Cisco.

Note To learn more about Cisco Validated Designs please visit: www.cisco.com/go/cvd

When you first log in to the APIC-EM controller, you will notice that there are multiple icons on the left side of the web page. Figure 8-4 shows the main page of the APIC-EM once you log into the controller. These icons represent the different tasks and applications that are available inside the APIC-EM controller.

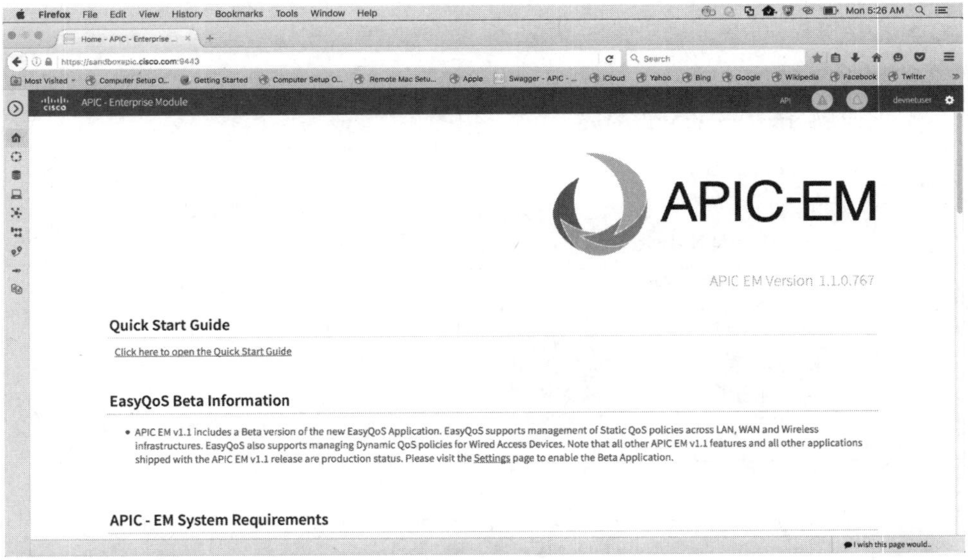

Figure 8-4 *Task icons on APIC-EM main page*

Note The APIC-EM main page may look different, depending on the version you are using.

Once on the main page of the APIC-EM controller, you can click the arrow on the upper left side. That will expand the menu names of the icons shown previously in Figure 8-4. Some of these available tasks and applications are:

- Home
- Discovery
- Device inventory

- Host inventory
- Topology
- IWAN
- Path trace
- Network plug and play

Now that you can see the names of the available tasks and applications listed on the main page, Figure 8-5 illustrates the steps on how to launch the IWAN application from the APIC-EM controller. The first step to start the configuration process using the IWAN application would be to configure a hub router. To do that, you could simply click the Set up Hub Site & Settings icon. Once you do that, it will begin the IWAN hub workflow to walk you through the necessary steps to configure a hub router. Within this workflow, you can set a variety of variables such as: Netflow, SNMP, DNS, IP address pools, QoS models, and so on.

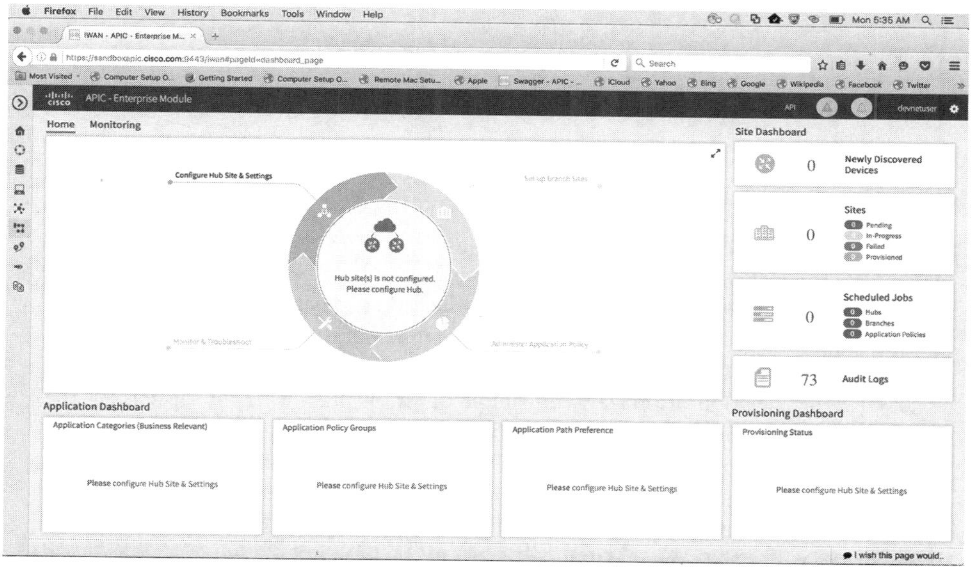

Figure 8-5 *Lauching the APIC-EM IWAN application*

As you can see from Figure 8-6, after you click the Set up Hub Site & Settings icon, the workflow begins. The key thing to notice here is that there are only five configuration categories in the Network Wide Settings of the IWAN application. These categories are all that are necessary to deploy a hub site in the APIC-EM IWAN application. This drastically reduces the time and complexity to deploy IWAN versus deploying it manually on hub devices.

Note This section of the chapter is neither a step-by-step guide on how to use the APIC-EM controller nor a step-by-step guide on how to deploy IWAN. This is to illustrate the simple and intuitive features of the applications within APIC-EM controller.

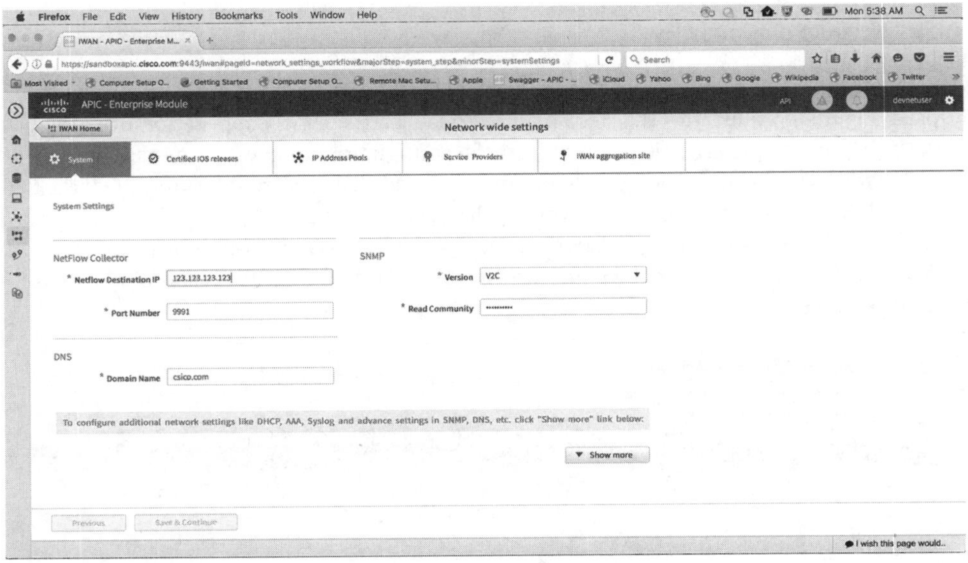

Figure 8-6 *First Step in the IWAN hub workflow*

Provisioning the hub routers in the IWAN application is designed to be easy and intuitive. Instead of having to go through the normal onboarding process of manually building a new hub router, you can simply use the IWAN application in a point-and-click fashion. The application asks you simple questions like, what interface is for the WAN, and what interface is for the LAN? What type of QoS model are the service providers using, for instance, 4 class model, 5 class model, 6 class model, and so forth? Figure 8-7 shows the Configure Router pop-up that you receive when you click on the hub during the deployment within the IWAN application. This pop-up lists what some of the parameters the controller asks for to deploy the hub. Figure 8-8 shows an example of the application policy in the IWAN application. These application policies are tied directly to the various application-based traffic classes configured in an IWAN environment.

Note Other QoS topics will be covered in a later section of this chapter.

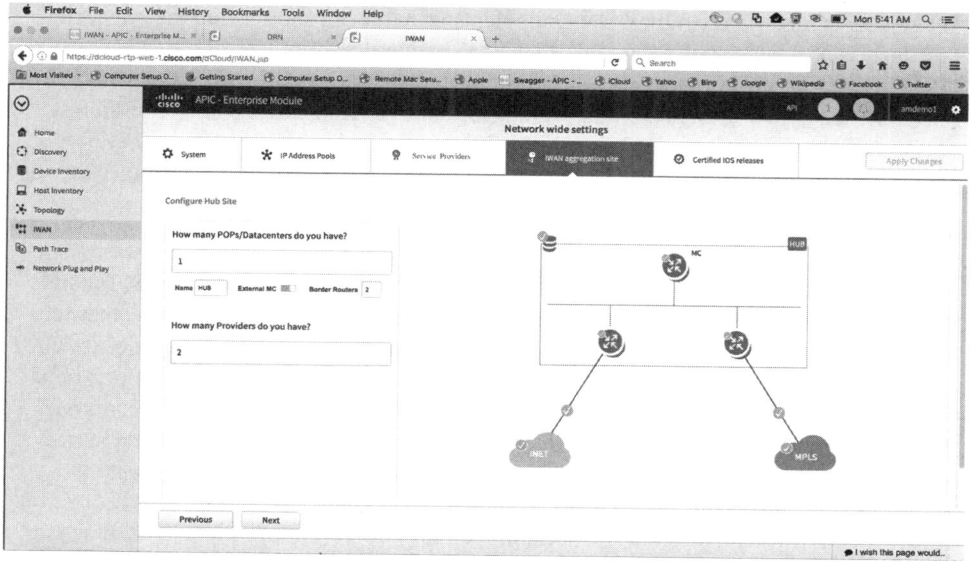

Figure 8-7 *Configure Router Pop-up during hub provisioning*

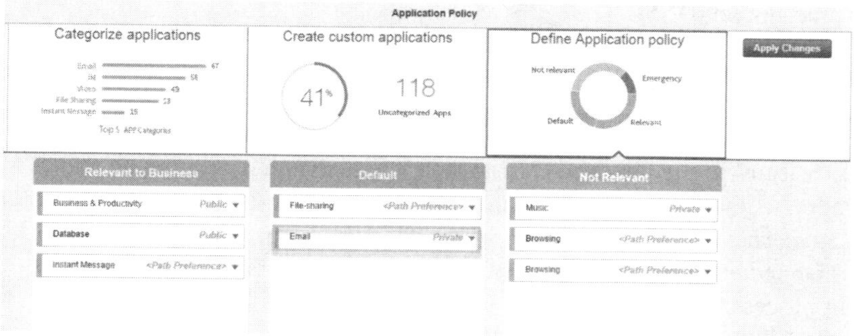

Figure 8-8 *IWAN application policy example*

> **Note** For more information on Cisco IWAN, please visit www.cisco.com/go/iwan to learn more about the IWAN and the different types of available management options.

Plug and Play (PnP) Application

Another common reason for automation techniques is when it comes to the deployment of network equipment throughout the campus environment. Commonly, the way most network operation teams deploy equipment is to send an experienced network engineer to the location where the equipment needs to be installed. Then the network engineer installs and configures the equipment so that it can successfully be connected to the rest of the enterprise network. One of the main disadvantages of this is that the experienced network engineer is taken away from more important tasks like monitoring network security or design planning and is put out in a remote location to configure a network device. This not only costs the business an exorbitant amount of money, it is also a tremendous waste of company resources, not to mention that it is serious waste of resources to install a network device.

The APIC-EM Plug and Play (PnP) application is designed to alleviate such a waste of resources and to make device deployment simple. Plug and Play offers a highly secure, seamless, and scalable way to deploy Cisco network equipment while doing so in a zero-touch manner across Cisco's entire enterprise network portfolio. This includes both wired and wireless devices. The Plug and Play application in APIC-EM reduces the operational overhead associated with device deployment. By automating device deployment, you can reduce travel costs, keep experienced engineers where they need to be, and in turn drastically reduce operating expenditures. This allows local installers to deploy new network devices without having any CLI or network administration skill. Devices can be provisioned in several different ways using the Plug and Play application. The following list defines some of those provisioning methods.

- Dynamic host configuration protocol (DHCP) discovery of APIC-EM controller
- Domain name system (DNS)
- Plug and Play (PNP) mobile application
- Mobile iOS or Android bootstrap application

There are many features to the Plug and Play application, such as a highly secure two-way authentication method that utilizes secure unique device identification (SUDI) and certificate-based mechanisms that are signed by trusted authorities. Plug and Play has an agent that is embedded in Cisco routers, switches, and access points to automate the deployment process. The PnP agent talks to a centrally located PnP server which is included with the APIC-EM software. The PnP server manages all the locations, devices, images, and licenses for all the different devices in the environment. The PnP server also provides northbound REST APIs for use with other software applications. The PnP server listens for PnP protocol requests from devices via HTTPS. Once a request is received, it then forces the devices to authenticate and be authorized based on their unique serial numbers. Once a device is authorized, it can then be provisioned with an IOS software image and device configuration. Because the PnP protocol uses HTTPS, remote branch devices can communicate with the PnP Server (APIC-EM) with a generic HTTP proxy. This removes the need for a gateway that converts the protocol. Another benefit of the PnP Mobile application is the monitoring and troubleshooting tools built into the application. You can also monitor installations from remote sites. Figure 8-9 illustrates an overview of the Cisco Plug and Play process.

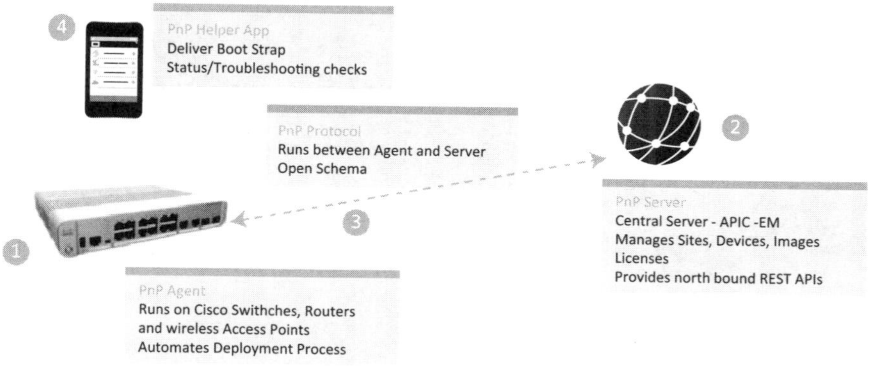

Figure 8-9 *Overview of the Cisco PnP process*

> **Note** PnP Agent is embedded into switches with IOS version 15.2(2) and IOS-XE 3.6.3E and newer. If you are running older versions of IOS on your switch, you will need to use the Cisco Smart Install (SMI) Proxy which converts Smart Install messages into PnP protocol messages. SMI Proxy is not available on router platforms.

There are multiple tabs you can navigate to within the Network Plug and Play application. Table 8-3 lists the tab names and some of the more common tasks you can accomplish on each tab.

Table 8-3 *Tabs and Descriptions with the Network Plug and Play Application*

Tab Name	Description
Dashboard	View overall status of devices and projects with errors
Projects	Device deployment projects
Unplanned Devices	Devices without pre-provisioning configuration applied.
Images	Software images by platform
Configurations	Device configurations
Bulk Import	Bulk import/export settings

Figure 8-10 illustrates the Network Plug and Play main dashboard page in APIC-EM. From the dashboard page you can see the status of the device deployments. These device deployments are called *Projects*. There are multiple states that a device can be in within the main dashboard page. They are as follows:

- Pre-Provisioned
- In-Progress
- Provisioned
- Projects with Errors

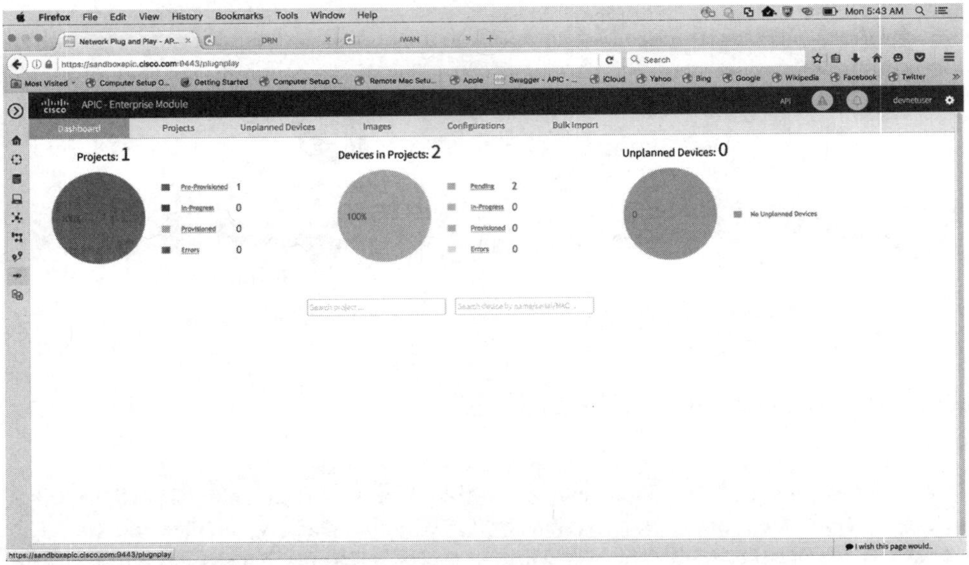

Figure 8-10 *Network Plug and Play dashboard*

Deployment projects are listed on the Projects tab. This is where you can create, clone, or delete projects. In this tab, we created a project named "CHIL-Router," and in that project we specify what devices we would like to deploy and any specific information on the devices that we are deploying. For example, device name, product ID, serial number/MAC address, device configuration and software image are some of the settings that can be selected on a device-by-device basis. Figure 8-11 illustrates the CHIL-Router project details.

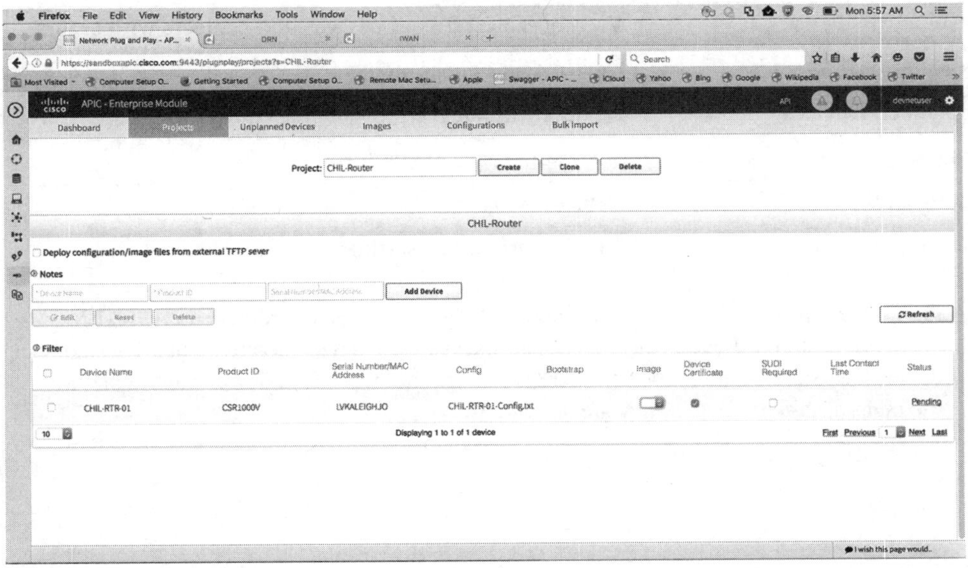

Figure 8-11 *CHIL-Router Project Details*

Once a project is completed successfully, the status will change to Provisioned. Clicking on the status of the device will bring up the history information window to show the complete progress of the device deployment with timestamps of when each step that took place. This is a good way to understand the flow and functions of the device provisioning. Figure 8-12 shows the History Info window that is called from clicking the Provisioned keyword in the Project tab next to the device about which you want to see more details. In addition, if you happen to be logged into the device while the PnP provisioning is taking place, you can see log entries that describe the PnP process and whether the provisioning has completed successfully or if something has failed. The following example illustrates the output from the **show log** command on a CSR1000V router. In the log, you can see that the PnP provisioning was successful. You can also see that if we issue the **show running-config | include pnp** command, we can see the zero-touch provisioning transport mode and profile used by the router to talk to the PnP Server on the APIC-EM.

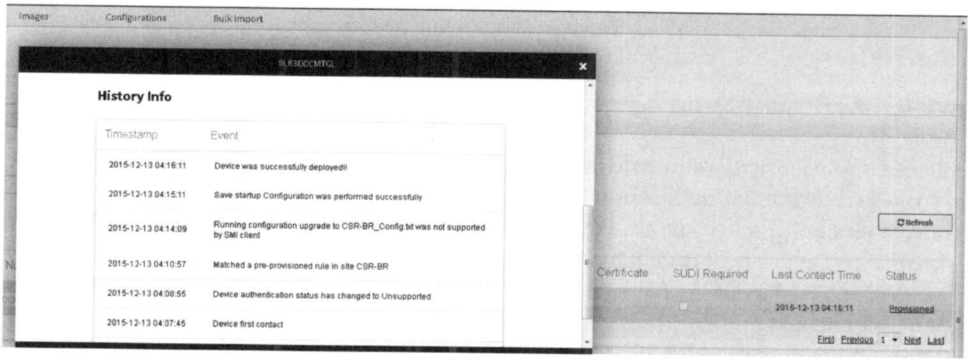

Figure 8-12 *Example of the Device History information window*

```
CHIL-RTR-01# show logging | include PNP
*Dec 13 04:07:20:144: %PNP-6-HTTP_CONNECTED: PnP Discovery connected to PnP server
http://192.168.129.100:80/pnp/HELLO
*Dec 13 04:07:21:168: %PNP-6-PROFILE_CONFIG: PnP Discovery profile pnp-zero-touch
configured
CHIL-RTR-01#
CHIL-RTR-01# show running-config | include pnp
!
pnp profile pnp-zero-touch
 transport https ipv4 192.168.129.100 port 443
end
CHIL-RTR-01#
```

Another status often seen on the Projects page is Pending. This means that the device has not fully been deployed or provisioned yet. There are multiple reasons for seeing the Pending status. One of the most common is that there is no communication to the device. Figure 8-13 shows the information page when the Pending status link is clicked in the Projects screen.

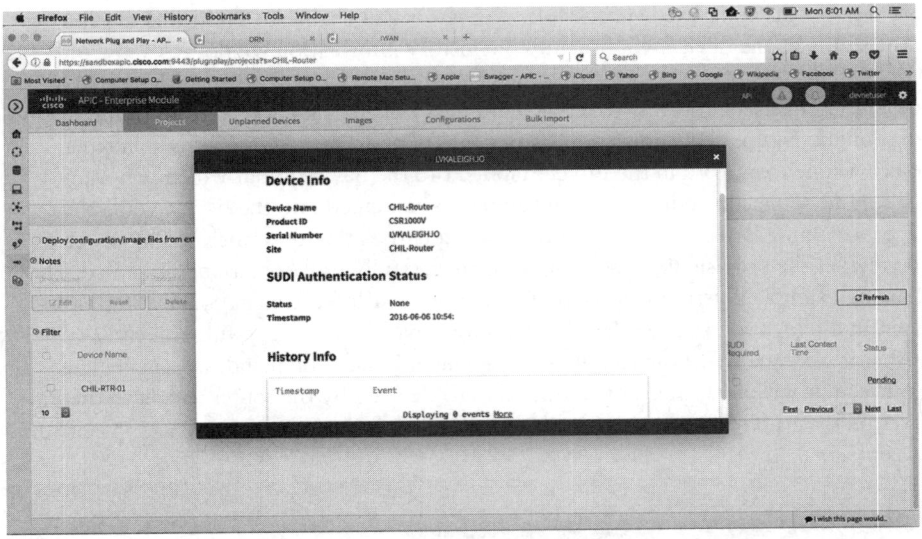

Figure 8-13 *Pending Status information page*

In order to manage the software images that each device type uses, we will look at the Images tab in the PnP application. The process to upload different types of software image files is quick and simple. First, click upload in the top left corner of the page, browse to the desired image file and click open to upload the file to the APIC-EM controller. Once an image file is uploaded, you will be able to see the size, platform information, and product ID associated to each specific image file. Figure 8-14 depicts the Images tab within the APIC-EM PnP application where software image files are managed.

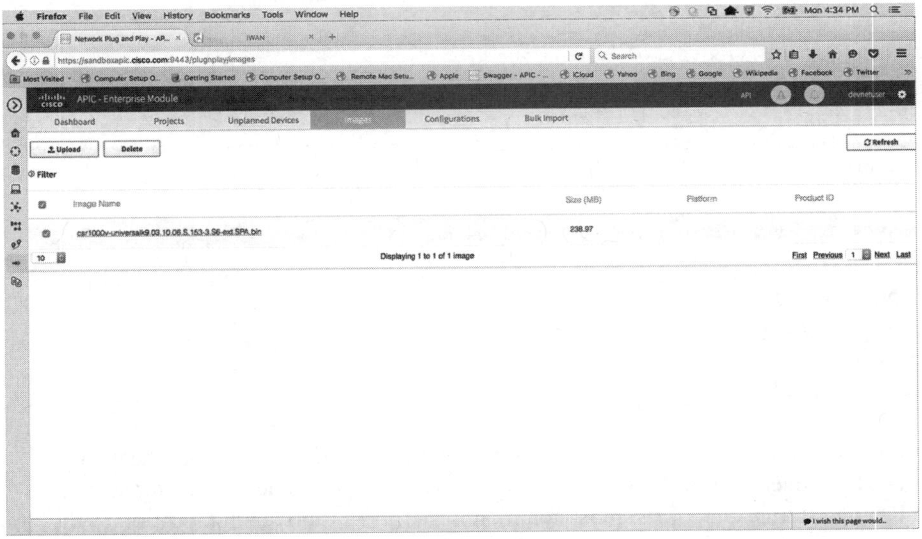

Figure 8-14 *Software Images tab in PnP application*

Managing the different configurations for various devices is just as easy as managing software image files. For this, look at the fifth tab called *Configurations*. In just a few simple clicks, you can upload a new configuration to the APIC-EM PnP application. Click Upload in the top left corner of the page, browse to the configuration file you want to upload to the APIC-EM, and then click open. Once the file is successfully uploaded, you will get a confirmation message at the bottom of the screen that the configuration files were uploaded as seen in Figure 8-15.

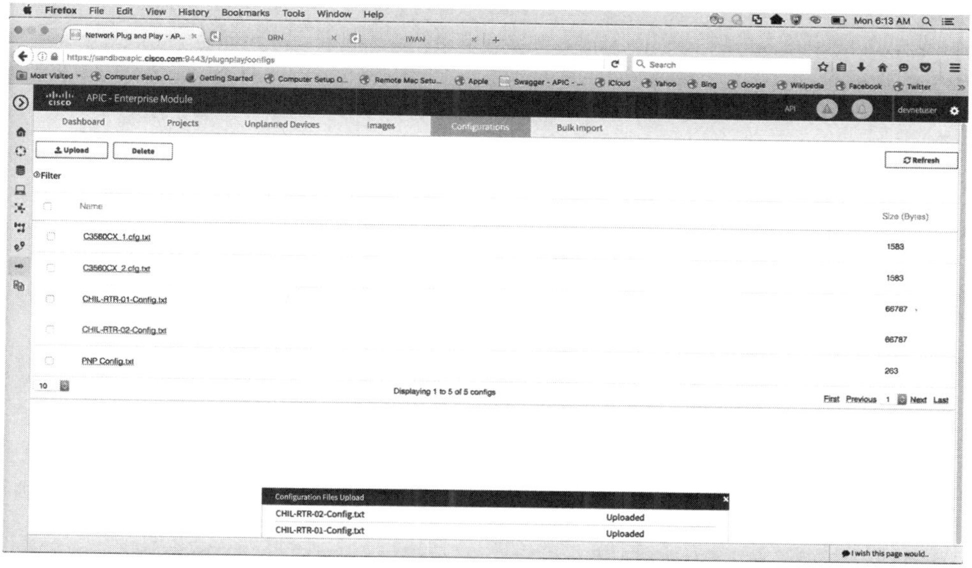

Figure 8-15 *Example of Configuration Upload page*

In certain cases, enterprise networks have sites that do not require pre-provisioning. In these instances, devices can be deployed without being previously setup in the Network Plug and Play application. This can be accomplished using the Unplanned Devices Workflow. Once a device is deployed manually, it can then be "claimed" as an unplanned device. This allows you to still be able to manage the device that wasn't pre-provisioned from within the PnP application. Inside the Network PnP application, there is a tab called *Unclaimed Devices*, this is where you can manage the devices that were not deployed using PnP. In this screen you will see three options that apply to any unclaimed devices. Those options are the following:

- Claim
- Ignore
- Delete

When a device connects to the PnP Server before it is provisioned by APIC-EM or the PnP Server was unable to match the device to an existing configuration, then the device will become an unclaimed device. To claim a device, you must select the device from the unclaimed devices screen. Then select the appropriate configuration file and software image for the device. Once those steps have been taken, you can click the Claim button to claim the device.

You can also choose to ignore a device and not manage it in the PnP application. If you do this, you can always decide to claim the device at a later time by moving the device back to the unclaimed device list and claiming it. To ignore an unclaimed device, simply select the device and click the Ignore button. Once a device is ignored, it will be moved automatically to the Ignored Devices tab in the top right corner of the Unplanned Devices screen.

The third option available under the Unplanned Devices screen is to delete the device from the PnP application altogether. To delete a device from the Unplanned Devices screen, select the device you wish to delete then click the Delete button. The device will be removed from the APIC-EM PnP application.

Path Trace Application

APIC-EM's Path Trace application automates some of the most common manual troubleshooting techniques used today. This increases the speed to find and diagnose network issues, which can save time and money. Path Trace also provides a detailed visual display and description of the flow paths between two endpoints anywhere within the entire enterprise network. Another key benefit of Path Trace is that it can look at traffic flows on a per-protocol basis. Figure 8-16 illustrates the Path Trace application within the APIC-EM.

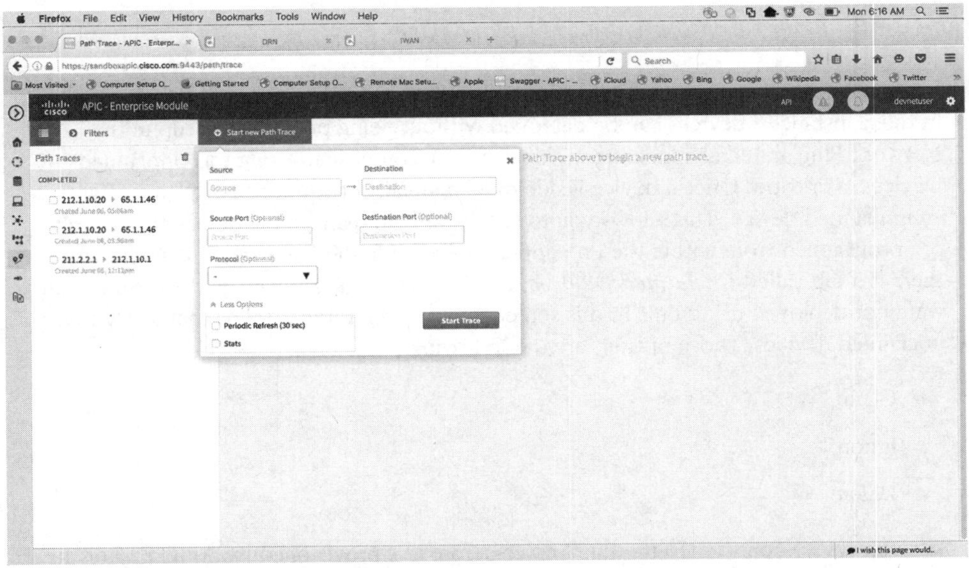

Figure 8-16 *Path Trace Application*

As seen in Figure 8-16, there are five fields in the Path Trace application that can be filled in. Of the five fields, two of them are mandatory, and three of them have optional values. Table 8-4 lists the available fields, if they are mandatory or optional, and a description of each field.

Table 8-4 *Path Trace Application Fields*

Field Name	Mandatory/Optional	Description
Source IP	Mandatory	Sender's forwarding interface IP address
Destination IP	Mandatory	Receiver's forwarding IP address
Source Port	Optional	Source port
Destination Port	Optional	Destination port
Protocol	Optional	Protocol

Starting with a valid source and destination IP, you can then click the Trace button to see the path visualization between the two host nodes. Once the path trace is completed, you can see a very detailed visual output that includes each hop that the trace passed through. Additionally, the device type, ingress interfaces, egress interfaces, and IP addresses of each device can be seen along the entire path. Figure 8-17 shows the exact path that was taken. As you can see from the output, there is a variety of details that even include information on wired and wireless clients. CAPWAP tunnels are also identified in the trace to show when wireless APs communicate to the wireless LAN controller (WLC). Another very important detail is that the method of packet delivery is specified, for instance, switched versus Inter-VLAN Routing.

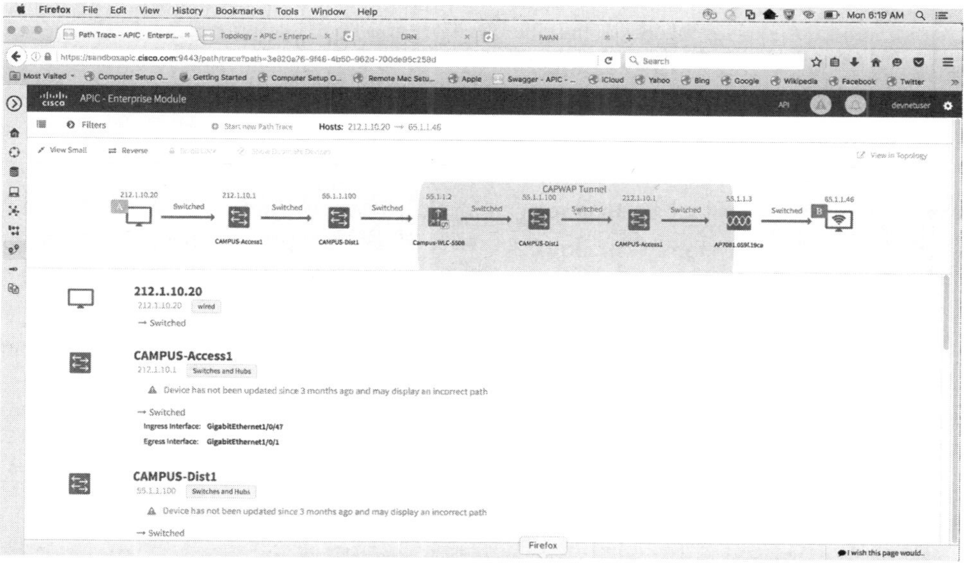

Figure 8-17 *Example of a Detailed Path Trace*

To further illustrate the versatility of this tool, you can click the Show Reverse button to see the traffic flow in the opposite direction from destination to source. This is especially useful to see if there are any asymmetrical traffic flows in the network. This is a crucial tool to find routing and switching path issues. Figure 8-18 illustrates an example of the reverse path trace in the Path Trace application.

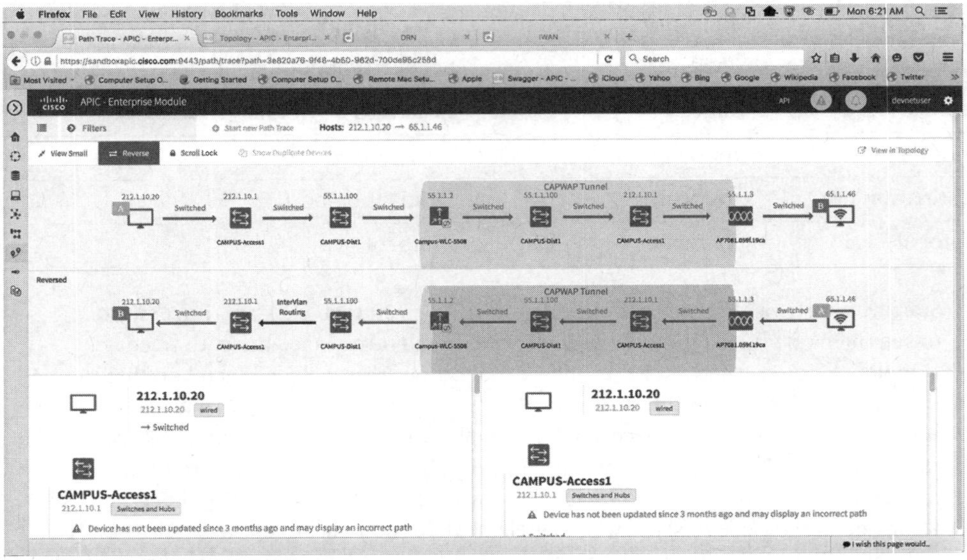

Figure 8-18 *Example of a reverse path trace*

> **Note** To see a smaller graphical representation of the path trace, click the View Small button in the top left corner of the Path Trace application.

> **Note** More applications are being developed for the APIC-EM controller and will continue to offer more robust features in the future. For the latest information on APIC-EM applications and features, please visit www.cisco.com/go/apicem

Additional APIC-EM Features

Other applications are available for APIC-EM and offer a multitude of benefits. Some of these applications are the following:

- Topology application
- Device inventory application
- Easy quality of service (EasyQoS)
- Dynamic QoS
- Policy application

Topology

Topology is a feature within APIC-EM that provides an interactive graphical layout of the entire campus network. Topology enables network operations teams to visually see the devices in the environment and how they connect to one another. Various different types of information can be displayed on the topology such as MAC addresses, IP addresses, and device names. Color-coded device types make it easy to distinguish between the different types of devices in the topology. Figure 8-19 illustrates the Topology tool within APIC-EM and the different color-coded device types.

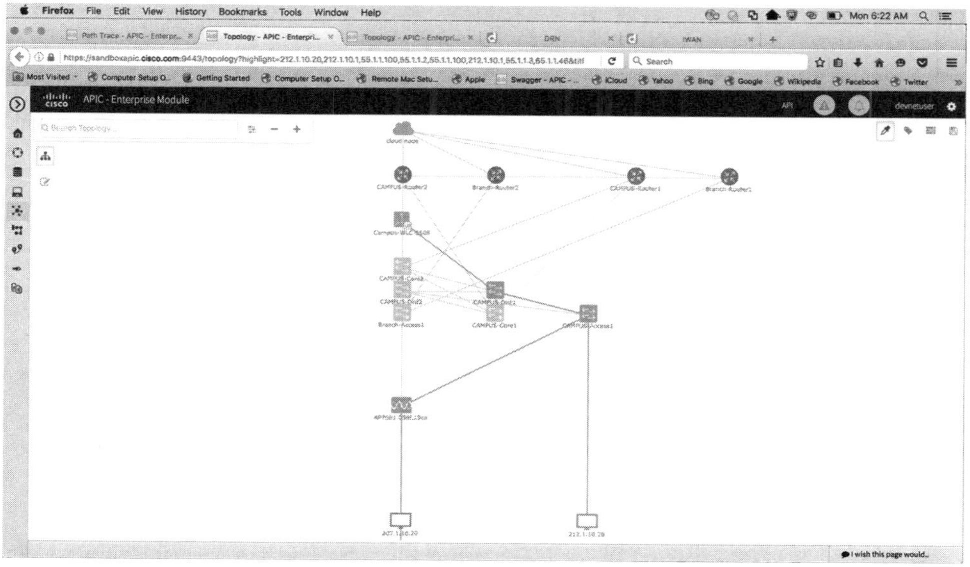

Figure 8-19 *Topology Overview Screen*

Topology gives network operators the ability to drill down on specific devices to get more information. Device type, role, IP address, and version are just some of the kinds of information shown when clicking on a device. Also, when a device is clicked in the topology screen, it then highlights all the links that the selected device has that connect to other devices. Another useful feature of topology is that all the device icons can be moved around in topology view to change the layout to something that fits the needs of the operator. Figure 8-20 illustrates the topology view with one of the switches selected and all the information that is available in the selected device view.

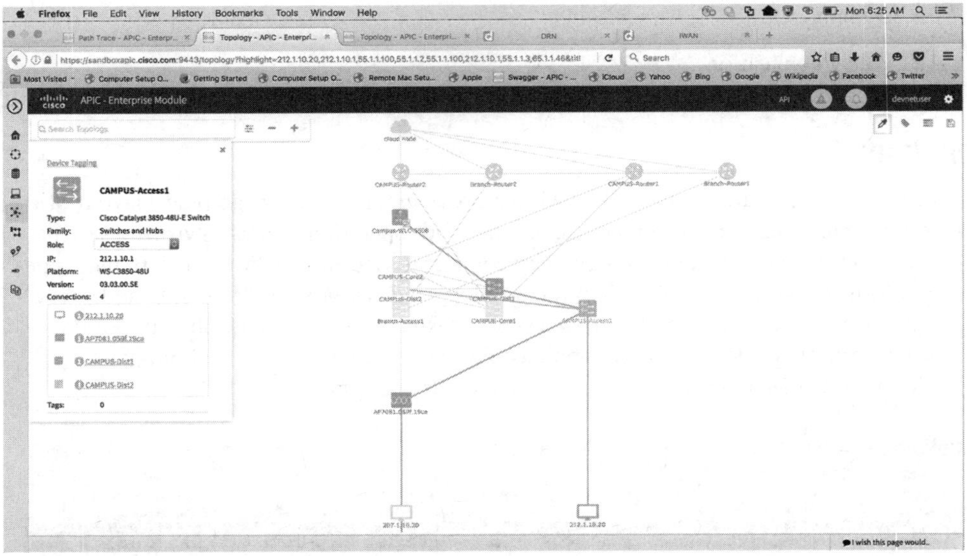

Figure 8-20 *Example of a Selected Device in Topology View*

Layering within the topology allows the network operators to highlight the specific devices that match the layer that is selected. For example, you could select a Layer 2 (L2) filter that only shows VLAN300, or you could select a Layer 3 (L3) filter that only highlights devices running a specific routing protocol like EIGRP, OSPF, ISIS, or static routing for that matter. This helps you visualize the network very simply and see which different network components are running what and where. The following example in Figure 8-21 shows the topology view with a L2 VLAN300 filter applied. Notice that only two devices are participating in L2 in regard to VLAN300. This can be seen easily because only two devices are highlighted and all the other devices are grayed out. To enable layers, click the Layers button in the top right corner of the topology view screen.

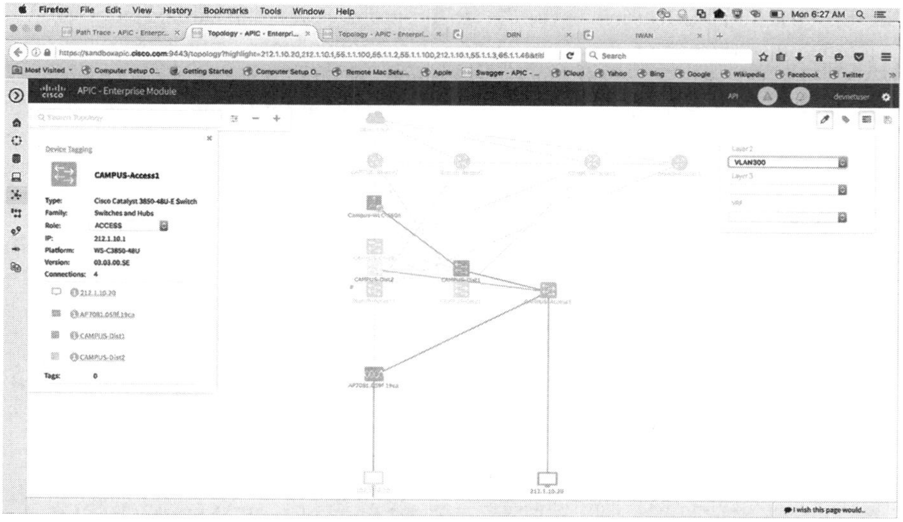

Figure 8-21 *VLAN Layer View in Topology*

Device Inventory

Device Inventory is a way to track all the managed devices with APIC-EM. This is a very simple way of gathering detailed information on multiple devices at one time. Device Inventory offers a convenient place to change the device role, location, tags, and device names. Columns in this view are customizable, and different options can be added or removed by changing the layout to Custom and picking the desired columns. Figure 8-22 illustrates the main Device Inventory page in APIC-EM. We will then cover some of the individual features of Device Inventory.

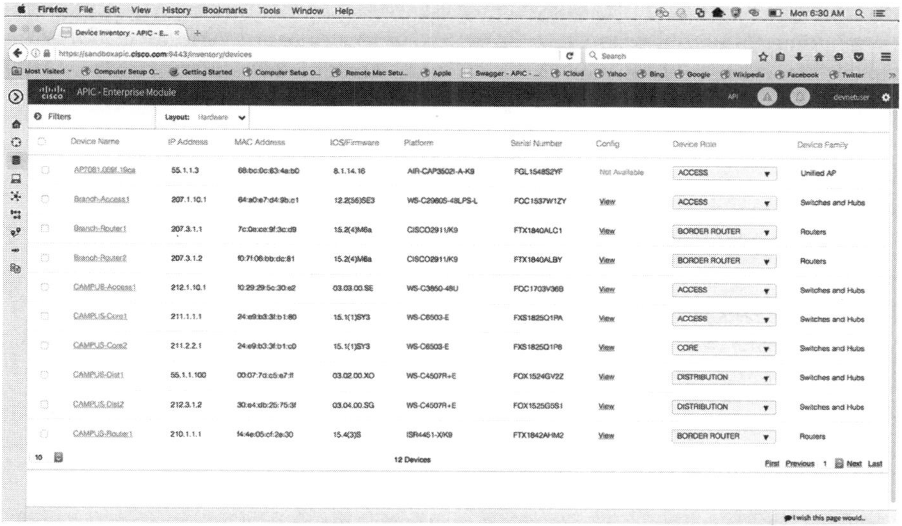

Figure 8-22 *Device Inventory page*

One of the most valuable features in the device inventory view is the amount of information you get when you click on a device. In the following example, we select one of the campus access switches. The output shown in Figure 8-22 shows the device overview screen, which has some of the following fields of information:

- Device name
- IP address
- MAC address
- OS version
- Up Time
- Product ID
- Memory

In addition to the device overview fields, you can see all the interfaces on the selected devices. This includes the total count of interfaces, interface names, MAC addresses, and the statuses of each of the interfaces on the device. By having this information at the click of a button, it drastically reduces the amount of time that would need to be taken to log into each device and issue show commands to try to gather the same device specific information. Figure 8-23 shows the detailed device overview of a campus access switch.

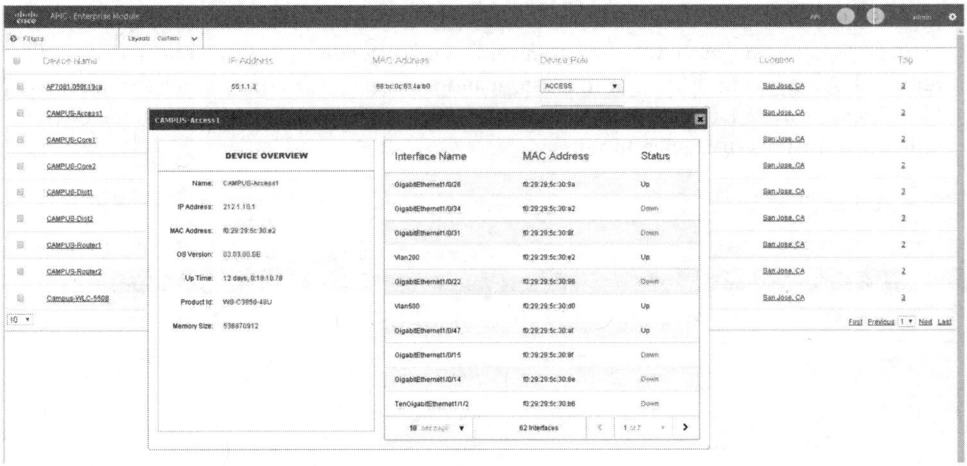

Figure 8-23 *Device overview of access switch*

Easy Quality of Service (Easy QoS)

One of the biggest sources of complexity within an enterprise campus network is around the topic of quality of service. There are many different options that can be set and policies that can be built, and it all varies, based on the specific device that QoS is being configured on. Catalyst switches and Cisco routers have very different QoS mechanisms, queues, thresholds, and so forth. QoS is designed to prioritize traffic across a network end-to-end from source to destination and back. This was seen previously in Figure 7-2, showing an end-to-end QoS example in Chapter 7 "On-Box Programmability and Automation Tools." The following is a brief list of steps needed to enable QoS on a Cisco device.

- Identify traffic to prioritize or set policy on
- Classify the identified traffic in a class-map
- Match the class-map in a policy-map
- Set actions in policy-maps like bandwidth or policing
- Apply policy-maps to interface in proper direction
- Monitor QoS policies to make sure they are performing properly

All of these steps require very careful and detailed planning to ensure proper implementation. If a setting is missed or a bandwidth statement is put in kbps, rather than mbps, it could have devastating impact on a network environment. Quality of Service is very time consuming, tedious to configure, and even more difficult to troubleshoot. QoS is typically configured on a box-by-box basis and has too many controls to keep track of. Commonly, businesses often simply do not deploy QoS because of its inherent complexity. Some businesses just over-provision all the circuits or network links and others just live with poor network performance by not deploying QoS. APIC-EM offers an application called Easy QoS. Easy QoS is a very clean and clear QoS deployment engine that significantly reduces the overall complexity of instantiating QoS in a campus environment. Easy QoS uses CVD templates to ensure a predictable, faster, and more reliable deployment. Easy QoS allows for creating categories of applications, such as real-time traffic. Under the real-time application, there can be multiple other applications with similar requirements like voice, softphones, and video. There also can be categories for default or scavenger traffic classes. Easy QoS also supports custom classification and marking templates to fit the business needs of the enterprise. Figure 8-24 illustrates the Easy QoS application dashboard. In this main screen, you can see the different traffic classifications on a single page.

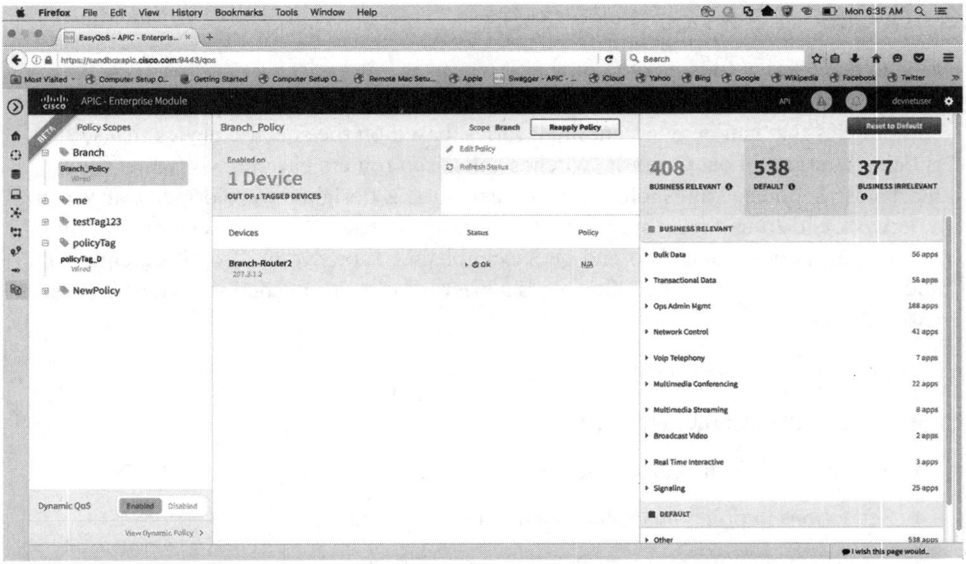

Figure 8-24 *Easy QoS application example*

APIC-EM acts as a central point of management for QoS across the campus. QoS policies get pushed down to devices in a simultaneous and uniform fashion. This limits the risk of issues and errors that can take place if you have mismatched QoS policies throughout your environment. Because QoS is end-to-end, this becomes especially important to the overall success of the design. Figure 8-25 depicts an overview of a centrally managed QoS policy deployment model that APIC-EM offers.

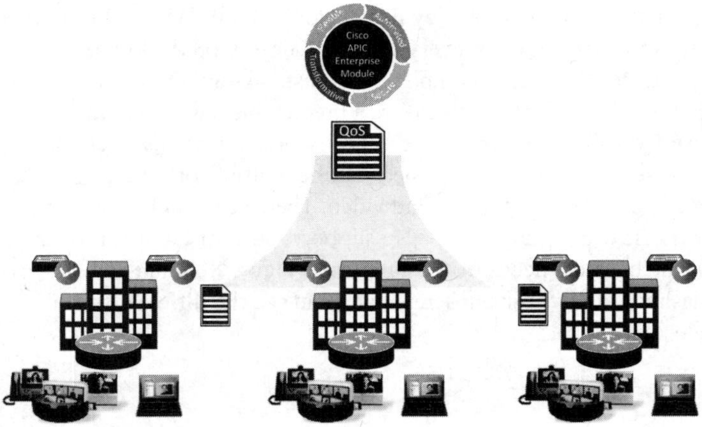

Figure 8-25 *Central QoS deployment model*

Another feature of Easy QoS is the capability to drag and drop different classifications and to mark settings for easy modification of existing class-maps and policy-maps. The drag-and-drop tool can also be used to create and apply new per-hop behaviors (PHB). These PHBs can contain new class maps and policy maps that can be populated with information based application or DSCP value—for example, voice traffic with a DSCP value of (46) EF versus bulk FTP data with a DSCP marking of Assured Forwarding (AF) or AF21.

Once QoS has been applied, APIC-EM offers enterprise-wide compliance checks for QoS. This means that the APIC-EM controller can constantly monitor the campus network to make sure that applied QoS policies are enforced and working as expected. This becomes increasingly more important to maintain the end-to-end QoS design that is needed for converged networks that run multiple traffic types such as real-time voice, interactive video, and various data streams. Figure 8-26 shows a deeper look at some of the different traffic types that are classified and the associated percentage of bandwidth that is allocated for each of classes within the APIC-EM Easy QoS application.

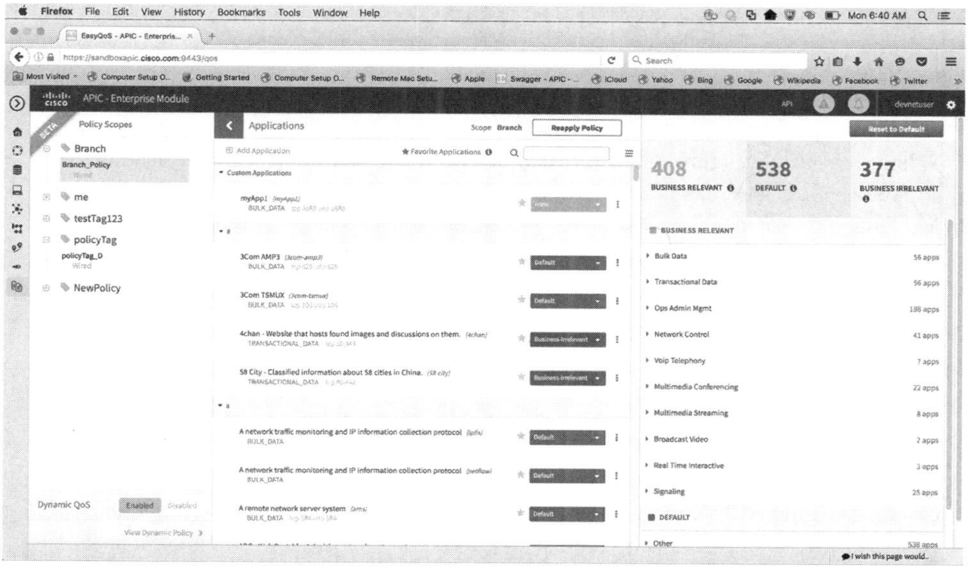

Figure 8-26 *Traffic classification and bandwidth allocation*

Dynamic QoS

Dynamic QoS is another feature that will apply QoS settings end-to-end across the enterprise network. However, this time it is done automatically, based on the application being used by the user. For example, a user is using Cisco Jabber as a softphone for communicating to other users within the organization. In this case, Client A calls Client B via a Jabber voice call. The Cisco Unified Communications Manager communicates via a REST API to the APIC-EM controller. Now the network will be automatically provisioned with the necessary classification and markings needed for that specific call flow. This is accomplished by the APIC-EM that pushes the QoS settings down to all the devices in the path dynamically. The QoS settings remain in place until the call has terminated. Once the call has terminated, the dynamic QoS settings are removed. This allows a single client, which has initiated a call, to engage the APIC-EM, automatically deploying a policy across all network devices in the call path and enabling a high-quality user experience. Figure 8-27 illustrates this concept in more detail.

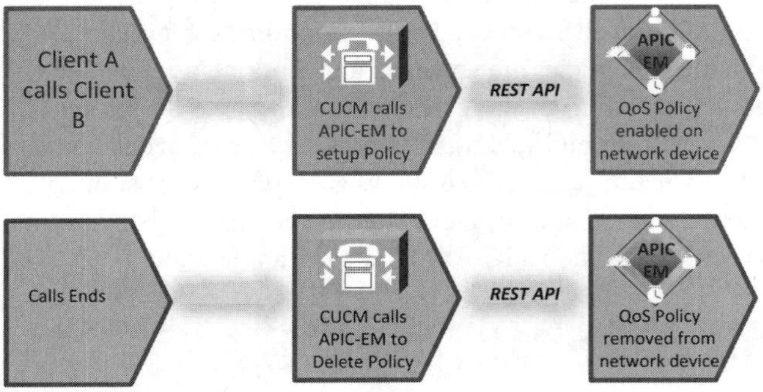

Figure 8-27 *Dynamic QoS overview*

When a client moves throughout the campus network environment, the dynamically applied QoS policies can move along with the client. This feature is called Follow-Me QoS and provides very powerful QoS enforcement to help support mobility in an enterprise network. This is becoming increasingly necessary for wireless clients and remote office workers.

Policy Application

The APIC-EM Policy application is the graphical Access Control List (ACL) manager. Oftentimes in networking, ACLs are deployed throughout the network to enhance security controls and perhaps influence traffic flows throughout the network. In many cases, managing ACLs can be a very tedious task that can eventually turn into an administrative nightmare. This happens frequently due to organic growth and lack of detailed network documentation. ACL entries can grow into the thousands, and over time, it is hard to be certain what each entry is used for and if it is even in use at all. The APIC-EM Policy not only gives you a graphical way of configuration and managing your ACLs, it can actually monitor existing ACL entries to see if and when they are in use. Figure 8-28 shows an example of the Policy application and the ACL tool.

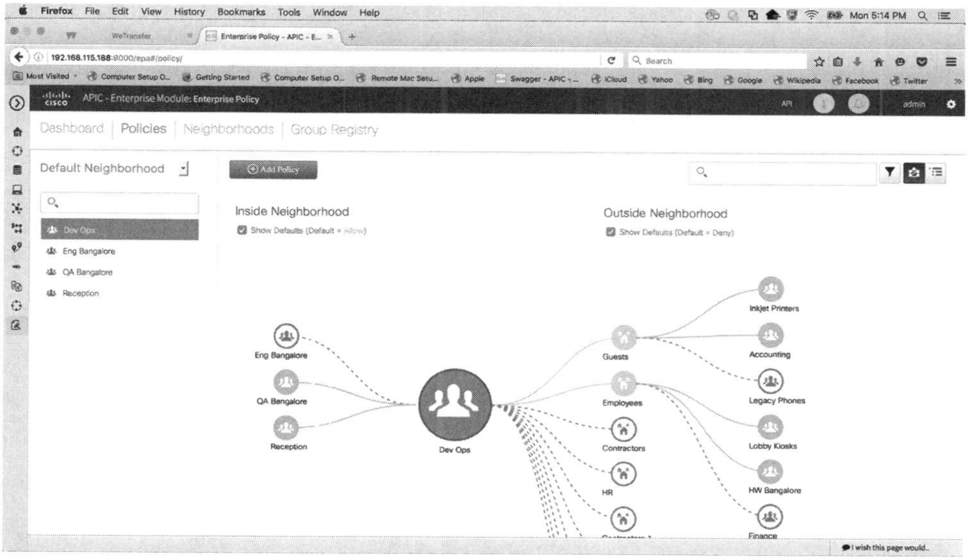

Figure 8-28 *APIC-EM Policy Application*

Another feature that the Policy application can assist with is helping facilitate Network Threat Defense. That means the Policy application can communicate with other network security platforms, for example, SourceFire sensors. This allows the APIC-EM to become an enforcer of the business security policy. For instance, when a SourceFire sensor in an enterprise network environment detects a malware attack, it can then report this to the APIC-EM controller via an API and the Policy application can take action by dynamically deploying an ACL to block or quarantine specific end points or host devices. This gives enterprise network operators a very robust method of network enforcement and helps to protect the business against malicious activity. Figure 8-29 shows a high-level example of a SourceFire network security sensor communicating with a centralized controller.

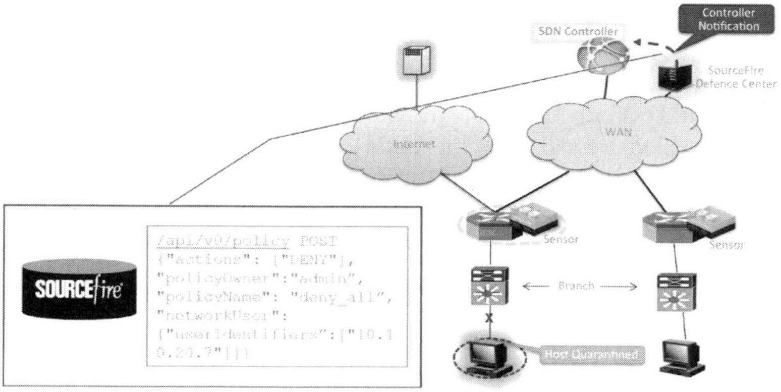

Figure 8-29 *Example of using Policy application for network security*

Note Figures shown in this section are of future or roadmap features. The actual look of the graphical user interface is subject to change. Also, the availability of these future features and applications is subject to change.

APIC-EM Programmability Examples Using Postman

APIC-EM has RESTful APIs that allow you to programmatically interact with the controller. These APIs will respond to the common HTTP requests such as GET, POST, PUT, and DELETE. This data is structured in JSON format. This section will cover how to authenticate to the system and how to access the list of available APIs within APIC-EM. This section will also cover some examples on using some of the APIs with Postman. The following APIs will be covered in particular:

- Ticket
- Host
- Network-device
- User

Note Cisco DevNet has an always on APIC-EM sandbox that you can use for learning and testing these APIs. Visit devnet.cisco.com for more information.

Ticket API

In order to authenticate to APIC-EM via the API, we will first have to create a service ticket. This is accomplished in the following example by using Google Postman to navigate to the "ticket" API within APIC-EM. Figure 8-30 illustrates the main Postman Builder window with ticket API in the URL path.

Using Postman, we will provide the credentials to authenticate to the APIC-EM. In order to do this, we will need to use a POST operation. After we select the POST operation we will then need to click on the "Body" tab in Postman, then select the "raw" radio button. Once that has been completed, we will insert the following in JSON format:

```
{
  "password": "Cisco123!",
  "username": "devnetuser"
}
```

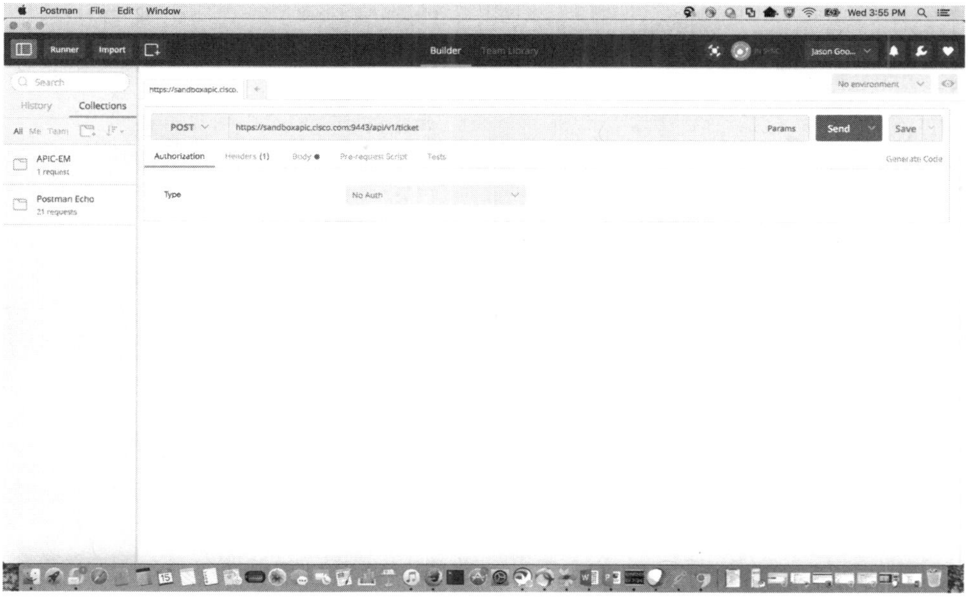

Figure 8-30 *Postman Builder window with the ticket API in the URL*

Figure 8-31 illustrates the process.

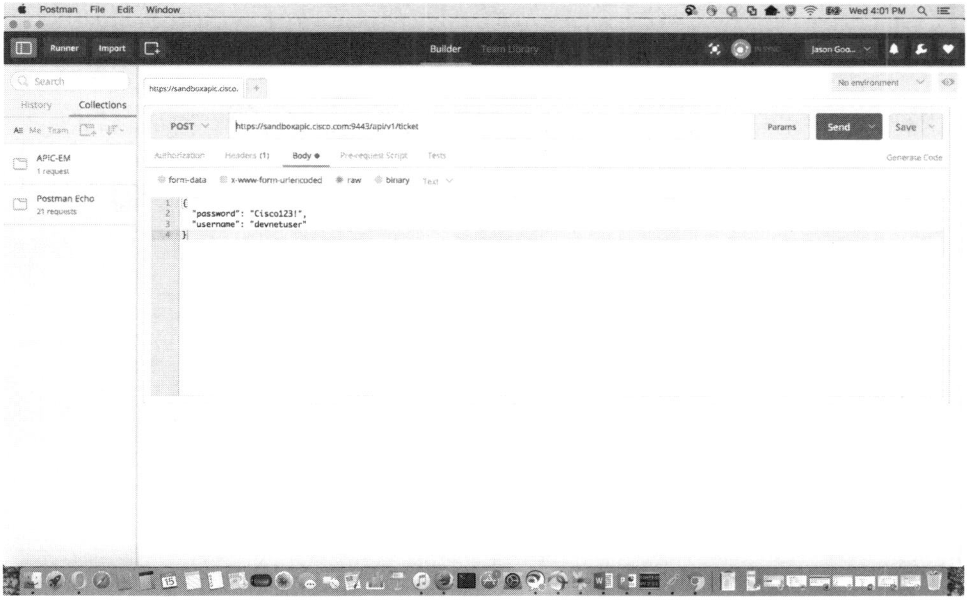

Figure 8-31 *Provide credential for authentication*

Next, we click on the **Headers** tab and specify "Content-Type" as the key value and "application/json" as the value as shown in Figure 8-32.

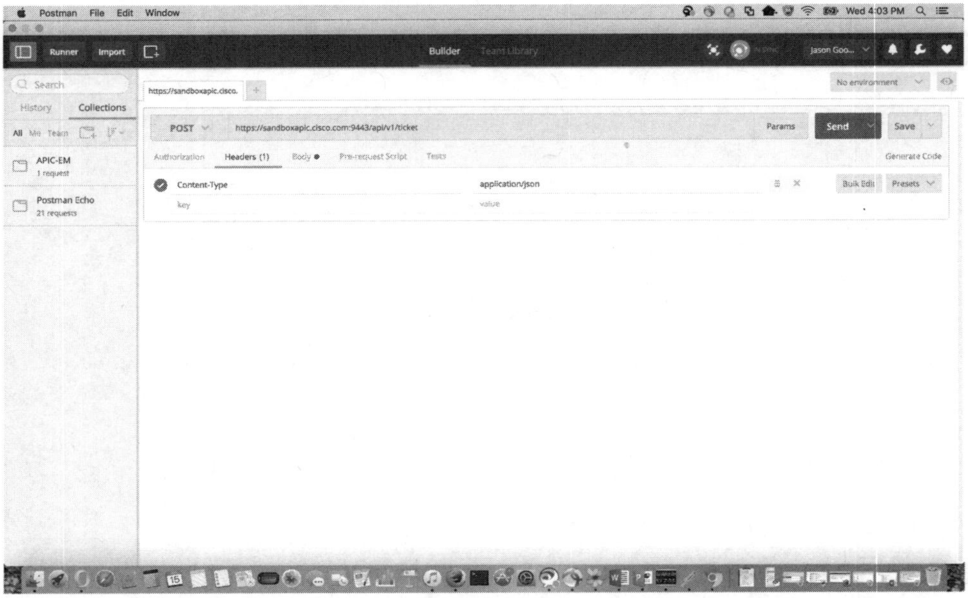

Figure 8-32 *Specify values*

Now that we have provided the credentials and specified the key and value under the Headers tab, we can send the POST command by clicking the Blue send button. Figure 8-33 illustrates the output received from the APIC-EM in response to the POST command.

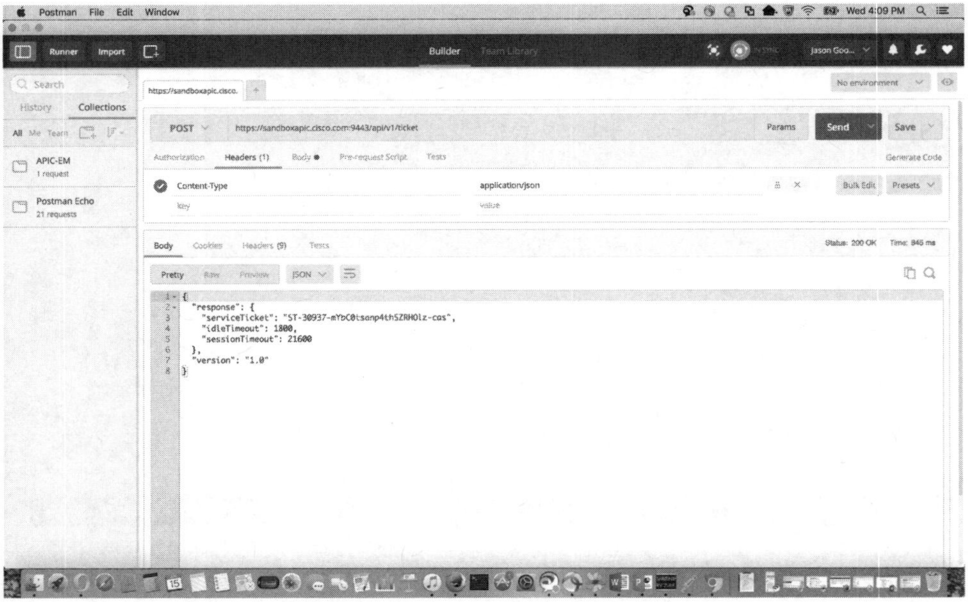

Figure 8-33 *Output from APIC-EM*

The response included a serviceTicket which in this case has a value of "ST-30937-mYbC0tsanp4thSZRHOlz-cas". This serviceTicket will be used when authenticating to the APIC-EM controller to run various different APIs calls. The serviceTicket value is unique to each session and has a default timeout of 1800 seconds. If the idle timer expires the process to authenticate and create another serviceTicket value will need to happen before any additional API calls can be made.

Host API

Once authenticated we can use the serviceTicket to interact with other APIs. In order to use this serviceTicket we need to add another header having the key called "x-auth-token" with the serviceTicket information "ST-30939-yHXZZYf7ivGI5PaQegkD-cas" in the value field. For the Host API, we will use an HTTP GET operation. Now that the values are entered, we can click the send button to retrieve the information from the controller. **Figure 8-34** shows the GET operation, x-auth-token key, and output of the host API call using Postman.

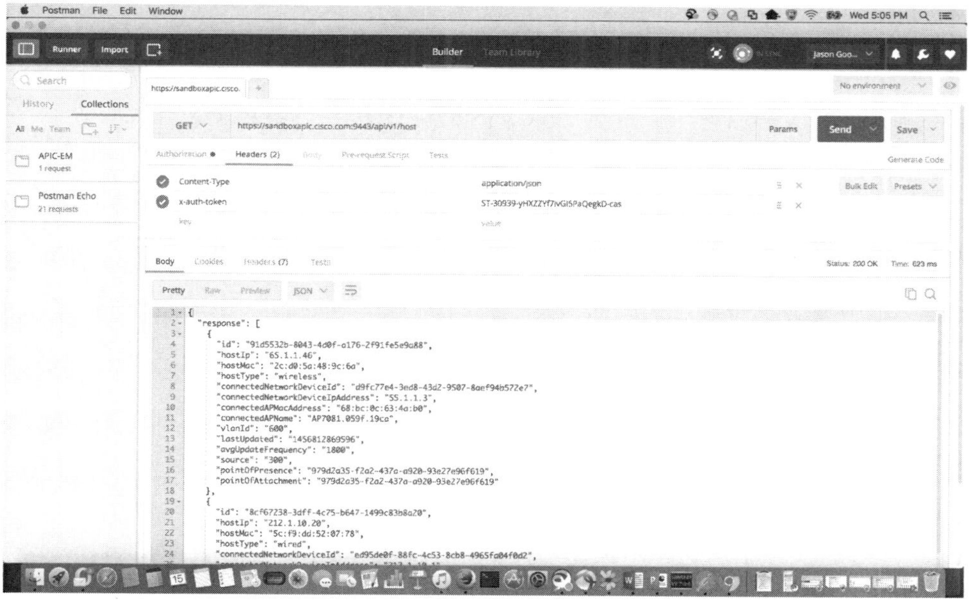

Figure 8-34 *GET operation, x-auth-token key, and output of the host API call using Postman*

Based on the output of the GET command, you can see that the information that was retrieved from the controller is very useful. Some of the information retrieved via the Host API are as follows:

- Host IP
- Host MAC
- Host Type

- Connected Network Device IP Address
- Connected AP MAC Address (If Host Type is Wireless)
- Connect AP Name (If Host Type is Wireless)

Network Device API

In this section, we are going to show an example of how to use the network-device API to get a list of network devices that are in the APIC-EM. These are the same values that we looked at in the Device Inventory section previously in this chapter. Using the same GET method as before, we will use Postman to retrieve a list of all the connected network devices. Figure 8-35 illustrates the output from the GET operation of the network-device API call.

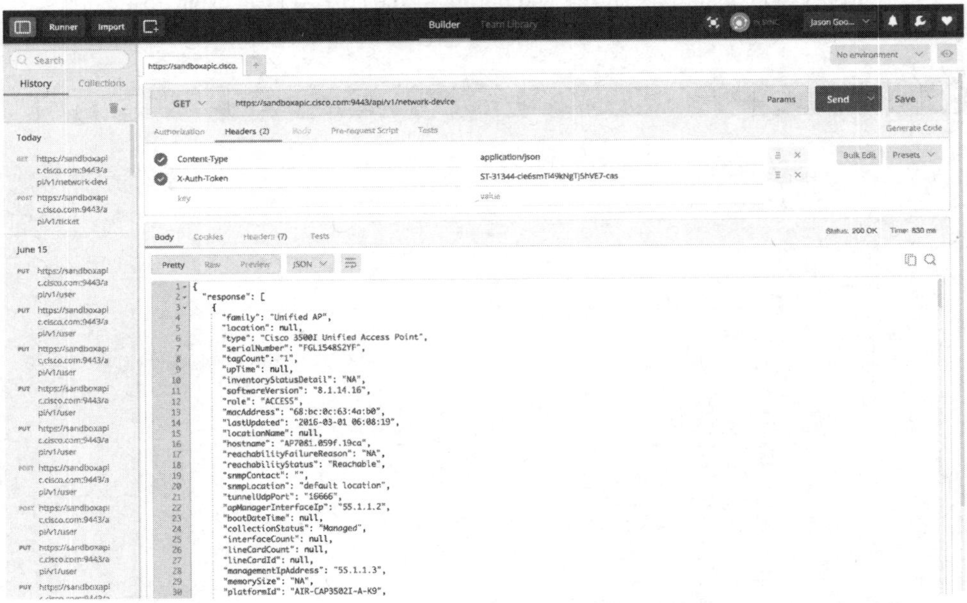

Figure 8-35 *Get operation of the network-device API call*

The APIC-EM REST API also allows for some filters to be applied to the output received from the controller. In the example shown in Figure 8-36, we will use the 3/1 filter at the end of the URL to start with the third device and only show a count of one device. Which is essentially calling out only the third device in the list. If we were to use the 3/3 filter, it would start with the third device in the list and show a total of 3 devices.

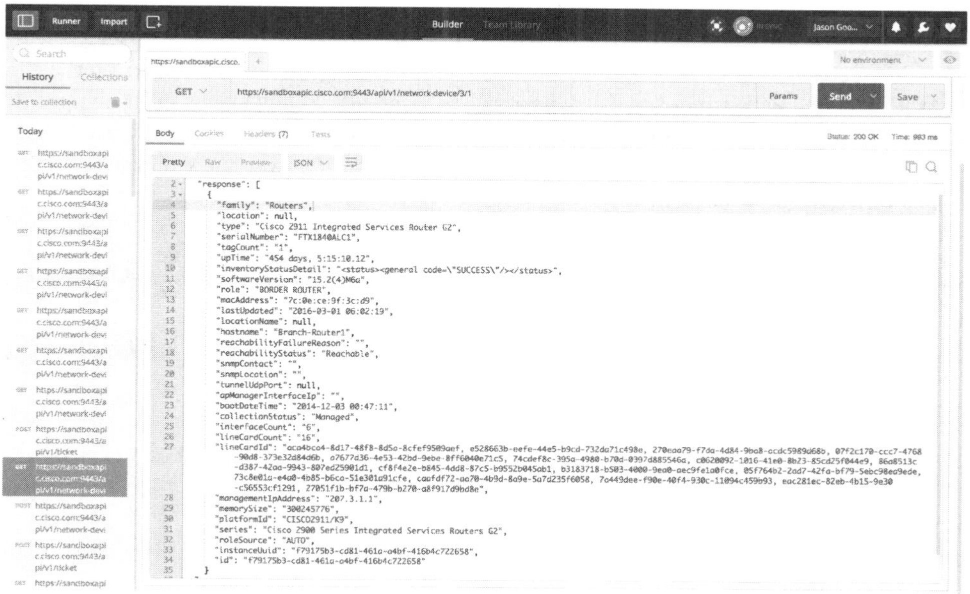

Figure 8-36 *Using the 3/1 filter*

Similar to the 3/1 filter, we can also use the limit and offset filter to accomplish the same outcome. Figure 8-37 depicts the use of the following filter *?limit=1&offset=3*.

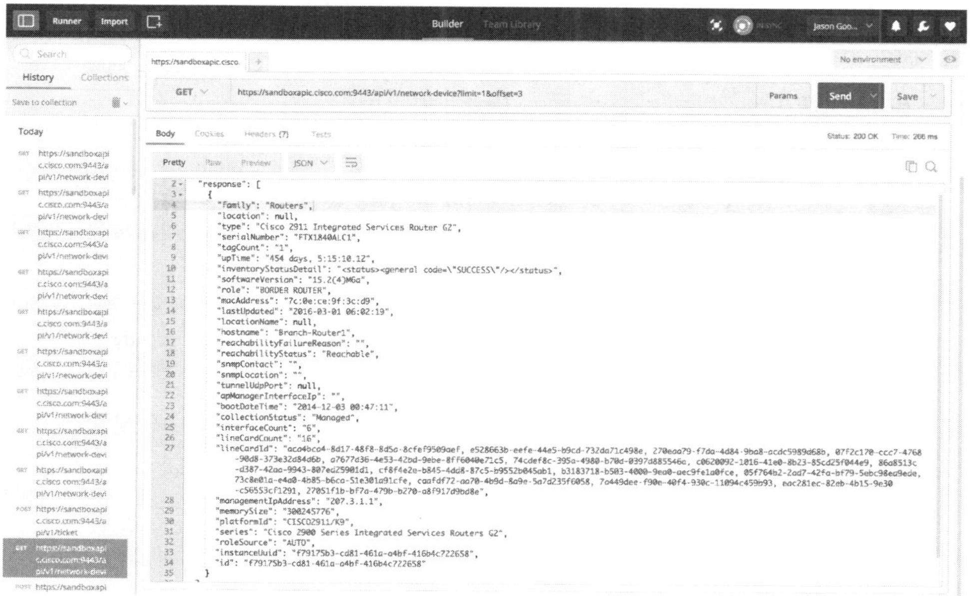

Figure 8-37 *Using the ?limit=1&offset=3 filter*

User API

In this section, we are going to cover an example of viewing the different users on the APIC-EM. We will also create a new user via the User API. Following a similar method as discussed in previous examples, we will use Postman to perform a GET operation to the User API. Figure 8-38 illustrates the information retrieved from the GET operation performed to the User API.

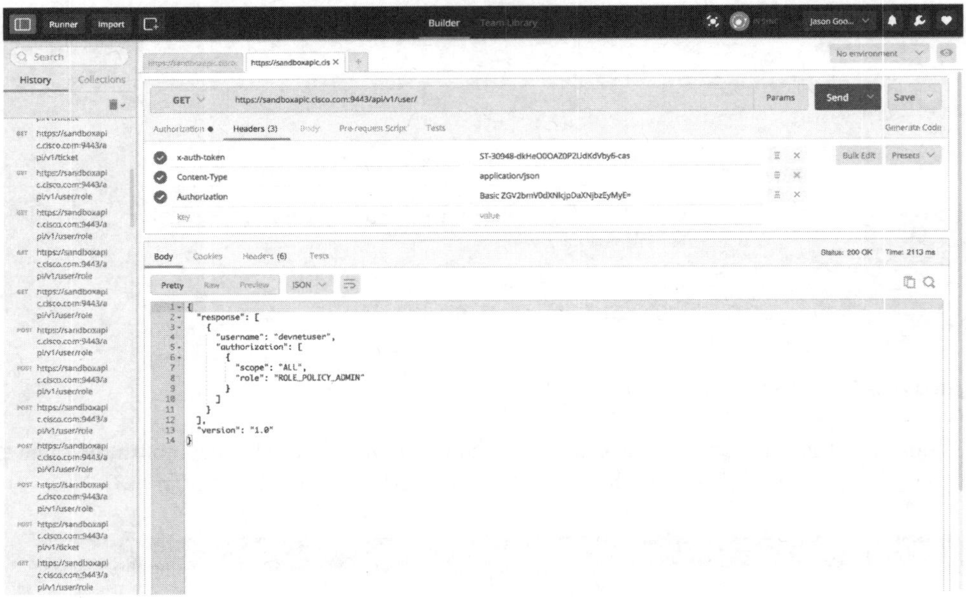

Figure 8-38 *GET operation performed to User API*

Based on the output from the GET, we can see that there is only a single user on the APIC-EM with the username of devnetuser and the role of ROLE_POLICY_ADMIN. The scope ALL refers to the entire APIC-EM platform. In the future, scopes may be used for multi-tenancy functions.

Now we will create a new user named Vince. Vince will have the role of ROLE_ADMIN. In order to create a new user, we now will use the POST operation again. Figure 8-39 depicts the successful creation of the user Vince.

To verify that the user was successfully created, we can issue another GET operation on the User API. Figure 8-40 illustrates the GET operation to the User API to verify the username "Vince" was created.

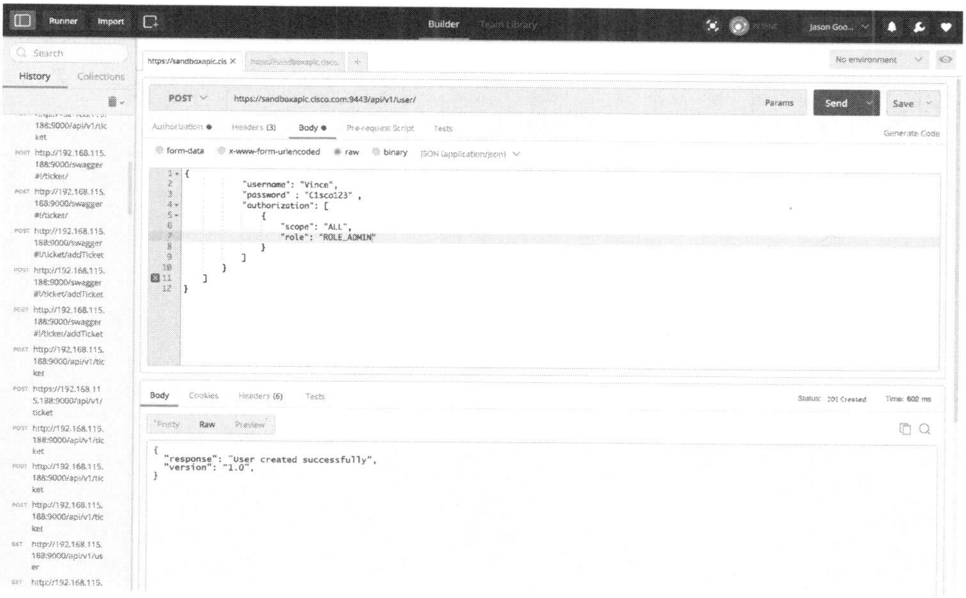

Figure 8-39 *Successful user creation*

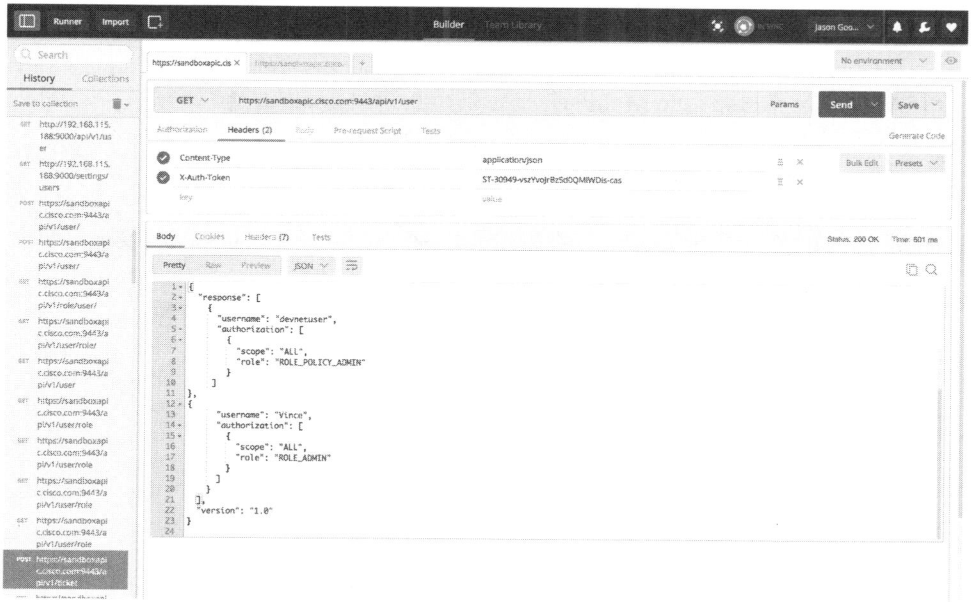

Figure 8-40 *Using GET to verify username*

Now that we have created a new user. We will change the password of one of the users by performing a PUT operation to the User API. Figure 8-41 illustrates a successful password change for the username "devnetuser."

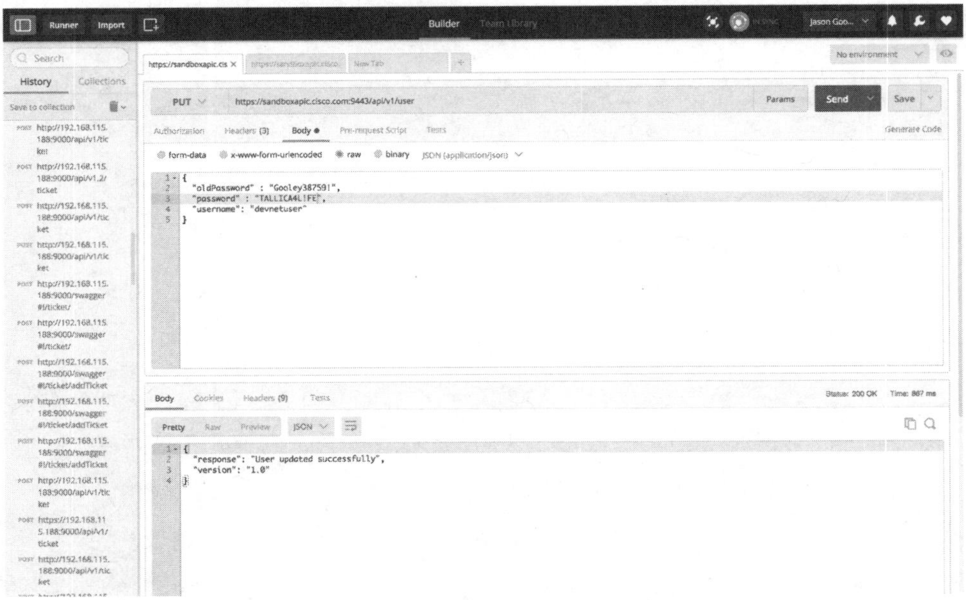

Figure 8-41 *Successful password change*

Available APIC-EM APIs

To see a list of all the available APIs on the APIC-EM and the corresponding syntax, click the API link at the top right of the screen next to the Alert icon as shown in Figure 8-42.

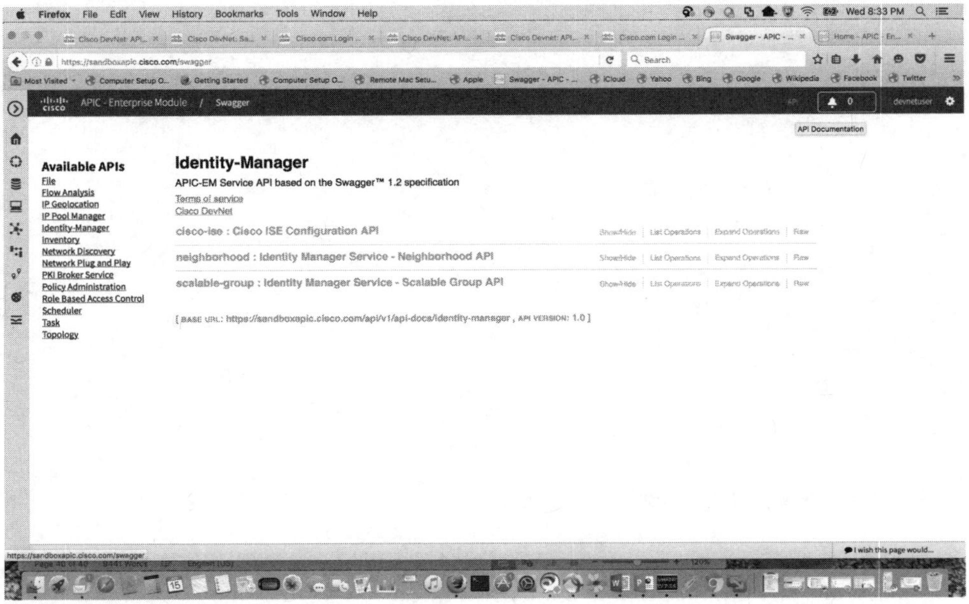

Figure 8-42 *List of available APIs on the APIC-EM*

APIC-EM Programmability Examples Using Python

In this section, we are going to cover an example of authenticating to APIC-EM using a Python script. Python also leverages the RESTful API of APIC-EM. This means that some of the information we covered in previously in this chapter will look familiar. For example, the JSON format for authentication is very similar. Using Python, we will achieve the same result when authenticating to APIC-EM as discussed in the previous Postman examples.

Ticket API

As discussed previously in this chapter, in order to use an API, we must first be authenticated to APIC-EM. To do this, we will use Python to perform a POST operation to the Ticket API. This will in turn create a service ticket. The following example illustrates the content of the APIC-EM-AUTH.py script that we will be using to authenticate to APIC-EM. See Chapter 2 Using PIP section for more information on how to install the requests module using PIP.

```
# This application authenticates to APIC-EM and prints the token

# Import libraries
import requests
import json
import sys


# It's used to get rid of certificate warning messages when using Python 3.
# For more information please refer to: https://urllib3.readthedocs.org/en/latest/
security.html
requests.packages.urllib3.disable_warnings() # Disable warning message

# Change apic-em IP to the one you are using
apicem_ip = "sandboxapic.cisco.com:9443"

# Enter user name and password to get a service ticket
username = "devnetuser"
password = "Cisco123!"
version = "v1"

# Format username and password for use with APIC-EM
r_json = {
    "username": username,
    "password": password
}
```

```
# Construct URL and content header
post_url = "https://"+apicem_ip+"/api/"+version+"/ticket"
    # All APIC-EM REST API query and response content type is JSON
headers = {'content-type': 'application/json'}
    # POST request and response

# This try / except block attempts to authenticate to APIC-EM
try:
    # Use python requests to post url with authentication header
    r = requests.post(post_url, data = json.dumps(r_json),
headers=headers,verify=False)

    # return service ticket and print output
    return_data = r.json()
    print (return_data)
    # just print serviceTicket
    print (return_data["response"]["serviceTicket"])
    #
except:
    # Something wrong, cannot get service ticket
    print ("Status: %s"%r.status_code)
    print ("Response: %s"%r.text)
    sys.exit ()
```

The APIC-EM-AUTH.py script contains some of the same information that was used in the previous Postman examples. The following is some of that information:

- JSON formatted username and password
- POST Operation and URL of API
- Headers

Now that we have examined the contents of the script, we will use PyCharm to test authentication to the APIC-EM by running the APIC-EM-AUTH.py script. Figure 8-43 illustrates the use of the APIC-EM-AUTH.py script to authenticate via the Ticket API. Notice that serviceTicket ST-31352-spLXNhybYi6xTLh9YhoB-cas was created as illustrated in the output returned from the APIC-EM-AUTH.py

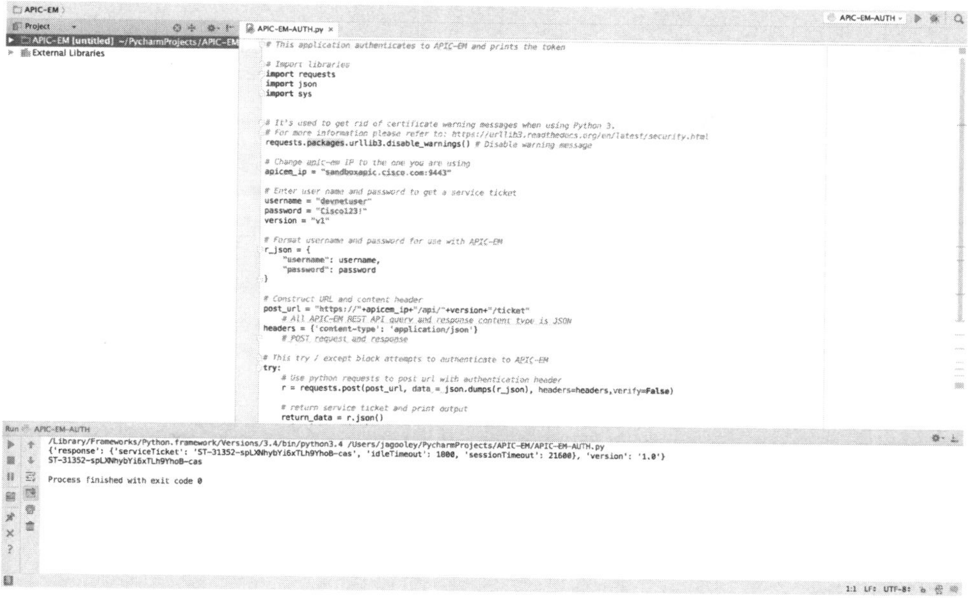

Figure 8-43 *Python authentication script for APIC-EM*

Host API

Similarly, to the previous Postman examples, we have authenticated to APIC-EM. Now we can use the available APIs in APIC-EM. The following example illustrates the contents of the next script that we will be using to do a REST API call to the Host API. The script is named APIC-EM-SHOW-HOST.py

```
# This application authenticates to APIC-EM, prints the token and uses a GET
operation to retrieve info from the HOST API


# Import libraries
import requests
import json
import sys



# It's used to get rid of certificate warning messages when using Python 3.
# For more information please refer to: https://urllib3.readthedocs.org/en/latest/
security.html
requests.packages.urllib3.disable_warnings() # Disable warning message


# Change apic-em IP to the one you are using
apicem_ip = "sandboxapic.cisco.com:9443"
```

```
# Enter user name and password to get a service ticket
username = "devnetuser"
password = "Cisco123!"
version = "v1"

# Format username and password for use with APIC-EM
r_json = {
    "username": username,
    "password": password
}

# Construct URL and content header
post_url = "https://"+apicem_ip+"/api/"+version+"/ticket"
    # All APIC-EM REST API query and response content type is JSON
headers = {'content-type': 'application/json'}
    # POST request and response

# This try / except block attempts to authenticate to APIC-EM
try:
    # Use python requests to post url with authentication header
    r = requests.post(post_url, data = json.dumps(r_json),
headers=headers,verify=False)

    # return service ticket and print output
    return_data = r.json()
    # create auth token formatted for APIC-EM with serviceTicket from previous
line
    auth_token = {"X-Auth-Token": return_data["response"]["serviceTicket"]}

except:
    # Something wrong, cannot get service ticket
    print ("Status: %s"%r.status_code)
    print ("Response: %s"%r.text)
    sys.exit ()

# Create working url to capture hosts in APIC-EM
working_url = "https://"+apicem_ip+"/api/"+version+"/host"

# Use requests to get data using working url and auth token
response2 = requests.get(working_url, headers=auth_token)
# Format data in json
working_data = response2.json()

# Iterate through list and print
host_ip_list=[]
```

```
for item in working_data["response"]:
    host_ip_list.append(item["hostIp"])
print ("\nThis is the list of host ip:\n",host_ip_list)
```

We can see that there is a "X-Auth-Token" value in the Python script which corresponds to the serviceTicket that was created in the previous example. We will again use PyCharm to run the APIC-EM-SHOW-HOST.py script. This time, instead of a POST operation, a GET operation will be performed. Figure 8-44 illustrates the use of the APIC-EM-SHOW-HOST.py script to retrieve data from the Host API with PyCharm.

Figure 8-44 *Python script used to retrieve host IP list from APIC-EM*

The APIC-EM-SHOW-HOST.py script is specifically retrieving the host IP addresses in APIC-EM. The output retrieved from the Host API are the following IP addresses:

10.1.1.46

10.1.10.20

10.1.20.20

The IP addresses were formatted into a list. The list is created with the follow portion of the Python script:

```
host_ip_list=[]
for item in working_data["response"]:
   host_ip_list.append(item["hostIp"])
print ("\nThis is the list of host ip:\n",host_ip_list)
```

Summary

This chapter covered many different network programmability and automation tools. These tools can help equip network operation teams with the ability to streamline day-to-day operations, increase the speed of deployment, reduce the amount of human error, and lower overall operating expenditures. By utilizing some of the tools discussed in this chapter, not only do the network operations teams benefit, but the business as a whole benefits, as well. Many times as network engineers, we get used to the stress of having to manage a network. Often, we wake up after hours for maintenance windows to deploy network changes or instantiate new features and applications. It's easy to have the mindset that these changes or features have to be deployed manually. However, doing things manually is very time consuming, repetitious, and error prone. We've been doing it this way for years. By using some of these automation tools, we can reduce the amount of manual effort, which in turn frees up time for us to focus on more critical aspects of the job, such as ongoing network design, ways to improve network performance, or how to align how the network functions as a whole to better meet objectives set by our business. These tools also help free up time in our personal lives. Less time up after hours making network changes equals enjoying more time off. It can be quite fun to learn more about these automation tools and begin to leverage them, rather than considering the tasks arduous or daunting. Most of all, these types of tools can benefit you, your business, and your work/life balance.

Chapter 9

Piecing It All Together

Network programmability changes how we deploy, operate, and manage network infrastructure. It enables the network to solve critical business problems and enhance application delivery. It also requires existing network professionals adopt a new skill set that encompasses, Linux, Python, and other skills that are normally outside of the network.

Over time, network programmability will be an important component of the required skill set for modern network engineers. More often than not, companies today are trying to accomplish more while having a very small or limited IT staff. This trend is called Lean IT. Having programming skills will help users and others to take over the multitude of daily operational tasks from engineers, allowing network engineers to focus on innovation. The methods discussed in this book are fundamental to enable the network to solve critical business problems and enhance application delivery.

It is a necessary change because the expectations of applications and application owners have changed to meet software driven-business initiatives. The next generation of network engineers will enter the work force with skills that have more resemblance to developers then network engineers. This is not to say that traditional network knowledge, for example, routing protocols operation, is no longer needed. However, those routing protocols are managed differently.

Ultimately, these network engineers work in a variety of different environments, such as public or private enterprises, healthcare, service providers, and value added resellers (VARs). Learning the fundamentals of network programmability and automation is a great step forward to helping network operators become more equipped to handle the daunting tasks that exist across all of these various environments. This will also give network operators the necessary knowledge that they will need to provide direction to their customers when asked how to be more agile and reduce time to market. This foundational skill set will be more instrumental moving forward as businesses begin focusing their attention on network programmability as it becomes more prevalent throughout the industry.

Although these types of skills are very different in nature than what a majority of typical network operators are familiar with, they will play an increasingly large part in how networks are managed. Current IT trends, including DevOps, SDN, and Cloud are accelerating the requirement for network engineers to think differently.

Software defined networking (SDN) is a broad term that can mean many different things. However, all definitions point to a streamlined operational model. The combination of network programmability and SDN eliminate arduous daily tasks that take up a majority of a network engineer's time. Cisco ACI eliminates the heavy lifting associated with moving to SDN with the use of abstracted policy. Holistic policy-based management of the network allows engineers to be more scalable while simultaneously reducing the amount of manual intervention or error caused by the current operational model. Abstracted IT policy enables organizations to move to a more centralized management of their networks as a whole, rather than the distributed management approach they are commonly used to.

DevOps, at the core, requires automation to achieve agility. To the network engineer, DevOps represents a shift in the consumption model of the network. This new consumption model dictates that the network engineer build network configurations but not deploy them. Deployment is left to the application owners as their software changes. Because application owners do not understand or want to understand complex network attributes, the consumption model requires an abstraction, normally via a controller or automation tool, to change the language of the network. Terms like VLAN, ACL, and BGP should never be heard by the application owner, in favor of segment, security, and Internet preference.

Network programmability is the foundation for the network participating in cloud operational models. Organizations are quickly adopting cloud operational models to decrease costs and increase agility. Network hardware can enhance Whatever as a Service (better known as XaaS) and hybrid cloud, using standard network features, for example security and QoS, but only when its configuration can be quickly changed and adopted, based on the requirements of the application or business. The Network Programmability toolset enables network configuration to be abstracted, which simultaneously provides agility, consistency, and quality.

The network is an essential component of application security. The network sees all traffic and, through network programmability and automation, can automatically react to traffic or security anomalies. Network hardware has low cost, high-performance security features, such as stateless ACLs, black hole routes, and policy-based routing that when managed with traditional CLI are too slow and expensive. Network programmability enables security managers to quickly evoke network features to security applications and response to attacks.

We hope that this book is the beginning of your pilgrimage from CLI to programmability, from conservative to agile, and from error prone to error free. This journey will require a time investment, constant retuning to current trends, and some frustration. That said, for most it will be enjoyable. Network programmability, automation, and SDN make the network sexy again, and moreover, they are necessary for the continued relevance of the network. We ask that you embrace this change, so the network continues to be the most important component to application delivery.

Our story continues. . .

Web traffic is up over 1000 percent after your company's mobile application is casually mentioned during the Superbowl. The web team, using orchestration tools, added twenty-five more servers to the cluster, and the network responded automatically. New customers, thrilled with the mobile application, spend millions of dollars and greatly accelerate the business.

As the lead network engineer, you continue watching the game, silently wondering how to spend the bonus check.

Index

Symbols

A

B

C

D

E

F

G

H

I

J

K

L

M

N

O

P

Q

R

S

T

U

V

W

X-Y-Z